Augsburg College

Y0-AJK-971

STATISTICS

OF

INDIAN TRIBES, AGENCIES, AND SCHOOLS,

1903.

Compiled to July 1, 1903.

WASHINGTON:
GOVERNMENT PRINTING OFFICE.
1903.

KRAUS REPRINT CO.
Millwood, New York
1976

Library of Congress Cataloging in Publication Data

United States. Bureau of Indian Affairs.
   Statistics of Indian tribes, agencies, and schools, 1903.

   "Compiled to July 1, 1903."
   Reprint of the 1903 ed.
   1. Indians of North America—Education—Statistics.
   2. Indians of North America—Statistics.   I. Title.
   E97.5.U597   1976   371.9'7'97073   76-21344
   ISBN 0-527-92020-7

Printed in U.S.A.

STATISTICS OF TRIBES, AGENCIES, AND SCHOOLS.

ABSENTEE SHAWNEE INDIANS, OKLAHOMA.

(Under School Superintendent.)

Tribe.	Population.
Absentee Shawnee	687

Area:	Acres.
Allotted	70,791.47
Reserved	510.63

Railroad station: Shawnee, on Choctaw, Oklahoma and Gulf Railroad; thence 2 miles to school.

Post-office address: Shawnee, Okla. Telegraphic address: Shawnee, Okla.

Absentee Shawnee School, Oklahoma.

Located 2 miles south of Shawnee, Okla., on high land; excellent drainage and healthful climate.

One frame school building, in which is included schoolrooms, boys' and girls' dormitories, and employees' quarters. Capacity, 60 pupils. Condition very poor. One frame commissary building for storing school subsistence and clothing; erected 1901; cost about $600 (estimated); present value, $500; condition good. One frame laundry building, old; used for school laundry purposes; present value (estimated), $300; condition poor. One frame barn, for sheltering school stock and storing supplies for issue to Indians; capacity, 10 horses and 10 cows; erected about 1890; present value (estimated), $200; condition poor.

Buildings are lighted by kerosene lamps and heated by wood stoves. No system of ventilation, water, or sewerage. No bathing facilities or fire protection. Water now used hauled in barrels from the river and from neighboring wells, but a well 10 feet in diameter is now being put down which, when completed, will furnish an adequate water supply, to be forced through pipes to school buildings by steam pump.

The school farm consists of 340 acres, mostly bottom land, of a black, heavy soil, which is very productive. The upland is of a sandy loam. About 160 acres in cultivation, balance in pasture and covered by timber.

This plant is well located, in a very productive belt, there being sufficient high, rolling land for the buildings and playgrounds and sufficient tillable land to make the school of little cost to the Government, provided a sufficiently large plant to accommodate 200 or 250 pupils is erected.

Little is known of the early history of this school. It was started by the Friends' Missionary Society, and received by the Government from them many years ago. It has been operated in the past for the Shawnees, but is now open to Shawnee, Kickapoo, and Potawatomi children alike.

BLACKFEET AGENCY, MONT.

Tribes.	Population.
Blackfeet, Bloods, and Piegan	2,082

Area, 900,000 acres, unallotted.

Railroad station: Durham, on Great Northern Railway; 3½ miles to agency by stage.

Nearest military post: Fort Assinniboine, Mont. Post-office address: Browning, Mont. Telegraphic address: Blackfoot, Mont.

Blackfeet Agency Boarding School, Montana.

Located 3½ miles northwest of Browning, Mont., on the Great Northern Railway. The site is an undesirable one for school purposes; it is on the east side of the Rocky Mountains, 7 miles therefrom, in a high, windy, desolate, and extremely cold section of country. The soil of the immediate site is rolling prairie intermingled with huge bowlders and gravel, and such portion thereof as is called tillable land is cold and wet and contains much alkali, thus rendering it absolutely unfit for agricultural purposes.

Girls' dormitory.—Character, two-story frame. Use, dormitory for girls and boys, employees' quarters, kitchen, and dining room. Capacity, 60 pupils. Erected in 1891. Cost, $12,000 (approximated). This building, with a similar one known as boys' dormitory, burned December, 1897, cost $20,620. Present value, worthless as a school building. Present condition, rotten and uninhabitable.

School building.—Character, one-story frame. Use, class rooms and assembly hall. Capacity, 125 pupils. Erected in 1894. Cost, $4,000. Present value, worthless for school purposes. Present condition, bad.

Warehouse.—Character, log. Use, storing supplies. Dimensions, 20 by 24 feet. Erected in 1892. Present value, $50. Condition, very bad.

Miscellaneous outbuildings.—Character, frame, with the exception of one log stable 19 by 37 feet. Use, stable, wood shed, ice house, well house, etc. Erected, 1892 to 1894. Cost, $700, including warehouse. Condition, very bad.

Bakery.—Character, one-story frame. Use, condemned as a bakery and used in connection with "dry room" for laundry purposes. Erected in 1894. Cost, $1,666. Present condition, fair.

Dry room.—Character, one-story frame. Use, drying clothes. Erected in 1896. Cost, $302.50. Present value, $250. Present condition, fair.

All buildings are lighted by kerosene, bracket lamps; heated by wood stoves. Ventilation of schoolrooms is by the system devised by the Indian Office. Other buildings have no modern system. The water supplied, though hard, is regarded pure. Its source is a well 16 feet deep on the gravel bar on which the buildings are located. The water from this well is pumped by hand and carried by hand to all parts of the buildings where used. There is no sewerage connected with the buildings. All waters are carried out by hand and emptied into a ditch which connects with Willow Creek, a fair-sized stream about 40 rods from the buildings and below the source of water supply. There is one small room in the girls' building in which are placed portable tubs for the use of the girls in bathing. For the same purpose the large boys use portable tubs in the laundry, while the small boys use tubs in the old wood shed, which serves for the boys' lavatory. Water buckets placed in the different buildings constitute the source of water supply for fire protection.

The school has 1,206 acres of land, all under fence. Twenty acres under cultivation used for growing garden truck, field vegetables, and tame hay. About 295 acres are used for summer pasturage and the remainder for hay and winter range.

This school was opened in the old agency stockade October 1, 1884, with 22 pupils and 4 employees. In January, 1892, it occupied buildings of present site. Number of pupils, about 40; employees, 4. Before the end of the fiscal year the enrollment reached adout 75 and the number of employees increased to 8. In 1894, probably the most prosperous year of the school, the enrollment reached 145, with an attendance at one time of 128 and an average attendance of 127.5. Since the boys' dormitory burned the attendance has been reduced from year to year until 60, the present number, is all the school can accommodate under the Indian Office rules.

CHEYENNE AND ARAPAHO INDIANS, OKLA.

(Under Three School Superintendents.)

Tribes.	Population.
Under superintendent Cheyenne and Arapaho schools:	
Cheyennes	794
Arapahos	557
Under superintendent Cantonment School:	
Cheyennes	558
Arapahos	239
Under superintendent Seger School:	
Cheyennes	607
Arapahos	139

Area:	Acres.
Allotted	529,682
Reserved—	
School lands	231,829
Military, agency, etc	32,344
Open for settlement	3,500,562

Railroad station: Darlington, Okla., on Chicago, Rock Island and Pacific Railway. One and one-quarter miles to agency by stage. Nearest military post: Fort Reno, Okla. Post-office address: Darlington, Okla. Telegraphic address: Darlington, Okla., via Fort Reno, Okla.

Arapaho School, Darlington, Okla.

Located 4 miles northwest of El Reno, Okla. The Rock Island Railroad, running north and south, passes within 1½ miles of the school, at Darlington station. The Choctaw, Oklahoma and Gulf Railroad, running east and west, passes within 1 mile of the school, at Fort Reno station. The site of the school is too flat for proper drainage, but is otherwise admirable. Soil of immediate site is prairie loam on a substratum of sand and gravel.

Girls' building.—Character, 2½-story brick with stone trimmings. Use, dormitory, sitting room, and sewing room. Capacity, 100 pupils, 4 employees. Erected in 1898. Cost, $15,000. Present value, $14,000. Present condition, good.

Dining hall, kitchen, and dormitory.—Character, 2½-story frame. Use, dining hall, kitchen, and boys' dormitory. Capacity: dining hall, 126; dormitory, 52. Erected in 1892. Cost, $6,500. Present value, $6,000. Present condition, good.

Manual-labor school.—Character, 2½-story frame. Use, schoolrooms, assembly hall, employees' dining room and kitchen, bakery, storeroom, employees' quarters. Capacity—assembly hall, 200; schoolrooms, 100. Erected in 1876. Cost, $10,000. Present value, about worthless (foundation gone). Present condition, very poor.

Employees' quarters.—Character, 1½-story frame. Use, residence of the carpenter and engineer, physician's office. Capacity, 7 rooms besides the physician's office. Erected in 1874. Cost, $1,200. Present value, $500. Present condition, fair.

Hospital.—Character, two-story frame. Use, superintendent's office, employees' quarters. Capacity, 1 office room, 6 dwelling rooms. Erected in 1889. Cost, $600. Present value, $450. Present condition, fair.

Teachers' cottage.—Character, one-story brick. Use, teachers' residence. Capacity, 4 rooms and a sitting room. Erected, two rooms and sitting room in 1882; others, 1894. Cost, $600. Present value, $1,000. Present condition, good.

Bakery.—Character, one-story frame. Use, employees' quarters. Capacity, 4 rooms. Erected in 1878. Cost, $500. Present value, $100. Present condition, fair.

Bath house.—Character, one-story frame. Use, bathing boys and for employees. Capacity, 10 rings for boys and 2 for employees; equipped with 2 Wilks's heaters and 2 tanks. Erected in 1897. Cost, $1,600. Present value, $1,200. Present condition, good.

Barn and crib, implement shed and granary, cowshed.—Character, two-story frame, with sheds for cattle and implements. Use, housing live stock, storing hay, grain, and implements. Capacity, 14 horses, 15 cows, 15 tons hay, 3,000 bushels grain. Erected, 1883, 1894, 1895. Cost, $1,350. Present value, $600. Present condition, fair.

Boiler house, laundry, and shop.—Character, one-story frame. Use, laundry and all mechanical work of the school. Capacity—shop, 4 pupils; laundry, 7. Erected in 1901. Cost, $1,360. Present value, $1,360. Present condition, good.

Miscellaneous outbuildings.—Character, all frame, except dairy, which is stone. Use, coal house, henhouse, water-closets, dairy, etc. Erected, 1874 to 1898. Cost, $2,000. Present value, $800. Present condition, from bad to good.

The girls' building, the dining hall, kitchen, and dormitory, the manual-labor school, and the teachers' cottage are lighted by gasoline gas manufactured on the premises. The plant was installed in 1899, at a cost of $2,500. Capacity, 250 lights; 150 in use. Condition, good; satisfactory. Girls' building is heated by steam plant located in the building. Cost of this included in cost of building. Other buildings heated by coal or wood stoves. Unsatisfactory for the large buildings. Girls' building is ventilated by system devised by the Indian Office. Satisfactory except in windy weather. Other buildings have ventilating shafts, but they are not effective.

The water supplied by the school waterworks is hard and impure, and during dry weather insufficient. The water is obtained for the greater portion of the year from a well near the river, and it is supposed that the water in it comes mostly from the river, as when the river is dry the well is mostly dry. The water from this well is pumped into the tank by a windmill. When there is water in the well, there is usually a sufficient supply in the tank. When this well fails, water is pumped into the tank by a steam pump. Both a well and sand points driven in the ground are used, but neither is effective, as it is very difficult to obtain sufficient water, even when the pump is run all day. This water is purer but harder than that from the other well. The water is pumped into a tank resting on a steel tower 60 feet high; capacity, 48,000 gallons. Pressure is ample to throw the water wherever required. The plant was installed in 1899, and, with improvements, cost $7,000. The agency is supplied from the tank at the school.

All the buildings except those used for employees' quarters are connected with a 6-inch general sewer pipe, which runs into the South Canadian River about one-half mile from the school. With the exception of two for night use in the girls' building, the water-closets are not connected with this. The sewage from them is hauled and dumped into the fields, which are on the same level with the school. There are 6 ring baths in the girls' building and 12 in the boys. There are standpipes in the girls' building with two hose on each floor. Buckets are the only protection for the other buildings. Fire hydrants in the grounds.

This school has 230 acres of fine agricultural land in its reserve. It was set apart by Executive order. Present value estimated to be $7,000. In addition to this, about 600 acres of the agency reserve are used for pasture in summer. All land used by the school is under fence. Two hundred acres under cultivation, all level bottom land; 100 additional acres could be cultivated. Twenty acres in addition to the 600 mentioned above. None irrigated; not necessary.

This school was organized as a day school in 1871. The following year the boarding school was opened; capacity of about 50, as far as can be ascertained. It now has a capacity of 150 pupils.

Cheyenne Boarding School, Darlington, Okla.

Located 3 miles north of Darlington, Okla., on the Chicago, Rock Island and Pacific Railway. Site beautifully situated for school purposes; climate subject to no very severe changes. Soil of surrounding country, prairie loam on a substratum of rock.

Boys' building.—Character, two-story brick with front porch. Use, dormitory, superintendent's and employes' quarters, office, music room, schoolroom, and tailor shop. Capacity, 70 pupils. Erected in 1892. Cost, $15,000. Present value, $12,000. Present condition, good.

Girls' building.—Character, three-story frame with front and back porches. Use, dormitory, dining room and kitchen, schoolrooms, chapel, sewing room, and bakery. Capacity, 70 pupils. Erected in 1879. Cost, $12,000. Present value, $7,000. Present condition, very bad.

Barn.—Character, 2½-story, frame. Use, housing horses and storing hay and grain. Capacity, 20 horses, 75 tons hay, 1,500 bushles oats, and 1,500 bushels wheat. Erected in 1893. Cost, $2,000. Present value, $2,000. Present condition, good.

Workshop and storeroom.—Character, 1¼-story frame. Use, carpenter and blacksmith shops and storeroom. Capacity, 6 pupils. Erected in 1885. Cost, $600. Present value, $250. Present condition, fair.

Spring house.—Character, one-story brick. Use, protection of water. Dimension, 8 by 16 feet. Erected in 1875. Cost, $250. Present value, $100. Present condition, excellent.

Laundry.—Character, one-story frame. Use, laundry and girls' bathroom. Capacity, 10 pupils. Erected in 1892. Cost, $500. Present value, $300. Present condition, bad.

Miscellaneous outbuildings.—Character, all frame. Use, cow barn, boys' play room, implement shed, windmill and tower, henhouse, etc. Erected, 1880 to 1896. Cost, $2,000. Present value, $1,200. Present condition, mostly very poor.

All buildings are lighted by kerosene-oil lamps. Heated by Smead system, which gives very unsatisfactory results. Buildings have no modern system of ventilation. The water supplied is fine, pure, and soft. Its source is the Caddo Spring, about 500 yards east of the buildings. The water from this spring is forced into a tank of 33,000 gallons capacity, on a steel trestle standing 60 feet high, by a steam engine and pump and by a windmill. None of the water is used for irrigation. Water system was installed in 1901, at a cost of $4,000. The buildings are not equipped with sewerage, but the natural drainage is excellent, the buildings being located on an elevation between two dry ravines. There are six ring baths in laundry building and six in boys' playroom building. Ring baths are in bad order. There are standpipes in the large buildings with hose on each floor, and water buckets and a few hand grenades in all the buildings. Fire hydrants on the grounds. Wooden ladders to second story for fire escapes.

This school has 4,800 acres of fine land in its reserve. This land was set aside by Executive order, and its present value is estimated to be about $50,000. The whole reserve is under fence. About 700 acres under cultivation. All except about 200 acres can be cultivated; 3,000 acres are used for pasture and hay land.

This school was opened in 1880, with a capacity of 70 pupils and 10 employees. It had an enrollment in 1900–1901 of 140. The Caddo Spring, on this reserve, is noted throughout this part of Oklahoma for furnishing the best water in this section of the country.

Cantonment Training School, Cantonment, Okla.

Located 18 miles southwest of Homestead station, on Choctaw Railroad, 60 miles northwest of Darlington and Okeene, 20 miles distant on Rock Island and Frisco railways. Site at an elevation of 150 feet above the North Canadian River, about one-fourth mile away. Elevation, 150 feet and admirably located for natural drainage. Most excellently arranged for school work. Climate a little better than the average, ordinarily dry and not subject to extreme changes. Soil, deep red and black loam, with substratum of red clay.

Dormitory and school; frame, two story.—Use, dormitory, schoolrooms, dining room, kitchen, boys' and girls' sitting rooms, storerooms, and chapel. Capacity, 120 pupils. Erected in 1898. Cost, $17,600. Present value, $17,300. Present condition, good.

Mess and laundry, one-story frame, consisting of 6 rooms.—Erected in 1898. Cost, $1,600. Present condition, good.

Hospital building, stone.—Use, general storage, warerooms, and doctor's residence. Capacity, 1 large storage and 6 smaller rooms. Erected, not definitely known, but probably in the year 1874. Cost, approximately $2,000 at present cost of material, but at that time must have cost much more. Cost to the school, $200. Present value, $1,000. Present condition, walls excellent, roof out of repair.

Barn, one-story frame.—Use, housing live stock and storing hay. Capacity, 10 head of stock and 3 tons of hay. Erected in 1899.

Windmill, tower, and tank.—Windmill, steel, 60 feet high; tank, steel, 65 feet high. Capacity, 20,000 gallons storage. Erected in 1898. Cost, $6,361.

Outhouses, 2, in good repair.

There is no record of the individual cost of sewer, water, tank, and tower systems. Buildings, cost not given, but according to the record of the total cost of the entire plant their cost was $8,400.

The buildings are lighted by means of kerosene-oil lamps, heated by wood stoves. An excellent flue and radiator ventilating system devised by the Indian Office. The water comes from a dug well 87 feet deep; the water is of the very best quality and pumped into the buildings. The water supply is quite deficient; have to haul water in barrels much of the time from the river. The sewerage would be good with some slight changes in the way of enlarging and changing the position of some of the piping and making connection with the water-closets (outhouses). The bathing is performed in washtubs during cold weather, owing to no hot-water facilities in connection with the spray system. The children are very well protected in case of fire by convenient exits, fire ladders, and standpipes on each floor connected with hose, buckets, and standpipes on the grounds.

There is now 1½ sections of land under school control, of good quality for both farming and grazing. It was set aside from the military reserve for school and subagency use. One and one-fourth acres are under fence. About 30 acres are cultivated by the school. Three hundred and twenty acres could be cultivated. All save the 30 acres are either grazed or reserved for hay. Not any irrigated. This section is much better adapted to stock raising than to agricultural purposes, and the school has a very good start in stock and can occupy all the grazing land in a few years. In addition to land above described, about 1,280 acres are leased for the benefit of the agency that can be utilized for school purposes whenever deemed best.

The school was organized in May, 1899, with the present capacity. Up to September 1, 1900, an enrollment of 102 children had been secured, with an average attendance of 76 for the year. During the year 1901 an enrollment of 120 pupils was maintained, with an average attendance of 112.

Seger Colony School, Colony, Okla.

Located 15 miles southeast of Weatherford, Okla., on the Choctaw, Oklahoma and Gulf Railway. Admirably situated in a beautiful grove on Cobb Creek, with good climate and fertile soil.

Barn.—Character, 1½-story frame. Use, housing live stock and storing grain and hay. Capacity, 14 horses, 20 tons hay, 1,000 bushels grain. Erected in 1894. Cost, $1,500. Present value, $1,200. Present condition, fair.

Carpenter and blacksmith shop.—Character, two-story frame, 18 by 52 feet, part brick. Use, carpenter and blacksmith shop and storeroom. Capacity, 1 pupil. Erected in 1898. Cost, $800. Present value, $800. Present condition, good.

Commissary.—Character, stone and brick, two stories. Use, storing supplies. Dimensions, 24 by 30 feet. Erected in 1896. Cost, $500. Present value, $500. Present condition, good.

Farmer's cottage.—Character, two-story frame. Use, employees' quarters. Capacity, 5 employees. Erected in 1892. Cost, $1,300. Present value, $1,300. Present condition, good.

Employees' cottage.—Character, brick, two stories, 28 by 36 feet. Use, employees' quarters, mess kitchen, and dining room, and guest chamber. Capacity, 5 employees. Erected in 1900. Cost, $1,030. Present value, $1,000. Present condition, good.

Girls' dormitory.—Character, 2½-story story brick, 36 by 100 feet. Use, dormitories and play rooms, lavatories, and clothing room. Capacity, 75 pupils. Erected in 1896. Cost, $10,629. Present value, $10,000. Condition, good.

Laundry.—Character, one-story frame. Use, laundering pupils' clothing. Dimensions, 22 by 42 feet. Erected in 1892. Cost, $1,000. Present value, $1,000. Present condition, fair.

Schoolhouse No. 1.—Character, two-story brick, with 1 one-story brick addition. Use, dormitory, dining room and kitchen, bakery, and sewing room. Capacity, 75 pupils. Erected in 1892. Cost, $12,000. Present value, $12,000. Present condition, good.

Schoolhouse No. 2.—Character, one-story brick. Use, superintendent's office and reading room. Dimensions, 24 by 26 feet. Erected in 1897. Cost, $320. Present value, $400. Present condition, good.

Schoolhouse No. 3.—Character, two-story brick, with stone basement. Use, class rooms and assembly hall; play rooms, museum, etc., in basement. Capacity, 150 pupils. Erected in 1901. Cost, $13,900. Present value, $13,900. Present condition, good.

Office.—Character, two-story brick, with stone basement. Use, school office and clerk's living room. Dimensions, 20 by 26 feet. Erected in 1900. Cost, $743. Present value, $800. Present condition, good.

Hospital.—Character, two-story stone and brick, with attic finished. Use, isolation and care of sick and instruction in nursing and domestic science. Capacity, 10 beds, single. Erected in 1901. Cost, $1,500. Present value, $1,500. Present condition, good.

Miscellaneous outbuildings.—Character, frame, stone, and brick. Use, henhouse, cattle sheds, outhouses, etc. Erected, 1892 to 1900. Cost, about $1,800. Present value, $1,500. Present condition, good.

The buildings are lighted by lamps with kerosene. Heated by stoves, wood and coal, except new schoolhouse, which is heated by steam. The new school building is ventilated as provided by the Indian Office. The boys' building has a ventilator about 3 feet from ceiling in each of the dormitory rooms. The girls' building is ventilated by leaving out the transoms over the doors of each dormitory and raising lower sash in the daytime and lowering upper sash at night.

The water supply is pure and soft, and flows from red sand rock. It is procured from a well 30 feet deep on a high point of ground above the drainage of the school. This well is supplemented from a well 100 feet deep, from which the water is pumped into the 30-foot well as is required. In the 30-foot well the water is usually about 10 feet deep, and in the 100-foot well there is 80 feet of water. The water is forced up into an iron tank of 1,000 barrels capacity, and the bottom of this tank rests on a stone tower 50 feet high. The water from this tank is conducted to the buildings through 4-inch galvanized-iron pipe, and to different parts of the buildings through a 2-inch pipe. The sewer system is composed of 4 and 6 inch vitalized earthen pipes, and only reaches the girls' and boys' dormitories. The sewer from each building is independent of the other, and discharges over the creek bank a short distance from the buildings. The sewer system is in good working order.

There are bath tubs in both the girls' and boys' dormitories, which are supplied from a hot-water heater located in the basement of the boys' building. There are standpipes in the girls' and boys' dormitories, with hose attached ready for use, sufficient to reach any room in the building. There are three hydrants on the grounds to which hose can be attached to reach any part of the buildings.

This school has 2,545 acres of excellent land for farming and grazing purposes. This land was set aside by Executive order, and is estimated to value $25,000. There are 2,545 acres under fence. There are 200 acres under cultivation. About 2,000 acres more could be cultivated. About 2,200 acres in pasturage. Irrigation plant sufficient to irrigate 1 acre of garden.

This school was opened January 11, 1892, with a capacity of 70 pupils, having at the time only one dormitory building.

STATISTICS OF INDIAN TRIBES, AGENCIES, AND SCHOOLS.

Red Moon School, Hammon, Okla.

(Under jurisdiction of superintendent of Seger School.)

Located 18 miles north and 2 miles east of Elk City, Okla., on the Choctaw, Oklahoma and Gulf Railroad. Climate without extreme changes. Soil a sandy loam of good fertility.

Main building.—Character, two-story frame. Use, dormitories (boys' and girls'), dining room and kitchen, schoolrooms, sewing room, superintendent's office, employee's rooms, bathrooms, lavatories, and official guest chamber. Capacity, 76 pupils. Erected in 1897. Cost, $13,498. Present value, $13,000. Present condition, good.

Laundry and bakehouse.—Character, one-story frame. Use, laundry and repair shop. Dimensions—laundry, 28 by 16 feet; bakehouse, 14 by 12 feet. Erected in 1900. Cost, about $500. Present value, $400. Present condition, excellent.

Storehouse.—Character, one-story frame. Use, storing supplies. Dimensions, 14 by 12 feet. Erected in 1900. Cost, $183. Present value, $183. Present condition, excellent.

Barn.—Character, 1½ stories frame. Use, housing live stock and storing hay. Capacity, 7 horses, 10 tons hay. Erected in 1897. Cost, $1,000. Present value, $1,000. Present condition, good.

Miscellaneous outbuildings.—Character, all frame. Use, cattle sheds, corn crib and implement shed, etc. Erected in 1897. Cost, $400. Present value, $400. Present condition, good.

Lamps burning kerosene furnish the necessary light. Stoves burning wood supply the necessary heat to the main building and laundry. Ventilation of main building is by the system devised by the Indian Office. The water supplied is good, but hard. Its main source is a well about 60 yards from the main building. The water is pumped by windmill to a wooden tank of 2,564 gallons capacity, on a metal tower standing 65 feet high. The pressure is ample to force the water wherever required. None of the water is used for irrigation, but it supplies a wooden tank in the barnyard. Water system was installed when plant was constructed, but has never been entirely satisfactory, principally owing to defective construction and the mill and pump being overtaxed. It is in a better state of repair than it has been since construction. Two cisterns, just finished, of about 200 barrels capacity, will no doubt supply a long-felt want in furnishing soft water for the laundry. To supply water for the kitchen in case of a breakdown in the water system a tubular well has recently been made and a hand pump attached. The water from this will always be pure and cool. The main building is connected with a 4-inch sewer pipe, which empties into a cesspool about 350 yards away. The outfall is 12 feet below the building. There are 8 ring baths located on the first floor of the main building. There are standpipes on each side of the main building, with hose on each floor. Water buckets are also used during fire drills. Two fire hydrants in grounds, and 250 feet of new hose for the same.

This school has 1,280 acres of good farming and grazing land. Seventy-five acres are under cultivation, 10 acres of which are seeded to alfalfa. Five hundred additional acres can be cultivated (unfenced). Three hundred and twenty acres are used for pasture.

This school was opened September, 1897, with a capacity of 76 pupils.

CHEYENNE RIVER AGENCY, S. DAK.

Tribes.	Population.
Blackfeet Sioux	
Minneconjou Sioux	2,471
Sans Arcs Sioux	
Two-Kettle Sioux	

Area: 2,867,840 acres, partly surveyed; unallotted.

Railroad station: Gettysburg, on Chicago and Northwestern Railroad. Twenty miles to agency by stage.

Nearest military post: Fort Yates, N. Dak. Post-office address: Cheyenne Agency, Dewey County, S. Dak. Telegraphic address: Gettysburg, S. Dak.

Cheyenne River Boarding School.

Located on the west side of the Missouri River, 20 miles west of Gettysburg, S. Dak., on the Chicago and Northwestern Railway. Site not a desirable one for such a plant, being situated right under a hill; climate subject to extreme changes. Soil of immediate site not very good, there being some "gumbo" in it.

Girls' building.—Character, two-story frame. Use, dormitory, dining room and kitchen, playrooms, bath, lavatory, bakery, mess dining room and kitchen, employees' rooms, and superintendent's office. Capacity, 50 pupils. Erected in 1892. Cost, $4,450 (one-third of contract for three buildings). Present value, $3,750. Present condition, good.

Schoolhouse.—Character, two-story frame. Use, two schoolrooms, one of which is used as assembly room, sewing room, and employees' rooms. Capacity, if used entirely as schoolrooms, 190. Erected 1892. Cost, $4,450 (one-third of contract for three buildings). Present value, $3,750. Present condition, good.

Boys' buildings.—Character, two-story frame. Use, dormitory, play rooms, lavatory, bath, sewing room, employees' rooms, and reading room. Capacity, 60 pupils. Erected 1892 and 1895. Cost, $4,450 (one-third of contract for three buildings). Present value, $4,000. Present condition, good.

Schoolhouse.—Character, one-story frame. Use, dormitory and kindergarten. Capacity, 50 in kindergarten, 50 in dormitory. Erected in 1881 as day school building, then removed to present site in 1895. Cost, $1,200. Present value, $1,000. Present condition, good.

Barn.—Character, frame horse and cow barn, with wagon shed, corral, and cow shed attached. Use, housing live stock and farming implements. Capacity, 4 horses and 15 cows' stable room. Extra shed room. Erected in 1893. Cost, $1,000. Present value, $800. Present condition, good.

Shop.—Character, 1½ story, frame. Use, shop. Capacity, five pupils. Erected in 1893. Cost, $500. Present value, $400. President condition, fair.

Outbuildings.—Character, frame. Use, henhouse, water-closets, and coal houses. Erected in 1893. Cost, $370. Present value, $350. Present condition, fair.

Lighted by lamps. Heated by stoves, some of them being for hard coal, some for soft coal, and some for wood. Ventilation is good. Water supply is from the Missouri River, and is good, except that it should be filtered before being pumped into the tank. Only two buildings are at present connected with the system. The water is pumped from the river by steam and stored in tank elevated about 20 feet above school buildings. The sewerage is carried from the school plant by an eight-inch sewer which connects with only two buildings and the outside closets. There are no closets in the buildings. Four-inch sewer pipes connect from the two buildings with the 8-inch main, about 100 feet to the south of the buildings. The sewerage is carried about 500 feet from the buildings. The boys have four tubs in their bathrooms and the girls have three tubs. As fire protection, we have 150 feet of 2-inch hose to fit outside hydrants. Water buckets are placed in buildings.

This school has about 10 acres set apart for gardening purposes. The quality of the soil is poor, being of alkali and gumbo character and has no present value, it being a part of the reservation. There are about 60 acres under fence. About 10 acres under cultivation for vegetables. No more available land that could be cultivated. About 50 acres used for pasture. About 2 acres will be irrigated during the coming season. This school was built in 1892, and opened in the spring of 1893, and has a capacity of 125 pupils, with a present enrollment of 148, and 16 employees.

No. 5 Day School.

Located on Moreau River, 55 miles from agency.

School building.—Character, one-story frame. Use, schoolroom, employees' quarters. Capacity, 20 pupils. Erected in 1887. Cost, $1,100. Present value, $800. Present condition, poor.

Outbuilding.—Character, frame. Use, water-closet. Erected in 1887. Cost, $5. Present value, $5. Present condition, poor.

Lighted by lamps. Heated by stoves. Ventilation, ordinary window. Water supply, from Moreau River. Fire protection, none.

No farm connected with the school.

No. 7 Day School.

Located on the Moreau River, 42 miles from agency.

School building.—Character, one-story frame. Use, schoolroom, employees' quarters. Capacity, 24 pupils. Erected in 1887. Cost, $1,185. Present value, $900. Present condition, fair.

Outbuilding.—Character, frame. Use, water-closet. Erected in 1887. Cost, $20. Present value, $20. Present condition, fair.

Lighted by lamps. Heated by stoves. Ventilation, ordinary window. Water supply from Moreau River. Fire protection, none.

No farm connected with the school.

STATISTICS OF INDIAN TRIBES, AGENCIES, AND SCHOOLS. 11

No. 8 Day School.

Located on Cherry Creek, 90 miles from agency.
School building.—Character, one-story frame. Use, schoolroom, employees' quarters. Capacity, 25 pupils. Erected in 1887. Cost, $1,185. Present value, $900. Present condition, fair.
Outbuilding.—Character, frame. Use water-closet. Erected in 1887. Cost, $12. Present value, $12. Present condition, fair.
Lighted by lamps.—Heated by stoves. Ventilation, ordinary window. Water supply from Cherry Creek. Fire protection, none.
No farm connected with the school.

COLORADO RIVER AGENCY, ARIZONA.

(Under School Superintendent.)

Tribes.	Population.
Mohave	523
Mohave at Needles	800
Mohave at Fort Mohave	1,000
Chemehuevi	300

Area: 240,640 acres, partly surveyed.
Railroad station: Needles, Cal., on Atlantic and Pacific Railroad. Ninety miles to agency by boat or sixty-three miles by land.
Nearest military post: Fort Whipple, Ariz. Post-office address: Parker, Yuma County, Ariz. Telegraphic address: Mellen, Ariz.

Colorado River Training School, Parker, Ariz.

Located about 86 miles south of Mellen station, Santa Fe Railway, on the Colorado River. Fairly well suited for school purposes. Soil a sandy loam, susceptible in the greater part to profitable cultivation under perfect irrigation.
Girls' building.—Character, two-story adobe, with 2 one-story additions. Use, dormitory and hospital of one room on upper floor, with matron and supply storeroom adjoining. Lower floor, two good-sized schoolrooms, sitting room for girls. Girls' bathroom and seamstress room in each of the one-story additions. Capacity.—Schoolrooms, 125; dormitory, about 60. Erected in 1891. Cost, $4,042. Present value, $3,500. Present condition, good.
Boys' building.—Character, one-story adobe. Use, dormitory and sitting room. Capacity, 60. Erected in 1879. Cost, unknown. Present value, $2,000. Present condition, fair.
Mess hall.—Character, two-story brick, with one-story addition. Use.—Lower floor, mess room; kitchen in one-story addition; upper floor divided into 4 rooms for school employees. Capacity, mess hall, 150. Erected in 1900. Cost, $3,000. Present value, $3,000. Present condition, good.
Laundry.—Character, one-story brick. Use, laundry work for school. Capacity, 150. Erected in 1899. Cost, $800. Present value, $800. Present condition, good.
School ice plant.—Character, one-story adobe. Use, manufacturing ice for use of school and school employees. Capacity, 1,500 lbs. per day. Erection, unknown. Cost, $2,000. Present value, plant and building, $2,000. Present condition, good.
School storeroom.—Character, one-story adobe. Use, storing school supplies. Dimensions, 21 by 36 feet. Erected, not known. Cost, not known. Present value, $500. Present condition, fair.
School pump and boiler house.—Character, one-story adobe and frame. Use, pumping water through underground pipes and elevating into two 5,000-gallon tanks, 30 feet high, thus providing a hydrant-water system for general use of school. Dimensions, 15 by 20 feet. Erected in 1892 and put in good repair fall of 1901, Cost to erect, about $500. Present value, with two school tanks, $1,000. Present condition, good.
Lighted by kerosene lamps. Fairly satisfactory. Heated by wood stoves. Ventilation of schoolrooms and dormitories is by Indian Office system. Other buildings no modern system. The water supplied is soft and apparently pure. Its source is from sheet of water 15 feet under surface, filtered through substrata of sand, 1 mile from Colorado River. Girls' dormitory, mess hall, kitchen, and laundry connected with 4-inch underground sewer drain tile, that empties into large open ditch one-fourth mile from buildings and away from water supply.
This school has probably 20,000 acres in reserve, chiefly pasture land. School has about 4 acres cleared, under fence and irrigation. Only the garden is fenced. Five hundred acres might be cultivated; 18,000 acres or more used for pasture. Value of land, $50,000.
This school was opened in March, 1879, with a capacity of 100 pupils.

COLVILLE AGENCY, WASH.

Tribes.	Population.	Tribes.	Population.
Colville	296	Columbia (Moses' band)	319
Cœur d'Alène	495	Okanogan	575
Upper and Middle Spokane (on Cœur d'Alène Reserve)	83	Nez Perces (Joseph's band)	128
		San Poil and Nespilem	400
Lake	306	Kalispel	150
Lower Spokane	374		
Upper and Middle Spokane, on Spokane Reserve	181	Total	3,307

Area:

	Acres.
Colville (allotted)	50,900
Columbia (unallotted)	24,220
Colville (unallotted)	1,300,000
Spokane (unallotted)	153,600

Railroad station: Davenport, on Central Washington Railroad (via Spokane). Twenty-seven miles to agency by stage.

Post-office address: Miles, Lincoln County, Wash. Telegraphic address: Fort Spokane, via Davenport, Wash.

Colville Agency Boarding School, Miles, Wash.

Located 20 miles north of Creston, Wash. (a station on the Washington Central Railroad), on the old Fort Spokane Military Reservation, now a part of the Spokane Indian Reservation. An excellent site for school purposes. Climate not severe. Soil a very sandy loam.

Small boys' dormitory.—Character, two-story frame (post barracks building). Use, dodmitory for small boys. Capacity, 50 pupils. Erected in 1884. Cost, $3,000. Present value, $1,500. Present condition, fair.

Small girls' dormitory.—Character, two-story frame (post barracks building). Use, dormitory for small girls. Capacity, 50 pupils. Erected in 1884. Cost, $3,000. Present value, $1,500. Present condition, fair.

Dining hall.—Character, two-story frame (post barracks building). Use, pupils' dining-room and kitchen. Capacity, 225 pupils. Erected in 1884. Cost, $3,000. Present value, $1,500. Present condition, fair.

Schoolhouse.—Character, two-story frame (post barracks building). Use, recitation rooms. Capacity, 150 pupils. Erected in 1884. Cost, $3,000. Present value, $1,500. Present condition, fair.

Gymnasium.—Character, two-story frame (post barracks building). Use, gymnasium. Capacity, 75. Erected in 1884. Cost, $3,000. Present value, $1,500. Present condition, fair.

Barracks No. 6.—Character, two-story frame (post barracks building). Use, one room used as a kindergarten; remainder unused. Capacity, same as other barracks buildings mentioned. Erected in 1884. Cost, $3,000. Present value, $1,500. Present condition, fair.

Headquarters building.—Character, two-story frame, interior partly unfinished. Use, superintendent's office, storerooms, dormitory for large boys. Capacity (for dormitory purposes), 36. Erected in 1883. Cost, $2,900. Present value, $1,450. Present condition, fair.

Guardhouse.—Character, one-story brick. Use, bathrooms, sewing room, guardrooms. Capacity, bathrooms, 12 rings, 2 tubs; sewing room, 12 pupils, 2 employees; guardrooms, 6 pupils. Erected in 1892. Cost, $5,240. Present value, $3,500. Present condition, good.

Large girls' dormitory.—Character, two-story frame residence. Use, dormitory for large girls. Capacity, 40 pupils. Erected in 1889. Cost, $8,000. Present value, $4,000. Present condition, good.

Employees' cottages, seven in number. Character, one and three-fourths-story frame residences. Use, one is used as a drug room and dispensary, and as the school physician's residence; one as a dormitory for large boys, and the remainder are partially occupied as employees' quarters. Otherwise unoccupied. Capacity, eight employees could be given one comfortable room each in each of the buildings not otherwise used. Erected in 1883 and 1884. Cost, $1,500 to $2,300 each. Present value, $700 to $1,000 each. Present condition, fair.

Employees' cottage.—Character, 1½-story frame residence. Use, employees' quarters. Capacity, for a small family. Erected in 1883. Cost, $700. Present value, $300. Present condition, fair.

STATISTICS OF INDIAN TRIBES, AGENCIES, AND SCHOOLS. 13

Warehouse, No. 1.—Character, two-story frame. Use, storing supplies. Dimensions, 24 by 80 feet. Erected in 1889. Cost, $2,300. Present value, $1,400. Present condition, good.

Warehouse, No. 2.—Character, two-story frame. Use, storing supplies. Dimensions, 24 by 60 feet. Erected in 1887. Cost, $826. Present value, $400. Present condition, fair.

Magazine.—Character, one-story brick. Use, storing flour. Dimensions, 24 by 32 feet. Erected in 1888. Cost, $735. Present value, $450. Present condition, good.

Stable.—Character, 1½-story frame. Use, housing live stock and storing hay. Dimensions, 34 by 132 feet. Erected in 1884. Cost, $1,600. Present value, $400. Present condition, poor.

Cavalry barn.—Character, one-story frame. Use, storing fuel. Dimensions, 34 by 200 feet. Erected in 1887. Cost, $1,176. Present value, $400. Present condition, poor.

Workshops.—Character, one-story frame. Use, school carpenter shop, agency blacksmith shop. Dimensions, 24 by 136 feet. Erected in 1885. Cost, $1,013. Present value, $150. Present condition, bad.

Oil house.—Character, low one-story brick. Use, storing kerosene. Dimensions, 15 by 18 feet. Erected in 1892. Cost, unknown. Present value, $75. Present condition, good.

Ice house.—Character, rough frame. Use, storing ice. Dimensions, 24 by 48 feet. Erected in 1882. Cost, unknown. Present value, $50. Present condition, bad.

Laundry.—Character, two-story frame. Use, laundry purposes. Dimensions, 34 by 50 feet. Erected in 1883. Cost, $2,000. Present value, $700. Present condition, fair.

Bakery.—Character, one-story frame, and brick oven. Use, as bakery. Capacity, for school of 400 pupils. Dimensions, 30 by 45 feet. Erected in 1890. Cost, $1,107. Present value, $600. Present condition, fair.

Pump house.—Character, one-story frame. Use, shelters pumping plant. Dimensions, 26 by 40 feet. Erected in 1899. Cost, $402. Present value, $200. Present condition, fair.

Chapel.—Character, one-story frame. Use, not used. Dimensions, 20 by 40 feet. Erected in 1885. Cost, $1,013. Present value, $300. Present condition, fair.

Reservoir.—Character, brick and cement basin, frame house. Use, storing water for distribution through pipes to buildings. Capacity, 1,900 barrels. Erected in 1883. Cost, unknown. Present value, $800. Present condition, good.

Reservoir.—Character, brick and cement basin, frame house. Use, not in use. Capacity, 1,650 barrels. Erected in 1883. Cost, unknown. Present value, $200. Present condition, bad.

Lighted by kerosene lamps. Heated by wood-burning stoves. In the three principal dormitories there are ventilating shafts, which conduct the air from near the floor of each sleeping room through the roof; and the windows are left open at the top and fitted with boards to give incoming air an upward movement. The windows in the schoolhouse and in the sewing room are also fitted in that manner. The bathrooms are ventilated by a shaft through the roof, which rests on a hood built over the bathing stalls. The other buildings are not ventilated in any systematic way.

The water supplied to the school is excellent and abundant. That which is ordinarily used comes from a spring which is on a hill 350 feet higher than the school premises. This is piped into the first reservoir above described, located about 100 feet above the principal school buildings, and is thence distributed into the said buildings, to the fire hydrants, etc. Water can also be pumped from the Spokane River into the same storage and distributing system when necessary. This becomes necessary when water is needed for irrigation, but not otherwise. The waterworks system was installed by the War Department. Data as to cost not available. Present value probably $15,000. Present condition, fairly good.

The school plant is practically surrounded by the main lines of an excellent sewer, laid by the War Department. Data as to when built and cost of construction not available. The lines surrounding the buildings are, at the upper end of the system, 6 inches in diameter; near the lower end, 8 inches. The line into which all branches converge is 10 inches in diameter, and the outlet is half a mile from the buildings, much below them, in a dry ravine which opens toward the river below the pumping plant, approximately a mile from said plant. The large girls' dormitory and the cottages are connected with this system, having toilet closets, etc. The other school buildings have connections with it only for disposal of waste water. There are six ring baths and one tub in each of the two bathrooms, both of which are located in the guardhouse building. There are fire hydrants near each important building. Fire hose is kept near each, and numerous water buckets are kept filled in each. Axes, ladders, and empty fire pails are kept in a central location.

The school has approximately 640 acres of land, but much of this is too rough for cultivation, and of little value. The section, unimproved, is worth about $2,000. There are but 80 acres under fence. Only about 10 acres were cultivated last year (in gardens). About 100 acres additional can be cultivated and will be worth cultivating. About 160 acres additional to that mentioned will probably be good pasture land when seeded to brome, or some other suitable grass. Is now almost worthless. No acreage has, as yet, been irrigated, excepting lawns.

This school opened April 1, 1900, with accommodations for 100 pupils. Capacity of the school is 200 pupils.

CROW AGENCY, MONT.

Tribe.	Population.
Crow	1,870

Area, 3,504,000 acres, partly surveyed; unallotted.
Railroad station: At agency, on Burlington and Missouri Railroad.
Nearest military post: Fort Custer, Mont. Post-office address: Crow Agency, Mont. Telegraphic address: Crow Agency, Mont.

Crow Boarding School.

Located at Crow Agency close to the Burlington and Missouri River Railroad depot. Is a beautiful location, with many shade trees and a beautiful lawn; climate, mild and healthful. Soil is very productive when irrigated.

Girls' building.—Character, two-story brick. Use, kitchen, dining room, dormitory, sitting room, and bathroom. Capacity, 70 pupils. Erected in 1895. Cost, $13,000. Present value, $10,000. Present condition, good.

Boys' building.—Character, two-story brick. Use, dormitory, bathroom, sitting room, employees' quarters, and superintendent's office. Capacity, 90 pupils. Erected in 1893. Cost, $14,000. Present value, $10,000. Present condition, good.

School building.—Character, wood and very old, having been moved to its present site from some other location. Use, two schoolrooms and chapel. Capacity, 100. Erected in 1886. Cost, $2,861. Present value, $500. Present condition, very poor.

Schoolhouse.—Character, 2½ stories frame. Use, employees' quarters. Capacity, 10 rooms. Erected in 1902. Cost, $4,790. Present value, $4,790. Present condition, excellent.

Laundry building.—Character, two-story frame. Use, laundry, sewing room, mess kitchen, and dining room, three class rooms, and employees' quarters. Erected in 1884. Cost, $9,000. Present condition, unfit for any purpose.

Barn and wagon shed.—Character, one-story wood. Use, hay, cattle, horses. Capacity, 20 head of cattle, 4 horses. Erected in 1893. Cost, not known. Present value, $500. Present condition, fair.

Miscellaneous outbuildings.—Character, all wood. Use, chicken house, coal building, outhouses. Erected in 1896. Cost, not known. Present value, $200. Present condition, fair.

Storehouse.—Character, one-story wood. Use, storing supplies. Erected in 1898. Cost, $1,000. Present value, $1,000. Present condition, good.

The lighting is done with coal-oil lamps. The heating is done with coal stoves. Ventilation of the boys' building is by special system and is good. The other buildings have no modern system. The water supply is ample and good. Its source is the Little Big Horn River, and is pumped into a large tank placed upon a hill near the school, which gives a great pressure and force to the water. This water system is also used by the agency, but none for irrigation. Erected in 1896. Cost, about $7,000. Present condition, excellent. All these buildings are connected with an 8-inch sewer pipe which empties into the river about one-half mile from any buildings and far below the source of the water supply. This sewer system is very good. There are two tubs for each of the two dormitories. Fire protection consists of 1 hose cart and 500 feet of 4-inch hose; 3 fire hydrants are close to the buildings, and water buckets are in all halls where they are easy of access.

Farm and garden consists of 50 acres, all under good substantial wire fence. About 12 acres are used for a garden, which produces an abundance of vegetables for the school; 30 acres is used for pasture for school cows.

This school was organized in 1883, and had a capacity for about 50 children with employees. Its present capacity is 150.

Pryor Creek Boarding School, Montana.

Location, 1 mile north of Pryor, Mont., on the Burlington Route. Site admirably suited for school purposes, climate without extreme changes, winters mild for latitude. Soil black loam on substratum of gravel.

Pryor schoolhouse.—Character, two-story brick with a one-story kitchen and laundry added to rear; a basement underneath the entire building. Use, dormitory, employees' quarters, dining room, kitchen, laundry, and schoolrooms. Capacity, 50 pupils. Erected in 1902. Cost, $23,632. Present value, $23,632. Present condition, excellent.

Gas house.—Character, one-story frame. Use, generating acetylene gas. Capacity, one room for generating and collecting gas; one room for heating the building. Erected in 1903. Cost, $1,080. Present value, $1,080. Present condition, excellent.

Lighted by acetylene gas, furnished by a generator in the gas house. There are 99 burners. It is in good condition and satisfactory. Heated by steam from a heater placed in the basement beneath the kitchen at time of erection of building, and the cost of same is included in the cost of building. The gas house is heated by hot water from a heater, separated by a partition from the gas-generating machine. Ventilation of school building is by a system devised by the Indian Office.

The water supplied is pure, slightly hard. Its source is a number of springs located in a reservoir 125 by 75 feet, which is of a uniform depth of 5 feet, and from thence is fed through a 6-inch pipe a distance of 8,800 feet to the school plant. There is a fall of 88 feet from reservoir to school. The pressure is ample to force the water wherever required. None of the water is used for irrigation. Water system was installed when plant was constructed. Cost, $5,879.17. The school building is connected with an 8-inch sewer pipe, which empties into Pryor Creek about 300 yards from the building. The outfall is about 20 feet below the building. There are 8 ring baths and 2 tubs located in the basement. There are standpipes with hose on each floor. Fire hydrants in grounds.

The school has no land at present. The land immediately surrounding the school is all under irrigation and cultivated by Indians. One hundred and sixty acres of the land is available for school purposes and will be sufficient. It is worth about $4,500.

This school was opened February 12, 1903, with a capacity of 50 pupils. It has an enrollment at present of 50 pupils.

CROW CREEK AGENCY, S. DAK.

Tribe.	Population.
Lower Yanktonai Sioux	1,020

Area:	Acres.
Allotted	172,413.81
Reserved	1,076.90
Unallotted	112,031.00

Railroad station, Chamberlain, on Chicago, Milwaukee and St. Paul Railway. Twenty-five miles to agency by stage. Nearest military post, Fort Niobrara, Nebr. Post-office address, Crow Creek, Buffalo County, S. Dak. Telegraphic address, Crow Creek, via Chamberlain, S. Dak.

Crow Creek Industrial Boarding School.

Located 25 miles north of Chamberlain, S. Dak. Site well suited for school. Soil of site, black loam, extending from the banks of the Missouri River.

Boys' building.—Character, 2½-story frame. Use, dormitory upstairs; playroom, superintendent's office, and matron's quarters downstairs. Capacity, 70 pupils. Erected in 1885. Cost, $4,800. Present value, $4,000. Present condition, fair.

Girls' building.—Character, two-story frame. Use, dormitory, matron's and cook's quarters, and storeroom in second story. Downstairs, dining room, kitchen, play room, girls' parlor, lavatory, bathroom, and sewing room. Capacity, 70 pupils. Erected in 1879. Cost, $8,400. Present value, nothing. Present condition, poor.

Schoolhouse.—Character, one-story frame. Use, class room, assembly room when partitions are raised. Capacity, 140 pupils at a single sitting. Erected in 1894. Cost, $900. Present value, $700. Present condition, good. Movable partition unsatisfactory.

Hospital.—Character, 1½-story frame. Use, care of sick. Capacity, 20 pupils; only two wards. Erected in 1892. Cost, $2,000. Present value, $1,750. Present condition, good.

Employees' quarters.—Character, two-story frame. Use, mess dining room and kitchen; occupied by five employees and mess cook. Capacity, 6 employees. Erected in 1879. Cost, $2,055. Present value, $2,000. Present condition, good.

Superintendent's quarters.—Character, three-room frame, with porch in front. Use, occupied by superintendent's family. Erected in 1900. Cost $750. Present value, $700. Present condition, good.

Laundry.—Character, one-story frame. Use, laundrying pupils' clothes and laundress' quarters. Dimensions, 38 by 42 feet. Erected in 1899. Cost $2,055. Present value, $2,000. Present condition, excellent.

Warehouse.—Character, one-story brick. Use, storing supplies. Dimensions, 20 by 50 feet. Erected in 1899. Cost, $1,845. Present value, $1,800. Present condition, excellent.

Horse barn.—Character, 1½-story frame. Use, housing horses and storing hay. Capacity, 12 horses and 8 tons of hay. Erected in 1891. Cost, $977. Present value, $650. Present condition, poor.

Cow barn.—Character, 1½-story frame. Use, housing cattle. Capacity, 20 cows and 12 tons of hay. Erected in 1899. Cost, $1,800. Present value, $1,650. Present condition, good.

Dairy.—Character, one-story frame. Use, storing and caring for milk. Dimensions, 16 by 28 feet. Erected in 1895. Cost, $411. Present value, $300. Present condition, good.

Woodhouse.—Character, one-story frame. Use, storing fuel. Dimensions, 20 by 40 feet. Erected in 1893. Cost, $400. Present value, $110. Present condition, poor.

Poultry house.—Character, frame. Use, housing poultry. Dimensions, 20 by 30 feet. Erected in 1893. Cost, $400. Present value, $300. Present condition, good.

Hog house.—Character, one-story frame. Use, housing hogs and storing feed. Dimensions, 24 by 50 feet. Erected in 1893. Cost, $307. Present value, $200. Present condition, good.

Lighted by oil lamps. Heated by stoves. Ventilation of schoolrooms is fair, but no modern systems in other buildings. The water is very hard and unfit for bathing purposes. Water is pumped from a well into a tank situated on a bench above school some 300 yards from school plant. The pressure is sufficient to force water to top of highest buildings. The supply is sufficient, if quality was tolerable. The laundry, dairy, lavatories, hospital, and kitchen have sewer pipes, all of which, except laundry and dairy, are entirely too small; these empty into a small creek which flows painfully near the well from which the water supply is furnished. There are five bath tubs for the boys and five for the girls. The fire department seems to be a relic of bygone days. There is a hand hose cart and 200 feet of hose.

This school has 160 acres of good land in its reserve. The present value is estimated to be $3,200. All of the land is under fence. About 100 acres are under cultivation. By cutting of a beautiful grove, 50 acres more can be cultivated. All can be irrigated from an artesian well, admirably situated, by proper ditching.

School was opened under auspices of Episcopal Church in 1874, with a capacity of 25 pupils. In 1879 the Government erected other buildings, it remaining under Episcopal management, the Government taking control in 1880.

DEVILS LAKE AGENCY, N. DAK.

Tribes.	Population.
Sioux	1,043
Turtle Mountain Chippewas:	
Full bloods	228
Mixed bloods	
Mixed bloods outside reserve	2,281
Mixed blood on reserve, unrecognized	
Total	3,552

Area:	Acres.
Allotted, Devils Lake Reserve	131,506
Reserved for agency, school, and church	921
Devils Lake, unallotted	144
Turtle Mountain, unallotted	304

Railroad station: Devils Lake, on Great Northern Railway; 14 miles to agency by boat and stage.

Nearest military post: Fort Yates, N. Dak. Post-office address: Fort Totten, Benson County, N. Dak. Telegraphic address: Devils Lake, N. Dak.

Day School No. 2, Turtle Mountain Reservation, N. Dak.

Located in township 162 north, range 70 west, and at Belcourt post-office. Site on a knoll, affording good drainage. Climate, pleasant and dry in summer, but extremely cold in winter. Soil, prairie loam with substratum of clay.

Scholhouse.—Character, one-story log. Use, schoolroom, kitchen and dining room. Capacity, 40 pupils. Erected in 1889. Cost, $900. Present value, $200. Present condition, bad.

CORRECTION—PAGE 16.

The following under Devils Lake Agency:

"Area:
>   Devils Lake, unallotted... 144
>   Turtle Mountain, unallotted .... 304"

Should read:
>   Devils Lake and Turtle Mountain reserves, unallotted 144, 304

STATISTICS OF INDIAN TRIBES, AGENCIES, AND SCHOOLS.

Teachers' quarters.—Character, one-story, frame. Use, teachers' quarters. Capacity, for one small family. Erected in 1893. Cost, about $375. Present value, about $225. Present condition, poor.

No lighting plant. Heated by wood stoves. No modern system of ventilation. The water supply consists of a spring dug out for a well, and is pure, but hard, and about 500 feet from the buildings. No sewerage. No baths. Twelve hand-grenade fire extinguishers.

There is about 1 acre of land connected with the school, which the teacher uses for a garden.

This school was built of logs in 1889. Several years later it was sided up and ceiled. In 1893 the teachers' quarters (frame building) were added.

A well was dug in order to have water nearer the building, but when water was struck, it was found to be impregnated with alkali and unfit for use, so the water is now obtained from natural springs, although it is a little far away.

Day School No. 3, Turtle Mountain Reservation, N. Dak.

Located in township 162 north, range 71 west, about 2½ miles from Laureate post-office. Site on a knoll, affording good drainage. Climate, pleasant and dry in summer, but extremely cold in winter. Soil, prairie loam with substratum of clay.

Schoolhouse.—Character, one-story log, sided, 40 by 22 by 10 feet. Use, school room 22 by 30 by 10 feet, kitchen and dining room 22 by 10 by 10 feet. Capacity, 40 pupils. Erected in 1889. Cost, about $900. Present value, $200. Present condition, bad.

Teacher's quarters.—Character, one-story frame 16 by 24 by 10 feet, partitioned into two rooms, 16 by 12 by 8 feet. Use, teacher's and housekeeper's quarters. Capacity, one small family. Erected in 1895. Cost, about $375. Present value, about $225. Present condition, poor.

No lighting plant. Heated by wood stove. No modern system of ventilation. The water supply consists of a spring dug out for a well, and is pure but hard, and about 600 feet from the buildings. No sewerage. No baths. Twelve hand-grenade fire extinguishers.

There is about 1 acre of land connected with the school, which is used by the teacher for a garden.

This school was built of logs in 1889. Several years later it was sided up and ceiled. In 1895 the teachers' quarters (frame structure) were added.

A well was dug in order to have water nearer the buildings, but when water was struck, it was found to be impregnated with alkali, and unfit for use, so the water is now obtained from natural springs, although it is a little far away.

Fort Totten School, Fort Totten, N. Dak.

This school, although within the jurisdiction of the Devils Lake Agency, is under the control of a bonded superintendent.

Located on the south shore of Devils Lake (Minnewakan-Haunted Water), 15 miles southwest of Devils Lake station on the main line of the Great Northern Railway, and 13 miles east of Oberon station on the Jamestown and Northern branch of the Northern Pacific Railway. The climate is one of extremes. The soil is a heavy black loam with heavy clay subsoil, very productive.

Offices.—Character, one-story brick. Use, superintendent's offices. Capacity, 4 rooms. Erected in 1868. Cost, $1,800. Present value, $1,500. Present condition, excellent.

Employees' cottage.—Character, 1½-story brick. Use, sewing rooms and employees' mess. Capacity, 11 rooms. Erected in 1868. Cost, $4,000 (estimated). Present value, $2,000. Present condition, fair.

Girls' quarters.—Character, two-story brick. Use, dormitory and sitting rooms. Capacity, 90 pupils. Erected in 1868. Cost, $7,000 (estimated). Present value, $4,000. Present condition, fair.

Superintendent's quarters.—Character, two-story brick. Use, superintendent's residence, guest chambers, and employees' living rooms. Capacity, 11 rooms. Erected in 1868. Cost, $5,500 (estimated). Present value, $3,000. Present condition, good.

Employees' quarters.—Character, two-story brick. Use, employees' quarters. Capacity, 15 rooms. Erected in 1878. Cost, $7,000. Present value, $4,000. Present condition, excellent.

Employees' cottage.—Character, 1½-story brick. Use, employees' quarters. Capacity, two small families. Erected in 1868. Cost, $4,000 (estimated). Present value, $2,000. Present condition, fair.

Employees' cottage.—Character, two-story brick. Use, employees' quarters. Capacity, 8 rooms. Erected in 1868. Cost, $5,000 (estimated). Present value, $1,750. Present condition, poor.

Dining hall.—Character, main portion, two-story brick; two wings, one-story brick. Use, dining room and kitchen and cook's and assistant cook's living rooms. Capacity, 180 pupils. Erected in 1868. Cost, $8,000 (estimated). Present value, $5,000. Present condition, good.

Storehouse.—Character, one-story brick. Use, storing supplies. Capacity, one room 15 by 18 feet. Erected in 1868. Cost, $800 (estimated). Present value, $100. Present condition, poor.

Shops, shoe and tailor.—Character, one-story brick. Use, shoe shop and tailor shop and band room. Capacity, two shops, size 40 by 30 feet; band room, 20 by 30 feet. Erected in 1868. Cost, $2,500 (estimated). Present value, $1,500. Present condition, fair.

Boys' quarters.—Character, two-story brick. Use, boys' sitting room, lavatory, bathroom, clothes room, reading room, and small boys' dormitory. Capacity, 125 pupils. Erected in 1868. Cost, $7,500 (estimated). Present value, $4,500. Present condition, good.

Boys' dormitory.—Character, two-story brick. Use, dormitory for large boys. Capacity, 90 pupils. Erected in 1868. Cost, $6,500 (estimated). Present value, $3,500. Present condition, poor.

Boys' dormitory.—Character, two-story brick. Use, vacant. Capacity, 90 pupils. Erected in 1868. Cost, $6,500 (estimated). Present value, $3,000. Present condition, poor.

Schoolrooms and assembly hall.—Character, two-story brick, with one-story brick addition. Use, class rooms and assembly hall. Capacity, 201 pupils in class rooms, 600 in new assembly hall. Erected in 1868 and 1902. Cost, $6,500 (estimated); addition, $5,000. Present value, $3,500; addition, $5,000. Present condition, fair; addition, excellent.

Commissary.—Character, one-story brick. Use, storeroom for school supplies. Capacity, 3 rooms, 33 by 30 feet. Erected in 1868. Cost, $3,000 (estimated). Present value, $500. Present condition, very poor.

Bakery.—Character, one-story brick. Use, vacant; one oven tumbled down. Erected in 1868. Cost, $500 (estimated). Present value, $100. Present condition, poor.

Engine house.—Character, one-story frame. Use, engine and boiler room and pump house. Capacity, 1 main room, size 35 by 26 feet; addition, 20 by 14 feet. Erected in 1893. Cost, $2,000 (estimated). Present value, $1,500. Present condition, fair.

Employees' cottage.—Character, one-story frame. Use, employees' quarters. Capacity, two small families. Erected in 1879. Cost, $1,000. Present value, $600. Present condition, fair.

Granary.—Character, one-story brick. Use, storing grain. Capacity, 4,000 bushels. Erected in 1868. Cost, $3,000 (estimated). Present value, $500. Present condition, poor.

Guardhouse.—Character, one-story brick. Use, storage room for worn and worthless property. Capacity, 3 rooms. Erected in 1868. Cost, $1,200 (estimated). Present value, $300. Present condition, poor.

Storehouse.—Character, one-story brick. Use, storage of old property. Capacity, 1 room, 60 by 25 feet. Erected in 1868. Cost, $3,000 (estimated). Present value, $1,000. Present condition, poor.

Laundry.—Character, one-story stone. Use, for laundry purposes. Capacity, main room, 70 by 20 feet; dry room, 20 by 20 feet; engine room, 20 by 20 feet. Erected in 1890. Cost, $2,500. Present value, $2,000. Present condition, good.

Shops, carpenter and blacksmith.—Character, one-story frame. Use, for carpenter and blacksmith shops, lumber and coal storage. Capacity, shop, 30 by 37 feet; shop, 30 by 21 feet; lumber storage, 30 by 36 feet; coal storage, 30 by 28 feet. Erected, original building in 1880, added to and improved in 1899 and 1900. Cost, $1,000. Present value, $1,200. Present condition, good.

Wagon sheds.—Character, one-story inclosed frame. Use, storage of wagons and farm machinery. Capacity, 100 by 18 feet. Erected in 1880; improved and inclosed in 1899 and 1900. Cost, $500. Present value, $500. Present condition, good.

STATISTICS OF INDIAN TRIBES, AGENCIES, AND SCHOOLS. 19

Hog house.—Character, 1½-story stone and frame. Use, care of hogs. Capacity, 60 hogs. Erected in 1894. Cost, $500. Present value, $400. Present condition, fair.

Barn.—Character, two-story stone and frame. Use, housing stock and storing hay. Capacity, 100 head of stock and 200 tons of hay. Erected in 1894. Cost, $4,000. Present value, $4,000. Present condition, good.

Ice house.—Character, one-story stone and frame. Use, storage of ice. Capacity, 125 tons. Erected in 1894. Cost, $600. Present value, $600. Present condition, good.

Lighted by electricity, installed in 1903; cost, $3,200. Heated by hot-water system, installed in 1903; cost, $23,650. Fuel, lignite and hard coal. There is no modern method of ventilation in any of the school buildings, except in the laundry, which is furnished with a modern system that is both satisfactory and sufficient. The water supplied is good, but very hard; its source is a number of springs in the hills about one-half mile south of the buildings, where it is assembled into an underground reservoir, thence piped into a cistern at the engine house by gravity, whence it is pumped by steam engine into a steel tank of 25,000 gallons capacity, on a steel tower standing 80 feet high. From the standpipe of this tank there are 4-inch cast-iron water mains extending around the entire square of buildings, from which a 2-inch pipe leads to the Sisters' department, 1¼ miles distant. The pressure is ample to force the water over any of the buildings at the post department. Water system was installed by the military department in 1882, but by 1893 it was so far gone that a new system was installed during that and the following years, not being completed until 1898, at a cost of about $13,000.

There is a general sewer system, constructed in 1903 at a cost of $2,639. A system of seven baths is now being installed in both the boys' and girls' dormitories. There are water connections in all the buildings in use and a fire hydrant on each of the four sides of the square and to the rear of the buildings, to which a 2-inch hose can be connected.

This school has 800 acres of fine land suitable for general farming, located on the Fort Totten Military Reserve, and its present value is estimated at $8,000. There are 450 acres under fence. About 250 acres under cultivation—small grain and vegetables. About 100 acres additional can be cultivated. About 400 acres are used for pasturage. No land is irrigated.

This school was organized in 1890 with a capacity of 175 pupils, and the department under the Gray Nuns was opened on October 27 with 9 employees in charge, while the school at the post was not opened until January 19, 1891.

GRAY NUNS' DEPARTMENT.

Located 1¼ miles north of the main department of the Fort Totton school on high, rolling ground near the lakeshore. Climate and soil the same as the main department of the school.

School building.—Character, 2½-story frame, with two two-story additions. Use, dormitory, boys' and girls' schoolrooms, dining hall, and kitchen. Capacity, 100 pupils. Erected about 1881. Cost, $18,000 (estimated). Present value, $10,000. Present condition, fair.

Ice house.—Character, stone, with shingle roof. Use, for storing ice. Capacity, 75 tons. Erected in 1882. Cost, $700. Present value, $400. Present condition, fair.

Barn.—Character, two-story frame. Use, housing live stock and storing hay. Capacity, 10 animals, horses, or cows. Erected in 1882. Cost, $600 (estimated). Present value, about $200. Present condition, poor.

The buildings are all lighted by kerosene lamps. Heating is done by coal and wood stoves. There is no modern method of ventilation. Water is furnished from the Fort Totten School proper. There is no regular sewer system; short lines of pipes are run from the different buildings that need them to cesspools, into which they empty. There are two bath tubs in the building, one for the use of the boys and one for the use of the girls. There is a standpipe in the building, with hose to connect in case of fire, also pails of water throughout, and hand grenades in the different rooms.

DIGGER INDIANS, IN CALIFORNIA.

These Indians are living on a reservation of 330 acres, 4 miles from Jackson, Cal. They are under the immediate control of a farmer and special disbursing agent. They have no school.

Population, 38.

EASTERN CHEROKEE AGENCY, N. C.

(Under School Superintendent.)

Tribe.	Population.
Eastern Cherokee	1,431

Area, 98,211 acres; unallotted.
Railroad station: Whittier, on Murphy division of the Southern Railroad. Six miles to school. Post-office address: Cherokee, N. C. Telegraphic address: Whittier, N. C.

Eastern Cherokee School, Cherokee, N. C.

Located 6 miles northeast of Whittier, N. C., on the Murphy division of the Southern Railway, connected by telephone with Whittier. Site in a little valley of the Ocona Lufty River, a stream of unsurpassed beauty; climatic conditions are good. Soil of the valley a sandy loam of the hills and mountains, clay mixed with fragmentary rock, mountains of granite rock.

Commissary and office.—Character, two-story frame, with basement under a small part. Use, superintendent's office, storage of supplies, and 3 rooms used for employees' quarters. Capacity, 2 office rooms, 3 living rooms, 2 storage rooms, and 1 basement for oils, etc. Erected in 1895. Cost, $1,000. Present value, $1,000. Present condition, good.

Teachers' quarters.—Character, two-story frame. Use, employees' quarters, dormitory, dining room, kitchen, sewing room, and employees' quarters. Capacity, 80 girls and 3 employees. Erected in 1895. Cost, $1,800. Present value, $2,000. Present condition, excellent.

School building.—Character, two-story frame. Use, class rooms and assembly hall. Capacity, 100 pupils. Erected in 1898. Cost, $3,999. Present value, $4,000. Present condition, good.

Kindergarten building.—Character, one-story frame. Use, kindergarten school. Capacity, 30 pupils. Erected in 1882. Cost, $600. Present value, $300. Present condition, good.

Shop, carpenter and shoe.—Character, one-story frame. Use, carpenter shop, shoe shop, and tool room. Capacity, 10 pupils. Erected in 1882; addition made in 1900. Cost, $700. Present value, $600. Present condition, good.

Boys' quarters.—Character, two-story frame. Use, dormitory, sitting room, and bathrooms. Capacity, 90 boys and 2 employees. Erected in 1882, with additions in 1895, 1897, and 1900. Cost, $3,250. Present value, $2,000. Present condition, good.

Barn.—Character, two-story frame. Use, sheltering stock, feed, and implements. Capacity, 6 horses, 18 cows, 20 calves, and 10 tons of hay. Erected in 1890. Cost, $400. Present value, $400. Present condition, good.

Superintendent's cottage.—Character, one-story frame. Use, superintendent's dwelling. Capacity, 4 dwelling rooms. Erected in 1898. Cost, $500. Present value, $500. Present condition, good.

Employees' cottages (2).—Character, 1½ story log, weatherboarded. Use, dwellings for employees. Capacity, 3 rooms each. Erected in 1884 and 1886. Cost, $150 each. Present value, $150 each. Present condition, good.

Laundry.—Character, 1½-story frame. Use, laundry. Capacity, 10 pupils and laundress. Erected in 1897. Cost, $400. Present value, $400. Present condition, fair to good.

Oil house.—Character, one-story stone. Use, storing oil. Capacity, 1,500 gallons. Erected in 1900. Cost, $75. Present value, $75. Present condition, excellent.

Smith shop.—Character, one-story log. Use, blacksmith work. Capacity, smith and 2 pupils. Erected in 1899. Cost, $25. Present value, $25. Present condition, good.

The school is lighted by oil lamps, heated by steam heating plant, installed in 1903, at cost of $1,897. School building ventilated by system devised by the Indian Office; other buildings have no modern system. The water supplied is pure, soft water. Its source is three springs; the water is brought in pipes direct to the various buildings; the supply is more than sufficient. The buildings are connected to three 6-inch sewers; each of these empty into brooks, one on either side of the grounds, and these empty into the river, which is on the third side. There are four ring baths and one tub in the boys' building. The girls at present have one bath tub, and use wash tubs. There are eight fire hydrants at convenient points over the grounds; hose and water buckets in the buildings. The water supply is drawn from a mountain brook and stored in an open reservoir on the mountain side. Water from springs and reservoir brought to school by gravity.

STATISTICS OF INDIAN TRIBES, AGENCIES, AND SCHOOLS. 21

This school has 120 acres (estimated) of land; about 30 acres fine bottom land, the remainder hillside and mountain. The first school site was donated; subsequent purchases have been made at a cost of $1,445. The present value is estimated at $2,000. The farm consists of 120 acres, all under fence; 20 acres in cultivation. Twenty acres additional can be cultivated. The 20 acres which can be cultivated and the mountain side 100 acres all told can be irrigated.

This school was originally under the control of the Society of Friends. It was organized by them in 1883 with a capacity for 20 pupils, girls; in 1884 was doubled, 20 of each sex, which capacity was afterwards increased to 40 boys and 40 girls. The school passed under the control of the Government in January, 1893.

FLATHEAD AGENCY, MONT.

Tribes.	Population.
Kootenai (from Idaho)	40
Flathead, Pend d'Oreilles, and Kootenai (confederated)	1,268
Spokane	74
Lower Kalispel	49
Carlos's Band of Flatheads	150
Total	1,581

Area, 1,433,600 acres; unallotted.

Railroad station: Arlee, on Northern Pacific Railway. Four and one-half miles to agency by team.

Nearest military post: Fort Missoula, Mont. Post-office address: Jocko, Mont. Telegraphic address: Arlee, Mont., and telephone to agency.

Flathead Agency Boarding School, Jocko, Mont.

Conducted in old buildings, situated right at rear of agency buildings, with no adjoining land. Rented from Jesuit Fathers.

Located 4½ miles east of Arlee, Mont., on the Northern Pacific Railroad. Site very poor for school purposes, having no available land near by. Climate very pleasant in summer, mild in winter. Soil very stony and fair for agricultural purposes.

School building.—Character, two-story frame, poorly built. Use, girls' dormitory, small boys' dormitory, employees' quarters, dining room, kitchen, schoolroom. Capacity, 45 pupils. Present condition, very poor.

Laundry.—Character, small one-story frame. Use, laundry purposes. Present condition, fair.

Warehouse.—Character, frame, two story. Use, boys' dormitory and warehouse purposes. Condition, fair.

Lighted by kerosene lamps. Heated with wood stoves. Ventilation, none. Water supply is good, being from agency water system. Bathing facilities, none. Fire protection, pipes in yard and kitchen only.

No farm or land connected with school.

This school was opened February 11, 1901, with 36 scholars, and has increased to 47, which is all the school can possibly accommodate.

FORT APACHE AGENCY, ARIZ.

(Under Bonded School Superintendent.)

Tribe.	Population.
White Mountain Apaches	1,959

Area, 1,681,920 acres; unallotted.

Railroad station: Holbrook, Ariz., on the Santa Fe Pacific Railroad. Eighty-six miles to agency by buckboard.

Nearest military post: Fort Apache, Ariz. Post-office address: White River, Ariz. Telegraphic address: Fort Apache, Ariz., via Holbrook, Ariz.

Fort Apache Boarding School, Whiteriver, Ariz.

Located 87 miles south of Holbrook, Ariz., on the Atchison, Topeka and Santa Fe Railway. Site only fairly well suited for school purposes, climate without extreme changes, pure air, good water. Soil of the immediate site is a sandy loam, sloping toward the east, affording excellent drainage; near the mountains on west side, and on edge of mesa land, about 200 feet above, and a half mile from Whiteriver.

Schoolhouse.—Character, one-story frame. Use, class room, assembly hall, employees' quarters for superintendent and two teachers. Capacity, 75 pupils. Erected in 1895. Cost, $1,500. Present value, $1,000. Present condition, fair.

Girls' dormitory.—Character, one-story frame. Use, dormitory, sitting room, sick room, schoolroom for kindergarten, and matron's quarters. Capacity, 30 pupils as a dormitory. Erected in 1893. Cost, $1,500. Present value, $500. Present condition, very poor.

Girls' dormitory.—Character, three-story stone. Use, living quarters for girl pupils. Capacity, 75. Erected in 1902. Cost, $18,631. Present value, $18,631. Present condition, excellent.

Boys' dormitory.—Character, one-story frame. Use, dormitory, sitting room, sick room, and quarters for the boys' matron and industrial teacher. Capacity, 40 pupils. Erected in 1892. Cost, $2,000. Present value, $500. Present condition, poor.

Laundry and kitchen.—Character, one-story frame. Use, laundry, kitchen, dining room, assembly hall, employees' quarters. Capacity, 75 pupils. Erected in 1894. Cost, $2,500. Present value, $700. Present condition, fair.

Employees' mess house.—Character, one-story frame of rough lumber. Use, dining room and kitchen for employees. Capacity, 12 employees. Erected in 1895. Cost, $200. Present value, $100. Present condition, poor.

Storehouse.—Character, rough lumber throughout. Use, to store school supplies. Capacity, sufficient for a school of 200 children. Erected in 1897. Cost, $1,400. Present value, $800. Present condition, fair.

Meat house.—Character, one-story frame, screened. Use, store meats. Capacity, sufficient for 150 children. Erected in 1899. Cost, $50. Present value, $50. Present condition, good.

Root house.—Character, dug-out, shingle roof. Use, storing vegetables. Capacity, about 300 bushels. Erected in 1900. Cost, $75. Present value, $75. Present condition, good.

Stable.—Character, rough lumber. Use, horses, and a wagon-shed. Capacity, 6 horses, 2 wagons. Erected in 1896. Cost, $500. Present value, $300. Present condition, fair.

Sewing-room building.—Character, one-story frame, good materials. Use, sewing room and apartment for seamstress. Capacity, school of 150 pupils. Erected in 1901. Cost, $750. Present value, $750. Present condition, excellent.

Miscellaneous outbuildings.—Character, all frames, made of rough lumber. Uses, chicken house, tool house, water-closets. Erected in 1892–1899. Present value, about $50. Present condition, poor to fair.

Each of the school buildings above noted, except the seamstress' building, is made of rough lumber, set upright as in an ordinary barn to inclose; the interiors of part of these buildings have been ceiled with lumber on which is tacked building paper which is painted. Both the interiors and exteriors of the buildings are either painted or whitewashed.

Electric lighting system installed in 1902. Heated by fire in wood stoves. Ventitation of schoolrooms and dormitories by means of windows, transoms, and ceiling ventilators. The water is the best; it is taken from White River about three-fourths of a mile from the school, and it is hauled from the river in tanks uphill more than 200 feet above the water in the river. Water and sewer systems installed 1902. Cost with electric light system, $18,994. There are bathing facilities. There is fire protection from new system.

This school has about 12 acres of very fine land for gardening, but it is in the canyon about one-half mile from the school; it should produce sufficient vegetables for a school of 200 pupils; yet, it has been a failure on account of the inability to obtain water for the purpose of irrigation; however, this important matter has been overcome lately in the making of a fine irrigating canal which will carry water in abundance to the garden as well as to several Indian farms. This garden is inclosed with a good wire fence. There is also about 15 acres of level land on the mesa, near the school buildings, that might be used for garden purposes; but as this land is a black tough adobe soil it would be better suited to the raising of fruit, when water is afforded by the water system proposed for the school; this tract is also fenced, and the fence incloses the school buildings and campus as well—in all, about 30 acres, not including the fine garden land in the canyon. Excepting about three months of year the cattle belonging to the school can find fair range grass in the vicinity of the school. Almost enough fodder forage may be produced on the school land for the milch cows.

This school was opened on January 27, 1894, with capacity of 28 children—11 girls and 17 boys. Its present capacity is 75 pupils.

FORT BELKNAP AGENCY, MONT.

Tribes.	Population.
Gros Ventre	548
Assinniboine	710
Total	1,258

Area, unallotted, 497,600 acres; surveyed.
Railroad station: Harlem Station, on Great Northern Railway. Four miles to agency by stage.
Nearest military post: Fort Assinniboine, Mont. Post-office address: Harlem, Choteau County, Mont. Telegraphic address: Harlem Station, Mont.

Fort Belknap Agency School.

Located 4 miles south of Harlem, Mont., on the Great Northern Railway, on the south bank of Milk River, the northern line of the reservation. Site, good for school purposes. Climate, dry and healthful, with long winters. Soil, sandy loam near the river, with some gravel on the higher bench land.

Girls' dormitory.—Character, two-story brick, with one two-story addition. Use, dormitory and girls' quarters, with sewing room, kitchen, dining room, employees' rooms, and office. Capacity, 55 pupils. Erected in 1890. Cost, $12,738.65. Present value, $6,000. Present condition, fair.

Boys' dormitory.—Character, two-story brick. Use, dormitory, boys' quarters, and employees' rooms. Capacity, 50 pupils. Erected in 1890. Cost, $8,000. Present value, $4,000. Present condition, fair.

Boys' dormitory.—Character, two-story frame. Use, employees' quarters. Capacity, 8 employees or 15 pupils. Erected in 1889 at agency (moved to school in 1900). Cost, $2,000. Present value, $750. Present condition, poor.

Warehouse.—Character, one-story frame. Use, storing supplies. Dimensions, 18 by 28 feet. Erected in 1889 at agency (moved to school later). Cost, $800. Present value, $300. Present condition, very poor.

School building.—Character, one-story brick. Use, class rooms and assembly hall. Capacity, 130 pupils. Erected in 1900. Cost, $11,989.60. Present value, $11,989.60. Present condition, excellent.

Barn (old).—Character, 1½-story frame. Use, housing stock and storing hay. Capacity, 16 head of stock and 8 tons hay. Erected in 1891. Cost, $1,800. Present value, $600. Present condition, fair.

Miscellaneous outbuildings.—Character, all frame. Use, laundry, shoe shop, engine room, fuel sheds, closets, etc. Erected in 1891 and later. Cost, $1,400 (approximately). Present value, $400. Present condition, poor to fair.

Barn (new).—Character, 1½-story frame. Use, housing stock and storing hay. Capacity, 36 heads of stock and 40 tons of hay. Erected in 1902. Cost, $1,500. Present value, $1,500. Present condition, excellent.

Cold-storage house.—Character, one-story frame. Use, ice house, meat room, milk room, carpenter shop, etc. Dimensions, 24 by 40 feet. Erected in 1902. Cost, $1,000. Present value, $1,000. Present condition, excellent.

The school building is lighted by a gasoline plant installed when the building was erected in 1900. This plant is safe and satisfactory. Kerosene lamps are used in all other buildings. The school building is heated by steam. The plant was put in when the building was constructed in 1900. It is in good condition. All other buildings are heated by coal stoves. Ventilation of school building is by the system devised by the Indian Office. Other buildings have no modern system.

The water supplied is alkaline and very hard. It is often unfit for use unless it has been filtered. It is pumped from Milk River by a steam engine and pump and forced into a 1,000-barrel wooden tank on a wooden trestle 40 feet high. The pressure is sufficient to force the water wherever necessary, but the water is only carried to one room in each building except the school building. None of the water is used for irrigation. The system was installed in 1898, costing about $2,000. All the brick buildings and laundry are connected with the water and sewer system. The frame boys' dormitory is connected with the water system only. The sewer empties into the irrigation ditch one-eighth of a mile below the school buildings and below the water supply. The outfall is about 15 feet below the buildings. There are no bathrooms. At present the bathing is done in bath tubs in the basement of the school building. There are hydrants on the grounds and a hose cart and hose for fire protection. Fire pails are kept in the buildings, but there are no fire hydrants or hose indoors.

This school has 420 acres of farming and grazing land. Four hundred acres are fenced; 20 acres are cultivated. The school garden can be enlarged if necessary. Twenty acres are irrigated for gardening, and 400 acres are used for pasture.

This school was opened September 14, 1891. Before that time the government school on this reservation was conducted as a day school.

FORT BERTHOLD AGENCY, N. DAK.

Tribes.	Population.
Arickaree	384
Gros Ventre	457
Mandan	247
Total	1,088

Area:

	Acres.
Allotted	80,340
Unallotted	884,780

Railroad station: Bismarck, on Northern Pacific Railway; thence by daily stage 120 miles to agency.

Nearest military post: Fort Yates, N. Dak. Post-office address: Elbowoods, via Bismarck, N. Dak. Telegraphic address: Bismarck, N. Dak.

Fort Berthold Agency School.

Located about 500 yards from Fort Berthold Agency, 71 miles north of Washburn, N. Dak., on the Bismarck, Washburn and Great Falls Railway. Site is well adapted for the purpose. Climate ranges from extreme cold in winter to extreme heat in summer. It is, however, bracing and healthy. Rainfall slight. Soil is a rich sandy loam and with sufficient moisture will raise large crops of grains and vegetables indigenous to North Dakota.

Dormitory and school building.—Character, two-story brick. Use, dormitory, schoolrooms, kitchen and dining room, bakery, assembly room. Capacity, 80 pupils. Erected in 1899. Cost, $29,990. Present value, $29,000. Present condition, good.

Teachers' residence.—Character, two-story frame. Use, sewing room, employees' rooms, mess dining room, and kitchen. Capacity, 4 employees. Erected in 1895. Cost, $1,600. Present value, $800. Present condition, poor.

Laundry and tank house.—Character, one-story frame, with tower and tank house of frame. Use, laundry. Capacity, entirely inadequate for work. Erected in 1894. Cost, $725. Present value, $200; worthless as a laundry. Present condition, very poor.

Barn.—Character, one-story frame, with stone basement. Use, housing stock and implements. Capacity, 4 horses and 6 cows. Erected in 1897. Cost, $500. Present value, $300. Present condition, fair.

Lighted from an acetylene-gas plant. Heated by hot water from low-pressure boiler in basement of dormitory building; unsatisfactory. The cottage or teachers' residence is heated by coal stoves. Ventilation is by system devised by Indian Office. No systematic ventilation in other buildings. Water is pumped from well by steam engine to new tank of 15,000 gallons' capacity, elevated on a new tower 76 feet high. Water conveyed to buildings by gravity through 4 and 6 inch mains. Cost of tank and tower, $6,440; installed in 1902. The main building and laundry are connected with an 8-inch sewer, which empties into the river bottoms below the school. It was intended that the sewage should be carried off by a ditch from the outlet of the sewer, but the fall is too slight to give a flow. No objectionable features to this plan have been observed so far. There are adequate bathing facilities in the main building. Both needle and tub baths are used. Fire buckets and hand grenades, distributed throughout the several buildings, are means of extinguishing fire in connection with water system just completed.

The school has one quarter section of land that compares favorably with any on the reservation in quality. It is level and suitable for agriculture or pasturage. Value is $2 per acre. Number of acres under fence, 100. Number of acres under cultivation, 30. Balance of land is more valuable for pasture than for planting purposes. Number of acres in pasturage, 80. Number of acres irrigated, none.

On April 1, 1900, the school, as now organized, was opened.

No. 1 Day School.

Located at Armstrong, 17 miles southeast of agency. Site well adapted to the purpose. Climate goes to extremes of heat and cold, but is healthy. Soil rich sandy loam, but lack of moisture makes anything but grazing unprofitable.

Schoolhouse.—Character, one-story frame. Use, schoolroom. Capacity, 40 pupils. Erected in 1894. Cost, $712. Present value, $500. Present condition, good.

Industrial cottage.—Character, one-story frame. Use, teachers' residence; also used for industrial work. Capacity, 2 employees. Erected in 1894. Cost, $843. Present value, $500. Present condition, good.

Lighted by kerosene lamps and heated by coal stoves. Ventilation is such as may be had in any ordinary building without any special system. Water for cooking and drinking is hauled from the Missouri River. For all other purposes it is taken from a well at the school. The supply is ample and of good quality. No sewerage. All refuse is carried off and thrown into river bottom, and is washed away by annual rise of river. No bathing facilities. Fire buckets and hand grenades are the only protection against fire.

The school is located on 40 acres of land, all of which is under fence. It is of fair quality, and its approximate value is $2 per acre. None of the land is cultivated, except a small garden about half an acre in extent, and none is irrigated. Balance of land is used as school grounds. It could be cultivated.

School was opened in 1895, and has been in operation continuously since that year.

No. 2 Day School.

Located at Independence, 22 miles northwest of agency. Site well adapted to the purpose. Climate goes from extremes of heat and cold, but is healthy. Soil, rich sandy loam, but lack of moisture makes agriculture uncertain and unprofitable.

Day school building.—Character, one-story frame. Use, schoolroom. Capacity, 50 pupils. Erected in 1894. Cost, $712. Present value, $500. Present condition, good.

Industrial cottage.—Character, one-story frame. Use, teachers' residence; also used as sewing room and for other industrial work. Capacity, 2 employees. Erected in 1894. Cost, $843. Present value, $500. Present condition, good.

Lighted by kerosene lamps. Heated by coal stoves. Only such ventilation as may be had in an ordinary house. Water for all purposes hauled from the Missouri River. No sewerage. Refuse is thrown into the river. No bathing facilities. Fire protection consists of buckets filled with water and hand grenades, which are placed in convenient places.

The school is located on 40 acres of land, on the west side of the Missouri River, all of which is under fence. The land is of fair quality and is worth about $2 per acre. Only a small garden is cultivated. None is irrigated. Balance of land is used as school grounds.

This school was built in 1894 and commenced work in 1895.

No. 3 Day School.

Located on Shell Creek, 25 miles northwest of agency, on the east side of the Missouri River, in close proximity to a large Grosventre settlement. The site is an excellent one in every respect. With a greater amount of rain the soil is capable of raising any grain or vegetable grown in the Temperate Zone in abundance.

Day school building.—Character, one-story frame. Use, schoolroom. Capacity, 46 pupils. Erected in 1896. Cost, $765. Present value, $500. Present condition, good.

Industrial cottage.—Character, one-story frame. Use, teachers' residence; also used as a workroom for the female pupils in various branches of household work. Capacity, 2 employees. Erected in 1896. Cost, $663. Present value, $500. Present condition, good.

Buildings lighted by kerosene lamps and heated by coal stoves. No special system of ventilation. A well close to the buildings furnishes an ample supply of pure water. It is a little hard, but is good for all domestic purposes. Garbage and other refuse is thrown into Shell Creek and carried away by the current. Have no bathing facilities. Hand grenades and buckets filled with water are the only means for extinguishing fire.

The school is located on 40 acres of land, all of which is under fence. It is of fair quality and is worth about $2 per acre. Only a small part used as a garden is under cultivation. The balance of land is used as school grounds.

The buildings at this school were completed in 1896, but school work did not commence until the following year.

FORT HALL AGENCY, IDAHO.

Tribes.	Population.
Bannock and Shoshoni	1,389
Not under an agent	200
Total	1,589

The tribes under this agency are known also as Fort Hall Indians.

Area:	Acres.
Allotted	6,172
Unallotted	447,940

Railroad station: Rossfork, on Oregon Short Line and Utah Northern Railroad.
Nearest military post: Fort Douglas, Utah.
Post-office address: Rossfork, Bingham County, Idaho.
Telegraphic address: Pocatello, Idaho.

Fort Hall School.

The school is located 10 miles east of Blackfoot, Idaho, and 18 miles northeast of the agency. The present site is all that could be desired for school purposes. The climate is rather severe in winter, but not changeable, and the soil is a black loam and one of the most fertile spots in the State of Idaho.

Office building.—Character, frame, one story. Use, general office. Size, 20 by 26 feet. Date of erection, 1891. Cost, $1,000. Present value, $800. Present condition, good.

Superintendent's and guests' quarters.—Character, story and half, frame. Use, superintendent's and guests' rooms. Size, 40 by 40 feet. Date of erection, 1870. Cost, $2,500. Present value, $500. Present condition, fairly good.

Mess kitchen and dining room and physician's rooms.—Character, story and half frame. Use, mess kitchen and dining rooms and physician's quarters. Size, 36 by 52 feet. Date of erection, 1870. Cost, $2,500. Present value, $500. Present condition, fairly good.

Employees' quarters.—Character, story and half, frame. Use, employees' quarters. Size, 38 by 40 feet. Date of erection, 1870. Cost, $2,400. Present value, $500. Present condition, fairly good.

Children's dining room, kitchen, bakery, storeroom, laundry and dry room, and employees' quarters.—Character, one-story frame. Use, children's dining room, kitchen, bakery, flour room, laundry, dry room, and employees' quarters. Size, 120 by 70 feet. Date of erection, 1870. Cost, $4,000. Present value, $500. Present condition, poor.

Girls' dormitory No. 1.—Character, two-story, frame. Use, girls' dormitory. Size, 36 by 44 feet. Date of erection, 1890. Cost, $4,000. Present value, $2,000. Present condition, fair.

Girls' dormitory No. 2.—Character, two-story, frame. Use, girls' dormitory. Size, 22 by 44 feet. Built in 1891. Cost, $1,500. Present value, $800. Present condition, fair.

Hospital.—Character, one story and half, frame. Use, hopital and nurses' quarters. Size, 30 by 40 feet. Built in 1891. Cost, $1,500. Present value, $800. Present condition, fairly good.

Schoolhouse.—Character, story and half, frame. Use, general schoolrooms and book room. Size, 60 by 75 feet. Built in 1891. Cost, $2,500. Present value, $600. Present condition, fair.

Boys' dormitory.—Character, two-story frame. Use, boys' dormitory and clothing room, and matron's quarters. Size, 50 by 50 feet. Built in 1891. Cost, $5,070. Present value, $2,000. Present condition, fair.

Employees' quarters.—Character, 1½-story frame. Use, employees' quarters, band room, harness shop, and sewing room. Size, 40 by 120 feet. Built in 1870. Cost, $3,000. Present value, $500. Present condition, poor.

Warehouse.—Character, one-story frame. Use, warehouse. Size, 30 by 100 feet. Built in 1870. Cost, $2,500. Present value, $400. Present condition, poor.

Barn.—Character, frame, 1½-story with basement. Use, for stock and storing hay and grain. Size, 60 by 80 feet. Built in 1891. Cost, $2,500. Present value, $1,500. Present condition, good.

Carriage house.—Character, one-story frame. Use, for storing carriages. Size, 16 by 24 feet. Built in 1891. Cost, $100. Present value, $30. Present condition, poor.

Oil house.—Character, one-story frame. Use, for oil and paint shop. Size, 12 by 20 feet. Built in 1871. Cost, $100. Present value, $20. Present condition, poor.

Ice house.—Character, 1½-story log building. Use, ice house. Size, 20 by 40 feet. Built in 1871. Cost, $200. Present value, $15. Present condition, poor.

Blacksmith shop.—Character, one-story frame, Use, blacksmith shop and carpenter shop. Size, 20 by 40 feet. Built in 1870. Cost, $500. Present value, $50. Present condition, poor.

Hog pen and house.—Character, one-story frame. Use, hog house. Size, 12 by 30 feet. Built in 1890. Cost, $150. Present value, $25. Present condition, fair.

Hen house.—Character, one-story frame. Use, poultry. Size, 12 by 20 feet. Built in 1890. Cost, $100. Present value, $20. Present condition, poor.

Wagon and implement house.—Character, one-story frame. Use, storing wagons and farming tools. Size, 30 by 40 feet. Built in 1890. Cost, $200. Present value, $50. Present condition, poor.

Wagon shed.—Character, 1½-story frame. Use, for storing wagons. Size, 20 by 40 feet. Built in 1896. Cost, $100. Present value, $50. Good condition.

Lime house.—Character, one-story frame. Use, for lime and brick. Size, 12 by 16 feet. Built in 1870. Cost, $75. Value, $5. Present condition, poor.

Two coal houses.—Character, one-story frame. Use, for storing coal. Size, each, 20 by 30 feet. Built in 1890. Cost, $100 each; total, $200. Present value, $40 each; total, $80. Present condition, fair.

Buildings lighted by kerosene oil lamps. Heated by stoves (coal). Dormitories and hospital ventilated by modern system. Water supply from springs. These springs are located about 5 miles above the school plant. The water is run into a reservoir about 1 mile above the school and conducted by pipes to the school and forced into the buildings by the gravity system. The sewerage system at this school consists of open ditches, with an abundance of running water, which run to Lincoln Creek below the school plant. There are no facilities for bathing, except by the use of washtubs in the laundry. The only fire protection is by means of water buckets and running water in ditches on three sides of the school campus.

The school farm is reservation land, set aside by the Department for school purposes, and the value is $25,000. Two thousand acres under fence; 250 acres under cultivation; 500 acres more could be placed under cultivation; 1,750 acres used for pasturage; 250 acres under irrigation.

This school was opened in the year 1882, with a capacity of 75 scholars, and its present capacity is 150.

A new school plant to be located near the agency is now under contract, to cost about $75,000.

FORT PECK AGENCY, MONT.

Tribes.	Population.
Yanktonai Sioux	1,136
Assinniboine	575
Total	1,711

Area, 1,776,000 acres; unallotted.

Railroad station: Poplar, on Great Northern Railway. One-half mile to agency.

Nearest military post: Fort Assinniboine, Mont. Post-office address: Poplar, Mont. Telegraphic address, Poplar, Mont.

Fort Peck Agency School, Poplar, Mont.

Located one-third of a mile north of Poplar, on the Great Northern Railway line. The site is high and dry and adapted for school purposes; climate subject to extreme changes. Soil in immediate vacinity of site is a drift formation situated over a hardpan and is not adapted to agriculture.

Employees' quarters.—Character, cottonwood pickets, one story. Capacity, 5 dwelling rooms, dining room, sitting room, and kitchen. Erected in 1881. Present value, $200. Present condition, fair.

Employees' quarters.—Character, one-story cottonwood picket with shingle roof. Capacity, 2 employees. Erected in 1881. Present value, $50. Present condition, poor.

Employees' quarters.—Character, one-story cottonwood picket with shingle roof. Use, employees' quarters. Capacity, 2 employees. Erected in 1881. Present value, $75. Present condition, poor.

Carpenter shop.—Character, one-story log, dirt roof. Use, carpenter shop. Dimensions, 38 by 90 feet. Erected in 1898. Cost, $1,200. Present value, $500. Present condition, good.

Employees' quarters.—Character, one-story cottonwood pickets, shingle roof. Use, employees' quarters, storeroom, and harness shop. Capacity, 3 employees, storeroom, and harness shop. Erected in 1881. Present value, $150. Present condition, poor.

Commissary building.—Character, one-story cottonwood picket, shingle roof. Use, storing supplies. Dimensions, 27 by 100 feet. Erected in 1881. Present value, $100. Present condition, very poor.

Employees' quarters and employees' laundry.—Character, one-story cottonwood picket, shingle and dirt roof. Use, employees' quarters and laundry. Capacity, 1 employee and use as above. Erected in 1881. Present value, $50. Present condition, very poor.

Employees' quarters, condemned room, and schoolroom.—Character, one-story cottonwood picket, shingle roof. Use, employees' quarters, condemned room, and schoolroom. Dimensions, 27 by 100 feet. Erected in 1881. Present value, $100. Present condition, very poor.

Dining room and kitchen.—Character, one-story cottonwood picket, shingle roof. Use, dining room, kitchen, and bakery. Dimensions, 24 by 182 feet. Erected in 1881. Present value, $200. Present condition, very poor.

Classroom, assembly, clothing rooms, boys' sitting rooms, and steam laundry.—Character, sawed logs, stone foundation, iron roof, ceiled with steel. Use, as above, class room, etc. Dimensions, 30 by 266 feet. Erected in 1895. Cost, $4,000. Present value, $4,000. Present condition, good.

School building.—Character, one-story cottonwood picket, shingle roof. Use, class rooms. Dimensions, 25 by 60 feet. Present value, $25. Present condition, very poor.

Employees' quarters.—Character, one-story frame, shingle roof. Use, 4 employees and superintendent's office. Capacity, as above. Erected in 1881. Present value, $1,000. Present condition, good.

Class room, tailor shop, and sewing room.—Character, one-story picket, shingle roof. Use, class room, sewing room, and tailor shop. Dimensions, 27 by 63 feet. Erected in 1881. Present value, $50. Present condition, very poor.

Boys' dormitory.—Character, two-story and basement, brick. Use, dormitory. Capacity, 80 pupils. Erected in 1899. Cost, $11,000. Present value, $11,000. Present condition, excellent.

Girls' dormitory.—Character, two-story brick, with basement. Use, dormitory. Capacity, 80 pupils. Erected in 1899. Cost, $11,000. Present value, $11,000. Present condition, excellent.

Barn and ice house.—Character, frame. Use, barn and ice house. Dimensions, 24 by 80 feet, with cow shed on one side. Erected in 1899. Cost, $600. Present value, $1,200. Present condition, good.

Two dormitories are lighted by gasoline gas, having about 100 tips. Plant installed with building in 1899. Condition good and fairly satisfactory. Balance of plant lighted by kerosene. Two dormitories heated by hot-water plant installed with building in 1899; condition, good; ideal system. Balance of plant heated with stoves. Fuel, soft coal and wood. Dormitories are ventilated by system devised by Indian Office, which is excellent. Other buildings have no modern system.

The water is soft and well adapted for all purposes. Its source of supply is a well located at the agency, one-half mile away. Water is pumped by steam into tank containing 100,000 gallons. This tank stands on steel tower 65 feet high. Four 2½-inch hydrants are located on school grounds. Pressure is sufficient to throw water on top of highest buildings. Sewerage system was constructed in 1899, at a cost of $2,759.76. Main pipes are 6 inches, branches 4 inches; condition, excellent. Discharge is into running stream below school. There are 6 ring baths and 1 tub in each of the dormitories. There are standpipes in the dormitories with hose attached. Hydrants are located in the grounds and an ample supply of hose.

The school has no separate farm. The agency, Indians and school have about 3,000 acres fenced, a large part of which can be irrigated. It is well fenced. The school cultivates about 20 acres, all of which is irrigated. The school has no pasture.

This school was burned in 1892, and was reopened in 1894. It has a capacity of 200, and during the last two years has been kept full.

GRANDE RONDE AGENCY, OREG.

(Under School Superintendent.)

Tribes.	Population.	Tribes.	Population.
Rogue River	52	Marys River	40
Santiam	24	Yam Hill	27
Clackamas	62	Umpqua	84
Lakmiut	29		
Cow Creek	26	Total	362
Wapeto	18		

STATISTICS OF INDIAN TRIBES, AGENCIES, AND SCHOOLS. 29

Area: Acres.
Allotted 33,148
Unallotted 26,111
Reserved for agency 440

Railroad station: Sheridan, Oreg. Fifteen miles to school.
Nearest military post: Fort Spokane, Wash. Post-office address: Grande Ronde, Oreg. Telegraphic address: Sheridan, Oreg.

Grande Ronde School.

Located 15 miles west of Sheridan, Oreg. Site well suited for school purposes. Climate without extreme changes. Soil, fair.

Schoolhouse.—Character, two-story frame. Use, dormitories, dining room, kitchen, 2 schoolrooms, mess dining room and kitchen, sewing room, girls' lavatory, sitting room for girls, 3 employees' rooms. Capacity, 90 pupils. Erected in 1876. Cost, $2,000. Present value, $800. Present condition, fair.

Boys' dormitory.—Character, two-story frame, with one-story old building attached. Use, dormitories, sitting room, industrial teacher and teachers' quarters, boys' lavatory. Capacity, 50 pupils. Erected in 1895. Cost, $1,000. Present value, $700. Present condition, good.

Woodshed and granary.—Character, one-story frame. Use, storing wood, potatoes, carrots, and all root crops. Dimensions, 60 by 30 feet. Erected in 1897. Cost, $200. Present value, $100. Present condition, fair.

Dwelling.—Character, one-story frame. Use, sawyer's quarters. Erected in 1880. Cost, $100. Present value, $25. Present condition, poor.

Dwelling.—Character, one-story frame. Use, vacant. Capacity, 3 dwelling rooms. Erected in 1878. Cost, $250. Present value, $25. Present condition, poor.

Dwelling.—Character, two-story frame. Use, superintendent's dwelling. Capacity, 6 dwelling rooms. Erected in 1860. Cost, $1,200. Present value, $300. Present condition, fair.

Office.—Character, 1½-story frame. Superintendent's office. Capacity, 1 office room, 1 drug room, three-room warehouse. Erected in 1895. Cost, $800. Present value, $800. Present condition, good.

Barns, two.—Character, 1½-story frame. Use, housing live stock and storing hay. Capacity, 7 horses, 14 cows, 75 tons hay. Erected in 1896. Cost, $800 and $300. Present value, $600 and $200. Present condition, fair.

Dwelling.—Character, 1½-story frame. Use, employees' quarters. Capacity, 5 rooms. Erected in 1887. Cost, $600. Present value, $150. Present condition, fair.

Blacksmith shop.—Character, one-story frame. Use, half vacant, one-half rented. Capacity, 2 rooms. Erected in 1890. Cost, $500. Present value, $100. Present condition, fair.

Grist and saw mills.—Character, one-story frame. Use, manufacturing lumber and flour. Erected in 1875. Cost, $3,000. Present value, $300. Present condition, fair.

Lighted by kerosene lamps. Heated by stoves, burning wood. Ventilation of dormitories is by the system devised by the Indian Office. Water obtained from wells. Sewerage is by wooden boxes under ground emptying into natural drain. Pupils are bathed in common wooden tubs. No fire protection.

This school has 200 acres in its reserve. Land is fair; estimated value, $2,000; all under fence. Fifty acres under cultivation, grain and garden; 50 acres more could be cultivated. All is used for pasturage except the 50 acres under cultivation.

Opened as a day school in 1855. From 1872 to 1895 was in charge of the Sisters of the Catholic Church, under supervision of United States Indian agent. Since 1895 by Government.

GREEN BAY AGENCY, WIS.

Tribes.	Population.
Oneida	1,977
Menominee	1,299
Stockbridge and Munsee	538
Total	3,814

Area of Menomonee and Stockbridge reserves, 243,483 acres, unallotted. All of Oneida lands allotted except 84 acres reserved for school purposes.

Railroad station: Shawano, on Chicago and Northwestern Railroad. Eight miles to agency by stage.

Nearest military post: Fort Snelling, Minn. Post-office address: Keshena, Shawano County, Wis. Telegraphic address: Shawano, Wis.

Green Bay Agency School (Menominee), Keshena, Wis.

Located 8 miles north of Shawano, Wis., on the Northwestern Railway. Site well suited for school purposes. Climate, fair. Soil, sandy.

Girls' building (sometimes called "boarding house").—Character, frame building, 2½ stories high, with wing on north end. Use, girls' dormitory, dining room, kitchen, office, toilet rooms, laundry, quarters for a few of the employees, sewing room. Capacity, 60 pupils. Erected in 1880. Cost, $7,000. Present value, $5,000. Present condition, poor.

Boys' building.—Character, frame building, 2½ stories high. Use, boys' dormitory, toilet rooms, bathrooms, schoolrooms, and quarters for a number of employees. Capacity, 80 pupils. Erected in 1892. Cost, $3,000. Present value, $3,000. Present condition, good.

Carpenter's quarters.—Character, frame building, 1½ stories high. Use, dwelling for carpenter. Capacity, 3 rooms. Erected in 1880. Cost, $250. Present value, $250. Present condition, good.

Industrial teacher's dwelling.—Character, frame building, 1½ stories high. Use, dwelling. Capacity, 3 rooms. Erected in 1880. Cost, $250. Present value, $50. Present condition, poor.

Industrial building.—Character, frame, two stories. Dimensions, 30 by 66 feet. Use, carpenter shop and storing supplies. Erected in 1884. Present value, $500. Present condition, good.

Oil house.—Character, frame building, one story. Use, storing oil. Dimensions, 16 by 20 feet. Erected in 1893. Cost, $100. Present worth, $75. Present condition, good.

Hog house.—Character, frame building, one story. Use, shelter for hogs. Dimensions, 16 by 40 feet. Erected in 1894. Cost, $150. Present value, $125. Present condition, good.

Wagon house.—Character, frame building, one story. Use, shelter for wagons. Dimensions, 20 by 67 feet. Erected in 1894. Cost, $150. Present value, $125. Present condition, good.

Barn.—Character, two stories, frame. Use, housing live stock and storing hay. Dimensions, 46 by 70 feet. Erected in 1888. Cost, $1,200. Present value, $1,000. Present condition, good.

Ice house.—Character, frame. Use, storing ice. Dimensions, 16 by 24 feet. Erected in 1895. Cost, $100. Present value, $75. Present condition, good.

Chicken house.—Character, frame. Use, chicken house. Capacity, 16 by 36 feet. Erected in 1895. Cost, $150. Present value, $125. Present condition, good.

Coal house.—Character, frame, one story. Use, storing coal. Capacity, 14 by 14 feet. Erected in 1895. Cost, $100. Present value, $75. Present condition, fair.

Root house.—Character, frame. Use, storing vegetables. Capacity, 20 by 24 feet. Erected in 1899. Cost, $100. Present value, $90. Present condition, good.

Woodhouse.—Character, one-story frame. Use, woodhouse. Capacity, 20 by 24 feet. Erected in 1900. Cost, $75. Present value, $75. Present condition, good.

Lighted by a gasoline gas plant. The plant has a capacity of 150 lights, of which 97 are in use, and was installed in June, 1898, at a cost of $950. It is in good condition and gives satisfaction. The girls' building is heated by an 8-section Gold's sectional safety boiler. Date of installation and cost unknown. The plant is in very poor condition and does not extend to all the rooms; some of them are provided with stoves. The boys' building is heated by a No. 7 and No. 6½ Furnam's boiler, which was constructed in 1895 at a cost of $482. The other buildings are heated by stoves. In the summer of 1898 a modern system of ventilation was constructed in the girls' building and in the boys' building by the Sanitary Construction Company, of Green Bay, Wis.

The water supply is pure and hard. The water is supplied from 4 driven wells and also from the creek, and is pumped into a tank, with a capacity of 500 barrels, by a steam pump. The tank stands on a steel trestle 40 feet high. The pressure is ample to force the water wherever required. None of the water is used for irrigation. The system was installed in 1898, at a cost of about $10,000, and improved in 1902, at an additional cost fo $1,400. The girls' building and the boys' building are connected with 10 or 12 inch sewer pipes, which empty into the Wolf River about 85 rods from the school. The outfall is about 20 feet below the buildings. There are 2 ring baths and 4 tubs in the girls' building and an equal number in the boys' building. There are standpipes in the girls' building and in the boys' building, with hose on each floor. The premises are well supplied with fire hydrants and buckets, and barrels of water have been distributed throughout the buildings.

This school has 320 acres of good land in its reserve. Its present value is estimated to be about $3,200. The land, with the exception of about 80 acres, is all fenced in.

About 120 acres are under cultivation; 120 additional acres can be cultivated; 200 acres are used for pasturage. None of the land is irrigated.

This school was opened in 1883. At that time the main building, now known as the "girls' building," constituted the only building. This building has a capacity of 60 scholars. From time to time new buildings have been added, until at present the school has a capacity for about 140 scholars. However, the enrollment has been as high as 199 scholars.

Stockbridge Day School.

Located on the Stockbridge Reservation, 8 miles southwest of the agency. Site well suited for school purposes. Climate, fair. Soil, sandy.

Day school.—Character, one-story frame. Use, schoolroom. Capacity, 40 pupils. Erected in 1894. Cost, $825. Present value, $825. Present condition, good.

Teacher's dwelling.—Character, 1½-story frame. Use, dwelling for teacher and school kitchen. Capacity, 5 rooms. Erected in 1896. Cost, $440. Present value, $440. Present condition, good.

Woodhouse.—Character, one-story frame. Use, storing wood. Dimensions, 20 by 24 feet. Erected in 1895. Cost, $140. Present value, $140. Present condition, good.

Lighted, when necessary, by lamps. Heated by stoves. Buildings have no modern ventilation. The necessary water is supplied from a well. The water is pure and wholesome. There is no sewer system connected with the buildings. There are no baths in connection with the buildings. Barrels of water with buckets and a near-by pump furnish the only fire protection.

This school has about 2 acres in connection with its buildings. The land is valued at about $15 per acre, or $30 for the tract. The whole of the school tract is under fence. None of this land is under cultivation. There is hardly sufficient land in connection with the school plant to make it practicable to use any of it for cultivation. There is no stock in connection with this school, and consequently none of the land is used for pasturage.

This school was constructed in 1894. During the year 1901 the school had an enrollment of 49 scholars.

The following schools, although within the jurisdiction of the Green Bay Agency, are under the control of a bonded superintendent:

Oneida Boarding School, Oneida, Wis.

Located at Oneida, 10 miles west of Green Bay, Wis., on the Green Bay and Western Railway. Soil varying from sandy ridges to sand and clay bottoms.

No. 1, girls' building.—Character, two-story brick; basement under part of it. Use, dormitory for girls, dining room, and kitchen; baths for girls in basement. Capacity, 100 pupils. Erected in 1892; enlarged in 1899. Cost, $12,000. Present value, $12,000. Present condition, good.

No. 2, boys' building.—Character, two-story brick. Use, boys' dormitory and wash rooms. Capacity, 30 boys and 3 employees. Erected in 1892. Cost, $5,000. Present value, $4,000. Present condition, fair.

No. 3, boys' building.—Character, two-story brick. Use, dormitory for boys. Capacity, 70 pupils. Erected in 1895. Cost, $6,764. Present value, $6,000. Present condition, good.

No. 4.—Character, two-story brick. Use, office, superintendent and employees. Capacity, 1 office and 7 rooms. Erected in 1897. Cost, $3,250. Present value, $3,000. Present condition, good.

School building.—Character, two-story brick; small basement. Use, school. Capacity, 4 schoolrooms and assembly hall. Erected in 1900. Cost, $12,314. Present value, $12,300. Present condition, good.

Hospital.—Character, one-story frame. Use, care of sick. Capacity, 6 pupils. Erected in 1899. Cost, $1,380. Present value, $1,300. Present condition, good.

Club house.—Character, two-story frame. Use, employees' quarters and mess. Capacity, 5 rooms and kitchen and dining room. Erected in 1898. Cost, $1,200. Present value, $1,000. Present condition, good.

Laundry, old.—Character, two-story frame. Use, laundry and employees. Erected in 1894. Cost, $580. Present value, $300. Present condition, poor.

Laundry.—Character, one-story and basement, brick. Use, laundry. Erected in 1891. Cost, $1,300. Present value, $1,300. Present condition, good.

Boiler house.—Character, one-story brick. Use, boiler and coal room and sewing room. Erected in 1895. Cost, $3,225. Present value, $3,000. Present condition, good.

32 STATISTICS OF INDIAN TRIBES, AGENCIES, AND SCHOOLS.

Barn.—Character, one story, wood, stone basement. Use, care of stock. Capacity, 5 horses and 12 cows. Erected in 1893. Cost, $1,000. Present value, $900. Present condition, good.

Carpenter shop.—Character, one-story frame. Use, workshop. Erected in 1897. Cost, $450. Present value, $400. Present condition, good.

Warehouse.—Character, one-story frame. Use, storage of supplies. Dimensions, 30 by 50 feet. Erected in 1893. Cost, $1,180. Present value, $1,000. Present condition, fair.

Blacksmith shop.—Character, one-story frame. Use, workshop. Erected in 1895. Cost, $85. Present value, $75. Present condition, fair.

Wagon house.—Character, one-story frame. Use, storing wagons and tools. Erected in 1894. Cost, $150. Present value, $125. Present condition, fair.

Wood and coal house.—Character, one-story frame. Use, store wood and coal. Erected in 1893. Cost, $200. Present value, $100. Present condition, poor.

Chicken house and outbuildings.—Character, one-story frame. Erected in 1893. Cost, $125. Present value, $100. Present condition, poor.

Hog house.—Character, one-story frame. Use, hog pens. Erected in 1895. Cost, $100. Present value, $50. Present condition, fair.

Ice house.—Character, one-story frame. Use, storage of ice. Erected in 1895. Cost, $100. Present value, $75. Present condition, fair.

Steam-heating plant building.—Erected, 1895 to 1897. Cost, $6,000. Present value, $4,000. Present condition, fair.

Electric-light plant building.—Use, lighting. Capacity, 200 lights, incandescent. Erected in 1898. Cost, $1,050. Present value, $900. Present condition, fair.

The school buildings are lighted by electricity. The dynamo is rated at 200 lights, is now in good repair and gives sufficient light. All buildings, except the new school building, are heated from the central plant. Heat, light, and power for laundry are supplied by two 40-horsepower boilers that are in fair condition. Ventilation is by registers in walls and floors opening into galvanized iron pipes extending to star ventilators on the roof.

Water is supplied from an artesian well about 250 feet deep, and is pumped into a 25,000-gallon wood tank on a 50-foot iron trestle, and is conducted to the various buildings through a 6-inch iron main. Sewage is carried away from buildings by two lines of 6-inch pipe, one extending about 1,500 feet and the other 500 feet from buildings. Both terminate in wood cesspools. These cesspools have not been offensive at any time within two years. Bathing facilities in the girls' building are good. The bathroom is warm, furnished with hot and cold water and both shower baths and tubs. Baths for boys are poor and inadequate; one building has one tub and the other has two. Fire protection consists of a 25,000-gallon wooden tank on a 50-foot iron trestle. A 6-inch cast-iron main conducts the water to five hydrants, each with two 2½-inch outlets. The three dormitory buildings are also supplied with 1½-inch standpipes, with lines of hose on suitable reels in the halls.

The school farm contains 80 acres, including ground occupied by buildings. More than half of this tract is bottom land from which the timber was recently cut. Stumps are still very numerous, and until they rot or are removed this part can only be used for pasture. The upland is rather thin and is quite rough, so that the available land for farm and garden work is limited. The value of the farm is about $1,500. About 25 acres are under cultivation.

The school was organized in 1892 as a boarding school under the Green Bay Agency. It was made a bonded school in 1897. The present capacity is 200.

Oneida Day School No. 2, Oneida, Wis.

Located 7 miles south from the boarding school.

Day school No. 2.—Character, one-story, wood. Use, class room. Capacity, 36, Cost, $762. Present value, $500. Present condition, fair.

Day school No. 1 is conducted in a building rented from the Methodist Episcopal Church.

HOOPA VALLEY AGENCY, CAL.

(Under School Superintendent.)

Tribes.	Population.
Hoopa	413
Klamath	540
Total	953

STATISTICS OF INDIAN TRIBES, AGENCIES, AND SCHOOLS. 33

Area: | Acres.
Unallotted, Hoopa Reserve 99,051
Allotted 29,143.38
Reserved for 3 villages... 68.74

Railroad station: Korbel, on Arcata and Mad River Railway. Forty-four miles to agency by team.
Nearest military post: Presidio, Cal. Post-office address: Hoopa, Humboldt County, Cal. Telegraphic address: Eureka, Cal.

Hoopa Valley Training School.

Located 29 miles northeast of Korbel, Cal., the terminus of the Arcata and Mad River Railroad, distance 44 miles by wagon road; site well adapted for school purposes, there being a gradual slope from the foot of the mountain range to Trinity River. Soil porous and gravelly, with alluvial deposit on foundation of bedrock near the river. Climate without extreme changes.

Dwelling.—Character, 1½-story frame. Use, superintendent's and employees' quarters. Capacity, 7. Erected by War Department previous to 1880. Present value, $1,750. Present condition, fair.

Dwelling.—Character, one-story frame. Use, physician's quarters and office; employees' quarters. Capacity, 2 employees in addition to physician. Erected in 1888. Present value, $1,250. Present condition, good.

Dwelling.—Character, 1½-story frame. Use, teachers' quarters and employees' mess. Capacity, 3 employees in addition to mess. Erected, date unknown; remodeled in 1889. Present value, $1,300. Present condition, good.

Dwelling.—Character, one-story frame and addition. Use, laborers' quarters. Capacity, one dwelling room and kitchen. Erected about 1865. Present value, nominal. Present condition, very poor.

Cottage.—Character, one-story frame. Use, baker's quarters and rooms for cooking class. Capacity, 2 employees. Erected, date unknown, about time military post was established. Present value, nominal. Present condition, poor.

Cottage.—Character, one-story frame, lathed and plastered. Use, hospital, isolation and care of sick. Capacity, 7 patients and nurse. Erected in 1888. Present value, $750. Present condition, good.

Girls' dormitory.—Character, one-story frame, partly lathed and plastered. Use, girl's home. Capacity, 80 pupils and 4 employees, Erected, main part previous to 1880, several additions since. Present value, $3,000. Present condition, fair.

Schoolhouse.—Character, two-story frame, woodwork painted inside and out. Use, class room and assembly hall. Capacity, 50 pupils at each session in class room. Erected in 1894. Cost, $1,500. Present value, $1,200. Present condition, good.

Laundry building.—Character, two-story frame. Use, laundry, bathroom, and sewing room. Dimensions, 24 by 60, with rear wing 24 by 56, and front wing 20 by 24. Erected in 1896. Cost, $1,200. Present value, $1,200. Present condition, good.

Commissary.—Character, one-story balloon frame. Use, storehouse for subsistence and school supplies. Dimensions, main building 24 by 50, addition 24 by 40. Erected, original building not known, addition 1885. Present value, $250. Present condition, main building poor, addition fair.

Storehouse.—Character, 1½-story balloon frame. Use, boys' dormitory (temporarily). Dimensions, main building 20 by 72, wing 20 by 28. Erected in 1897. Present value, $400. Present condition, fair.

Kindergarten.—Character, one-story frame. Use, kindergarten and primary school. Capacity, 45 pupils at each session. Erected, not known, remodeled 1895; was old military guardhouse. Present value, $800. Present condition, good.

Office.—Character, one-story frame, painted inside. Use, offices superintendent and clerk and repository of records. Dimensions, 23 by 24. Erected previous to 1885, exact date not known. Present value, $400. Present condition, good.

Cottage.—Character, one-story frame, unfinished inside. Use, clerk's quarters (temporarily). Capacity, 1 employee. Erected in 1900. Cost, $200. Present value, $200. Present condition, good.

Cottage.—Character, one-story frame. Use, employees' quarters. Capacity, 1 employee. Erected in 1898. Present value, $500. Present condition, good.

Adobe building.—Character, one-story adobe. Use, agency employees' dwelling. Capacity, 2 employees. Erected previous to 1870, exact date not known. Present value, $1,000. Present condition, fair.

Carpenter shop.—Character, 1½-story, balloon frame. Use, agency carpenter and pupil apprentices. Dimensions, 30 by 34 feet. Erected previous to 1880, exact date not known. Present value, $100. Present condition, poor; foundation rotten.

8193—03——3

Blacksmith shop.—Character, frame, rough. Use, agency blacksmith and pupil apprentices. Dimensions, 20 by 50 feet. Erected in 1896. Present value, $100. Present condition, fair.

Barn.—Character, two-story frame, rough. Use, barn and stable. Dimensions, 32 by 70 feet. Erected, date not known. Present value, $1,600. Present condition, good.

Bakery.—Character, one--story frame. Use, school bakery. Dimensions, 15 by 16 feet, and extension, 12 by 28 feet. Erected, date not known. Present value, $100. Present condition, fair.

Drying room.—Character, one-story frame. Use, small boys' dormitory. Dimensions, 24 by 56 feet. Erected in 1894. Present value, $500. Present condition, good.

Old sewing room.—Character, one-story frame. Use, small boys' sitting room. Dimensions, 18 by 24 feet. Erected in 1889. Present value, $225. Present condition, fair.

Old fish hatchery.—Character, log and frame. Use, band practice and reading room. Dimensions, 18 by 45 feet. Erected, date unknown; very early; formerly belonged to Fish Commission. Present value, nominal. Present condition, poor; foundation rotten.

Miscellaneous outbuildings.—Character, all frame. Use, henhouse, cattle sheds, covered walks, implement and tool shed. Dimensions, sufficient. Erected, 1889 to 1901. Present condition, fair to good.

Buildings lighted by kerosene lamps. Heated by box stoves using hard wood as fuel. Ventilation of all buildings is by means of doors and windows, and in some cases by openings in the ceilings to attics. Some windows are fitted with ventilating boards to prevent direct drafts.

An abundant supply of pure mountain water is carried from Supply Creek to the school by a ditch and flume nearly a mile long to a tank about 30 feet up the hillside, from which the water is conveyed by pipes to all parts of the school grounds. The sewerage from the boys' and girls' buildings (excepting the small boys' quarters) is carried by a stream of water constantly flowing through the closets, thence underground through 8-inch pipe some distance from the buildings, and thence to the Trinity River, across the fields in open ditches. Several of the unsanitary and offensive privy vaults are still in use. There are several open running ditches in the grounds which help to carry away the sewage. Bathing is by a system of ring baths in the laundry building. There are also two tubs in the hospital building and one in the girls' dormitory. In the winter there is much difficulty in heating sufficient water for bathing purposes.

This school has 99.73 acres of land in its reserve. It is poor in quality, the entire value being about $2,000.

Practically all of the land set aside for the school is under fence. About 30 acres of the school land is under cultivation—18 acres as garden, orchard, and oat field, 11 acres seeded to alfalfa and grain, and about 1 acre planted to berries and small fruit. There is no other school land available for cultivation, the remainder of the allotment being occupied by buildings, playgrounds, etc. There is no pasture land. All of the school land can be irrigated—some of it not very successfully because of the porous nature of the ground and lack of sufficient water during the dry season.

This school was opened in July, 1892, with a capacity of 100 pupils; reorganized September, 1893; capacity increased to 120 in September, 1894, and further increased in 1899 to 160.

HUALAPAI AGENCY, ARIZ.

(Under Superintendent of School at Truxton Canyon.)

Tribes.	Population.
Hualapai	533
Yava Supai	233
Total	766

Area, 730,880 acres, unsurveyed.

Railroad station: Hackberry, Ariz., on Atlantic and Pacific Railway.

Nearest military post: Fort Apache, Ariz. Post-office address: Hackberry, Ariz. Telegraphic address: Hackberry, Ariz.

Truxton Canyon Training School.

Located at Truxton, Ariz., directly on the Santa Fe Pacific Railroad, 5 miles east of Hackberry. Site, in a recess of Truxton Canyon; protected from cold winds by mountains. Well-drained soil, sandy, fertile in valley. Climate, dry. Altitude, about 4,500 feet.

STATISTICS OF INDIAN TRIBES, AGENCIES, AND SCHOOLS. 35

Barn.—Character, frame. Erected in 1898. Cost, $200. Present value, $100. Present condition, fair.

Dormitory.—Character, two-story brick, with basement. Use, dormitory for boys and girls, dining room and kitchen, 2 schoolrooms, bakery, 2 play rooms, 2 clothes rooms, furnace, 2 bathrooms, water-closets, lavatories, etc. Capacity, 80 pupils. Erected in 1901. Cost, $34,400. Present value, $33,000. Present condition, excellent.

Schoolhouse.—Character, one-story brick. Use, schoolrooms. Capacity, 80 pupils. Erected in 1902. Cost, $11,989. Present value, $11,989. Present condition, excellent.

Employees' quarters.—Character, brick, two stories. Use, employees' living quarters. Capacity, 7 small bedrooms, 1 small sitting room, kitchen, dining room, cellar, 2 bathrooms. Erected in 1901. Cost, $5,490. Present value, $5,000. Present condition, excellent.

Employees' quarters, old.—Character, frame, one story. Use, employees' rooms. Capacity, four rooms. Erected in 1883. Cost, $500. Present value, $75. Present condition, very poor.

Laundry.—Character, one-story brick. Use, laundry work for school and sewing room. Capacity, 2 rooms. Erected in 1901. Cost, $2,700. Present value, $2,500. Present condition, excellent.

Office, old.—Character, frame, one story. Use, not used. Capacity, 2 small rooms. Erected in 1898. Cost, $200. Present value, $25. Present condition, very poor.

Pump house.—Character, brick. Use, contains boiler for pump that throws water into tank. Capacity, 1 room. Erected in 1901. Cost, $7,390, including the water and sewer system. Present value, $7,000, including water and sewer system. Present condition, excellent.

Shops.—Character, brick, one story. Use, carpenter and blacksmith shops. Capacity, 20 by 80 feet. Erected in 1901. Cost, $2,950. Present value, $2,700. Present condition, excellent.

Wagon shed.—Character, shed, iron roof, boarded on two ends, open on both sides. Use, shelter for school wagons. Capacity, 2 or 3 wagons. Erected in 1901. Cost, $25. Present value, $20. Present condition, good.

Warehouse.—Character, one-story brick. Use, storing supplies and goods of different kinds for school and Indians. Capacity, 50 by 20 feet. Erected in 1901. Cost, $2,010. Present value, $1,900. Present condition, excellent.

Lighted by acetylene plant. Dormitory heated by steam; others by stoves. Ventilation only by windows and doors. Water from wells, pumped into steel tank by steam, into buildings by gravity.

The school farm is quite small. About 15 acres under fence. Cost, about $450. About 2 acres cultivated. All will be cultivated when there is enough water. No pasturage. About 6 acres irrigated now.

This is a new school plant and was opened for the first time October 24, 1901. It has 160 pupils; 57 girls, 103 boys.

Havasupai Day School.

Located in Cataract Canyon, a spur of the Grand Canyon of the Colorado. Soil fertile. Water plentiful. Timber scarce. Climate dry.

School building.—Character, stone, one story. Use, day school. Capacity, 25 by 40 feet. Erected in 1900. Present value, $2,000. Present condition, good.

Farmer's house.—Character, one-story stone. Use, farmer's residence. Capacity, 14 by 24 feet. Erected; finished in 1898. Present value, $800. Present condition, good.

Jail.—Character, stone. Used as an office and drug store. Capacity, 14 feet square. Erected; finished in 1901. Present value, $500. Present condition, good.

Teacher's residence.—Character, stone, one story. Residence for school employees. Capacity, 4 rooms, each 14 feet square. Erected; finished in 1895. Present value, $1,500. Present condition, good.

Pump house.—Character, frame, one story. Use, for gasoline engine. Capacity, 8 by 10 feet. Erected in 1900.

Five acres in school farm. Good land; 6 acres under fence, including pasture; 10 acres can be cultivated. Plenty of water.

JICARILLA AGENCY, N. MEX.

(Under Superintendent of School.)

Tribes.	Population.
Jicarilla Apache	802

Area:

	Acres.
Allotted	129,313.35
Unallotted	286,400.00
Reserved for mission, school, and agency	280.44
Total	415,993.79

Railroad station: Dulce, N. Mex., on Denver and Rio Grande Railroad.
Nearest military post: Fort Wingate, N. Mex. Post-office address: Dulce, N. Mex. Telegraphic address: Lumberton, N. Mex.

Jicarilla Training School.

Located 1½ miles north of Dulce, N. Mex., on the Denver and Rio Grande Railroad. Site is ideal for school purposes; climate, extreme changes. Soil, adobe on a substratum of rock and shale.

Dormitory.—Character, two-story wood, with stone basement and ell one-story wood addition. Use, dormitory, dining room, kitchen, bakery, schoolrooms. Capacity, 125 pupils. Erected in 1901. Cost, $31,095. Present value, $31,095. Present condition, excellent.

Employees' cottage.—Character, two-story wood. Use, employee's quarters and mess hall. Capacity, 8 employees. Erected in 1901. Cost, $3,990. Present value, $3,990. Present condition, excellent.

Warehouse.—Character, one-story wood. Use, storing supplies. Dimensions, 20 by 49 feet. Erected in 1901. Cost, $1,550. Present value, $1,550. Present condition, excellent.

Laundry building.—Character, one-story wood. Use, laundry. Dimensions, 22 by 46 feet. Erected in 1901. Cost, $2,275. Present value, $2,275. Present condition, excellent.

Lighted by gasoline gas furnished by a Mathews gas machine, capacity 150 lights. There are 123 lights. Plant was installed in 1901. It is in good condition and satisfactory. Heated by steam from a steam heater, American Radiator Company, Chicago, located in basement. It was installed in 1901. The cottage is heated by coal stoves. Ventilation of schoolrooms and dormitories is by the system devised by the Indian Office. Cottage has no system of ventilation except windows and doors.

The water supply is the Navajo River, 1 mile northeast of plant. A ditch and flume 1 mile in length furnishes power for two turbines, which force 1,000 gallons per minute into a reservoir of about 3,000,000 gallons capacity, 112 feet above the level of the plant. From this the water is conducted by 4-inch main to the plant. This water will also be used for irrigation. The cost is $28,990. All the buildings are connected by 4 and 6 inch sewer pipe to an 8-inch main, which empties on the valley below the plant. There are 12 ring baths and 2 tubs on first floor of dormitory. There are standpipes in the dormitory, with hose on each floor and basement.

This school has 100 acres of sagebrush land, which will be converted into a school farm.

This school opened for pupils October 19, 1903.

KIOWA AGENCY, OKLA.

Tribes.	Population.
Kiowa	1,134
Comanche	1,407
Apache	164
Wichita, and affiliated tribes	596
Total	3,301

Area:

	Acres.
Kiowa, Comanche, and Apache Reservation, unallotted	480,000
Wichita and affiliated tribes, allotted	152,991

Railroad station: Anadarko, on Chicago, Rock Island and Pacific Railway.
Nearest military post: Fort Sill, Okla. Post-office address: Anadarko, Okla. Telegraphic address: Anadarko, Okla.

Fort Sill Indian Boarding School.

Location, 40 miles south of Anadarko, Okla., on Chicago, Rock Island and Pacific Railway (Enid and Anadarko Branch), 3½ miles south of Fort Sill, and 1½ miles north of Lawton, Okla.

STATISTICS OF INDIAN TRIBES, AGENCIES, AND SCHOOLS. 37

The site of the plant is a choice selection; the climate is good and mild, but subject to quick changes and droughts. The soil is sandy loam in the creek bottom (Cache Creek) and very fertile. Prairie hard, but generally fertile.

Girls' dormitory.—Character, two-story frame. Use, girls' dormitory, employees' quarters and sewing room. Capacity, 75. Erected in 1890. Cost, $8,000. Present value, $1,000. Present condition, poor.

Boys' dormitory.—Character, two-story stone. Use, dormitory for boys and 3 rooms for employees' quarters. Capacity, 75. Erected in 1893. Cost, $7,500. Present value, $4,000. Present condition, poor.

Superintendent's cottage.—Character, one-story frame. Use, quarters for superintendent and family. Capacity, 4 rooms, including dining room and kitchen. Erected in 1897. Cost, $1,200. Present value, $1,200. Present condition, excellent.

Schoolhouse.—Character, brick, with stone foundation, 1½ stories, and basement for storing coal, and for a heating plant. Use, class rooms and assembly hall, office for superintendent, and quarters for 1 employee. Capacity, 225. Erected in 1899. Cost, $12,986. Present value, $12,986. Present condition, excellent.

Mess hall.—Character, one-story brick, with stone foundation and cellar. Use, dining hall, kitchen, bakery, and employees' quarters. Capacity, 200. Erected in 1899. Cost, $4,900. Present value, $4,900. Present condition, excellent.

Laundry.—Character, two-story frame. Use, laundry and drying room, also room for 2 employees in second story. Capacity, 150. Erected in 1891. Cost, $700. Present value, $350. Present condition, fair.

Wareroom.—Character, one-story frame; two buildings connected. Use, storage room for supplies. Dimensions, 18 by 36 and 14 by 28 feet. Erected in 1891. Cost, $600. Present value, $300. Present condition, good.

Boiler house (pump house).—Character, one-story frame. Use, pumping water, shoe shop, and storing coal. Dimensions, 20 by 40 feet. Erected in 1900. Cost: Is part of water and sewer system, and included in cost thereof. Present condition, excellent.

Coal house.—Character, one-story frame. Use, storing coal supply. Capacity, 100 tons coal. Erected in 1901. Cost, $200. Present value, $200. Present condition, excellent.

Shop.—Character, one-story frame. Use, tool house and repair shop. Erected in 1895. Cost, unknown. Present value, $20. Present condition, poor.

Horse barn.—Character, 1½-story frame. Use, stabling horses and storing hay and grain. Capacity, 12 horses, 2,000 bushels grain, 30 tons hay. Erected in 1898. Cost, $1,200. Present valuation, $1,100. Present condition, excellent.

Implement shed.—Character, one-story frame. Use, shelter for agricultural implements. Erected in 1898. Cost, $200. Present value, $150. Present condition, good.

Barn.—Character, one-story frame with small loft. Use, storing grain, hay, and stabling 4 horses. Capacity, 4 horses and feed. Erected in 1896. Cost, $350. Present value, $150. Present condition, good.

Miscellaneous, poultry house, cistern house, buggy shed, and meat house.—Character, all frame. Use, protection of poultry, for storage of beef, protection of vehicles, etc. Erected from 1896 to 1900. Cost, unknown. Present value, unknown. Present condition, good.

Electric lights installed in 1903, costing $556. All buildings are heated by wood and coal stoves, except the schoolhouse, which is heated by steam. Ventilation of school building is modern and excellent; all other buildings are ventilated by means of doors and windows only. The girls' and boys' dormitories are poorly ventilated because of this fact.

The water is supplied from a well near the buildings, is excellent, and the supply sufficient; but the capacity of the well being entirely too small, causes use of pump oftener than if well was larger. The water is pumped by steam into a steel standpipe, 65 feet high, of 24,000 gallons capacity. From the standpipe the buildings are supplied with water by means of mains, underground. In addition to this there is another well with hand pump and 3 cisterns. The sewerage system was installed in 1900 by contractor. The system's outfall discharges by means of a 6-inch main into Cache Creek about 400 yards from the plant. Outfall is 20 feet. Cost of water and sewer system, $6,752.72. The bathing facilities of this school are as sorry as could well be imagined. Eighty boys have one bath tub supplied with water heated in an adjoining room. The facilities for bathing in girls' quarters not much better. Temporary tubs, without modern conveniences. There are 8 fire hydrants at convenient points on the grounds, and the school is supplied with one hose reel and 300 feet of 2-inch hose.

This school has 2,068.72 acres of land reserved for exclusive school purposes. Estimated value, $25,000. All except 468.72 acres is under fence, and 320 acres of this will be fenced in the near future. One hundred and sixty acres is under cultivation, with 30 acres sodded in alfalfa and 10 acres planted in fruit and grapes. One hundred acres of excellent land can be added to the farm. About 1,300 acres are used to pasture school cattle.

This school was opened for pupils January 25, 1891, with a capacity of 40. The school farm is one of the best in the country, and special stress is laid on the agricultural and stock raising features of the institution.

Riverside Indian Boarding School.

Located 1½ miles north of Auadarko, Okla. Situation well suited for school purposes; climate mild and subject to droughts. Soil light, sandy, yet productive. Surface rolling.

Girls' building.—Character, two-story brick. Use, dormitory, reading room, and sewing room; also employees' quarters. Capacity, 100 pupils. Erected in 1899. Cost, $14,100. Present value, $14,100. Present condition, excellent.

Boys' building.—Character, 1½-story brick. Use, dormitory, boys' play room, and employees' quarters. Capacity, 60 pupils. Erected in 1882. Cost, about $10,000. Present value, $2,500. Present condition, poor.

School building (schoolhouse).—Character, one-story brick. Use, class rooms and assembly hall and quarters for two employees. Capacity, 225 pupils. Erected in 1900. Cost, $12,964.67. Present value, $12,964.67. Present condition, excellent.

Dining hall and kitchen (mess hall).—Character, one-story brick. Use, children's dining room, kitchen, bakery, and employees' quarters. Capacity, 200 pupils. Erected in 1899. Cost, $4,900. Present value, $4,900. Present condition, excellent.

Superintendent's cottage.—Character, 1½-story frame. Use, superintendent's office and dwelling. Capacity, 1 office room, 4 dwelling rooms. Erected about 1880. Cost, about $600. Present value, about $150. Present condition, very poor.

Storehouse.—Character, one-story frame. Use, storing supplies. Capacity, dimensions 16 by 28 feet. Erected about 1880. Cost, about $300. Present value, $100. Present condition, poor.

Barn.—Character, 1½-story frame. Use, housing live stock and storing hay and grain. Capacity, 12 horses, 30 tons hay, 800 bushels of grain. Erected in 1899. Cost, $800. Present value, $700. Present condition, good.

Laundry.—Character, 1½-story frame, with one-story addition. Use, laundry and band room. Capacity, dimensions 16 by 32; one-story addition, 18 by 20 feet. Erected about 1892. Cost, about $1,000. Present value, $400. Present condition, poor.

Employees' mess building.—Character, 1½-story frame. Use, employees' kitchen and dining room and quarters for mess cook. Capacity, dimensions 20 by 28 feet. Erected about 1880. Cost, about $600. Present value, worthless. Present condition, old, dilapidated.

Miscellaneous outbuildings.—Character, all one-story frame. Use, implement shed, coal house, boiler house, etc. Erected from 1897 to 1901. Cost, about $1,000. Present value, about $700. Present condition, fair to good.

The girls' building, school building, dining hall, and kitchen are all lighted with gasoline gas. The lighting plant was installed at the completion of the buildings and was a part of the cost thereof. It is in good condition and satisfactory. The girls' building and school building are heated by steam from plants installed at completion of buildings and part of cost thereof. All the other buildings are heated by wood stoves and lighted by kerosene lamps. The girls' building and school building are ventilated by the system devised by the Indian Office. The other buildings have no modern system of ventilation.

The water supply has heretofore been taken from the Washita River and pumped into a steel standpipe 75 feet high and 8 feet in diameter, having a capacity of 28,350 gallons, thus affording a pressure of 33 pounds to the square inch. The source of supply is now being changed and the water will hereafter be pumped from a well now about completed. This well will be 50 feet deep and 10 feet in diameter, and will furnish an abundant supply of water for the school. The character of the water is not the best, as it contains some gypsum. The water from the well is better and purer, however, than that in the river. All the buildings are connected with a 6-inch sewer main which empties into the Washita River about 300 yards from the buildings. The outfall is 15 feet below the buildings, and is below the source of water supply. Cost of water and sewer system, $7,092. There are 10 ring shower baths and 2 tubs in the girls' building, and 5 bath tubs in the boys' building, located on first and second floors in girls and first floor in boys' building. There are standpipes with hose attached in girls' building, water buckets and chemical fire extinguishers in all other buildings, also hydrants in grounds, with hose and hose cart.

STATISTICS OF INDIAN TRIBES, AGENCIES, AND SCHOOLS. 39

This school has 2,350.72 acres of rolling land, most of which is suitable only for grazing. Its present value is about $23,000. There are 1,200 acres under fence. About 200 acres under cultivation. Two hundred additional acres could be cultivated. One hundred acres are used for pasture.

This school was opened under the name of Wichita School in the early fall of 1871, with 18 pupils and 1 teacher.

Rainy Mountain Boarding School.

Located 6 miles south of Harrison, Okla., a station on the Chicago, Rock Island and Pacific Railway. Site, high and healthful. Climate, warm for the greater part of the year, but in winter subject to extreme changes. Soil, hard clay, cold and tenacious in wet weather and very hard in dry weather. Difficult to cultivate and yielding poor returns.

Boys' building.—Character, two-story stone, with two-story ell. Use, boys' dormitory, play rooms, chapel, schoolroom, and employees' quarters. Capacity, 38 pupils. Erected in 1893. Cost, $12,000. Present value, $8,000. Present condition, good.

Girls' building.—Character, two-story brick, with basement. Use, dormitory, sitting room, kindergarten room, sewing room, play room, and employees' quarters. Capacity, 64 pupils. Erected in 1899. Cost, 3 buildings, $24,000. Present value, 3 buildings, $24,000. Present condition, excellent.

Mess hall.—Character, one-story brick. Use, dining room, kitchen, bakery, employees' quarters. Capacity, 200. Erected in 1899. Cost (see cost of girls' building). Present value (see girls' building). Present condition, excellent.

Superintendent's cottage.—Character, one-story frame. Use, superintendent's quarters. Capacity, 4 dwelling rooms. Erected in 1898. Cost (see girls' building). Present value (see girls' building). Present condition, excellent.

Laundry building.—Character, two-story frame, with one-story ell. Use, wash room, ironing room, drying room, and storeroom. Capacity, 12 pupils. Erected in 1894. Cost, unknown. Present value, unknown. Present condition, good.

Employees' mess hall.—Character, one-story frame. Use, employes' dining room and kitchen. Carpenter shop in rear. Capacity, 14 employees. Erected in 1897. Present condition, good.

Barn.—Character, 1½-story frame, with basement. Use, housing live stock, storing hay and grain. Capacity, 10 horses, 6 cows, 25 tons hay. Erected in 1894. Cost, $600. Present value, $500. Present condition, good.

Miscellaneous outbuildings.—Character, all frame. Use, storerooms, machinery shed, chicken house, etc. Erected, 1894 to 1899. Cost, about $800. Present value, $600. Present condition, good.

Lighted by kerosene lamps, except girls' building, which has a 100-light gas machine. Gas machine is satisfactory. Girls' building heated with an 11-section Ideal steam boiler; all other buildings by wood and coal stoves. The girls' building is provided with system of ventilation. No means of ventilating other buildings except by windows.

Water is soft and of excellent quality. It is furnished by a well 400 yards west of buildings, raised by steam pump 75 feet up the mountain side to a reservoir of 800 barrels capacity; from thence is carried by pressure where needed. Water system installed in 1900. Cost, $5,430.86. A 6-inch sewer leads from the girls' building to small ravine northeast of school buildings and in an opposite direction from water supply. The outfall is 20 feet below buildings. There are two bathrooms, each having 5 ring baths and 1 tub, in the girls' building. Superintendent's cottage also has bathroom; other buildings have no bathing facilities of any description. Girls' building is supplied with hose on each floor. Water buckets and chemical fire extinguishers in other buildings. Fire hydrants on grounds, equipped with 300 feet hose and reel.

This school has 2,560 acres of land set apart for its use from the original Apache, Kiowa, and Comanche Reservation. The land is of poor quality, more suitable for grazing than for agricultural purposes. Its present value is estimated to be about $15,000. There are 1,000 acres under fence. There are 100 acres under cultivation. There are 500 additional acres that can be cultivated. There are 900 acres used for pasturage. None irrigated. One corner of school reserve is used for agency purposes.

Rainy Mountain School was opened September, 1893, with 11 employees and an average attendance of 19 pupils.

KLAMATH AGENCY, OREG.

(Under School Superintendent.)

Tribes.	Population.
Klamath	736
Modoc, Paiute and Pitt River	405
Total	1,141

Area:	Acres.
Allotted	177,719.62
Reserved for agency, school, and church	6,094.77
Unallotted	872,186

Railroad station, Ager, Cal., on Southern Pacific Railway. Eighty-five miles to agency.

Nearest military post, Vancouver Barracks, Wash. Post-office address, Klamath Agency, Klamath County, Oreg. Telegraphic address, Klamath Falls, Oreg.

Klamath Boarding School.

Located 89 miles northeast of Ager, Cal., shipping station on the Southern Pacific Railroad. Site admirable. Climate without extreme changes.

Girls' building.—Character, two-story frame, rock foundation. Use, dormitory, dining room, kitchen, sitting room, employees' room. Capacity, 50 girls. Erected in 1893. Cost, $6,000. Present value, $6,000. Present condition, good.

Boys' building.—Character, 2½ story frame. Use, dormitory, sitting room, mess quarters, employees' rooms. Capacity, 60 pupils. Erected in 1883. Cost, $1,000. Present value, $2,000. Present condition, good.

Schoolhouse.—Character, two-story frame. Use, class room and assembly hall. Capacity, 150. Erected in 1892. Cost, $3,126. Present value, $3,500. Present condition, good.

Hospital.—Character, 1½ story frame. Use, quarters for sick pupils. Capacity, 12 beds. Erected in 1901. Cost, $993. Present value, $1,500. Present condition, good.

Laundry.—Character, 1½ story frame. Use, laundry, sewing room, and bathrooms. Erected in 1895. Cost, $360. Present value, $800. Present condition, fair.

Dairy.—Character, one-story frame. Use, storage for milk and butter. Erected in 1900. Present value, $100. Present condition, good.

Barn.—Character, 1½ story frame. Use, housing live stock. Capacity, 12 horses, 21 cows, 21 calves, 100 tons hay. Erected in 1901. Present value, $800. Present condition, good.

Wood sheds (2).—Character, frame. Erected in 1896. Cost, $78. Present value, $150. Present condition, fair.

Miscellaneous buildings.—Character, all frame. Use, poultry house, pigpens, ice house, oil house. Erected, 1900 and 1901. Present value, $300. Present condition, good.

Lighted by coal-oil lamps. Heated by wood stoves. Hospital only building belonging to school plant that has modern system of ventilation. The water supply is brought to the school from a clear, cold spring, a distance of 2,200 feet, in a wooden flume. There is no kind of a water system. The water used in the buildings is carried in buckets from the flume. What sewerage there is consists of wooden guttering above ground, with no means of flushing. The sewage is supposed to pass off into a creek below the school. There are eight bath tubs. The water, hot and cold, is carried to these in buckets by hand. The only fire protection consists of buckets distributed through the various buildings.

This school has 3,229.26 acres of land. There are 2,659.36 acres under fence. There are 87 acres being cultivated, and 580 acres more could be cultivated with an irrigation system. Spring pasturage, 960 acres; fall pasturage, 2,659.26 acres; meadow, 160 acres.

The Klamath School was opened July 1, 1875, with 2 employees and 12 pupils. The number of pupils had increased by the end of the month to 23. Before this period a day school had been maintained during the winter and spring with not to exceed 10 pupils. The growth of the school has been steady and satisfactory and has kept pace with the increase of national interest in the cause of Indian education. The Klamath School now has a capacity of 110 pupils. An enormous spring of clear, cold water rises near the school, and furnishes water for use and all the power necessary for machinery.

Yainax Boarding School.

Located 40 miles east of Klamath Agency and about 95 miles from Ager, Cal., on the Southern Pacific Railroad. Climate without extreme changes, summers pleasant, with occasional frosts at night.

Main building.—Character, two-story frame. Use, boys' and girls' dormitories, sitting rooms, kitchen and dining room, schoolroom, and employees' quarters. Capacity, 90 pupils. Erected in 1882. Cost, $800. Present value, $1,200. Present condition, fair.

Warehouse.—Character, 1½-story frame. Use, storing supplies. Dimensions, 24 by 48 feet. Erected in 1894. Present value, $400. Present condition, good.

Employees' cottages.—Character, 4 one-story frames. Use, employees' quarters, mess, and dispensary. Capacity, 12 employees. Erected, 1894 to 1897. Cost, average $160 each. Present value, average $400 each. Present condition, good.

Laundry.—Character, 1½-story frame. Use, Laundry and sewing room. Dimensions, 36 by 36 feet. Erected in 1896 (unfinished). Cost, $300. Present value, $250. Present condition, good.

Barns.—Character, 3 frame structures. Use, housing live stock and storing hay. Capacity, 12 cows, 10 horses, 175 tons hay. Erected in 1881, 1882; and 1899. Present value, $600.

Miscellaneous buildings.—Character, all frame. Use, dairy house, blacksmith shop, harness shop, chicken house, etc.

The buildings are lighted by coal-oil lamps and are heated by wood stoves. The ventilation of the buildings is by a system recommended by the inspecting officials of the Indian Department. The water for cooking and drinking purposes is supplied from wells. A small pipe carries the water to the school kitchen. A spring supplies water for the laundry and for irrigating purposes. There is no sewerage system. Stationary washtubs are used for bath tubs. Buckets filled with water are placed throughout the buildings for protection against fire.

This school has four sections of land in square form, 2,560 acres, of which about half is hilly or mountainous, and for the most part covered with pine timber. About half the area is level, fertile land, of which 120 acres are in wild meadow, 60 acres in cultivation under the plow, and the remainder pasture land. There are about 860 acres under fence, and 60 acres cultivated, exclusive of natural meadow. About 100 acres, mostly wild meadow, improved by irrigation. This can be increased by careful ditching to about 160 acres. Inclosed spring pasture about 200 acres; fall pasture (exclusive of spring pasture and plow land), 600 acres; wild meadow, approximately, 120 acres.

The Yainax Industrial Boarding School was opened November 1, 1882. The average attendance during the first month—November—was 31. By February 28, 1883, 30 additional pupils had applied for admission, but there was no room for them. The history of the school since its organization has been one of steady growth and prosperity.

LA POINTE AGENCY, WIS.

Tribes.	Population.
Chippewa at Red Cliff	237
Chippewa at Bad River	833
Chippewa at Lac Court d'Oreilles	1,145
Chippewa at Lac du Flambeau	755
Chippewa at Fond du Lac	833
Chippewa at Grand Portage	323
Chippewa at Boise Fort	773
Chippewa at Rice Lake	191
Total	5,090

Area:	Acres.
Allotted	139,907.85
Unallotted	137,577.85
Reserved for schools	40.10

Railroad station: Ashland, on Chicago and Northwestern Railway, and Wisconsin Central Railway.

Nearest military post: Fort Snelling, Minn. Post-office address: Ashland, Wis. Telegraphic address: Ashland, Wis.

Lac du Flambeau School.

Located 3 miles west of Chicago and Northwestern Railway station, on the Lac du Flambeau Reservation, Wis. The site is a peninsula comprising about 18 acres, and bounded on the north, south, and west by three beautiful lakes, making an admirable location. Climate is rather cold in winter and mild in summer. Soil is light and sandy, but well suited to the raising of vegetables and small fruits.

Dormitory.—Character, two-story frame. Use, dormitories, dining rooms, kitchen, lavatories, play rooms, rooms for 5 employees, one office room. Capacity, 124 pupils. Erected in 1895. Cost, $10,164.43; with recent improvements, $12,893.66. Present value, $12,230. Present condition, good.

Laundry.—Character, two-story frame. Use, laundrying purposes. Capacity, sufficient. Erected in 1895. Cost, $1,279.99. Present value, $1,000; with machinery, $1,500. Present condition, good.

School.—Character, one-story frame. Use, class rooms. Capacity, 160 pupils. Erected in 1895. Cost, $3,789.85. Present value, $3,400. Present condition, good.

Warehouse.—Character, one-story frame. Use, storing supplies. Dimensions, 20 by 60 feet. Erected in 1895. Cost, $1,257. Present value, $1,257. Present condition, good.

Barn.—Character, two-story frame. Use, housing live stock and storing feed, hay, etc. Capacity, 6 horses, 36 head cattle, 50 tons hay, 30 tons feed. Erected in 1897. Cost, $2,001.64. Present value, $1,800. Present condition, good.

Dormitory.—Character, two-story frame. Use, dormitories, sewing room, reading room, 2 rooms for employees. Erected in 1897. Capacity, 26 pupils. Cost, $2,833.69. Present value, with late improvements, $3,000. Present condition, good.

Employees' building.—Character, two-story frame. Use, employees' quarters. Capacity, 6 employees. Erected in 1897. Cost, $2,232.40. Present value, $2,200. Present condition, good.

Hospital.—Character, one-story frame. Use, isolation and care of sick. Capacity, 14 pupils. Erected in 1897, addition in 1901-2. Cost, $3,839.28 without heating plant. Present value, $3,840. Present condition, good.

Superintendent's residence.—Character, two-story frame. Use, dwelling for superintendent's family and room for visiting officials. Capacity, 6 rooms. Erected in 1897. Cost, $1,533.40. Present value, $1,500. Present condition, good.

Blacksmith shop.—Character, one-story frame. Use, for blacksmith work and instruction. Dimensions, 26 by 36 feet. Two forges. Erected in 1897. Cost, $784.89. Present value, $800. Present condition, good.

Carpenter shop.—Character, one-story frame. Use, carpenter and paint shops. Dimensions, 42 by 88 feet. Erected in 1897. Cost, 1,221.21. Present value, $1,200. Present condition, good.

Carpenter shop.—Character, one-story frame. Use, band room and guardhouse. Dimensions, 16 by 40 feet. Erected in 1895. Cost, $105.55. Present value, $200. Present condition, good.

Cold storage.—Character, two-story frame. Use, preservation of meats, milk, and butter. Dimensions, 13 by 22 feet. Erected in 1897. Cost, $346.48. Present value, $340. Present condition, good.

Hose house.—Character, frame. Use, to house fire hose and carts. Dimensions, 8 by 12 feet. Erected in 1899. Cost, $27.91. Present value, $40. Present condition, good.

Ice house.—Character, one-story frame. Use, storing ice. Dimensions, 16 by 24 feet. Erected in 1895. Cost, $58.78. Present value, $125. Present condition, good.

Oil house.—Character, frame. Use, storing oils, paints, etc. Dimensions, 14 by 22 feet. Erected in 1895. Cost, $70. Present value, $125. Present condition, good.

Fire engine house.—Character, frame. Use, at present, to store unserviceable property, etc. Dimensions, 18 by 22 feet. Erected in 1895. Cost, $66.06. Present value, $130. Present condition, good.

Miscellaneous outbuildings.—Character, all frame. Uses, hog house, chicken house, three coal houses. Dimensions, 18 by 60, 18 by 48, 8 by 20, 12 by 16, and 6 by 12 feet. Erected in 1895-1898. Cost, about $579. Present value, $700. Present condition, good.

Lighted by electricity furnished by the Flambeau Lumber Company, there being 70 lights in dormitory and school buildings, at a cost of 50 cents per light per month. Hospital is lighted by kerosene lamps at present. Dormitories and school are heated from a central steam station, which system was installed in 1901 at a cost of $5,675. The hospital is heated by a low-pressure individual steam system, installed in 1901-2, at a cost of $646.35. Direct indirect radiation in wards. Shops and cottages are heated by stoves. Ventilation of schoolrooms, dormitories, and hospital is by the system devised by the Department. Other buildings have no modern system.

Water supply from a lake is pure and soft. The water is forced by a steam pump into a tank of 800 barrels capacity, which is supported by a steel tower 70 feet in height, giving sufficient pressure for fire protection. The dormitories, school building, cottages, hospital, and barn are supplied from the system. The system was installed in 1898, and, including plumbing done in the different buildings at the time, cost $4,589.16. Dormitories and laundry are connected with 6-inch branches leading into an 8-inch sewer which empties into Flambeau Lake, about 1,100 feet below water supply. A separate 6-inch sewer from the hospital empties into Long Lake, where the current is from the buildings. The employees' building and superintendent's residence are connected with box sewers which empty into Long Lake. The box sewers are unsatisfactory. There are 6 ring baths and 2 tubs for girls and 5 ring baths and 2 tubs for boys in main dormitory building. One tub in hospital, none in cottages. There are standpipes and hose on both floors of main building, and on one floor of other buildings, excepting shops and outbuildings. Fire hydrants in grounds.

This school has, as nearly as can be ascertained, 490 acres of land, which has never been set aside by Executive order, but which were in 1897, by the agent, ordered to be used as a school farm. Estimated value, $3,000. (No accurate way of ascertaining the value.) All under fence. There are 45 acres under cultivation, and 50 additional acres can be cultivated. About 445 acres are used for pasturage. None irrigated.

This school was opened November 18, 1895, with a capacity of 124.

Hayward Boarding School.

Located 2 miles north of the village of Hayward, Sawyer County, Wis., on the Chicago, St. Paul, Minneapolis and Omaha Railroad. Site is well situated for school purposes, on a moderate elevation overlooking a small lake, and is well timbered with a growth of white, jack, and Norway pines. Soil consists principally of bowlders interspersed with just sufficient soil to keep the bowlders separated from each other. What little soil there is is of a clayey loam. Climate is subject to extreme changes of heat and cold.

Girls' dormitory.—Character, two stories and basement, brick with stone foundation, tin roof. Use, dormitory, sewing room, sitting room, and play room. Capacity, 65 pupils. Erected in 1900. Cost, $9,500. Present value, $9,000. Present condition, good.

Boys' dormitory.—Character, two stories and basement, brick with stone foundation, tin roof. Use, dormitory, sitting room, and play room. Capacity, 65 pupils. Erected in 1900. Cost, $9,500. Present value, $9,000. Present condition, good.

Schoolhouse.—Character, two-story, brick, with stone foundation, tin roof. Use, schoolrooms and chapel. Capacity, 100 pupils. Erected in 1900. Cost, $17,000. Present value, $16,500. Present condition, good.

Mess hall.—Character, two stories and partial basement, brick with stone foundation, tin roof. Use, first floor, general dining room, general kitchen, employees' dining room, employees' kitchen, and laundry; second floor, employees' sitting room and bedrooms. Capacity, 130 pupils and 10 employees. Erected in 1900. Cost, $16,000. Present value, $15,500. Present condition, good.

Warehouse.—Character, one-story brick with stone foundation, tin roof. Use, storing supplies. Dimensions, 22 by 52 feet. Erected in 1900. Cost, $1,500. Present value, $1,400. Present condition, very good.

Pump house.—Character, one-story brick with stone foundation, shingle roof. Use, to house gasoline engine to pump water from well under pump house to water tank. Dimensions, 10 by 12 feet. Erected in 1902. Cost, $150. Present value, $150. Present condition, good.

Miscellaneous buildings.—Character, all frame, consisting of dwelling, two stories, 14 rooms; barn, 16 by 30 feet; granary, 14 by 20 feet, and woodhouse, 12 by 16 feet. These buildings are located on the school farm about one-half mile from the school buildings, and are known as the Sawyer County poor-farm buildings. Use, dwelling for isolated hospital; barn, housing live stock and storing hay. Erected in 1890. Cost, $2,000. Present value, $300. Present condition, poor.

Lighted by gasoline gas, the gas being generated by a gas machine located in the basement of the schoolhouse, gasoline being supplied from a 500-gallon tank sunk in the ground a short distance from the schoolhouse. The plant was installed at time the buildings were erected, at a cost of about $2,500. It is in good condition and is entirely satisfactory. Heated by steam, with a separate heating plant in each of the dormitories, schoolhouse, and mess hall, at a cost of about $4,000. The several heating plants were installed at the time the buildings were erected; all are now in good condition. The warehouse and pump house are heated by stoves. Ventilation of schoolhouse, dormitories, and mess hall is by a system devised by the Indian Office. Other buildings have no modern system.

The water supplied is pure and soft. Its source is a well 36 feet deep sunk under the pump house, from where it is pumped by a gasoline engine into a wooden water tank of 700 barrels' capacity on a timber tower 50 feet high, which gives ample pressure to force the water wherever required. Water system was installed when buildings were erected, and afterwards improved by sinking the present well and building a new pump house at a cost of about $3,000. The dormitories, schoolhouse, and mess hall are all connected with a 6-inch sewer pipe, which empties into a small stream about 60 rods from the buildings. There are 5 needle baths and 1 tub for each of the two dormitories and 2 tubs for the mess hall. The baths for the two dormitories are located in the basements and for the mess hall on the second floor. There are lavatories in the basements of the two dormitories and on the second floor of the mess hall. There are hose attachments in the buildings and fire hydrants in the grounds.

The school has 640 acres of land in its reserve, and its present value is estimated to be $5,000, exclusive of buildings. There are 40 acres under very poor fence, 30 acres under cultivation, and 560 additional acres can be cultivated. Land donated by citizens of Hayward. School established out of specific appropriation made by Congress in 1900.

This school was opened September 2, 1901, with a capacity for 130 pupils.

Fond du Lac Day School.

Located on the Fond du Lac Reservation, Minn., about 2 miles from the town of Cloquet and 90 miles west of Ashland, Wis.

Schoolhouse.—Character, one-story frame. Use, class room and dwelling rooms for the teacher and family. Capacity, 1 class room, 2 dwelling rooms. Erected in 1896. Cost, $777.92. Present value, $780. Present condition, good.

The capacity of the Fond du Lac day school is 30 pupils.

Normantown Day School.

Located on the Northern Pacific Railway line, Fond du Lac Reservation, Minn., about 10 miles from the town of Cloquet and 90 miles west of Ashland, Wis., the agency headquarters. The climatic conditions are peculiar to the latitude in which the school is located, the winters being cold and the summers moderately warm.

Schoolhouse.—Character, one-story frame. Use, class room. Capacity, 42 pupils. Erected in 1891. Cost, $585. Present value, $580. Present condition, good.

Teacher's residence.—Character, one-story frame. Use, teacher's dwelling. Capacity, 3 dwelling rooms. Erected in 1891. Cost, $515. Present value, $500. Present condition, good.

Grand Portage Day School.

Located on the Grand Portage Reservation, Minn., on the north shore of Lake Superior, about 230 miles northeast of Ashland, Wis. The winters are severe, the summers short and pleasant.

Schoolhouse.—Character, 1½-story frame. Use, class room and dwelling rooms for teacher and family. Capacity, 1 class room, 5 dwelling rooms. Erected in 1896. Cost, $1,292. Present value, $1,295. Present condition, good.

This school has a capacity of 30 pupils.

Redcliff Day School.

Located on the Redcliff Reservation, 3 miles from Bayfield, a town on the Chicago, St. Paul, Minneapolis and Omaha Railway, and about 30 miles from the agency headquarters.

The buildings and equipment at this school belong to the Roman Catholics, and the sum of $100 is paid annually by the Government for their use.

The Franciscan Sisters have always had charge of the Redcliff school, the capacity of which is 50 pupils.

Odanah Day School.

Located on the Bad River Reservation, Wis., 12 miles east of the city of Ashland, Wis., on the Chicago and Northwestern line.

The buildings and equipment at this school are the property of the Roman Catholics and are leased by the Government at the rate of $100 per annum.

STATISTICS OF INDIAN TRIBES, AGENCIES, AND SCHOOLS. 45

This school has always been operated by the order of Franciscan Sisters. Its present capacity is 125 pupils.

The following school, although within the jurisdiction of the La Pointe Agency, is under the control of a bonded superintendent:

Vermilion Lake School, Tower, Minn.

Located 3 miles northwest of Tower, Minn., and on the opposite side of Vermilion Lake. Tower is on the Duluth and Iron Range Railroad, 96 miles north of Duluth, Minn. During the summer season the school can be reached only by boat. Site is fairly well suited for school purposes. The climate during the winter months is severe. The soil is only fairly productive and this, with the short season, makes extensive farming impossible, though garden truck does well.

Dormitory.—Character, two-story frame. Use, dormitory for both boys and girls, dining room, kitchen, sitting rooms, sewing room, employees' quarters, etc. Capacity, 150 pupils. Erected in 1898. Cost, $16,400. Present value, $15,000. Present condition, good.

Schoolhouse.—Character, one-story frame. Use, class rooms and assembly hall. Capacity, 150 pupils. Erected in 1898. Cost, $5,740. Present value, $5,000. Present condition, good.

Superintendent's residence.—Character, two-story frame. Use, employees' quarters and mess dining room and kitchen. Capacity, quarters for two small families, or six employees without families. Erected in 1898. Cost, $3,390. Present value, $3,000. Present condition, good.

Warehouse.—Character, one-story frame. Use, storing supplies. Dimensions, 20 by 60 feet. Erected in 1898. Cost, $1,390. Present value, $1,300. Present condition, good.

Laundry.—Character, two-story frame. Use, laundry. Dimensions, 21 by 36 feet. Erected in 1898. Cost, $1,490. Present value, $1,300. Present condition, good.

Pump house.—Character, one-story frame. Use, boiler and steam-pump room, etc. Dimensions, 21 by 27 feet, with two wings each 12 by 16 feet. Erected in 1898. Cost, $1,140. Present value, $1,000. Present condition, good.

Stable.—Character, 1½-story frame. Use, housing stock and storing hay and feed. Capacity, 6 horses, 12 cows, 20 tons hay. Erected in 1898. Cost, $1,389. Present value, $1,200. Present condition, good.

Ice house.—Character, one-story frame. Use, storing ice. Capacity, 75 cords ice. Erected in 1898. Cost, $1,500. Present value, $1,000. Present condition, fair.

Sheds (2).—Character, one-story frame. Use, storing wood and coal. Dimensions, 14 by 20 feet. Erected in 1899. Cost, $123.64 each. Present value, $120 each. Present condition, good.

Guardhouse.—Character, one-story brick. Use, confining drunken Indians and unruly pupils. Dimensions, 12 by 16 feet. Erected in 1900. Cost, $135. Present value, $135. Present condition, good.

In addition to the buildings described, there are four old buildings, known as teacher's residence, farmer's house, warehouse, and schoolhouse, about half a mile from the school. These are one story, log or frame. The date of their erection and their cost are unknown. Their present condition is very poor and their present value nothing.

Plant.—Lighted by gasoline gas, produced by 300-light gas machine; Detroit Heating and Lighting Company's manufacture. The system was installed in 1899 at a cost of $1,470. It is in good condition, and has given satisfaction. Dormitory and schoolhouse are heated by steam, each building having a boiler in the basement. The other buildings are heated by stoves. The heating plants were put in when the buildings were erected, at a cost of $3,500. They have given satisfaction from every standpoint but that of expense, and are in excellent condition. Ventilation of dormitory and schoolhouse is by system prescribed by the Indian Office. Other buildings have no modern system.

Water is filtered from the lake through sand, gravel, brick, and charcoal into a well, thence pumped by steam into a steel standpipe 60 feet high and 12 feet in diameter. The base of the standpipe is not above the level of the first floor of the buildings, consequently the pressure is not so great as it would be if the standpipe were on higher ground. The water supply is pure and ample, and the system is in good condition. The water and sewer systems were constructed in 1898 under one contract at a cost of $5,665. All main buildings are connected with an 8-inch general sewer pipe, which empties into the lake 100 yards from the nearest building and about a quarter of a mile below the point from which water is taken. The system is in good condition, but the main line has very little fall, and requires close attention. At certain seasons of the year the mouth of the sewer is below the water level of the lake. There are five ring baths for each sex, located on the first floor of the dormitory. There are two standpipes in the dormitory, with hose on two floors. Three fire hydrants are located at convenient points. Other buildings have only pails.

The reservation on which this school is located comprises 1,080 acres and was set apart "for warehouse and shipping purposes" by Executive order in 1887. The value of the land for agricultural purposes would not exceed $2 an acre at this time, but including value of timber of all kinds its value is estimated at $15,000. There are 15 acres under fence, 12 acres under cultivation. All land not under cultivation is covered with heavy brush or timber. The major portion of the reservation could be used for certain agricultural purposes if cleared. No pasture land proper, though cattle find good pasturage here and there in the timber or along the marshes. No land irrigated.

The school was opened October 16, 1899, with an attendance of 13 pupils. Capacity, 125 pupils.

LEECH LAKE AGENCY, MINN.

Tribes.	Population.
Cass Lake, Pillager, and Lake Winnibigoshish bands of Chippewa	1,283
Mdewakanton Sioux, Red Lake, Pembina, and White Oak Point bands of Mississippi Chippewa	1,934

Area:	Acres.
Allotted	91,883.92
Unallotted	801,100.99
Reserved for school, etc	321.60

Railroad station: Walker, Minn.
Nearest military post: Fort Snelling, Minn.
Post-office address: Onigum, Minn. Telegraphic address: Walker, Minn.

Leech Lake Agency School.

Located 2½ miles east of Walker, Minn., on the Great Northern, and Minnesota and International railroads. An arm of Leech Lake separates the school from Walker, and all going and coming is by boat, and in winter by sled over the ice.

Main building.—Character, two-story frame with basement under the entire building. Use, dormitory for boys and girls, schoolrooms, dining room, kitchen, laundry, engine room, employees' quarters, boys' play room, girls' play room, lavatories, mess kitchen and dining room, closets, and sewing room. Capacity, 60 pupils. Erected in 1900. Cost, $20,000. Present value, $17,000. Present condition, good.

Employees' quarters.—Character, two-story frame. Use, employees' sleeping rooms, dining room, and kitchen. Capacity, 8 employees. Erected, 1902. Cost, $4,938. Present value, $4,000. Present condition, good.

Miscellaneous outbuildings.—Character, all frame. Use, housing acetylene gas generator, and small building used as a barn. Capacity of barn, 2 cows and 3 tons of hay. Erected in 1900–1902. Cost, approximately, $300. Present value, approximately, $200. Present condition, excellent to fair.

Lighted by acetylene gas, there being 75 jets in the system, gas being generated in building located 50 feet from main building. Plant was installed April, 1901, at a cost of $436. It is in good condition and satisfactory. Heated by steam from a low-pressure boiler located in basement. There is no ventilating system other than by opening windows and doors.

The water is of good quality, being pumped from a well into a wooden tank on a 40-foot tower, located 200 feet south of building. The pumping is done by a 4-horsepower gasoline engine, and the water system meets all requirements. The building is connected with a 6-inch sewer pipe, which empties into Leech Lake 300 feet north of the building. There are 6 needle baths, located on second floor. Two hose are on each floor and connected for immediate use in case of fire.

There are 400 acres reserved for school and agency purposes, all heavily timbered. Farming is not practical by reason of the great expense necessary to put the land in condition for farming. There are no acres under fence. The school has no land under cultivation. This school was opened November 1, 1900, with a capacity of 60 pupils.

Red Lake Boarding School.

Located 45 miles, by wagon trail, north of Solway, Minn., the nearest railroad station. The immediate site is well selected, but latitude and other conditions are such that the school is exposed to the severest climatic changes possible within the United States. The soil is a fine sand, black on top from the amount of iron it contains, but fertile only when made so artificially.

Dormitory.—Character, two-story frame with basement and a one-story addition. Use, dormitory, dining room, kitchen, schoolrooms, dwelling rooms, sewing room, and carpenter shop. Capacity, 80 pupils. Erected in 1901. Cost, $35,000. Present value, $35,000. Present condition, excellent.

Employees' building.—Character, two-story frame. Use, dwelling for employees. Capacity, 6 employees. Erected about 1875. Present value, $500. Present condition, poor.

Laundry.—Character, one-story frame. Use, school laundry. Erected about 1875. Present value, $400. Present condition, good.

Warehouse.—Character, two-story frame. Use, storehouse for school supplies. Erected in 1901. Cost, $700. Present value, $700. Present condition, excellent.

Stable.—Character, old log shed. Use, housing live stock. Capacity, 2 horses, 14 head of cattle, 1 ton hay. Present value, $20. Present condition, poor.

Pump house.—Character, one-room frame. Use, housing gasoline pump engine. Erected in 1901. Cost, unknown. Present value, $100. Present condition, excellent.

The dormitory or main building is designed to be lighted by gasoline gas, which system was installed during the erection of the building. The main building is heated by steam from a boiler in the basement. Employees' building is heated by stoves. Ventilation of schoolrooms and dormitories is by the system installed at the erection of the building and is sufficient.

The water supplied is very hard and contains a great deal of iron and other constituents that render it unfit for drinking purposes during the warm weather of summer. Its source is a shallow well located alongside a small stream about 300 yards west of the schoolhouse. It is often found necessary to pump directly from this stream, since the well does not supply the demand when the weather is hot. The stream above the intake receives the drainage from the village of Red Lake. The water is pumped by a 4-horse Charter gas engine into a tank, from which water is easily forced to any part of the building. The system was installed when the school plant was constructed, and a separate account of its cost is not known. The sewage is carried from the main building by a 4-inch pipe emptying into a creek west of the building about 100 yards below the water intake. The outfall is about 30 feet below the building. There are five ring baths and one tub for each of the two dormitories. They are located on the first floor. There are standpipes in the main building with hose on each floor. One fire hydrant is placed outside at each extremity of the building.

This school has about 100 acres of land, all under fence. There are 15 acres under cultivation, 5 acres in meadow, 5 acres for grain, and 5 acres for potatoes and garden. About 85 acres are used as pasture for school cattle.

This school was originally opened about the year 1875, but moved into the new plant during the last week in January, 1901. It has a capacity of 80 pupils.

Cass Lake Boarding School.

Located 6 miles north of Cass Lake, Minn., on the Duluth branch line of the Great Northern coast line. Site admirably situated for school purposes; climate with extreme changes. Soil, sandy on high ground, and loam or what may be properly termed "sandy loam" on low ground.

School building.—Character, two-story frame. Use, dormitories for boys and girls, dining room, kitchen, schoolroom, sewing room, 2 sitting rooms, and employees' dwelling. Capacity, 40 pupils. Erected in 1900. Cost, $4,245. Present value, $4,380. Present condition, good.

Warehouse.—Character, one-story frame. Use, storing supplies. Dimensions, 18 by 30 feet, 10-foot posts. Erected in 1900. Cost, $360. Present value, $360. Present condition, excellent.

Laundry.—Character, one-story frame. Use, laundering clothes. Dimensions, 16 by 24 feet. Erected in 1900. Cost, $200. Present value, $200. Present condition, good.

Barn.—Character, two-story frame. Use, housing live stock and storing feed and hay. Capacity, 4 horses and 4 cows. Erected in 1900. Cost, $360. Present value, $360. Present condition, good.

Miscellaneous outbuildings.—Character, frame and log. Use, oil shed, privy, and ice house (log). Erected in 1900. Cost, $70 (privy alone). Present value, $70. Present condition, poor to good.

Buildings lighted by oil lamps and heated by box stoves, wood as fuel. Ventilation of the school building has no modern system.

48   STATISTICS OF INDIAN TRIBES, AGENCIES, AND SCHOOLS.

The water supply is obtained from a 40-foot well of wholesome quality. There is a 60-barrel water tank, whose base is 16 feet above the ground, provided with a wind mill and force pump. The tank is useless in its present condition, having no connection by means of pipes with any building. There is no sewer connected with the building, except with the bath tub located on the second floor. There is one good bath tub located on the second floor of the school building, which is used both by boys and girls. There is no fire protection, except with cans of water placed in different parts of the building.

This school has about 140 acres of timber and brush land out of five 40's reserved for school purposes, the rest being of lakes. No acres under fence, and none under cultivation. Ten acres can be cultivated without much labor. No acres used for pasturage.

This school was opened January 1, 1901, with a capacity of 40 pupils.

Cross Lake Boarding School.

Located between the north and south lakes, together known as Red Lake. Beautiful site. Climate is severe in winter, but not uncomfortable in summer. Soil is mostly of a rich loam, slightly sandy near lake shore.

Schoolhouse.—Character, two-story frame. Use, dormitory, dining room and kitchen, school room, sewing room, employees' rooms, pupils' living rooms. Capacity, 40 pupils. Erected in 1900. Cost, $5,075. Present value, $5,000. Present condition, good.

Warehouse.—Character, 1½-story frame. Use, storing supplies. Dimensions, 16 by 24 feet. Erected in 1901. Cost, $289. Present value, $289. Present condition, excellent.

Barn.—Character, 1½ story frame. Use, housing live stock and storing hay. Capacity, 3 horses, 4 cows, 5 tons hay. Erected in 1901. Cost, $352. Present value, $352. Present condition, excellent.

Laundry.—Character, one-story frame. Use, laundry. Dimensions, 16 by 24 feet. Erected in 1901. Cost, $275. Present value, $275. Present condition, good.

Root cellar.—Character, 1½-story, stone and frame. Use, storing garden produce Dimensions, 16 by 20 feet. Erected in 1901. Cost, $90. Present value, $150. Present condition, excellent.

Carpenter shop.—Character, one-story log, shed roof. Use, workshop. Dimensions, 16 by 20 feet. Erected in 1901. Present value, $75. Present condition, good.

Ice house.—Character, one-story log, shed roof. Use, storing ice. Dimensions, 12 by 16 feet. Erected in 1901. Present value, $40. Present condition, good.

Lighted by lamps. Heated by stoves. Ventilation of buildings is poor. The water supplied is good. It is hauled from the lake. No system of any sort has ever been installed. No sewage system whatever. Ordinary wash tubs are used for bathing. Pails, filled with water, in different parts of building furnish fire protection.

This school has about 190 acres reserved for school purposes, all heavily timbered. The land was loaned by the Indians. There are about 30 acres under fence and 3½ acres under cultivation, all in garden. About 2 acres more can be cultivated without any expense. The balance is very heavily timbered. Ten acres are used for pasturage. No irrigation.

This school was opened January 21, 1901, with a capacity of 40 pupils.

Bena Boarding School.

Located one-fourth mile north of Bena, Minn., on the Eastern Minnesota Railroad. Site well suited for school purposes. Climate in winters extremely cold; mild in summers. Soil of immediate site very sandy.

Schoolhouse.—Character, two-story frame. Use, boys' and girls' dormitories, schoolroom, dining room, and kitchen, sewing room, play rooms, office, and employees' rooms. Capacity, 40 pupils. Erected in 1900. Cost, $4,225. Present value, $4,225. Present condition, good.

Laundry.—Character, one-story frame. Use, for laundry and bath room. Dimension, 16 by 24 feet. Erected in 1900. Cost, $200. Present value, $180. Present condition, good.

Warehouse.—Character, one-story frame. Use, storing supplies. Dimension, 18 by 30 feet. Erected in 1900. Cost, $310. Present value, $300. Present condition, good.

Barn.—Character, 1½-story frame. Use, housing live stock and for storing hay. Capacity, 4 horses, 4 cows, and 2 tons hay. Erected in 1900. Cost, $360. Present value, $350. Present condition, good.

Storm sheds and privies.—Character, all frame. Use, protection to entrances of schoolhouse, etc. Dimension, sheds 4 by 6, one privy 6 by 12, one 4 by 6 feet. Erected in 1900–1901. Cost, $110. Present value, $100. Present condition, good.

Lighted by oil lamps. Heated by wood stoves. Schoolhouse not ventilated by any modern system. The water supplied is hard. Its source is from a driven well 10 feet east of the building. A galvanized tank elevated 16 feet is connected with a force pump in the well. Water is forced into the tank by windmill power. Tank has no connection with any of the buildings, and is not used in winter on account of water freezing in it. This system was installed when the school was constructed, at the cost of $215. The present system is insufficient and very unsatisfactory. No sewerage system. All refuse from kitchen is hauled away in barrels and emptied in Cedar Swamp, one-fourth mile east of the school. No bathing facilities. Bathe children in washtubs. Water buckets placed in hallways.

This school has 40 acres of pine land in its reserve, which was an allotment and was relinquished by an Indian in exchange for another 40. Twenty acres of it is swamp land, and is worthless. The remaining 20 acres is estimated at $100. There are 20 acres under fence, and 2 acres under cultivation. All in vegetables. Eight additional acres can be cultivated. None pastured nor irrigated.

This school opened January 1, 1901, with a capacity of 40 pupils.

LEMHI AGENCY, IDAHO.

(Under School Superintendent.)

Tribes.	Population.
Shoshone	291
Sheepeater	93
Bannock	95
Total	479

Area, 64,000 acres; unallotted.

Railroad station: Redrock, on Union Pacific Railroad. Seventy miles to agency by stage.

Nearest military post: Fort Harrison, Mont. Post-office address: Lemhi Agency, Lemhi County, Idaho. Telegraphic address: Redrock, Mont.

Lemhi Boarding School.

Located 70 miles west of Redrock, Mont., nearest railroad point on the Oregon Short Line Railroad. Situation on the western slope of the Bitter Root Range, not far from the summit. Climate, cool in summer and generally mild in winter. Soil, good, producing grains and hardy vegetables.

Girls' building.—Character, 1½-story cottage, ceiled walls. Use, dormitory, sewing room, girls' sitting room, sick room, school parlor, quarters for one employee. Capacity, 14 pupils. Erected in 1886. Present vaule, $800. Present condition, poor.

Boys' hall.—Character, two-story frame building. Use, dormitory, boys' sitting room, quarters for three employees. Capacity, 13 pupils. Erected in 1897. Cost, $3,314. Present value, $3,000. Present condition, good.

Dormitory and mess building.—Character, two-story frame. Use, dormitory, sitting room, sewing room, dining room, and kitchen. Capacity, 40 pupils. Erected, under construction July 1, 1903. Cost, contract price, $10,425.25.

Schoolhouse.—Character, one-story frame, one room. Use, for school literary work. Capacity, 23 pupils. Erected in 1883. Present value, $50. Present condition, very bad.

Mess hall and kitchen.—Character, one-story frame. Use, dining rooms and kitchens for school and employees' mess. Capacity, 50 pupils. Erected in 1897. Cost, $2,850. Present value, $2,800. Present condition, good.

Laundry.—Character, frame, one story. Use, for school laundry work. Dimensions, 18½ by 20½ feet. Erected in 1900. Cost, $350. Present value, $350. Present condition, good.

School warehouse.—Character, log built, weather boarded. Use, storing school supplies. Dimensions, 18 by 21 feet. Erected in 1898. Cost, $160. Present value, $150. Present condition, excellent.

Various outbuildings, chicken house, cellar, etc.—Character, log and frame buildings. Use, housing chickens, storing vegetables, etc. Erected, various dates. Present condition, fair to good.

Lighted by kerosene lamps. Heated by wood stoves. Ventilation: Only girls' building has roof ventilators. Other buildings depend upon windows and the chinks and crevices due to defective construction and lack of repair.

Water supply: Excellent water is furnished by a large mountain stream flowing through the grounds. The water used by the school is obtained by the primitive method of dipping from the creek in buckets and conveying by hand to wherever needed. Sewerage: Practically none, except that naturally furnished by the creek. Bathing facilities, none. Fire protection, none.

The school farm consists of 210 acres of land generally good for the production of such crops as are adapted to the region. There are 210 acres under fence; 40 acres under cultivation. Thirty acres additional could be cultivated. There are 40 acres in pasturage and 40 acres irrigated. The estimated value of the farm is $2,100.

The capacity of the school will be 60 when new building is finished.

LOWER BRULE AGENCY, S. DAK.

Tribe.	Population.
Lower Brule Sioux	469

Area:	Acres.
Allotted	151,856
Unallotted	200,694

Railroad station: Chamberlain, on Chicago, Milwaukee and St. Paul Railroad. Thirty-two miles to agency by stage.

Nearest military post: Fort Crook, Nebr. Post-office address: Lower Brule, Lyman County, S. Dak. Telegraphic address: Chamberlain, S. Dak.

Lower Brule Agency School.

Located 35 miles north of Chamberlain, S. Dak., on the west bank of the Missouri River. No railroad, telegraph, or telephone communication nearer than Chamberlain, S. Dak. Site well suited for school purposes. Cold in winter but climate dry, bracing, and healthful. Soil a fertile prairie loam. Crops very uncertain without irrigation.

Girls' building.—Character, two-story brick. Use, dormitory, play room, reception room, lavatory, employees' quarters, mess hall, and kitchen. Capacity, 60 pupils. Erected in 1894. Cost, $14,000. Present value, $12,000. Present condition, good.

Boys' building.—Character, two-story frame. Use, dormitories, lavatory, sewing room, play room, and employees' quarters. Capacity, 70 pupils. Erected in 1894. Present value, $4,000. Present condition, good.

Schoolhouse.—Character, one-story frame. Use, class room and assembly hall. Capacity, 150 pupils. Erected in 1894. Present value, $3,000. Present condition, good.

Superintendent's quarters.—Character, two-story frame. Use, superintendent's office and dwelling. Capacity, 2 office rooms and 4 dwelling rooms. Erected in 1894. Cost, $1,300. Present value, $1,000. Present condition, good.

Hospital.—Character, one-story frame. Use, isolation and caring for sick. Capacity, 10 pupils. Erected in 1898. Present value, $800. Present condition, good.

Dining room and kitchen.—Character, one-story frame. Use, dining room and kitchen. Capacity, 150 pupils. Erected in 1894. Present value, $3,000. Present condition, good.

Laundry.—Character, one story and basement. Use, not used on account of imperfect sewerage. Capacity, large enough for present needs. Erected in 1894–95. Present value, $150. Present condition, good.

Warehouse.—Character, one-story frame. Use, storing supplies and for shoe shop. Dimensions, 48 by 32 feet. Erected in 1894. Present value, $500. Present condition, good.

Stable.—Character, 1½-story frame. Use, housing horses, storing hay. Capacity, 4 horses and 2 tons of hay. Erected in 1894. Present value, $100. Present condition, fair.

Coal house.—Character, one-story frame. Use, storing coal. Capacity, 100 tons. Erected in 1895. Present value, $100. Condition, fair.

Creamery-milk house.—Character, one-story and basement frame. Use, not used on account of imperfect sewerage. Capacity, enough for needs. Erected in 1898. Present value, $500. Present condition, good.

Miscellaneous buildings.—Cow shed, hog house, and henhouse. Character, all frame. Use, housing live stock. Capacity, 25 head cattle, 25 of hogs, and 50 to 100 chickens. Erected in 1895. Present value, $100. Present condition, good.

STATISTICS OF INDIAN TRIBES, AGENCIES, AND SCHOOLS. 51

Lighted by kerosene lamps. Heated by hard-coal stoves. Ventilation of schoolroom and dormitories is satisfactory. The system was devised by the Indian Office. The water supplied is good. It is pumped by a steam engine into a tank which holds 12,000 gallons. The pressure is ample to force the water into the various buildings. The system was installed in 1895, not fully completed till 1896. All the buildings are connected with an 8-inch general sewer pipe, which empties into the river below the source of the water supply. There are four bath tubs in each of the dormitories. There are pipes in the large buildings with hose in case of fire, water buckets and chemical fire extinguishers in other buildings, and fire hydrants on the grounds near the buildings.

This school has about 800 acres of land, which is a fertile soil and fine pasture land, but not adapted to farming without irrigating. There are 800 acres under fence. About 30 acres in cultivation, the greater part to corn, but a part used for potato and garden patches.

This school was opened in 1895 with 130 pupils.

MACKINAC AGENCY, MICH.

Tribes.	Population.
L'Anse and Vieux Désert	690
Potawatomi of Huron	78
Ottawa and Chippewa (scattered)	5,587
Total	6,355

Area: Acres.

Unallotted, at L'Anse and Ontonagon 8,317
Allotted to L'Anse and Vieux Désert 145,302

Railroad station: L'Anse, Mich., on Duluth, South Shore and Atlantic Railroad. Post-office address: L'Anse, Mich. Telegraphic address: L'Anse, Mich.

No Government schools for these Indians.

MDEWAKANTON SIOUX, IN MINNESOTA.

Population, 929.

They have no reservation, but are living on land in the vicinity of Redwood, Minn., which was purchased for them individually.

They have no school, and are not under the control of any agent.

MESCALERO AGENCY, N. MEX.

(Under Superintendent of School.)

Tribes.	Population.
Mescalero Apache	447

Area, 474,240 acres; unallotted.

Railroad station: Tularosa, on El Paso and Northeastern Railroad. Eighteen miles to agency.

Nearest military post: Fort Bliss, Tex. Post-office address: Mescalero, N. Mex. Telegraphic address: Tularosa, N. Mex.

Mescalero Indian School.

Located 18 miles northeast of Tularosa, a station on the Chicago, Rock Island and El Paso Railroad. Site admirably suited for school purposes, being situated in the well-watered, fertile, and picturesque Tularosa valley. Altitude, about 7,000 feet. Climate, salubrious. Water, abundant, pure, clear, and cold. Soil, highly productive, consisting of decomposed vegetable matter which has been washed down from the mountain sides for centuries past.

Dormitory for boys and girls.—Character, two stories; lower story of main building, adobe; upper story, frame. Use, dormitory, kitchen and dining room, hospital, sewing room, and quarters for matron, assistant matron, cook, and industrial teacher. Capacity, 104 pupils. Erected in 1884-1886. Cost, said to be $7,200. Present value, $1,000. Present condition, very poor.

Schoolhouse.—Character, one-story adobe. Use, class room. Capacity, 40 pupils. Erected in 1893. Cost, $1,000. Present value, $200. Present condition, poor.

Assembly.—Character, one-story adobe. Use, class room and assembly hall. Capacity, 140 pupils. Erected in 1897. Cost, $1,000. Present value, $3,000. Present condition, good.

Superintendent's house.—Character, two-stories adobe. Use, superintendent's office and dwelling, employees' mess hall and dining room, dispensary, physician's quarters, and post-office. Capacity, two office rooms, dispensary, four dwelling rooms, dining room, and kitchen. Erected in 1882. Cost, $2,782. Present value, $1,000. Present condition, poor.

Employees' cottages.—Character, 1 one-story adobe, and 1 one-story frame. Use, adobe occupied bo the clerk, frame by kindergartner and seamstress. Dimensions, adobe 20 by 30 feet, frame 16 by 32 feet. Erected, adobe 1879, frame 1885. Cost, adobe unknown, frame $600. Present value, adobe $150, frame $150. Present condition, both buildings very poor.

Warehouses.—Character, 1 one-story adobe, and 1 one-story frame. Use, storing supplies. Dimensions, adobe 18 by 24, frame 23 by 42 feet. Erected, frame 1882, adobe 1884. Cost, adobe $300, frame $800. Present value, adobe nothing, frame $100. Present condition, very poor.

Bath house.—Character, one-story adobe. Use, bathing and laundering. Capacity, two rooms, one for bathing and one for laundry work. Erected in 1896. Cost, $1,996. Present value, $150. Present condition, very poor.

Barn.—Character, 1½ story frame. Use, housing stock and storing hay and grain. Capacity, 10 horses, 20 cows, 40,000 pounds oats, and 60 tons hay. Erected in 1899 and 1900. Cost, $1,000. Present value, $1,800. Present condition, good.

Buildings lighted by electricity. Plant is operated by water power, and the capacity is 210 incandescent lights. Plant was installed in 1900, at a cost of $2,500. It is in good condition and satisfactory. Heated by wood stoves. Ventilation, good when all the doors and windows are open.

Water is abundant, clear, cold, and pure, but very hard. Its source is a number of springs about one-fourth of a mile east of the the school. The water from these springs is carried to the school grounds by means of a ditch, and is conducted from the ditch into a 27,000-gallon wooden tank by hydraulic pressure. The tank serves its purpose, but its dissolution is near at hand. The water system was installed several years ago, but the records of the office are too incomplete to show the cost.

The dormitory and superintendent's house are connected with a 6-inch general sewer pipe which empties into a cesspool in the rear of the grounds. There are 3 water-closets and 2 bath tubs in the dormitory, and a water-closet and tub in the superintendent's house. This system was installed during 1901–2, at a cost of $310. There are 5 tubs in the laundry building for the use of the pupils. There are standpipes in the dormitory. Fire hydrants in the grounds.

The school farm embraces about 200 acres of rich valley land. The pasture lands are limited only by the reservation lines.

This school was opened in 1884, with accommodations for 15 pupils.

MISSION-TULE RIVER AGENCY, CAL.

Tribes.	Population.
Tule River	143
Mission	2,682
Total	2,825

Area:	Acres.
Unallotted	229,194.00
Allotted	1,689.70
Reserved for school use	2.70

Railroad station: San Jacinto, on Southern California Railroad.
Nearest military post: Presidio, Cal. Post-office address: San Jacinto, Riverside County, Cal. Telegraphic address: San Jacinto, Cal.

Coahuilla Day School.

Located 35 miles from agency headquarters.
Post-office: Coahuilla. Climate, cold, and some snow in winter.
School building.—Character, one-story frame structure. Use, schoolroom and three living rooms for teacher's family. Capacity, 24 pupils. Cost, unknown. Present value, $300. Present condition, poor.

Water supply deficient; supply carried in buckets from springs.
Heated by stove; lighted by lamp.

STATISTICS OF INDIAN TRIBES, AGENCIES, AND SCHOOLS. 53

Capitan Grande Day School.

Located 12 miles from Lakeside, Cal., on the Capitan Grande Reservation, 145 miles from the agency headquarters (by rail).

Post-office and railroad station at Lakeside, Cal.

School building.—Character, 1½-story frame structure. Use, schoolroom and three living rooms for the teacher's family. Capacity, 30 pupils. Cost, unknown. Present value, $800. Present condition, fair.

Water supply poor, carried in buckets from shallow well in creek bed some distance away.

Heated by stove; lighted by lamp.

La Jolla Day School.

Located at Potrero Reservation, 80 miles from agency headquarters.

Post-office: Amago. Nearest railroad depot: Escondido, 30 miles from school. Climate good.

New school building.—Character, 1½-story frame structure. Use, schoolroom and two living rooms for teacher. Capacity, 30 pupils. Erected in 1896. Cost, unknown. Present value, $1,000. Present condition, good.

Old school building.—Character, one-story frame. Use, kitchen, noonday lunch room, and council room. Present value, $50. Present condition, very poor.

Water, abundant, supplied in iron pipe from mountain stream.

Heated by stove; lighted by lamp.

Martinez Day School.

Located at Torres Reservation, 4 miles from Walters, Cal., Southern Pacific railroad station and post-office, 120 miles from agency headquarters. Climate, excessively hot during eight months of the year.

School building.—Character, adobe. Use, schoolroom and one living room for teacher's family. Capacity, 28 pupils. Erected in 1895. Cost, $1,250. Present value, $500. Present condition, poor.

Water poor; obtained from surface well.

Heated by stove; lighted by lamp.

This school is said to be mislocated and not on the reservation.

Mesa Grande Day School.

Located at Santa Ysabel Reservation, 80 miles from agency headquarters.

Post-office and telephone: Mesa Grande. Nearest railroad station: Foster, San Diego County, 40 miles from school.

School building.—Character, one-story frame. Use, schoolroom and three small rooms for teacher's use. Capacity, 24 pupils. Cost, unknown. Present value, $300. Present condition, very poor.

All the water used is carried in buckets some distance from spring.

Heated by stove and lighted by lamp.

Location of this building is very poor.

Pechanga Day School.

Located 35 miles from agency headquarters, on Temecula Reservation.

Post-office and nearest railroad depot: Temecula, Cal., 6 miles from school.

School building.—Character, 1½-story frame structure. Use, schoolroom and two small living rooms. Capacity, 32 pupils. Erected in 1895. Cost, unknown. Present value, $850. Present condition, good.

Water supply sufficient; supplied by well and windmill pumping plant.

Heated by stove; lighted by lamps.

Potrero Day School.

Located at Morongo Reservation, 4 miles northeast of Banning, Cal.

Post-office and railroad station 25 miles from agency headquarters. Climate, good.

School building.—Character, frame. Use, schoolroom and three small living rooms for teacher's use. Capacity, 28 pupils. Erected in 1895. Cost $1,500. Present value, $1,000. Present condition, good.

Water furnished in open ditch.

Heated by stove; lighted by lamp.

Rincon Day School.

Located at Rincon Reservation, 70 miles from agency headquarters.
Post-office: Valley Center. Nearest railroad station: Escondido, Cal., 20 miles from school. Climate, equable. School building.—Character, one-story frame structure. Use, schoolroom and two rooms for kitchen purposes, cooking lunch and serving noonday lunch. Capacity, 25 pupils. Cost, unknown. Present value, $350. Present condition, fair.
Water plentiful, but poor, furnished in pipe from open mud reservoir.
Heated by stove; lighted by lamp.

Soboba Day School.

Located at San Jacinto Reservation, 4 miles south of the town of that name.
Post-office and nearest railroad station: San Jacinto.
School building.—Character, one-story frame structure. Class room and 4 living rooms for teacher's family. Capacity, 38 pupils. Cost, unknown. Present value, $1,000. Present condition, good.
Water supply from well and windmill pump.
Heated by wood stove; lighted by lamp.
Bath house in connection with school.
This school has small orchard and 5 acres of garden land in connection.

Tule River Day School.

Located 20 miles east of Porterville, Cal
Post-office and nearest railroad depot: Porterville, Cal.
School building.—Character, 1½-story frame structure. Use, schoolroom and 2 small living rooms for teacher's family. Erected in 1895. Cost, $1,000. Present value, $850. Present condition, good.
Water abundant, supplied in open ditch.
Heated by stove; lighted by lamp.
Small garden in connection with school.

MOAPA RIVER RESERVATION, NEV.

(Under Charge of Industrial Teacher.)

Tribe.	Population.
Paiute	200

Area, 1,000 acres, unallotted.
Railroad station, Chloride, Ariz., on Arizona and Utah Railroad; thence 90 miles by stage to St. Thomas; thence 28 miles by team to reservation.
Post-office address, Moapa, Nev.
Day school building and cottage for teacher under contract.

MOQUI AGENCY, ARIZ.

(Under Superintendent of Training School.)

Tribes.	Population.
Moqui	1,845
Navaho	1,837

Area, unallotted, 2,472,320 acres.
Railroad station, Holbrook, on the Atchison, Topeka and Santa Fe Railroad.
Post-office address, Keams Canyon, Ariz. Telegraphic address, Holbrook, Ariz.

Moqui Training School.

Located 85 miles due north of Holbrook, Ariz., on the Santa Fe Railroad. Site is in narrow canyon. Climate equable. Soil sandy loam.
Dormitory building.—Character, 2½-story stone. Use, boys' living quarters. Capacity, 75. Erected in 1901–2. Cost, $15,000. Present value, $15,000. Present condition, excellent.
Dormitory building.—Character, 2½-story stone. Use, girls' living quarters. Capacity, 75. Erected in 1901–2. Cost, $15,000. Present value, $15,000. Present condition, excellent.
Mess hall and employees' quarters.—Character, three-story stone. Use, dining hall and kitchen for pupils; mess hall, kitchen, and quarters for employees. Capacity, 150 pupils, 10 employees. Erected in 1901–2. Cost, $19,400. Present value, $19,400. Present condition, excellent.

Schoolhouse.—Character, one-story stone. Use, schoolrooms, play rooms, and assembly rooms. Capacity, 80. Erected in 1901–2. Cost, $13,690. Present value, $13,690. Present condition, excellent.

Laundry building.—Character, one-story stone. Use, general laundry work of school. Dimensions, 68 by 36 feet. Erected in 1901–2. Cost, $5,360. Present value, $5,360. Present condition, excellent,

Warehouse.—Character, one-story stone. Use, storing supplies for school. Dimensions, 50 by 20 feet. Erected in 1901–2. Cost, $2,200. Present value, $2,200. Present condition, excellent.

Steam heating and electric-light plants installed in 1902 at a cost of $13,901, also sewer and water systems at a cost of $12,017.

The water is the finest in the world. Ten good springs supply an unlimited amount.

This school was opened in 1897 with a capacity of 55. Was removed to new plant on completion of the buildings in 1902. The enrollment during December, 1902, was 183.

Oraibi Day School.

Located about 75 miles north of Winslow, Ariz., on Santa Fe Pacific Railroad. Site good. Climate, very hot in summer, with violent sand storms in spring. Atmosphere dry.

Schoolhouse.—Character, one-story adobe; roof, tin and shingles. Use, class rooms. Capacity, 50. Erected about 1892. Cost, unknown. Present value, $100. Present condition, fair.

Teacher's cottage.—Character, one-story stone. Use, teacher's residence. Capacity, four living rooms. Erected in 1897. Cost, unknown. Present value, $500. Present condition, good.

Teacher's cottage, old.—Condemned and useless.

Lighted by oil lamps. Heated by coal and wood stoves. Ventilated by doors and windows. Water supply furnished by two wells; one about a mile from buildings, furnishing an almost inexhaustible supply of pure water, and the other one near the school plant, but furnishing very small supply. No sewerage. Bathing facilities consist of washtubs. No fire protection.

Owing to arid conditions and the entire absence of irrigating facilities there is no farm or garden work done.

This school was opened about 1892. During the first nine years only a very small attendance was had. The last two years the attendance has reached an average of 122, and when facilities are provided an attendance of 200 can be had.

Polacca Day School.

Located 14 miles west of Keams Canyon, Ariz., the seat of the agency. Site excellent for school purposes, climate warm in summer and cold in winter. Many sand storms. Soil entirely consists of sand dunes.

School building.—Character, one story adobe brick. Use, school, kitchen, dining room and storeroom. Erected about 1890. Cost, $350. Present value, $300. Present condition, excellent.

Teacher's cottage.—Character, one story, stone. Use, teacher's residence. Capacity, 4. Erected about 1890. Cost, $200. Present value, $200. Present condition, excellent.

Laundry or washhouse.—Character, one story, stone. Use, laundry and sewing room. Capacity, 25. Erected about 1890. Cost, $100. Present value, $100. Present condition, excellent.

Lighted by lamps. Heated by wood and coal stoves. Ventilated by windows only. Water is supplied by well. Quality good. No sewerage.

Attendance about 35 since the beginning of the school.

Second Mesa Day School.

Located 25 miles west of Keams Canyon near the great Toreva Spring, at the head of a deep mountain arroya. Site admirable for a day school, being nearly equidistant from the three villages from which its support is derived. Soil, deep drifting sand, rock and adobe.

Teacher's cottage.—Character, one-story stone. Use, residence for employees and sewing room. Erected about 1896. Cost, $500. Present value, $500. Present condition, good.

Old school building.—Character, one-story stone. Use, schoolroom, kitchen, and dining room. Capacity, 30 pupils. Erected in 1897. Cost, $700. Present value, $700. Present condition, good.

New school building.—Character, one-story stone. Use, schoolroom, laundry, and storeroom. Capacity, 30 pupils. Erected in 1900. Cost, $1,500. Present value, $1,500. Present condition, good.

Lighted by kerosene lamps. Heated by wood and coal stoves. Ventilation, doors and windows. Water supply abundant, free from organic pollution, but strongly impregnated with alkali; supplied by buckets. No sewerage. Bathing done in tubs. This school has an enrollment of 102.

NAVAHO AGENCY, ARIZ.

(Under School Superintendents.)

Tribes.	Population.
Navaho on reserve	6,000
Navaho off reserve	8,000
Moqui (Hopi)	150
Navaho (under Western Navaho superintendent)	6,000
Paiute	350
Papago	2,000
Total	22,500

Area, unallotted, 9,442,240 acres.

Railroad station, Gallup, on Atlantic and Pacific Railway. Thirty miles to agency.

Nearest military post, Fort Wingate, N. Mex. Post-office address, Fort Defiance, Ariz. Telegraphic address, Gallup, N. Mex.

NOTE.—This reservation was divided August 20, 1903, by a line drawn east and west through the center of the reservation. The northern half is placed under superintendent of training school to be erected on San Juan River, New Mexico, and the southern half under superintendent of training school at Fort Defiance.

Navaho Agency School.

Located 30 miles northwest of Gallup, N. Mex., on Santa Fe Pacific Railway. Site not the best, as it is located at the mouth of a canyon that extends through the mountain, thus creating a cold draft of wind which is almost continuous, creates colds and has a tendency to bring on pneumonia; with the above exception the climate is excellent. The soil is adobe, and bakes hard as a brick.

Boys' building.—Character, stone basement with two-story brick. Use, dormitory, reading room, play room for small boys, employees' rooms, superintendent's office; lighting and heating apparatus in basement. Capacity, 100 pupils. Erected in 1900. Cost, $28,150. Present value, $28,000. Present condition, good.

Girls' building.—Character, two-story stone. Use, dormitory, sitting room, bathroom, and employees quarters. Capacity, 60 pupils. Erected about 1890. Present value, $4,000. Present condition, good.

Kitchen building.—Character, two-story stone, with one story adobe, and frame additions. Use, school and mess kitchen, school and mess dining rooms, bakery, sewing room, and employees quarters on second floor. Capacity, 160 pupils. Erected about 1889. Present value about $4,000. Present condition, fairly good.

Boys' old building.—Character, two story of stone and mansard roof comprising third story. Use, 3 schoolrooms, 2 sick rooms, 2 employees' rooms. Erected about 1882. Present value, nominal. Present condition, poor.

Laundry.—Character, one story frame. Use, laundry. Capacity, 160 pupils. Erected in 1894. Present value, $600. Present condition, fair.

Chapel.—Character, one-story stone. Use, schoolroom and assembly hall. Capacity, 160 pupils. Erected about 1883 or 1884. Present value, possibly, $400. Present condition, fair.

Stable.—Character, one-story adobe. Use, stable and feed room. Capacity, 4 horses. Condition, poor.

Boys' building lighted by gasoline gas; capacity, 100 jets. Plant was put in when building was erected in 1900, is in good condition, and fairly satisfactory. All other buildings lighted by kerosene-oil lamps. Boys' building heated by steam. Plant put in when building was erected in 1900. All other buildings heated by coal stoves. Ventilation of boys' building, modern; others none, except through windows.

Water supplied is good but hard. Its source is springs, distant 1¼ miles in the canyon; conducted to buildings through iron pipes; 1,000 feet of main pipe is 4-inch, balance 2-inch; this does not furnish a sufficient supply. The pressure is not sufficient to force the water to the second floor, neither is it available for fire protection.

STATISTICS OF INDIAN TRIBES, AGENCIES, AND SCHOOLS. 57

The boys' building, girls' building, kitchen, dining hall, and laundry are all connected with a 6-inch sewer, which empties into the creek one-fourth mile below the school and below the source of water supply. The fall of the sewer is very slight, but it might be sufficient if the water supply was abundant. There are 5 ring and 1 tub baths on each floor of the boys' building, but those on the second floor can not be used on account of insufficient pressure of water. There are also 4 bath tubs in the girls' building. There are hose on each floor of the boys' building, but for lack of water pressure can not be used. Fire buckets are in all the buildings. No fire hydrants in the grounds.

This school has 5 acres for school garden, which is fenced and watered by ditches leading from the dam across the creek.

School was started about 1872.

Little Water School.

Located 35 miles northeast of agency, 30 miles North of Gallup, N. Mex., on Santa Fe Pacific Railway. Site not near as favorable as might have been selected. Climate good. Soil poor, only about one-half acre near the school that can be utilized.

Boys' building.—Character, one-story abode on good rock foundation, dirt roof. Use, dormitory, schoolroom, bathroom, clothes room, 3 employees' rooms. Capacity, 38 pupils. Erected in 1898. Cost about $6,000. Present value, $5,500. Present condition, good.

Girls' building.—Character, one-story abode, good rock foundation, metal roof. Use, dormitory, kitchen, dining room, clothes room, sitting room, 2 employees' and bath rooms. Capacity, 38 pupils. Erected in 1900. Cost, $9,200. Present value, $9,100. Present condition, good.

Stone building.—Character, one-story stone building with dirt roof. Use, ironing room, boys' sitting room, 1 employees' room. Capacity, 25 people. Present value, about $300. Present condition, poor.

Warehouse.—Character, one-story frame, 24 by 16 feet. Use, storing supplies. Capacity insufficient. Erected in 1899. Cost, no cash outlay. Lumber from agency mill, work done by employees. Present value, $100. Present condition, fair.

The entire plant lighted by kerosene lamps. All buildings heated by stoves, wood fuel. Ventilation, no modern appliances. The water supply is inadequate; its source is a well 3½ by 10½ feet, about 24 feet deep, located about 400 feet from the school. The water is raised by windmill and forced to a tank near the school. The tank has a capacity of 3,000 gallons. The tank is not elevated sufficiently to give force to put the water in the upper rings of the bath. The tank is placed on a stone tower about 28 feet high. The quality of the water is very good. The water system was installed when the plant was constructed in 1898, at a cost of about $500. Each dormitory is connected with a 6-inch sewer that empties into the bed of the creek some distance below the entire school plant. There are 3 ring and 1 tub bath in each dormitory, with tank and hot water heater.

This school has about one-half acre of ground that may be used for garden, but can be irrigated only when the water is running freely in the creek, which will only be in wet seasons and when the snow is melting in the mountains. No other lands near the school suitable for farming.

This plant was ready for occupancy in the fall of 1898, with a capacity of 38 pupils. It now has an enrollment of 81 pupils.

The following school, although within the territory of the Navaho Reservation, is under the control of a bonded superintendent, located at Tuba City. He has jurisdiction of the Navaho Indians residing on the western portion of the reservation, between the Moqui Reservation and the western border of the Navaho Reservation.

Western Navaho Training School.

Location 90 miles nearly due north of Winslow, Ariz. Site poor on account of the limited supply of water and opportunity for farm, garden, or pasture. Climate excellent.

School building.—Character, one-story stone (30 by 100 feet outside), 9 rooms. Use, 1 room schoolroom and dormitory, 1 room clothes room, 7 rooms used as employees' quarters and mess dining room and kitchen. Capacity, 16 pupils in dormitory. Erected, date not known, probably between 1880 and 1885, by trader. Cost, purchased by Government in 1897 for $2,000. Present value, $1,000. Present condition, walls good, roof worthless.

Dining room.—Character, one-story stone (16 by 48 feet inside). Use, kitchen and dining room. Capacity, 40 pupils. Erected in 1900. Built by employees and

58   STATISTICS OF INDIAN TRIBES, AGENCIES, AND SCHOOLS.

school children. Present value, $200. Present condition, walls fair, roof worthless, and no floor; windows made by putting glass in shoe boxes, doors made from goods boxes.

Girls' building.—Character, one-story stone (18 by 30 feet inside). Use, girls' dormitory and sitting room. Capacity, 14 pupils. Erected in 1901. Built by employees and school children. Present value, $100. Present condition, walls, good, roof worthless, windows made from sewing-machine crates.

Office.—Character, one-story stone, connecting girls' building and school building. Use, office and quarters of superintendent and matron. Capacity, one room, 16 by 19 feet inside. Erected in November, 1901. Cost (see note). Present value, $100. Present condition, walls good, roof poor.

Dispensatory.—Character, one-story stone, addition to school dining room. Use, drug room. Dimensions, 7 by 16 feet inside. Erected in November, 1901. Cost (see note). Present value, $50. Present condition, walls good, roof poor.

Boys' room.—Character, one-story stone, connecting school dining room and school building. Use, boys' wash and sitting room. Capacity, 16 by 16 feet inside. Erected in December, 1901. Cost (see note). Present value, $100. Present condition, walls good, roof poor.

Wareroom.—Character, one-story stone on south end of school building. Use, storeroom and meat room. Dimensions, 2 rooms, each 9 by 10 feet inside. Erected in November, 1901. Cost (see note). Present value, $40. Present condition, walls good, roof poor.

Warehouse.—Character, one-story stone. Use, storing supplies. Dimensions, 12 by 22 feet inside. Erected, date unknown. Cost, part of original purchase. Present value, $75. Present condition, walls good, roof worthless.

Warehouse.—Character, one-story stockade (cottonwood logs). Use, storing supplies. Dimensions, 16 by 30 feet inside. Erected in January, 1902. Present value, $25. Present condition, walls fair, roof poor.

NOTE.—For the erection of the buildings put up during October, November, and December, 1901, there was authorized an expenditure of $90 for irregular labor. The rest of the work was done by the employees and pupils. The material for the floors, doors, and windows was carried over from last year.

Lighted by kerosene lamps. Heated by wood and coal stoves. No system of ventilation except by doors and windows. The water supply is very meager, but what there is is pure and soft, being supplied by a spring about 40 yards below the school building and carried from there to the buildings in pails. There is no sewerage system; the slops and waste water are carried to the bank and thrown over. The bathing is done in ordinary wash tubs. Our stone walls and dirt roofs are our only protection against fire, except pails of water.

No farm, garden, or pasture, for want of water to irrigate with.

This school was opened September 1, 1898, under the name of Blue Canyon School, with a capacity of 20 pupils and with 2 employees. December 31, 1900, the enrollment was 60. At the beginning of the present fiscal year the name of the school was changed to Western Navaho Training School and it was placed under a bonded superintendent. December 31, 1902, the enrollment was 124.

This school will be abandoned when the new plant is erected at Tuba City.

NEAH BAY AGENCY, WASH.

(Under School Superintendent.)

Tribes.	Population.
Makah	382
Quileute	46
Hoh	67
Makah at Ozette	235
Total	730

Area, 24,517 acres; unallotted.

Railroad station: Seattle. One hundred and thirty-eight miles to agency by steamer.

Nearest military post: Vancouver Barracks, Wash. Post-office address: Neah Bay, Clallam County, Wash. Telegraphic address: Neah Bay, Wash.

Neah Bay Indian Training School.

Located 6 miles east of Cape Flattery, on slight elevation at south edge of Indian village, at the terminus of steamer line. Fine summers, but wet winters; rainfall 80 to 120 inches annually.

STATISTICS OF INDIAN TRIBES, AGENCIES, AND SCHOOLS. 59

Schoolhouse.—Character, one-story frame. Use, class room. Capacity, 28. Erected in 1896. Cost, about $200. Present value, $150. Present condition, fair.

Water-closets, 3. Character, frame. Cost, about $25. Erected in 1898–1902. Present value, $15. Condition, good.

Lighting, coal-oil lamps. Heating, wood stove. Ventilation, by windows. Water supply, from brook about 40 rods distant.

No school farm at this agency.

Quileute Day School.

Located 30 miles south from Cape Flattery and 35 miles from Neah Bay Agency, close to the ocean beach, and one-half mile from the mouth of the Quileute River. Climate, rainy all winter; cool and pleasant all summer.

Schoolhouse.—Character, a rented frame building 20 by 36 feet, located 200 yards from nearest Indian house. Capacity, 42. Condition, good.

Teacher's residence.—Character, 1½-story frame. Use, superintendent's office and dwelling; 10 rooms; 1 room used as reading room, band practice, and weekly evening meeting of ex-pupils. Capacity, 20 for this room. Cost unknown, probably $3,000 or $4,000. Present value unknown, probably $2,000 to $2,500. Erected in 1885 by private citizens, who lost it in legal contest with the United States Government. Condition, fair.

Woodhouse.—Dimensions, 18 by 20 feet, with 10-foot wall, frame. Present value, $150. Present condition, good.

Barn.—Character, one-story, with basement, frame, 24 by 42 feet. Capacity, 3 horses and 2 cows. Erected by private capital, like all the other buildings of this place, and lost to the Government by court proceedings. Present value, about $300. Present condition, fair.

This school was opened November 16, 1883, with a capacity of 24 pupils.

NEVADA AGENCY, NEV.

(Under School Superintendent.)

Tribe.	Population.
Pah-Ute at Pyramid Lake	646

Area, 641,815 acres; unallotted.

Railroad station: Wadsworth, on Central Pacific Railroad. Eighteen miles to agency.

Nearest military post: Presidio, Cal. Post-office address: Wadsworth, Washoe County, Nev. Telegraphic address: Wadsworth, Nev.

Nevada Agency Training School.

Situated on Truckee River, 18 miles north of Wadsworth, Nev. Splendid location for school. Altitude 4,000 feet. Climate equitable; atmosphere dry. Sandy soil overlying gravel.

Dormitory.—Character, two-story frame, stone foundation. Use, dormitory for boys and girls, contains class rooms, dining room, kitchen, sewing room, and two play rooms. Capacity, 60 pupils. Erected in 1900. Cost, $19,234. Present value, $18,271. Present condition, excellent.

Employees' quarters.—Character, frame building of two stories. Use, quarters for school employees. Capacity, 5 living rooms, sitting room, and bath. Erected in 1900. Cost, $2,488. Present value, $2,363. Present condition, excellent.

Bath house.—Character, one-story frame, brick foundation. Use, bathing purposes for pupils and employees. Capacity, 2 tubs for employees and 8 showers for pupils. Erected in 1897. Cost, $1,990. Present value, $1,592. Present condition, good.

Laundry.—Character, two-story frame, rough, battened. Use, laundry, workroom, and condemned rooms. Capacity, 4 rooms. Erected in 1891. Cost, $500. Present value, $300. Present condition, poor.

Ice house.—Character, rough one-story frame. Use, storing ice. Capacity, 60 tons of ice. Erected in 1894. Cost, $150. Present value, $50. Condition, bad.

Pump house.—Character, one-story frame. Use, to protect pumping plant. Erected in 1900. Cost, $450. Present value, $400. Present condition, good.

Miscellaneous outbuildings.—Character, all frame. Use, henhouse, cow shed, and stable. Erected at various dates. Present value, $25. Present condition, good to poor.

Dormitory lighted with gas manufactured from gasoline, capacity, 100 jets. Plant was installed at the time of the erection of the dormitory. Other buildings are lighted by kerosene lamps. The plant is satisfactory and in good condition. The dormitory is heated by a hot-water system installed at time of erection of building; is very efficient and in good condition. The other buildings are heated by coal and wood stoves. The dormitory building is ventilated by a system designed by the Indian Office at the time of the construction of the building. The other buildings of the plant have no organized system.

The water system in use at this school was installed at the time of the construction of the dormitory and employees' quarters in 1900. The water is.pumped from a well situated on the banks of the Truckee River, and from thence it is forced by a gasoline engine into a wooden tank 65 feet above the surface of the ground, the total elevation above the source of supply being approximately 120 feet. Water filters from river into the well through a large bed of sand and gravel, is soft, pure, and healthful. The plant is very satisfactory and in good condition. The sewerage system was also placed in operation in 1900. It is made with 6-inch glazed terra cotta pipe laid well below the surface, so as to be free from danger of freezing. It discharges the sewage of the dormitory and employees' quarters into the Truckee River some three-eighths of a mile below the buildings and pumping plant. There are six catch basins along the line, so that the sewer may be flushed out when necessary. The outlet is about 30 feet below the level of the buildings. The system is very complete and gives little trouble, therefore is satisfactory. The bathing facilities afforded by the bath house are ample, there being two tubs and eight shower rings. This building is located about 400 feet north of the dormitory. The equipment for fighting fire is quite complete. There are four standpipes, with hose attached, in the dormitory, and on the school grounds are three hydrants. The piping is arranged in such a manner that direct pressure from the pump is obtainable. There are also two hose carts which are kept in readiness for use at the shortest notice. The system is complete and should give satisfaction if necessary to call it into use.

The school has a garden of 15 acres under irrigating ditch and a pasture of 40 acres. The soil is a sandy loam, being an alluvial deposit. This soil is easily cultivated and very productive in favorable seasons. The estimated value of the land under ditch is $40 per acre and of the pasture $20 per acre. There are about 60 acres of land under fence; 15 acres under cultivation; about 7 acres in alfalfa. Ten to 15 acres additional can be cultivated. Pasture contains 40 acres, none of which is under irrigation.

The Nevada Agency Boarding School was opened in 1882 with a capacity of 30 and an average attendance of 33 for the first year of its existence. The plant was entirely destroyed by fire in May, 1899, and the buildings now occupied were completed and occupied in March, 1900.

NEW YORK AGENCY, N. Y.

Tribes.	Population.
Seneca	2,689
Onondaga	555
Cayuga	176
St. Regis	1,208
Oneida	276
Tuscarora	368
Total	5,272

Area, 87,677 acres.
Railroad station: Salamanca, on New York, Lake Erie and Western Railroad.
Post-office address: Salamanca, N. Y. Telegraphic address: Salamanca, N. Y.
No United States Government school at this agency. Schools maintained and controlled by the State of New York.

NEZ PERCE AGENCY, IDAHO.

(Under School Superintendent.)

Tribe.	Population.
Nez Percé	1,592

Area:	Acres.
Allotted	180,370.09
Reserved for agency, school, mission, and cemetery	2,170.47
Timber land reserved	32,020.00

STATISTICS OF INDIAN TRIBES, AGENCIES, AND SCHOOLS. 61

Railroad station: North Lapwai, on branch of Northern Pacific Railway. One mile to agency.

Nearest military post: Fort Sherman. Post-office address: Lapwai, Idaho. Telegraphic address: North Lapwai, Idaho.

Fort Lapwai Indian Training School.

Located 3½ miles south of Spalding, Idaho, and one-half mile south of Lapwai, Idaho. A short branch of the Northern Pacific Railroad runs right through the school farm. The climate is very hot and dry in summer and wet and disagreeable in winter. The location is admirably suited for school purposes. The soil on bottom is rich loam, and the pasturage contains about 1,000 acres.

Girls' home.—Character, two-story frame. Use, dormitory and matron's quarters. Capacity, 100 pupils. Erected in 1884 and 1892. Cost, $8,000. Present value, $5,000. Present condition, poor.

Dining hall.—Character, two-story frame with one-story ell. Use, dining room and kitchen. Capacity, 200 pupils. Erected in 1896. Cost, $4,790. Present value, $4,000. Present condition, good.

School building.—Character, two-story frame. Use, school rooms and chapel. Capacity, 200. Erected in 1891. Cost, $4,500. Present value, $2,500. Present condition, fair.

Office.—One-story frame. Use, office. Capacity, 2 office rooms. Erected in 1897. Cost, $800. Present value, $250. Present condition, fair.

Shoe and harness shop.—Character, one-story frame. Use, repair shop. Capacity, 6 benches. Erected in 1897. Cost, $810. Present value, $250. Present condition, fair.

Three employees' quarters.—Use, quarters for employees. Capacity, 15 employees. Erected in 1863. Present value, $1,200. Condition, one is fair and two poor.

Warehouse.—Character, one-story box, board. Use, storing school supplies. Capacity, sufficient to supply school. Erected in 1868. Present value, $300. Present condition, poor.

Small boys' home.—Character, two-story brick with basement. Use, small boys' home. Capacity, 70 pupils. Erected in 1895. Cost, $5,850. Present value, $4,000. Present condition, good.

Large boys' home.—Character, one-story frame. Use, large boys' home. Capacity, 30 pupils. Present value, $400. Present condition, good.

Barn.—Character, one-story box, board. Use, stabling stock and storing feed. Capacity, 12 horses and 15 cows and 75 tons feed and oats. Present value, $800. Present condition, fair.

The buildings are lighted with kerosene lamps, heated with common iron stoves, ventilated by lowering the upper windows. Water is supplied from a spring, pumped into a reservoir, the gravity force being sufficient to throw water on top of any building. There is no sewerage. Bathing facilities are crude. Water is carried in washtubs to big caldrons and heated. Bathing is done in washtubs. For fire protection there are hose carts, hose, and hydrants.

The farm is worth about $15,000. There are at least 700 acres under fence. About 100 acres have been cultivated. Possibly 50 more could be cultivated. There are 600 acres under pasture and 25 acres irrigated.

OMAHA AND WINNEBAGO AGENCY, NEBR

(Under School Superintendents.)

Tribes.	Population.
Winnebago	1,089
Omaha	1,218
Total	2,307

Area:	Acres.
Allotted	207,760.66
Unallotted	52,592

Railroad station: Dakota, on Chicago, St. Paul, Minnesota and Omaha Railroad. Twenty miles to agency.

Nearest military post: Fort Crook, Nebr. Post-office address: Winnebago, Thurston County, Nebr. Telegraphic address: Sioux City, Iowa.

Omaha Boarding School.

Post-office, Omaha Agency, Nebr.
Located 10 miles southeast of Omaha and Winnebago Agency; 18 miles northeast of Bancroft, Nebr. Main building is on a knoll, which makes a particularly desirable location. Weather variable; climate, somewhat dry; healthful. Soil, prairie loam on clay.

School building and dormitory.—Character, two-story frame, made up of several additions built at different times. Use, dormitory, dining room, and kitchen for pupils; also for mess, bathroom, playrooms, and employees' quarters. Capacity, 54 pupils, 10 employees. Erected in 1889 and 1891. Present value, $5,000. Present condition, good.

Schoolhouse.—Character, one-story frame. Use, class rooms and employees' room. Capacity, 77 pupils and 2 employees. Erected in 1890. Present value, $1,000. Present condition, good.

Storehouse.—Character, 1½-story frame. Use, storing supplies. Dimensions, 16 by 44 feet. Erected in 1889. Cost, $395. Present value, $300. Present condition, good.

Barn and addition to barn.—Character, 1½-story frame. Use, housing live stock and storing hay. Capacity, 6 horses, 12 cows, 12 tons hay. Erected in 1889 and 1891. Present value, $425. Present condition, fair.

Laundry.—Character, 1½-story frame. Use, school laundry work. Dimensions, two parts in ell shape, each part 16 by 24 feet. Erected in 1889. Present value, $350. Present condition, excellent.

Wagon and blacksmith shop.—Character, 1½-story frame. Use, shopwork and storing supplies. Dimensions, 24 by 80 feet. Erected in 1891. Present value, $1,100. Present condition, good.

Cottages (2).—Character, one-story frame. Use, for employes with families, when necessary. Dimensions, 20 by 30 and 22 by 26 feet. Erected in 1896. Present value, $300 each. Present condition, fair.

Physician's office.—Character, one-story frame. Use, for physician's office and agency payment room. Dimensions, 14 by 20 feet. Erected in 1890. Present value, $150. Present condition, good.

Miscellaneous outbuildings.—Character, 3 frame, 3 brick, 1 earth. Use, henhouse, hog shed, etc. Erected in 1896, 1897, and 1900. Present value, $350. Present condition, fair to good.

Lighted by kerosene lamps. Heated by stoves. Have no modern system of ventilation. Dormitories and class rooms have sloping board near top of windows.

The present water supply is inadequate. A windmill pumps water into a reservoir high enough up a hillside to force the water to the kitchen, but not upstairs. The pipe is 1 inch. The well is weak. It furnishes enough water for drinking and cooking, but not for dishwashing, scrubbing, nor laundry work. Water for those uses is hauled in barrels in a wagon from a tank in the pasture about one-fourth of a mile away. A well was dug which has a very strong flow of water, but no pump, engine, nor pipe connections have been furnished yet. All the water is of good quality. The main building has a 4-inch sewer which empties into a ravine that is dry most of the time. The outlet is about 20 rods from the building. The laundry has a board sewer pipe about 50 feet long, which empties onto the surface of the sloping ground where the water spreads and dries up. The boys, except the little ones, bathe in two bath tubs in the basement of the main building. The girls and small boys bathe in washtubs in the girls' wash room. There are 11 barrels of salt walter in the buildings with buckets kept near them for instant use in case of fire.

The school farm is a half section. More than half of this is good soil for cultivation, and even the most hilly parts furnish pasture. It is reservation land set aside for school purposes. Estimated value, $16,000. About 250 acres are fenced in. About 75 acres are under cultivation for raising corn, oats, millet, potatoes, and garden. About 200 acres more can be cultivated. About 175 acres are used for pasture. There is no irrigation.

This school was opened in 1881. The present dormitory rooms measure to accommodate 54 pupils. The school farm produces fairly good crops of corn, oats, millet, potatoes, and garden products.

Winnebago School.

Located 20 miles south of Dakota City, Nebr., on the Chicago, St. Paul, Minneapolis and Omaha Railway. Site, fairly well adapted to school purposes; climate, good; soil of site, a deep prairie loam

STATISTICS OF INDIAN TRIBES, AGENCIES, AND SCHOOLS. 63

Addition to school building.—Character, one-story brick. Use, assembly room and schoolroom. Capacity, 50 pupils. Erected in 1901. Cost, $3,400. Present value, $3,400. Present condition, excellent.

Dormitory.—Character, two-story brick. Use, dormitory, kitchen, dining room, employees' rooms, bathrooms, closets, lavatories, sitting and play rooms for both sexes. Capacity, 85 pupils and 5 employees. Erected in 1900–1901. Cost, $21,750. Present value, $21,750. Present condition, excellent.

School building.—Character, two-story brick. Use, schoolroom, sewing room, superintendent's office, and employees' rooms. Capacity, 40 pupils and 4 employees. Erected in 1892–3. Cost, unknown. Present value, $2,500. Present condition, fair to good.

Laundry.—Character, one-story brick. Use, washing for pupils. Capacity, 85 to 90 pupils. Erected in 1900–1901. Cost, $2,950. Present value, $2,950. Present condition, excellent.

Commissary.—Character, one-story brick. Use, storing supplies. Dimensions, 20 by 50 feet. Erected in 1901. Cost, $2,198.10. Present value, $2,198.10. Present condition, excellent.

Barn (cow).—Character, 1½-story frame. Use, housing cows and storing hay. Capacity, 14 cows and 8 to 10 tons hay. Present value, $150. Present condition, poor.

Barn (horse).—Character, 1½-story frame. Use, housing horses and storing hay. Capacity, 6 horses and 10 tons hay. Present value, $125. Present condition, fair.

Granary.—Character, 1½-story frame. Use, storing corn, oats, and ground feed. Capacity, 800 bushels corn, 600 bushels oats, and 1,800 pounds ground feed. Erected in 1891. Present value, $200. Present condition, fair to good.

Hog house.—Character, frame. Use, housing swine. Capacity, 20 to 30 hogs. Present value, $40. Present condition, poor.

Pump house.—Character, frame. Use, housing the gasoline engine. Erected in 1900–1901. Present value, $200. Present condition, excellent.

Miscellaneous outbuildings.—Character, all frame. Use, chicken house, coal, hose and gasoline house. Erected in 1880 to 1889. Present condition, fair.

Lighted by gasoline gas from carburetter and mixer. There are 161 lights installed in the plant, in the two main buildings. The plant is in good condition and satisfactory. Same was put in August, 1901. The dormitory and school building are heated by steam from a boiler under each building. The heating plant was put in when the buildings were being constructed in 1900. The heating plant is excellent, giving splendid results. The ventilation of the dormitory and school building is by the direct-indirect system, with ventilating flues to roof. This system was designated to be put in by the Indian Office. The same is very efficient and satisfactory.

The water is supplied from an 8-foot open well about 60 feet deep. The water is pumped from this well by a gasoline engine to a 1,300-barrel reservoir about 650 feet distant, on a hill 50 feet above the top of buildings. So far the water system and supply are quite adequate. The water is very harsh, or hard. The system was put in simultaneously with the construction of plant. The dormitory, school building, and laundry are connected with a general sewer pipe which at buildings is 6 inches, when past buildings it is 8 inches, and this is enlarged to 10 inches to outfall, which is 20 feet below buildings and fully 1,000 feet from them. The outfall is into a running stream. The system was installed at the same time the buildings were being constructed and is satisfactory. There are 10 ring baths and 2 bath tubs in the basement of the dormitory building. There is 1 bath tub in the school building on the second floor, but is not connected with hot water. The bath system is quite satisfactory. There are standpipes on each side of the dormitory with hose on each floor, which makes six fire lines in this building, which is ample for inside fire protection. Four fire hydrants are favorably distributed about the grounds.

The Winnebago School has 155 acres. It is only fair as a farm, there being too much waste land. This land is reserved or set apart for school purposes from Winnebago tribal land and is worth about $2,000. Practically all under fence. Fifty acres are under cultivation. No more is suitable for cultivation. One hundred acres are used for pasture. No irrigation.

The Winnebago School was installed as such about thirty years ago. The first school plant was constructed of brick and had a capacity of about 85 pupils; this plant was destroyed by fire February 24, 1892. A new plant was constructed in 1893 with about the same capacity, which was also destroyed by fire April 26, 1898. The present modern plant was erected in 1900–1901 and has a capacity of about 90 pupils, and cost nearly $35,000.

OSAGE AGENCY, OKLA.

Tribes.	Population.
Osage	1,833
Kaw (or Kansas)	222
Total	2,055

Area, 1,570,195 acres; unallotted.

Railroad station: Elgin, Kans., on Atchison, Topeka and Santa Fe Railway. Distance to agency, 25 miles.

Nearest military post: Fort Reno, Okla. Post-office address: Pawhuska, Okla. Telegraphic address: Pawhuska. Okla., via Elgin, Kans.

Osage Agency School.

Located at Pawhuska, 27 miles south of Elgin, Kans., on the Atchison, Topeka and Santa Fe Railway. Site well suited for school purposes. Climate without extreme changes.

Girls' building.—Character, three-story and basement stone, with one two-story and basement stone addition. Use, dormitory, dining room, and kitchen for 80 girls, dining room and kitchen for 14 employees, 12 rooms for employees, commissary, and laundry. Capacity, 90 pupils, 12 employees, 1 large room for commissary and 1 large room for laundry purposes. Erected in 1892. Cost, $16,800. Present value, $15,000. Present condition, fair.

Boys' building.—Character, three-story and basement stone, with one two-story frame addition. Use, dormitory, 10 rooms for employees, carpenter shop, bakery, dining room, and kitchen. Capacity, 100 pupils, 10 employees, 1 large room each for carpenter shop, bakery, dining room, and kitchen. Erected in 1873. Cost, $30,000. Present value, $20,000. Present condition, fair.

Hospital.—Character, one-story frame. Isolation and care of sick. Capacity, 10 patients. Erected in 1892. Cost, $1,195. Present value, $600. Present condition, fair.

Schoolhouse.—Character, two-story stone. Use, assembly hall and class rooms. Capacity, 150 pupils. Erected in 1892. Cost, $6,400. Present value, $6,000. Present condition, fair.

Barn.—Character, two-story stone. Use, sheltering stock and storing grain and hay. Capacity, 8 horses, 15 cows, 600 bushels grain, and 30 tons of hay. Erected in 1894. Cost, $1,850. Present value, $1,800. Present condition, fair.

Boiler house.—Character, one-story stone. Use, steam heating and manufacturing ice. Capacity, heating plant. Manufactures 4 tons of ice per day. Erected in 1892. Cost, $1,875. Present value, $800. Present condition, poor.

Engineer's and farmer's houses.—Character, both one-story frame. Use, quarters for engineer and farmer. Capacity, one small family each. Erected in 1895 and 1891. Cost, engineer's house, $650; farmer's house, $250. Present value engineer's house, $500; farmer's house, $250. Present condition, fair.

Laundry.—Character, two-story frame. Use, dining room and kitchen for 8 employees and 2 rooms for employees. Capacity, dining room and kitchen for 8 employees and 2 employees' quarters. Erected in 1882. Present value, $200. Present condition, poor.

Privy, tool and wood sheds, and ice house.—Character, frame. All small buildings. Use, name designates use. Capacity of ice house 25 tons. Erected in 1893, 1899, 1877, 1893, respectively. Cost, $70. Present value, $50, $250, $200, respectively. Present condition, ice house very bad, others fair.

Lighted by gasoline gas; 230 lights are in use. Plant was installed in 1899; cost, $2,875. Is in fair condition. Heated by steam from boiler house, which was installed in 1892; cost $4,000, estimated. Ventilation of buildings is by windows and doors. No modern system in use.

The small creek from which water supply is furnished has running water about half the year. The water is pumped from this creek by a steam engine and pump into a reservoir of 7,000 barrels capacity which is 70 feet above school grounds and 1,400 yards west of buildings. The pressure is ample to force water where needed. None of the water is used for irrigating purposes. Water system was installed in 1893 at a cost of $4,500. Cistern water is used for drinking purposes. Hydrant water used for all other purposes. The boys' and girls' buildings, hospital, schoolhouse, boiler house, and privy are connected with a 10-inch sewer pipe which empties into a small ravine about 100 rods from buildings and flows into creek above mentioned 1,000 yards below point where water is pumped into reservoir. The sewer empties 25 feet below buildings. In basement of boys' building there are 4 ring baths and 2 bath tubs; on third floor in girls' buildings 3 bath tubs. There are stand pipes in boys' and girls' buildings and schoolhouse with hose on all the floors except third floor of boys' building. Chemical fire extinguishers are in all buildings. Fire hydrants in grounds.

The school has about 800 acres. Soil of 160 acres is very much impregnated with alkali on a substratum of hardpan; 640 acres rolling pasture land of light soil on a substratum of rock. This land cost the school nothing and its present value is estimated at $10,000. Eight hundred acres are under fence; 85 acres under cultivation, of which 5 are in orchard; 120 acres additional can be cultivated; 715 acres are in pasture. No land irrigated.

The school was opened in 1874 with a capacity of 75 pupils. Its present capacity is 180 and it is one of the best-equipped agency boarding schools in the service.

Kaw Training School.

Located 35 miles west of Osage Agency, on the Arkansas River, 15 miles east of Kildare, Okla., on the Atchison, Topeka and Santa Fe Railway, which is the shipping point for the school supplies. Site is admirably adapted to school purposes; climate equable. Soil is a sandy loam, being the deposit of the flood plain of the Arkansas River.

Mission building.—Character, 2½-story stone building, with a 2½-story addition joined to the main building by a one-story addition used as pupils' dining room. Use, assembly rooms, children's dining room and kitchen, sewing room, dormitories, infirmary, employees' quarters, employees' sitting room, laundry and drying room, bath rooms. Capacity, 44 pupils. Erected, main building, 1873; addition, 1885. Cost, estimated, $8,000. Present value, $6,000. Present condition, good.

School building.—Character, one-story stone. Use, class room, chapel, and assembly hall. Capacity, 44 pupils. Erected in 1873. Cost, $2,000. Present value, $1,500. Present condition, good.

Barn.—Character, 1½-story stone. Use, storing of hay, corn, farm machinery, wagons, and buggies; shelter for horses and cattle. Capacity, 10 horses, 15 cattle, 2 wagons, 2 buggies, 1,000 bushels corn or wheat, 40 tons hay, and the farm's complement of machinery. Erected in 1873. Cost, estimated, $2,000. Present value, $2,000. Present condition, excellent.

Doctor's house.—Character, 1½-story frame. Use, school farmers' quarters. Capacity, 5 rooms. Erected in 1873. Cost, $800. Present value, $500. Present condition, good.

Commissary.—Character, one-story stone. Use, school offices, school warehouse. Capacity, 3 rooms. Erected in 1901. Cost, $2,000. Present value, $2,000. Present condition, excellent.

Agent's house.—Character, 2½-story stone. Use, physician's residence. Capacity, 7 rooms. Erected in 1873. Estimated cost, $2,500. Present value, $2,000. Present condition, fair to good.

Doctor's office.—Character, 1½-story frame. Use, pharmacy. Capacity, 2 rooms and attic. Erected in 1873. Cost, $400. Present value, $300. Present condition, fair to good.

Lighted by kerosene lamps. Heated by wood stoves. Ventilated by doors, transoms, and windows.

The water supplied is pure but hard. Its source is a well located about 60 feet south of mission building. It is pumped into a galvanized iron tank, 3,500 gallons capacity, supported by a 38-foot steel trestle. The pressure is insufficient for fire protection, but answers as supply for domestic, drinking, and sewerage purposes for the school. The tank was erected in 1901. The total cost of water system, including tank, windmill, piping to all floors of mission building, $600. The mission building is connected with an 8-inch sewer pipe which empties into a sand ravine about 150 yards southeast of building. The outfall is 10 feet below building. There are two bath tubs, with hot and cold water. There is no special provision for fire protection.

The school has a farm of 640 acres. Its present value is estimated at $5,000. There are 500 acres under fence. Nearly 100 acres are under cultivation. Two hundred additional acres can be cultivated. Two hundred and sixty acres are used for pasture.

This school was opened in 1873 with a capacity of 44 pupils.

PAWNEE INDIANS, OKLAHOMA.

(Under Superintendent of School.)

Tribe.	Population.
Pawnee	638

Area, 112,860 acres, allotted.

Railroad station: Pawnee, on Atchison, Topeka and Santa Fe Railway, thence by team 1 mile.

Post-office address: Pawnee, Okla. Telegraphic address: Pawnee, Okla.

Pawnee Training School.

Located 1 mile east of Pawnee, Okla., on the Atchison, Topeka and Santa Fe Railway. Site is high. Drainage excellent in all directions. The climate is very hot in summer, with cool nights. Healthy.

Boarding school and appendages.—Character of material, stone and wood. Use, girls' home, dormitories, bakery, kitchen, dining room, schoolrooms, wash rooms, bathroom, rooms for employees. Capacity, 82 girls are housed. Normal capacity as figured by the architect, 45. Can reasonably accommodate 60. Erected about 1879. Present value, possibly $2,000. Present condition, poor.

Laundry.—Character of material, part wood and part stone.

Boys' dormitories.—Character of material, stone. Use, boys' dormitories, play rooms, bathrooms, and employees' rooms. Erected in 1892. Cost, $10,000. Present value, $10,000. Present condition, excellent.

Commissary.—Character, two-story wood. Present use, shoe shop, sewing room, hospital; sufficient for these purposes. Erected in 1892. Present value, $800. Ceiled building, allowing cold and dust to penetrate.

Barn.—Character of material, story and a half, wood. Use, horses and storage of hay, 25 tons. Capacity, 9 horses. Erected in 1902. Cost, $500. Present value, $500. Present condition, good.

Cow shed.—Character of material, wood. Use, for cows. Capacity, 15 cows. Erected about 1895. Cost, probably $200. Present value, $100. Present condition, fair.

Coal house.—Character of material, wood. Capacity, 60 tons. Erected in 1901. Use, coal house. Cost, possibly $150. Present value, $150. Present condition, good.

Engine house.—Character of material, wood. Use, engine house. Capacity, sufficient. Erected in 1901. Cost, $125. Present condition, good. Present value, $125.

Granary and corn crib.—Character of material, wood. Use, granary and corn crib. Capacity, 3,000 bushels. Erected in 1902. Cost, $200. Present value, $200. Present condition, good.

Wareroom and shop.—Character of material, wood. Use, wareroom and workshop. Capacity, about one-half as large as needed. Erected in 1902. Cost, $350. Present value, $350. Present condition, good.

Lighted by coal-oil lamps. Heated by coal and wood stoves. Ventilated by open doors and windows. Water supply good. Sewerage good. Bathing facilities good. Fire protection good. The water is supplied from a well 40 feet deep, walled in cement and mortar. The well is sunk 9 feet into sandstone rock. Quality good. Pumped to tank by gasoline engine. Base of tank, 60 feet high. Supply main, 3-inch galvanized pipe. Distributing main, 4-inch galvanized pipe. Sewerage-main pipe, 8 inches. Empties in Black Bear Creek. Fall in 1,500 feet, about 100 feet or over. Branch pipes, 4 inches and 6 inches.

School farm.—Acreage, 640. Quality, good. Character, pasturage and tillage. Government reserve. Present value, about $6,000. Under fence, 640 acres. Under cultivation, 200 acres. Additional acres that can be cultivated, none. Number of acres in pasturage, 360. Number of acres irrigated, none.

PIMA AGENCY, ARIZ.

(Under School Superintendent.)

Tribes.	Population.
Pima	4,400
Maricopa	350
Papago	640
Papago at San Xavier	2,516
Papago, nomadic	1,200
Total	9,106

STATISTICS OF INDIAN TRIBES, AGENCIES, AND SCHOOLS. 67

Area: Acres.
    Unallotted... 453,797
    Allotted 41,622.65
    Reserved for school 14

Railroad station: Casa Grande, on Southern Pacific Railway. Fifteen miles to agency.
Nearest military post: Whipple Barracks, Ariz. Post-office address: Sacaton, Pinal County, Ariz. Telegraphic address: Casa Grande, Ariz.

Pima Training School.

Located on the Gila River Reservation, 16 miles north of Casa Grande, Ariz., on the Southern Pacific Railway. The site is a good one for a school, except that there is no water for irrigating. The climate is very mild, with extreme heat in summer. The air is exceedingly dry. The soil has been formed by the decay of granitic rock, and is extremely productive when irrigated. The school is about 2½ miles from the Gila River. The elevation is about 1,200 feet.

Bakery.—Character, one-story adobe, with brick addition. Use, baking bread, etc., for subsistence of pupils. Dimensions, old building 14 by 26 feet; brick addition 14 by 14 feet. Erected in 1890 (addition new). Old building $200; addition about $100. Present value, $200. Present condition, old building not in very good repair.

Girls' dormitory.—Character, two-story adobe with two-story brick addition. Use, girls' dormitory, kitchen, dining room, employees' quarters, sewing room, superintendent's office. Capacity, dormitory 125, dining room 225. Erected in 1890 (brick addition built in 1900). Cost, adobe building, $8,000; brick addition, $3,225. Present value, $10,000. Present condition, good.

Boys' dormitory.—Character, one-story adobe. Use, boys' dormitory. Capacity, 125 pupils. Erected in 1890. Cost, $3,500. Present value, $3,500. Present condition, good.

Dwelling.—Character, one-story adobe cottage. Use, superintendent's dwelling. Capacity, 3 rooms. Erected in 1897. Cost, $300. Present value, $300. Present condition, bad.

Employees' quarters.—Character, two-story brick. Use, living quarters for employees. Capacity, 6 employees. Erected in 1902. Cost, $6,275. Present value, $6,275. Present condition, excellent.

Dwellings (2).—Character, one-story adobe cottages (double). Use, employees' quarters. Capacity, 6 rooms each, 3 on each side of central hall. Erected in 1895. Cost, $600 each. Present value, $600 each. Present condition, good.

Hospital.—Character, one-story adobe. Use, care of sick (one room used as quarters for nurse). Capacity, 8 patients. Erected in 1892. Cost, $1,000. Present value, $500. Present condition, very bad.

Laundry.—Character, one-story brick. Use, washing pupils' clothes, bedding, etc. Dimensions, 24 by 50 feet, 2 rooms. Erected in 1900. Cost, $3,600. Present value, $3,600. Present condition, excellent.

Oil house.—Character, one-story adobe. Use, storing kerosene, paints, oil, etc. Dimensions, 20 by 36 feet. Erected in 1900. Cost, $300. Present value, $300. Present condition, good.

Poultry house.—Character, frame. Fence of yard, wire net. Use, care of school poultry. Dimensions, 12 by 16 feet (yard 140 by 160 feet). Erected in 1900. Cost, $200. Present value, $200. Present condition, good.

Schoolhouse.—Character, one-story brick. Use, class rooms and assembly hall. Capacity, 200 pupils. Erected in 1900. Cost, $10,000. Present value, $10,000. Present condition, excellent.

Shop.—Character, one-story adobe. Use, blacksmith and carpenter shops, shoe and harness maker's shop, and storeroom. Dimensions, 43 by 46 feet; 4 rooms (one room is agency blacksmith shop). Cost, $3,000. Present value, $1,500. Present condition, fair.

Stable.—Character, one-story adobe with frame wagon shed. Use, housing of stock and storing fodder. Dimensions, 22 by 67 feet; 3 rooms; wagon shed 14 by 80 feet. Erected in 1899. Cost, $500. Present value, $500. Present condition, good. (This building is also used for agency stock.)

Store.—Character, one-story adobe. Use, storing supplies. Dimensions, 64 by 24 feet and 55 by 24 feet (ell-shaped building); 3 rooms, one of which is agency store. Erected in 1899. Cost, $3,000. Present value, $2,000. Present condition, fair.

Well house.—Character, one-story brick. Use, covering well. Dimensions, 13 by 13 feet. Erected in 1900. Cost, $200. Present value, $200. Present condition, excellent.

Ice and cold-storage building.—Character, one-story brick. Use, ice making and cold storage. Dimensions, 21 by 32 feet; 4 rooms. Erected in 1901. Cost, $900. Present value, $900. Present condition, excellent.

Boiler house.—Character, one-story brick. Use, housing boiler for laundry machinery. Dimensions, 15 by 21 feet. Erected in 1901. Cost, $200. Present value, $300. Present condition, excellent.

Shed —Character, adobe. Use, storing lumber, wagon timber, etc. Dimensions, 16 by 45 feet. Erected in 1901. Cost, $50. Present value, $100. Present condition, good.

Water-closets (2).—Character, brick. Use, employees and pupils. Dimensions, 14 by 17 feet (girls); 14 by 25 feet (boys). Erected in 1900. Cost, $3,555. Present value, $3,555. Present condition, good.

The schoolhouse is lighted by gas furnished by a small gas plant in the building. This plant is not entirely satisfactory. The other buildings and the grounds are lighted with oil lamps. Wood stoves and open fireplaces are used for heating all buildings when artificial heat is required, and are all that is necessary in this mild climate. The rooms of the school buildings are large and the ceilings high. There are many doors and windows, which can be kept open nearly all the time. There appears to be no need of other ventilation.

The source of the water supply is a well 11 feet in diameter and 30 feet deep. The water is pumped into two tanks, one of 10,000 and one of 20,000 gallons capacity, the larger being elevated about 40 feet above the ground, and is piped wherever needed, none of the buildings being more than two stories high. The pumping is done by steam furnished by the boiler of the mill engine. The water is seepage water, and is apparently very good but hard. The supply is ample for present needs. Closets and sinks are connected by 5 and 6 inch sewer pipes with 8-inch sewer pipe which empties into the Little Gila, an arm of the Gila River. The Little Gila is usually dry, but is well flushed several times a year. The sewage outfall is about 600 feet from the main school building. The fall is about 20 feet. There are three ring baths for pupils, and a tub for the women employees in the girls' dormitory. The water is heated by exhaust steam from the boiler of the laundry. There is also a sink with a number of faucets. This bath is in good condition. There are six ring baths and a sink with faucets for pupils in the boys' dormitory, the water being heated in a boiler with brick furnace near the bathroom but outside of the building. This bath is in bad repair. There are fire plugs near all buildings and 1,000 feet of fire hose. The large tank being, as before stated, 40 feet above ground, there is a good head of water at all times, and the force of the steam can be made still greater by direct pumping. Steam can be had in a short time at any hour.

There is no school farm, there being no water for irrigating purposes. There are about 160 acres set aside for the school and fenced. All of this could be cultivated if water could be had, but at present none of it is cultivated. There is no pasture whatever.

Pima boarding school was opened in the fall of 1881 with 75 pupils enrolled.

Gila Crossing Day School.

Located at Gila Crossing, on the Gila River Reservation, about 35 miles from the agency at Sacaton, and about 15 miles from Phoenix, Ariz. The climate is very mild, the elevation being low. The land around it would be very productive but for lack of water.

Schoolhouse.—Character, one-story adobe. Use, class room and teacher's dwelling. Capacity, 40 pupils. Dimensions, 27 by 44 feet; 3 rooms, 1 class room and 2 living rooms. Erected in 1899. Cost, $1,000. Present value, $1,000. Present condition, good.

The building is lighted with oil lamps; is heated in winter with wood stoves. No further ventilation is required than that afforded by windows and doors. The source of water supply is a well 25 feet deep, provided with bucket and windlass. The water is seepage water, good, though very hard, and there is plenty of it for school needs. No sewerage. There are no bathing facilities. There is practically no protection against fire.

There is no school farm, as there is no water for irrigation. About 4 acres are fenced for the school; there is no pasture.

Gila Crossing Day School was opened December 11, 1899, with 40 pupils enrolled.

Salt River Day School.

Located on the Salt River Reservation, about 3 miles from Scottsdale, Ariz., 12 miles from Phoenix, and about 30 miles from the agency at Sacaton. The site is a good one for the purpose of the school. The climate is very mild, the elevation being a little over 1,000 feet. The soil is exceedingly productive when irrigated.

STATISTICS OF INDIAN TRIBES, AGENCIES, AND SCHOOLS.

School building.—Character, one-story adobe. Use, class room and teacher's residence. Capacity, 44 pupils. Dimensions, 23 by 43 feet; 2 rooms, schoolroom and teacher's dwelling. Erected in 1899. Cost, $600. Present value, $400. Present condition, only fair.

Lighted by oil lamps. Heating, with small wood stoves. Doors and windows can be left open most of the time at any season, giving sufficient ventilation. Good water in plenty is supplied by a well 25 feet deep, and provided with windlass and buckets. There is no sewerage. There are no bathing facilities. There is practically no protection against fire.

There is no school farm, as there is no water for irrigating. About 4 acres are fenced, but there is no pasture.

This school was opened September 11, 1899, and in a few days there were 44 pupils enrolled.

Maricopa Day School.

Located in the extreme western part of the Gila River Reservation, among the Maricopa Indians, about 50 miles from the agency at Sacaton, and 12 miles from Phoenix. The climate is dry and mild, as in all the lower parts of southern Arizona. The school is well placed, in the midst of the Maricopa farm. The soil is extremely productive.

Schoolhouse.—Character, one-story adobe. Use, class room and teacher's dwelling. Capacity, 44 pupils. Dimensions, 27 feet by 56 feet 6 inches; 4 rooms, class rooms and living rooms. Erected in 1901. Cost, $1,200. Present value, $1,200. Present condition, excellent.

Lighted with oil lamps. Heating is done with wood stoves. Windows and doors give sufficient ventilation. Plenty of seepage water of good quality is supplied by a well 25 feet deep, and provided with windlass and bucket. There is no sewerage. There are no bathing facilities. There is practically no protection against fire.

About 4 acres have been set aside for school and fenced. This land is all irrigable and considerable water can be secured.

Maricopa Day School was opened October 1, 1901.

Blackwater Day School.

Located 12 miles east of Sacaton, Ariz. Climate hot and dry.

Schoolhouse.—Character, one-story brick. Use, day school. Capacity, 40 pupils. Completed January 1, 1903. Cost, $1,500. Present value, $1,500. Present condition, good.

Lighted with lamps. Heated with stoves. Ventilation by windows. Water supplied by well. Sewerage, none. Bathing facilities, none. Fire protection, water from well.

Number of acres under fence, 4; acres under cultivation, 4 (plowed). Additional acres that can be cultivated, none. Number of acres under pasture, none. Number of acres irrigated, none. Four acres will be irrigated when there is water.

Brick for this building was burned at Sacaton by Indian labor. Material purchased in open market. Labor performed by whites and Indians.

Casa Blanca Day School.

Located 10 miles west of Sacaton, Ariz. Climate hot and dry.

Schoolhouse.—Character, one-story brick. Use, day school. Capacity, 40 pupils. Completed January 1, 1903. Cost, $1,500. Present value, $1,500. Present condition, good.

Lighted with lamps. Heated with stoves. Ventilation by windows. Water supplied by well. Sewerage, none. Bathing facilities, none. Fire protection, water from well.

Number of acres under fence, 4; acres under cultivation, 4 (plowed). Additional acres that can be cultivated, none. Number of acres in pasture, none. Number of acres irrigated, none. Four acres will be irrigated as soon as there is water to use.

Brick for this building was burned at Sacaton by Indian labor. Material purchased in open market. Labor performed by whites and Indians.

Lehi Day School.

Located 6 miles northeast of Mesa, Ariz., on Salt River Reservation. Climate hot and dry.

Schoolhouse.—Character, one-story brick. Use, day school. Capacity, 40 pupils. Completed, January 1, 1903. Cost, $1,500. Present value, $1,500. Present condition, good.

Lighted with lamps. Heated with stoves. Ventilation by windows. Water supplied by well. Sewerage, none. Bathing facilities, none. Fire protection, water from well.

Number of acres under fence, 4; acres under cultivation, 4 (plowed). Additional acres that can be cultivated, none. Number of acres irrigated, none. Four acres will be irrigated as soon as there is water to use. Number of acres in pasture, none.

Brick for this building was burned on the site by Indian labor. Material purchased in open market. Labor performed by whites and Indians.

PINE RIDGE AGENCY, S. DAK.

Tribes. Population.
Oglala Sioux 6,616

Area, 3,155,200 acres; unallotted.

Railroad station: Rushville, Nebr., on Fremont, Elkhorn and Missouri Valley Railway. Twenty-five miles to agency.

Nearest military post: Fort Robinson, Nebr. Post-office address: Pine Ridge, S. Dak. Telegraphic address: Pine Ridge, S. Dak.

Pine Ridge Agency School.

Located 25 miles northwest of Rushville, Nebr. Site well suited for school purposes; climate mild; soil sandy; rainfall light; irrigation necessary.

School building.—Character, two-story-and-basement brick. Use, class rooms and assembly hall. Capacity, 200 pupils. Erected in 1897. Cost, $12,908. Present value, $12,500. Present condition, excellent.

Boys' dormitory.—Character, two-story-and-basement brick. Use, dormitory, offices of superintendent and disciplinarian. Capacity, 100 pupils. Erected in 1897. Cost, $12,258. Present value, $11,500. Present condition, good.

Girls' dormitory.—Character, two-story-and-basement brick. Use, dormitory. Capacity, 100 pupils. Erected in 1897. Cost, $12,258. Present value, $11,750. Present condition, good.

Mess hall, kitchen, and bakery.—Character, 1½-story brick. Use, dining room, kitchen, bakery, and employees' rooms. Capacity, 200 pupils. Erected in 1897. Cost, $4,793. Present value, $4,500. Present condition, good.

Boiler house and laundry.—Character, two-story-and-basement brick. Use, boiler house and laundry. Erected in 1897. Cost, $5,503. Present value, $5,250. Present condition, good.

Employees' mess cottage.—Character, two-story brick. Use, employees' mess and employees' rooms. Erected in 1900. Cost, $1,242. Present value, $1,200. Present condition, excellent.

Employees' cottages.—Character, 2 two-story brick. Use, employees' quarters. Capacity, 14 employees. Erected in 1897. Cost, $7,448. Present value, $7,400. Present condition, excellent.

Warehouse.—Character, one-story brick. Use, storing supplies. Dimensions, 20 by 48 feet. Erected in 1897. Cost, $1,547. Present value, $1,500. Present condition, excellent.

Barn.—Character, one-story-and-basement frame. Use, housing stock and storing grain. Capacity, 6 horses, 4 cows, and 15 tons of hay. Erected in 1891. Cost, $1,800. Present value, $1,000. Present condition, poor.

Workshop.—Character, one-story frame. Use, carpenter and shoe and harness shops. Capacity, 16 pupils. Erected in 1900–1901. Present value, $750. Present condition, excellent.

Miscellaneous outbuildings.—Character, one brick, others frame. Use, meat house, tool house, etc. Erected in 1897–1901. Present condition, good.

Lighted by electricity furnished by a dynamo in the boiler room. There are 300 incandescent lamps and 2 arc lights. Plant was installed in 1897, at a cost of $3,380. It is in good condition and satisfactory. Heated by steam from a central station which was installed in 1897, at a cost of $10,277. Ventilation of school rooms and dormitories is by the system devised by the Indian Office. Other buildings have no modern system.

The water supplied is fairly good. It is filtered from a small running stream, which is mainly fed from springs, into a cistern, and from thence forced by a steam engine and pump into a steel standpipe 60 feet high with a capacity of 50,000 gallons. The pressure is sufficient to force the water wherever required. Water system was installed when plant was constructed, and, with sewer system and pumping station, cost $7,590. All the buildings are connected with a nine-inch general pipe which empties into the small stream above referred to, about 100 rods from the buildings

STATISTICS OF INDIAN TRIBES, AGENCIES, AND SCHOOLS. 71

and below the source of the water supply. The outfall is 35 feet below the buildings. There are 10 needle baths in each of the two dormitories, 5 on each of the main floors. There are standpipes in each of the dormitories with hose on each floor. Water buckets in the other buildings and hydrants on the ground.

This school has about 480 acres of land reserved for its use. Its estimated value is $1,920. All school land is under fence. There are 80 acres under cultivation. One hundred and sixty additional acres can be cultivated. About 400 acres are used for pasturage and hay. Sixty-five acres are partially irrigated. This school was organized in 1883. In 1894 the buildings were burned and school was suspended. It was reopened in the new buildings February 7, 1898.

No. 2. Day School.

Located 5 miles west from agency. Is poorly located for gardening and farming. Climate good.

Buildings consist of one schoolhouse, one industrial building, one wood shed, and one water-closet. Are all one-story, frame, weatherboarded, shingled. Use, day school purposes. Capacity, 33. Erected in 1892. Cost, school building, $999.44; industrial cottage, $999.37; wood shed, $97.46; water-closet, $105.62. Present value, same as the cost. Condition of each building, good.

Lighting, common lamps. Heating, stoves. Ventilation, none. Water supply, from wells; supply, poor; water, poor. Sewerage, none, and none needed. Bathing facilities, none, except common tubs. Fire protection, none.

Farm, none. Number of acres under cultivation, none. About half under fence could be cultivated. About one-half acre under fence, used for pasture. None irrigated.

School opened in 1892.

No. 3. Day School.

Located 14 miles west of agency on White River.

Consists of four buildings, viz: One school building, one industrial cottage, one wood shed, and one water-closet. Are all one-story, framed, weatherboarded, and shingled. Schoolhouse is plastered with Baker hard wall plaster; cottage with common plaster. Capacity, 40. Schoolhouse was erected in 1892, cottage in 1894. Cost, schoolhouse, $999.44; industrial cottage, $999.37; wood shed, $97.46; water-closet, $105.62. Present value, same as cost.

New cistern put in this year. Well with pulley and buckets, but well dry. Stoves, ample.

No farm. About 40 acres under fence. No irrigation.

School opened in 1892.

No. 4. Day School.

Located 10 miles north of agency on White Clay Creek.

Consists of four buildings, viz: One school building, one industrial cottage, one wood shed, and one water-closet. Are all one-story, framed, weatherboarded, and shingled. Schoolhouse is plastered with Baker hard wall plaster; cottage with common plaster. Capacity, 35. Erected in 1901. Cost, schoolhouse, $1,177.77; industrial cottage, $1,144.04; wood shed, $97.46; water-closet, $105.62. Present value, same as cost. Present condition, excellent.

Stoves, ample. Well with pulley and buckets, supply ample. Bath room 8 by 8 feet.

No farm. About 40 acres under fence. No irrigation.

School opened in 1885. Building burned by lightning, 1900; rebuilt in 1901.

No. 5. Day School.

Located 20 miles northwest of the agency at the mouth of White Clay Creek. Excellently located for school purposes, and well located for irrigating a garden. Climate is good.

Buildings consist of one school building, one industrial cottage, one wood shed, and one water-closet. Are all one-story, framed, weatherboarded, and shingled. Buildings plastered with Baker hard wall plaster. Use, day-school purposes. Capacity, 35. Erected in 1892. Cost, school building, $999.44; industrial cottage, $999.37; wood shed, $97.46; water-closet, $105.62. Present value, same as cost. Present condition of each building, good.

Lighting, common lamps. Heating, stoves. Ventilation, none. Water supply, well with pulley and buckets, ample. Sewerage, none. Bathing facilities, none, except common tubs. Fire protection, none, and none needed.

About 80 acres under fence, used by teacher for pasture. Two acres under cultivation, for garden.

School opened in 1892.

No. 6. Day School.

Located 25 miles northwest of the agency on White River. Well located. Climate is good.

Buildings consist of one large school building, one industrial building (cottage), one wood shed, and one water-closet. Are all one-story, framed, weatherboarded and shingled. Buildings are plastered with Baker hard wall plaster. Use, day school purposes. Capacity, 40. Erected in 1892; cottage in 1894. Cost, schoolhouse, $990.44; industrial cottage, $999.37; wood shed, $97.46; water-closet, $105.62. Present value, same as cost. Present condition of each building, good.

Lighting, common lamps. Heating, stoves. Ventilation, none. Well with pulley and buckets. Water supply ample. Sewerage, none. Bathing facilities, none, except ample room and common tubs. Fire protection, none, and none needed.

Farm, none. About an acre used for garden. Nearly all under fence could be cultivated. About 40 acres under fence used for pasture and hay. None under irrigation.

School opened in 1892.

No. 7. Day School.

Located 15 miles northeast of agency on Wounded Knee Creek. Well located. Soil is good, and the school has been a success in raising a garden. Climate is good.

Buildings consist of one school building, one industrial cottage, one wood shed, and one water-closet. Are all one-story. The school building is a frame building, weatherboarded and shingled. The cottage is the old log building first built for school and cottage, but has been ceiled inside and is withal comfortable and roomy. Use, day-school purposes. Capacity, 33. Schoolhouse erected in 1892; industrial cottage, 1878. Cost, schoolhouse, $999.44; industrial cottage, $600; wood shed, $97.46; water-closet, $105.62. Present value, same as cost. Present condition of each building, good.

Lighting, common lamps. Heating, stoves, except industrial building heated by a furnace, constructed by the teacher. Ventilation, none. Water supply, two wells, one with pulley and rope, the other with a windmill furnished by the teacher. Water good and ample, and supplies water for the greenhouse and a small garden. Sewerage, none. Bathing facilities, none, except common tubs. No fire protection, and none needed.

Farm, none. Number of acres under cultivation about 5, used for garden. Nearly all that is under fence could be plowed. About 40 acres under fence, used for pasture and hay. None under irrigation, except amount mentioned above.

School opened in 1881.

No. 8. Day School.

Located 16 miles northeast of agency, on Wounded Knee Creek. Unusually well located for a garden without the need of irrigation. The school site is within a native grove. Climate is good.

Buildings consist of one school building, one industrial cottage, one wood shed, and one water-closet. Are all one story, framed, weatherboarded, and shingled and plastered. Use, day school purposes. Capacity, 40. Schoolhouse erected in 1892, cottage in 1894. Cost, schoolhouse, $999.44; industrial cottage, $999.37; wood shed, $97.46; water-closet, $105.62. Present value, same as cost. Present condition of each building, good.

Lighting, common lamps. Heating, stoves. Ventilation, none. Water supply, well with pulley and rope. Water, good and ample. A good spring near the schoolhouse. Sewerage, none and none needed. Bathing facilities, none except common tubs. Fire protection, none.

Farm, none. Number of acres under cultivation, about 2, used for a garden. About half that is under fence could be cultivated. About 40 acres under fence, used for pasture, not suitable for hay. None under irrigation.

School opened in 1892.

No. 9. Day School.

Located 18 miles north-northeast of agency, on Wounded Knee Creek. Well located for a garden which can usually be grown without irrigation, or can be irrigated without much expense. Climate, good. School within one-fourth mile of Manderson, the post-office and telephone station.

STATISTICS OF INDIAN TRIBES, AGENCIES, AND SCHOOLS.   73

Buildings consist of one school building, one industrial cottage, one wood shed, and one water-closet. Are all one story, framed, weatherboarded, shingled, and plastered with Baker hard-wall plaster. Use, day school purposes. Capacity, 33. Erected in 1892. Cost, schoolhouse, $999.44; industrial cottage, $999.37; wood shed, $97.46; water-closet, $105.62. Present value, same as cost. Present condition of each building, good.

Lighting, common lamps. Heating, stoves. Ventilation, none. Water supply, well being dug, probably pipe in the old drill well will be used for lifting the water. Sewerage, none, none needed. Bathing facilities none, except common tubs. Fire protection none.

Farm, none. About an acre under cultivation, used for a garden. Probably one-fourth of that is under fence could be cultivated. About 75 acres fenced, used for pasture and hay. None at present under irrigation.

School opened in 1881.

No. 10. Day School.

Located 22 miles north-northeast of agency, on Wounded Knee Creek. Climate is good. Situated 3 miles from Manderson.

Buildings consist of one school building, one industrial cottage, one wood shed, and one water-closet. Are all one story, framed and weatherboarded, and have just been replastered with Baker hard-wall plaster; also school building refloored. Use day school purposes. Capacity, 35. Schoolhouse erected in 1892, cottage in 1894. Cost, schoolhouse, $999.44; industrial cottage, $999.37; wood shed, $97.46; water-closet, $105.62. Present value, same as cost. Present condition of each building, good.

Lighting, common lamps. Heating, stoves. Ventilation, none. Water supply, good and ample; well with pulley and buckets. Sewerage, none. Bathing facilities, two small rooms cut off from the school building for bath rooms, common tubs used. Fire protection, none.

Farm, none. None under cultivation at present. Nearly all under fence. About 40 acres could be cultivated. None under irrigation.

School opened in 1892.

No. 11. Day School.

Located 30 miles north of agency, on Grass Creek. Is the best situated for grass and hay, not very reliable for gardening on account of the creek being dry during the summer. Climate is good.

Buildings consist of one school building, one industrial cottage, one wood shed, and one water-closet, are all one story, framed, weatherboarded, shingled, and plastered with Baker hard-wall plaster. Use, day school purposes. Capacity, 33. Erected in 1892. Cost, school house, $999.44; industrial cottage, $999.37; wood shed, $97.46; water-closet, $105.62. Present value, same as cost. Present condition of each building, good.

Lighting, common lamps. Heating, stoves. Ventilation, none. Water supply ample and good; well with pulley and bucket. Sewerage, none. Bathing facilities, none except common tubs. Fire protection, none.

Farm, none. Three acres have been under cultivation for garden, but too high and dry to make much success. Nearly all under fence. About 60 acres could be cultivated. None under irrigation.

School opened in 1892.

No. 12. Day School.

Located 32 miles north of agency, on Wounded Knee Creek. Located near a small stream which will afford irrigation for a garden. Climate is good.

Buildings consist of one school building, one industrial cottage, one wood shed, and one water-closet. Are all one story, framed, weatherboarded, and plastered. Use, day school purposes. Capacity, 33. Erected in 1892. Cost, schoolhouse, $999.44; industrial cottage, $999.37; wood shed, $97.46; water-closet, $105.62. Present value, same as cost. Present condition of each building, good.

Lighting, common lamps. Heating, stoves. Ventilation, none. Water supply, ample and good. Well with suction pump. Sewerage, none. Bathing facilities, none except common tubs. Fire protection, none.

Farm, none. A fraction of an acre, for garden, cultivated. Nearly all under fence. About 40 acres could be cultivated. None under irrigation.

School opened in 1892.

No. 13. Day School.

Located 35 miles north-northeast of agency, on Porcupine Creek. Unusually well located for irrigation. Climate, good.

Buildings consist of one school building, one industrial cottage, one wood shed, and one water-closet. Are all one story, framed, weatherboarded, shingled, and recently replastered with Baker hard-wall plaster. Use, day school purposes. Capacity, 33. Erected in 1894. Cost, schoolhouse, $999.44; cottage, $999.37; wood shed, $97.46; water-closet, $105.62. Present value, same as the cost. Present condition of each building, good.

Lighting, common lamps. Heating, stoves. Ventilation, none. Water supply, well with pulley and buckets. Sewerage, none. Bathing facilities, none except common tubs. Fire protection, none.

Farm, none. About 5 acres cultivated, mainly for garden. Nearly all under fence, can be plowed. About 50 acres, for pasture and hay. Five acres have been under irrigation.

School opened in 1894.

No. 14. Day School.

Located 52 miles east of agency, on Lake Creek. Is well situated for water, irrigation, and hay. Climate, good.

Buildings consist of one schoolhouse, one industrial cottage, one wood shed, and one water-closet. Are all one-story, framed, weatherboarded, shingled, walls replastered. Use, school purposes. Capacity, 33. Erected in 1894. Cost, school building, $999.44; cottage, $999.37; wood shed, $97.46; warer-closet, $105.62. Present value, same as cost. Present condition of each building, good.

Lighting, common lamps. Heating, stoves. Ventilation, none. Water supply, ample. Drilled well with force pump. Sewerage, none. Bathing facilities, none. Fire protection, none.

Farm, none. About an acre used for garden. Nearly all under fence. About 40 acres for pasture and hay. None irrigated.

School opened in 1894.

No. 15. Day School.

Located 30 miles north-northeast of agency, on Porcupine Creek. Well situated in a natural grove and a good place for a garden. Climate good.

Buildings consist of one schoolhouse, one industrial cottage, one wood shed, and one water-closet. Are all one-story, framed, weatherboarded, shingled, and plastered with Baker hard-wall plaster. Use, day school purposes. Capacity, 33. Erected in 1892. Cost, schoolhouse, $999.44; cottage, $999.37; wood shed, $97.46; water-closet, $105.62. Present value, same as cost. Present condition of each building, good.

Lighting, common lamps. Heating, stoves. Ventilation, none. Fire protection, none.

Farm, none. About an acre used for garden. About half under fence. About 60 acres used for pasture and hay. None irrigated.

No. 16 Day School.

Located 25 miles northeast of agency, on Porcupine Creek. Climate, good. Very well situated for irrigation, especially a garden, if the dam can be made strong enough to resist a flood.

Buildings consist of one schoolhouse, one industrial cottage, one wood shed, and one water-closet. Are all one-story, framed, weatherboarded, shingled, and plastered. Use, day school purposes. Capacity, 35. Erected in 1894. Formerly a log building used for school and cottage. Cost, schoolhouse, $999.44; industrial cottage, $999.37; wood shed, $97.46; water-closet, $105.62. Present value, same as cost. Present condition of each building, good.

Lighting, common lamps. Heating, stoves. Ventilation, none. Fire protection, none. Water supply, ample and good. Dug well. Sewerage, none. Bathing facilities, none except common tubs.

Farm, none. About 1 acre used for garden. About one-half under fence. About 75 acres used for hay and pasture. None irrigated.

School opened in 1881.

No. 17 Day School.

Located 40 miles northeast of agency, on American Horse Creek. Climate, good. Very well situated for irrigation.

STATISTICS OF INDIAN TRIBES, AGENCIES, AND SCHOOLS. 75

Buildings consist of one schoolhouse, one industrial cottage, one wood shed, and one water-closet. Are all one-story, framed, weatherboarded, shingled, and plastered. Use, day school purposes. Capacity, 33. Erected in 1894. Formerly log building used for school. Cost, schoolhouse, $999.44; industrial cottage, $999.37; wood shed, $97.46; water-closet, $105.62. Present value, same as cost. Present condition of each building, good.

Lighting, common lamps. Heating, stoves. Ventilation, none. Fire protection, none. Water supply, ample and good. Drill well. Sewerage, none. Bathing facilities, none except common tubs.

Farm, none. About 2 acres used for garden. About three-fourths under fence. About 50 acres used for hay and pasture. None irrigated.

School opened in 1881.

No. 18. Day School.

Located 45 miles north-northeast of agency, on Medicine Root Creek. Climate, good. Very well situated for irrigation.

Buildings consist of one schoolhouse, one industrial cottage, one wood shed, and one water-closet. Are all one story, framed, weatherboarded, shingled, and plastered. Use, day-school purposes. Capacity, 40. Erected in 1892. Cost, schoolhouse, $999.44; industrial cottage, $999.37; wood shed, $97.46; water-closet, $105.62. Present value, same as the cost. Present condition of each building, good.

Lighting, common lamps. Heating, stoves. Ventilation, none. Fire protection, none. Water supply, ample and good. Sewerage, none. Bathing facilities, none, except common tubs.

Farm, none. About 2 acres used for garden. About all under fence. About 40 acres used for hay and pasture. None irrigated.

School opened 1892.

No. 19. Day School.

Located 40 miles northeast of agency on Little Wound Creek. Climate, good. Very well situated for irrigation.

Buildings consist of one schoolhouse, one industrial cottage, one wood shed, and one water-closet. Are all one story, framed, weatherboarded, shingled, and plastered. Use, day-school purposes. Capacity, 40. Erected, schoolhouse, 1892; cottage, 1894. Cost, schoolhouse, $999.44; industrial cottage, $999.37; wood shed, $97.46; water-closet, $105.62. Present value, same as the cost. Present condition of each building, good.

Lighting, common lamps. Heating, stoves. Ventilation, none. Fire protection, none. Water supply, ample and good. Dug well. Sewerage, none. Bathing facilities, none, except common tubs.

Farm, none. About 2 acres used for garden. About one-half under fence. About 40 acres used for hay and pasture. None irrigated.

School opened 1885.

No. 20. Day School.

Located 45 miles northeast of agency, on No Flesh Creek. Climate, good. Very well situated for irrigation.

Buildings consist of one schoolhouse, one industrial cottage, one wood shed, and one water-closet. Are all one story, framed, weatherboarded, shingled, and plastered. Use, day-school purposes. Capacity, 33. Erected in 1893 and 1894. Cost, schoolhouse, $999.44; industrial cottage, $999.37; wood shed, $97.46; water-closet, $105.62. Present value, same as the cost. Present condition of each building, good.

Lighting, common lamps. Heating, stoves. Ventilation, none. Fire protection, none. Water supply, ample and good. Dug well. Sewerage, none. Bathing facilities, none, except common tubs.

Farm, none. About 1 acre used for garden. About one-twentieth under fence. About 75 acres used for pasture. None irrigated.

School opened 1893.

No. 21. Day School.

Located 50 miles east-northeast of agency, near Corn Creek. Climate, good. Very well situated for irrigation, especially a garden, if the dam can be made strong enough to resist a flood.

Buildings consist of one schoolhouse, one industrial cottage, one wood shed, and one water-closet. Are all one story, framed, weatherboarded, shingled, and plastered. Use, day-school purposes. Capacity, 33. Erected in 1892. Cost, schoolhouse, $999.44; industrial cottage, $999.37; wood shed, $97.46; water-closet, $105.62. Present value, same as the cost. Present condition of each building, good.

Lighting, common lamps. Heating, stoves. Ventilation, none. Fire protection, none. Water supply, ample and good. Drilled well. Wind pump. Sewerage, none. Bathing facilities, none, except common tubs.

Farm, none. About 2 acres used for garden. About one-half under fence. About 60 acres used for hay and pasture. None irrigated.

School opened 1892.

No. 22. Day School.

Located 65 miles northeast of agency, on Bear Creek. Climate, good. Very well situated for irrigation, especially a garden.

Buildings consist of one schoolhouse, one industrial cottage, one wood shed, and one water-closet. Are all one story, framed, weatherboarded, shingled, and plastered. Use, day-school purposes. Capacity, 33. Erected in 1893–94. Cost, schoolhouse, $999.44; industrial cottage, $999.37; wood shed, $97.46; water-closet, $105.62. Present value, same as the cost. Present condition of each building, good.

Lighting, common lamps. Heating, stoves. Ventilation, none. Fire protection, none. Water supply, ample and good. Drilled well, force pump. Sewerage, none. Bathing facilities, none, except common tubs.

Farm, none. About 1 acre used for garden. About three-fourths under fence. About 40 acres used for hay and pasture. None irrigated.

School opened 1893.

No. 23. Day School.

Located 60 miles north-northeast of agency, on Potato Creek. Climate, good. Very well situated for irrigation, especially a garden.

Buildings consist of one schoolhouse, one industrial cottage, one wood shed, and one water-closet. Are all one story, framed, weatherboarded, shingled, and plastered. Use, day-school purposes. Capacity, 33. Erected in 1893–94. Cost, schoolhouse, $999.44; industrial cottage, $999.37; wood shed, $97.46; water-closet, $105.62. Present value, same as the cost. Present condition of each building, good.

Lighting, common lamps. Heating, stoves. Ventilation, none. Fire protection, none. Water supply, ample and good. Dug well. Sewerage, none. Bathing facilities, none, except common tubs.

Farm, none. About 5 acres used for garden. About one-half under fence. About 50 acres used for hay and pasture. None irrigated.

School opened 1893.

No. 24. Day School.

Located 80 miles northeast of agency, on Lone Tree Creek. Climate, good. Very well situated for irrigation, especially a garden.

Buildings consist of one schoolhouse, one industrial cottage, one wood shed, and one water-closet. Are all one story, framed, weatherboarded, shingled, and plastered. Use, day-school purposes. Capacity, 33. Erected in 1893 and 1894. Removed to present location in 1896 at a cost of $1,440.50. Cost, schoolhouse, $999.44; industrial cottage, $999.37; wood shed, $97.46; water-closet, $105.62. Present value, same as the cost. Present condition of each building, good.

Lighting, common lamps. Heating, stoves. Ventilation, none. Fire protection, none. Water supply, ample and good. Dug well. Sewerage, none. Bathing facilities, none, except common tubs.

Farm, none. About one-half acre used for garden. About one-half under fence. About 45 acres used for hay and pasture. None irrigated.

School opened present location 1896.

No. 25. Day School.

Located 15 miles northwest of agency, on White Clay Creek. Climate, good. Very well situated for irrigation, especially a garden, if the dam can be made strong enough to resist a flood.

Buildings consist of one schoolhouse, one industrial cottage, one wood shed, and one water-closet. Are all one story, framed, weatherboarded, shingled, and plastered. Use, day-school purposes. Capacity, 33. Erected in 1893 and 1894. Cost, schoolhouse, $999.44; industrial cottage, $999.37; wood shed, $97.46; water-closet, $105.62. Present value, same as the cost. Present condition of each building, good.

Lighting, common lamps. Heating, stoves. Ventilation, none. Fire protection, none. Water supply, ample and good. Dug well. Sewerage, none. Bathing facilities, none, except common tubs.

Farm, none. About one-fourth acre used for garden. About one-fourth under fence. About 40 acres used for hay and pasture. None irrigated.

School opened 1893.

STATISTICS OF INDIAN TRIBES, AGENCIES, AND SCHOOLS. 77

NO. 26. Day School.

Located 30 miles north of agency, on White River. Climate, good. Very well situated for irrigation, especially a garden.

Buildings consist of one schoolhouse, one industrial cottage, one wood shed, and one water-closet. Are all one story, framed, weatherboarded, shingled, and plastered. Schoolhouse and cottage united. Use, day-school purposes. Capacity, 33. Erected in 1896. Cost, schoolhouse, $999.44; industrial cottage, $999.37; wood shed, $97.46; water-closet, $105.62. Present value, same as the cost. Present condition of each building, good.

Lighting, common lamps. Heating, stoves. Ventilation, none. Fire protection, none. Water supply, ample and good. Dug well. Sewerage, none. Bathing facilities, none, except common tubs.

Farm, none. About 1 acre used for garden. Abont one-fourth under fence. About 75 acres used for hay and pasture. None irrigated.

School opened 1896.

No. 27. Day School.

Located 6 miles north of agency, on White Clay Creek. Climate, good. Very well located for irrigating a garden by putting in a dam in the creek at the school.

Buildings consists of one school building, one industrial cottage, one wood shed, one water-closet. School buildings have a kitchen and a storeroom. Are all one story, framed, weatherboarded, shingled, and plastered. Use, day-school purposes. Capacity, 33. Erected in 1898. Cost, school building, $1,023.47; cottage, $1,023.47; wood shed, $97.46; water-closet, $105.62. Present value, same as the cost. Present condition of each building, good.

Lighting, common lamps. Heating, stoves. Ventilation, modern. Water supply, ample and good. Dug well. Sewerage, none. Bathing facilities, none, except common tubs. Fire protection, none.

Farm, none. About an acre used for garden. A good part of all under fence. About 40 acres for pasture and hay. None irrigated.

School opened 1898.

No. 28. Day School.

Located 5 miles east of agency, on Wolf Creek. Climate, good. Very well located for irrigating a garden by putting in a dam in the creek at the school.

Buildings consist of one school building, one industrial cottage, one wood shed, and one water-closet. School buildings have a kitchen and a storeroom. Buildings are all one-story, framed, weatherboarded, shingled, and plastered. Use, day school purposes. Capacity, 33. Erected in 1898. Cost, school building, $1,023.47; cottage, $1,023.47; wood shed, $97.46; water-closet, $105.62. Present value, same as the cost. Present condition of each building, good.

Lighting, common lamps. Heating, stoves. Ventilation, modern. Water supply, ample and good. Dug well. Sewerage, none. Bathing facilities, none except common tubs. Fire protection, none.

Farm, none. About an acre used for garden. A good part of all under fence. About 40 acres for pasture and hay. One acre irrigated.

School opened 1898.

No. 29. Day School.

Located 50 miles northeast of agency, on Medicine Root Creek. Climate, good. Very well located for irrigating a garden by putting in a dam in the creek at the school.

Buildings consist of one school building, one industrial cottage, one wood shed, and one water-closet. School buildings have a kitchen and a storeroom. Buildings are all one-story, framed, weatherboarded, shingled, and plastered. Use, day school purposes. Capacity, 33. Erected in 1898. Cost, school building, $1,023.47; cottage, $1,023.47; wood shed, $97.46; water-closet, $105.62. Present value, same as the cost. Present condition of each building, good.

Lighting, common lamps. Heating, stoves. Ventilation, modern. Water supply, ample and good. Dug well. Sewerage, none. Bathing facilities, none except common tubs. Fire protection, none.

Farm, none. About an acre used for garden. A good part of all under fence. About 40 acres for pasture and hay. None irrigated.

School opened 1898.

No. 31. Day School.

Located 40 miles east of agency on Flint Bull Creek. Climate, good. Very well located for irrigating a garden by putting in a dam in the creek at the school.

Buildings consist of one school building, one industrial cottage, one wood shed, and one water-closet. School buildings have a kitchen and a storeroom. Buildings are all one-story, framed, weatherboarded, shingled, and plastered. Use, day school purposes. Capacity, 33. Erected in 1898. Cost, school building, $1,023.47; cottage, $1,023.47; wood shed, $97.46; water-closet, $105.62. Present value, same as the cost. Present condition of each building, good.

Lighting, common lamps. Heating, stoves. Ventilation, modern. Water supply, ample and good. Drilled well. Sewerage, none. Bathing facilities, none except common tubs. Fire protection, none.

Farm, none. About an acre used for garden. A good part of all under fence. About 40 acres for pasture and hay. None irrigated.

School opened 1898.

No. 32. Day School.

Located 28 miles east of agency, on Little White River. Climate, good. Very well situated for irrigation, especially a garden.

Buildings consist of one schoolhouse, one industrial cottage, one wood shed, and one water-closet. Buildings removed to present site 1898. Are all one-story, framed, weatherboarded, shingled, and plastered. Use, day school purposes. Capacity, 33. Erected in 1892. Cost, schoolhouse, $999.44; industrial cottage, $999.44; water-closet, $105.62 (and wood shed combined). Present value, same as the cost. Present condition of each building, good.

Lighting, common lamps. Heating, stoves. Ventilation, none. Fire protection, none. Water supply, ample and good. Drilled well. Sewerage, none. Bathing facilities, none except common tubs.

Farm, none. About one-fourth acre used for garden. About all under fence. About 20 acres used for hay and pasture. None irrigated.

School opened 1892.

PONCA, OTO, AND OAKLAND AGENCY. OKLA.

(Under School Superintendent.)

Tribes.	Population.
Ponca	557
Oto and Missouria	370
Tonkawa	54
Total	981

Area:	Acres.
Allotted	133,244
Unallotted	90,747
Reserved	2,244

Railroad station: Whiteagle, on Atchison, Topeka and Santa Fe Railway. By team to agency, 3 miles.

Nearest military post: Fort Reno, Okla. Post-office address: Whiteagle, Okla. Telegraphic address: Whiteagle, Okla.

Ponca School.

Located at Ponca Agency 3 miles south of Whiteagle, Okla., a station on the Atchison, Topeka and Santa Fe Railroad. Site is well suited for school purposes; climate without extreme changes. Soil of good quality.

Schoolhouse.—Character, three-story brick, third story frame, court running to center. Use, dormitories, dining room and kitchen, schoolrooms, chapel, employees quarters and superintendent's office. Capacity, 100 pupils. Erected in 1882. Cost, $19,500. Present value, $15,000. Present condition, good.

Commissary and sewing room.—Character, 1½-story frame. Use, wareroom, sewing room, and seamstress quarters. Dimensions, 20 by 40 feet. Erected in 1897. Cost, $755. Present value, $700. Present condition, fair.

Bath house.—Character, one-story frame. Use, pupils bathroom. Dimensions, 18 by 22 feet. Erected in 1896. Cost, $175. Present value, $175. Present condition, poor.

STATISTICS OF INDIAN TRIBES, AGENCIES, AND SCHOOLS. 79

Laundry house.—Character, 1½ story frame. Use, contains steam-laundry plant. Dimensions, 30 by 60 feet. Erected in 1901. Cost, $1,000. Present value, $1,000. Present condition, good.

Employees' quarters.—Character, one-story frame. Use, employees kitchen and dining room and four sleeping rooms. Dimensions, 28 by 50 feet. Erected in 1894. Cost, $600. Present value, $800. Present condition, fair.

School barn.—Character, 1½-story frame. Use, housing live stock and storing forage. Capacity, 6 horses, 8 cows, 25 tons hay, and 2,000 bushel grain. Erected in 1888. Cost, $770. Present value, $500. Present condition, poor.

Miscellaneous outbuildings.—Character, all frame except meat house which is brick. Use, poultry house, meat house, coal sheds, etc. Erected in 1892–1901. Present value, $750. Present condition, good to fair.

Lighted by kerosene lamps and heated by coal and wood stoves. No system of ventilation, the only method being by the opening of windows and doors.

The water supply is pure and soft. Water is pumped from a well by a steam engine and pump and forced into a wooden tank of 300 barrels capacity standing on a wooden trestle about 20 feet high. The tank is not very good and the pressure is sufficient to force the water to the second story only. No water is used for irrigation. The steam pump has been only recently installed and has not yet been fairly tested, but is thought to be satisfactory. The sewerage system is of the crudest, consisting of a 4-inch pipe laid from the center of the court to the surface about 100 yards from the building. The bathing system is most unsatisfactory, there being four old zinc tubs in the bath house for use of both boys and girls. Water buckets and chemical fire extinguishers are placed throughout buildings for fire protection. The water tank stands so low that it is not available in case of fire.

This school has 480 acres of fine farming land in its reserve. The land was set aside for the school when the Indians were allotted in 1894. Its present value is estimated to be about $10,000. All of this land is under fence. About 90 acres are in cultivation, probably 10 acres being in orchard. All of the school farm can be cultivated. Three hundred acres are used for pasturage. None of the land is irrigated.

This school was established as a boarding school January 1, 1883.

Tonkawa Day School.

Located 3 miles east of the city of Tonkawa in Kay County, Okla., on the Atchison, Topeka and Santa Fe Railway, near the Chikaskie River. Good climate and soil prairie loam.

Tonkawa Day School.—Character, frame building, one story, size 20 by 30 by 10 feet. Use for school and chapel purposes. Capacity, 24 pupils. Built in 1902. Cost, $354. Present value, $354. Present condition, excellent.

Being a day school no lights are needed. Heated by wood-burning stove. Ventilated by opening windows. Good well near school building. No sewerage. No bathing facilities. No fire protection.

No school farm, but part of agency farm can be used for gardening purposes.

This school was organized October 1, 1902, to enable the Tonkawa children to attend school, and has been in operation since that time.

Oto Boarding School.

Located at Oto Subagency, about 11 miles from Ponca; railroad station, Redrock, on Atchison, Topeka and Santa Fe Railway, thence by private team 7 miles. The climatic conditions are similar to those at Ponca. The plant was almost entirely destroyed by fire September 10, 1902, and on petition of the Oto Indians Congress, in the appropriation act for 1904, allowed the use of $30,000 of their trust funds for rebuilding at the old site.

On September 11, 1903, contract was awarded for rebuilding plant, as follows: Combination school, dormitory, mess hall building, acetylene generator house, water and sewer system, $22,181. Brick construction.

School farm contains 640 acres under fence.

POTAWATOMI RESERVATION, KANS.

(Under School Superintendent.)

Tribe.	Population.
Potawatomi prairie band	590

Area:	Acres.
Allotted	58,298.51
Unallotted	19,059

Railroad station: Hoyt, on Chicago, Rock Island and Pacific Railroad; thence by private team; distance, 10 miles.

Nearest military post: Fort Riley, Kans. Post-office address: Nadeau, Kans. Telegraphic address: Hoyt, Kans.

Potawatomi Training School.

Located 10 miles west of Hoyt, Kans., on the Chicago, Rock Island and Pacific Railway, situated on upland rolling prairie. The climate is without extreme change except during the months of January and February, when the temperature frequently reaches from 15° to 20° below zero.

Dormitory building.—Character, two-story frame building, with attic. Use, dormitory, dining room, kitchen, play rooms, sleeping rooms for employees, reception room, and mess quarters. Capacity, 57 pupils. Erected in 1893. Cost, $17,250. Present value, $15,000. Present condition, good.

Schoolhouse.—Character, one-story frame structure. Use, 3 schoolrooms and 1 assembly hall. Capacity, 110 pupils. Erected in 1896. Cost, $4,000. Present value, $3,700. Present condition, good.

Warehouse or schoolhouse (old).—Character, one-story frame. Use, storing supplies. Dimensions, 26 by 60 feet. Erected in 1875. Cost, $4,000. Present value, $1,000. Present condition, fair.

Barn.—Character, two-story; lower story stone, upper story frame. Use, housing live stock and storing hay and grain. Capacity, 14 horses, 25 tons hay, 400 bushels corn, 500 bushels oats. Erected in 1875. Cost, $2,000. Present value, $800. Present condition, fair.

Cow barn.—Character, one-story, with basement. Use, housing cattle and storing hay and grain. Capacity, 18 cows, 15 tons of hay, 200 bushels grain. Erected in 1901. Cost, 350. Present value, $350. Present condition, excellent.

Miscellaneous outbuildings.—Character, all frame. Use, coal houses, laundry, ice house, etc. Capacity—ice house, 100 tons; coal house, 60 tons; laundry, 50 pupils. Erected, 1893 to 1896. Cost, about $1,000. Present value, about $700. Present condition, fair.

Lighted by oil lamps. Heated by steam from boiler located in basement under dormitory; all other buildings are heated by coal stoves. None of these buildings have modern systems of ventilation.

The water supplied is pure and hard. Its source is a number of wells connected in one supply well located about three-fourths of a mile from the dormitory building. The new water system is nearing completion at this school and will cost about $10,000. The water will be forced into a steel tank, of about 20,000 gallons capacity, on a steel trestle standing 60 feet high. The water will be forced into this tank by a gasoline engine and windmill; the pressure should be ample to afford fire protection. The dormitory and laundry are connected with an 8-inch sewer pipe which empties into a small ravine about 1,400 feet north of the dormitory building, which is about 30 feet below the said buildings. There are 6 bath tubs in the basement of the dormitory. Water is carried to the first and second floors through 2-inch pipes to which cotton hose is attached; buckets are also kept in the halls and dormitory buildings. Fire hydrants are located in the grounds near the buildings.

This school has a 160-acre farm, 100 acres of which is under cultivation, the remainder in pasture. This land was set aside by the tribe for school purposes and its present value is about $30 per acre.

This school opened in 1872 with a very small and irregular attendance.

KICKAPOO, IOWA, SAUK AND FOX, AND GREAT NEMAHA RESERVATIONS, KANS.

(Under School Superintendent.)

Tribes.	Population.
Kickapoo	258
Iowa	220
Sauk and Fox of Missouri	78
Munsee } Chippewa }	92
Total	648

Area:

	Acres.
Allotted	35,672.5
Unallotted	8,589
Reserved for school and cemetery	362

STATISTICS OF INDIAN TRIBES, AGENCIES, AND SCHOOLS. 81

Railroad station: Horton, Kans., on Chicago, Rock Island and Pacific Railway; hence by team, 7 miles.
Post-office address: Germantown, Kans. Telegraphic address: Horton, Kans.

Kickapoo Training School.

Location: On Kickapoo Reservation, Brown County, Kans.
Dormitory.—Character, frame, stone foundation, drop siding, lathed and plastered, painted inside and out. Use, dormitories, schoolrooms, children's dining room and kitchen, employees' quarters, furnace room, toilet rooms, baths, and cellar. Capacity, 60 pupils. Erected in 1899. Cost, $13,184. Present value, $13,184. Present condition, good.
Employees' cottage.—Character, two-story frame, stone foundation. Use, employees' quarters. Capacity, 7 employees. Erected in 1902. Cost, $2,490. Present value, $2,500. Present condition, excellent.
Storeroom (old).—Character, frame. Use, storing school supplies. Capacity, 20 by 30 feet floor space. Erected in 1899. Cost, $250. Present value, $250. Present condition, good.
New storeroom.—Character, frame. Use, storing school supplies. Capacity, 20 by 32 feet floor space. Erected in 1900. Cost, $900. Present value, $900. Present condition, excellent.
Laundry (old).—Character, frame. Use, boys' play room. Capacity, 24 by 32 feet floor space. Erected in 1899; remodeled, 1900. Cost, $300. Present value, $300. Present condition, good.
Laundry (new).—Character, frame. Use, laundering. Capacity, 24 by 36 feet floor space, embraces washing room, drying room, and ironing room. Erected in 1900. Cost, $925. Present value, $925. Present condition, excellent.
Coal house.—Character, frame, one story. Use, storing coal. Capacity, 100 tons. Erected in 1899. Cost, $80. Present value, $80. Present condition, good.
Wagon house.—Character, frame. one story. Use, housing wagons, carriages, machinery, etc. Capacity, 20 by 34 feet floor space. Erected in 1899. Cost, $125. Present value, $125. Present condition, good.
Stable.—Character, 1½-story frame. Use, housing live stock and storing feed. Capacity, 6 horses, 3 tons hay, and 200 bushels corn. Erected in 1899. Cost, $250. Present value, $250. Present condition, good.
Cow barn.—Character, frame, 1½ stories. Use, housing live stock and storing feed. Capacity, 5 cows, 3 tons of hay, and 800 bushels corn. Erected in 1899. Cost, $200. Present value, $200. Present condition, good.
The dormitory building is lighted by gasoline gas. The plant was installed in March, 1900, at a cost of $900. It is in good condition and satisfactory. Heated by hot water from central station or furnace; was installed in 1899 as part of the building contract. The employees' cottage is heated by stoves and lighted by gasoline gas conducted from plant in dormitory. Ventilation of dormitory building is by the system devised by the Indian Office. Other buildings have no modern system.
The water supplied is pure, but slightly hard. Its source is a spring located about three-eighths of a mile from the buildings. The water is accumulated in a reservoir, and from thence by windmill and gasoline-engine power forced into a wooden tank of 1,600 gallons capacity on a steel trestle 50 feet high; from thence distributed by gravity where needed in dormitory and laundry. Some of the water is used for irrigating lawns; the supply is sufficient. The water system was installed in 1901 at a cost of $3,800. A stock well at the barn furnishes a plentiful supply for stock. The dormitory laundry and employees' cottage are connected with a 6-inch sewer pipe which empties into a gully about 30 rods from buildings. The outfall is about 20 feet below buildings. There are 3 ring baths and 1 tub bath for each of the dormitories. They are located in the second story of the building. In the dormitory building there are standpipes with hose on each floor; also water buckets; fire hydrants in the grounds.
This school farm has 240 acres of good land. This land was set aside by Executive order, and its present value is estimated at $10,000. The whole of the farm is under fence. There are 130 acres under cultivation. Nearly the whole of the farm can be cultivated. Eighty-five acres are used for pasturage; 25 acres are in meadow.
This school was opened October 15, 1899, with a capacity for 60 pupils.

Great Nemaha Day School.

(This school under charge of superintendent of Kickapoo Training School.)

Located 6 miles west of Whitecloud, Kans., on the Burlington and Missouri Railroad. Site, high, rolling prairie, black loam soil.

8193—03——6

82 STATISTICS OF INDIAN TRIBES, AGENCIES, AND SCHOOLS.

Great Nemaha Day School.—Character, two-story frame building. Use, for day school and residence of day-school teacher. Capacity, 50 pupils. Erected in 1880. Cost, $5,500. Present value, $1,000. Present condition, bad.

This boarding school was abandoned July 1 of last year, and the farm is leased for the maintenance of the day school; all other buildings and Government property was sold at public auction or transferred to the Kickapoo and Potawatomi boarding schools.

Sauk and Fox Day School.

(This school under charge of superintendent of Kickapoo Training School.)

Located on the Sauk and Fox Reservation. It is a small church building, frame, about 24 by 32 feet, erected by the Catholics in 1900 at a cost of $600, and is in good condition. Capacity, 25.

It is lighted with lamps and heated with stoves. There is no water or sewerage system, bathing facilities, or fire protection.

There is no school farm connected with this school.

PUEBLOS OF NEW MEXICO.

(Under the superintendents of Albuquerque and Santa Fe, N. Mex., schools.)

Tribe.	Population.
Pueblo	6,794

Area, 691,805 acres, unallotted.

Railroad station: Santa Fe, on Atchison, Topeka and Santa Fe Railway.

Nearest military post: Fort Wingate, N. Mex. Post-office address: Santa Fe, N. Mex. Telegraphic address: Santa Fe, N. Mex.

The following day schools, while situated upon the Pueblos in New Mexico, are under the supervision of the superintendent of the Albuquerque Training School:

Acoma Day School, Acomita, N. Mex.

Located 70 miles west of Albuquerque, and 12 miles west of Laguna, the nearest railway station. Site quite well suited for school purposes, climate dry and without very extreme changes. Soil sandy, with a substratum of rocks.

Acoma Day School.—Character, 1½-story building through the center; stone and clay; shingled roof. Use, schoolroom and 3 living rooms for the teacher. Capacity, 35. Erected about ten years ago. Present value, $1,200. Present condition, fairly good.

Lighted by kerosene lamps and heated by wood stoves. Ventilation is by the ordinary way of opening doors and windows. Water is procured from San Jose River, about one-fourth mile from school. A great quantity of alkali in the water. No sewerage. For bathing purposes the river and main irrigation ditch are used. The fire protection consists of a barrel of water and a ladder.

The building was erected by the Catholic Church and the school maintained by them for about seven years, when it was converted into a Government school. The building is now owned by the Catholic Church and is rented to the Indian agent for day-school purposes.

Isleta Day School, Isleta, N. Mex.

Located about 13 miles southwest of Albuquerque, N. Mex., on the Atchison, Topeka and Santa Fe Railway. Site poor. Climate warm and dry without extreme changes.

Isleta Day School and teacher's quarters.—Character, one-story adobe, with three rooms. Use, one room used for class exercises and industrial work, and two rooms used as a dwelling by teacher. Capacity, 32 pupils. Erected in 1892. Cost, $1,200. Present value, $400. Present condition, poor.

Lighted by kerosene lamps and heated by coal stoves. Ventilation obtained by opening doors and windows. Water obtained from wells of adjoining properties; good. No sewerage. No bathing facilities. No fire protection.

No farming land connected with the school.

The school was built in 1892 and opened in September of that year. It was then under the supervision of the Right Reverend Archbishop of Santa Fe and supported partly by Government aid. In 1897 the school building was rented to the United States Indian agent for day-school purposes.

Laguna Day School, Laguna, N. Mex.

Located 66 miles west of Albuquerque, on main line of Santa Fe Pacific Railroad. Site is poor. Climate fine, dry, and sunny. Soil of immediate site poor, but that surrounding the pueblo is good for farming when water can be obtained for irrigation.

Laguna Day School building.—Character, one-story rock building, with one room. Use, class room and industrial work. Capacity, 36. Present value, $300. Present condition, fair.

Teacher's quarters.—Character, one-story adobe, with three rooms. Use, teacher's dwelling. Capacity, three rooms. Present value, $250. Present condition, fair.

Lighted by kerosene lamps and heated by wood stoves. Ventilation obtained by opening windows and doors. Water obtained by carrying it from railway hydrant. No sewerage. No bathing facilities. No fire protection.

No farming land connected with the school.

Pahuate Day School, Pahuate, N. Mex.

Located 12 miles north of Laguna, N. Mex., the nearest point to the Santa Fe Pacific Railroad. The pueblo is on a mesa. Climate mild, dry, and delightful.

Pahuate Day School building.—Character, one-story, three-room adobe. Use, class room and teacher's quarters. Capacity, 20 pupils. Present value, $200. Present condition, good.

Lighted by kerosene lamps and heated by wood stoves and fireplace. Ventilation by opening windows. The water furnished is good and soft. Source, mountain-spring water. It is obtained from the open irrigation ditch or from the village reservoir. No sewers. No bathing facilities. No fire protection.

There is no land connected with the school.

School building owned by the Indians and rented to United States Indian agent for day-school purposes.

Paraje Day School, Paraje, N. Mex.

Located about 7 miles northwest of Laguna, N. Mex. Laguna is the nearest railway station and post-office. Site good. Climate warm, mild, and dry.

Paraje Day School building.—Character, one-story stone building. Use, class room, storeroom, and teacher's dwelling. Capacity, good-sized schoolroom, accommodates 32 pupils; good sized storeroom and two dwelling rooms. Erected in 1900. Present value, $600. Present condition, good.

Lighted by kerosene lamps and heated by wood stoves and fireplace. Ventilation obtained by opening windows. Water is hauled in barrels from a spring about 2 miles distant. No sewerage. No bathing facilities. Water barrel and buckets for fire protection.

No farming land in connection with the school.

The Paraje school was opened May 1, 1899, in a small building rented from an Indian, and both schoolroom and teacher's room had only dirt floors. The Indians have recently put up a good-sized building with board floors, which they now rent to the Government. This new building has been occupied since January 1, 1902.

San Felipe Day School, San Felipe, N. Mex.

Located 10 miles southwest of Thornton, N. Nex., on the Atchison, Topeka and Santa Fe Railway, on west bank of Rio Grande, about 400 feet from water. Site well suited for school purposes. Climate excellent. Soil of immediate site is adobe earth on a bed of coarse gravel.

San Felipe Day School building.—Character, one-story adobe, 15 by 60 feet, 9 feet ceiling. Use, class room and sewing room. Capacity, 45. Erected about 1760. Present value, $50. Present condition, very bad.

Teacher's residence.—Character, one-story adobe. Use, teacher's dwelling. Capacity, one room, 12 by 30 feet. Erected in 1895. Cost, about $30. Present value, $25.

Lighted by kerosene lamps and heated by coal and wood stoves. Ventilation obtained by opening doors and windows. Water obtained from Rio Grande; carried in pails. No sewerage. No bathing facilities; washtubs used. No fire protection. No farming land in connection with this school.

A mission school (Catholic) was maintained at this place, beginning at a very early date. A school was opened by authority of the Indian Office in December, 1897.

Santa Ana Day School, Santa Ana Pueblo, N. Mex.

Located 4 miles north of Bernalillo, N. Mex. Site is in the Indian pueblo and is convenient for the pupils, but is unhealthful, especially in summer. Climate dry and mild.

Santa Ana Day School.—Character, small adobe building, 13 by 19 feet. Use, class room and sewing room. Capacity, 12 pupils. Present value, $50. Present condition, bad.

Not lighted. Heated by one wood stove. Ventilated by opening windows. Water obtained from the Rio Grande. Water muddy and impure. No sewerage. No bathing facilities. No fire protection.

School has no land.

The history of the organization of the school not known.

Seama Day School, Seama, N. Mex.

Located 8 miles west of Laguna, N. Mex. Site good. Climate warm and dry, without extreme changes.

Schoolhouse.—Character, one-story stone. Use, class room and domestic instruction. Capacity, 40 pupils. Cost, about $300. Present value, $300. Present condition, good.

Teacher's quarters.—Character, one-story stone. Use, teacher's residence and storeroom. Capacity, two employees. Cost, about $250. Present value, $250. Present condition, good.

Lighted by kerosene lamps and heated by wood stoves. Ventilation by means of windows and doors. Water obtained from a near stream, very hard, but fairly good. No sewerage. No bathing facilities. No fire protection.

No farming land connected with this school.

This school has been a mission school for some years, but in February, 1902, it was organized as a Government school, and opened with 34 pupils. The buildings are rented from the Indians.

The following day schools, while situated upon the Pueblos in New Mexico, are under the supervision of the superintendent of the Santa Fe Training School.

Cochiti Day School.

Located 9 miles north of Thornton, in Rio Grande Valley. Climate, pleasant, and soil productive when irrigated.

Schoolhouse, rented by Government.—Character, adobe. Use, class room. Capacity, 30 pupils. Erected in 1891. Present condition, good.

Two living rooms, rented by Government.—Character, adobe. Use, housekeeping. Capacity, 1 employee or small family. Erected in 1891. Present condition, good.

Outhouses (2).—Character, 1 frame, 1 adobe. Use, pupils' closets, employee's closet. Erected in 1891 and 1901. Present condition, good.

Lighted by kerosene lamps and heated by wood stove and fireplace. Ventilated by fireplaces and windows. Water obtained from well 65 feet deep near school. No sewerage. No bathing facilities. No fire protection.

No school farm.

The school was organized in 1891. The school building is rented from an Indian. All the children of the pueblo between the ages of 5 and 16 are attending school.

Jemes Day School, Jemes, N. Mex.

Located 45 miles north of Albuquerque, N. Mex. Site very well suited for a day school. Climate, dry and no extreme changes. Soil, sandy.

School building, rented by Government.—Use, class room and teachers' quarters. Character, one-story adobe. Capacity, 35 pupils. Erected in 1878. Cost, $1,500. Present value, $1,000. Present condition, fair.

Lighted by kerosene lamps and heated by stove and fireplace. Ventilated by windows. Water is good. Taken from a well located about 50 yards from school building; carried by hand in pails. No sewerage. No bathing facilities. No fire protection.

The school has a fraction less than 2 acres for playground. The land was given to the Presbyterian board of home missions by the Indians to be used for school purposes.

The school, as a mission, was opened in 1879, and continued mission and contract until December, 1896. Since that time has been rented by the Government for school purposes.

STATISTICS OF INDIAN TRIBES, AGENCIES, AND SCHOOLS. 85

Nambe Day School.

Located 18 miles northwest of Santa Fe, N. Mex., in the valley of Nambe Creek. Climate good, without extreme change.

Schoolhouse, rented by Government.—Character, one-story adobe. Use, class and study room. Capacity, 28 pupils. Present condition, good.

Teacher's quarters, rented by Government.—Character, one-story adobe. Use, teacher's dwelling. Capacity, 2 rooms. Present condition, good.

Lighted by kerosene lamps and heated by wood stoves. Ventilated by windows. The water is pure and soft; is carried from running stream about 250 yards.

The school was opened September 4, 1899, with an enrollment of 19 pupils.

Picuris Day School, Picuris, N. Mex.

Located 4 miles northwest from Penasco and 15 miles north-northeast from Embudo, the nearest railroad station on the Denver and Rio Grande Railroad. Site excellent. Above the Rio Chico. Pure air. Few storms. Cool summers, although winters are cold. Soil rocky, but rich and productive in the valleys when irrigated.

Schoolhouse.—Character, one-story adobe. Use, schoolroom, teacher's quarters. Capacity, 16 pupils. Erected in 1899. Cost, about $400; rented by Government. Present value, $400. Present condition, good.

Lighted by kerosene lamps and heated by a fireplace and stoves. Ventilated by doors, windows, and open fireplace. Water supply, soft pure spring and mountain river water, carried to school by buckets. No sewers. Bathing facilities, the ditches and river. Fire protection, none.

Farm, none.

History of organization of school, opened to pupils April 26, 1899, with 12 pupils.

San Ildefonso Day School.

Located 25 miles northwest of Santa Fe, N. Mex. Climate dry and healthful and without extreme changes.

Schoolhouse, rented by Government.—Use, school rooms and teacher's quarters. Capacity, 21 pupils and 1 teacher's room. Present condition, fair.

Lighted by kerosene lamps and heated by woodstoves. Ventilated by windows. Water is secured from well near school. No sewerage. No bathing facilities. No fire protection.

No school farm.

This school was opened about January, 1898, with its present capacity. It provides a noonday lunch for pupils.

San Juan Day School, San Juan Pueblo, N. Mex.

Located about 45 miles northwest of Santa Fe, N. Mex., and one-half mile east of the Denver and Rio Grande Railway station of Chamita. A very good place for a school. The climate is about the same as at Santa Fe, only a little warmer in summer and not quite so cold in winter.

Schoolroom.—Character, one-story adobe room. Use, schoolroom. Capacity, 32 pupils. Erected in 1886. Cost, $450. Present value, $550. Rented by Government. Present condition, excellent.

Lighted by lamp and heated by wood stove. Water is obtained from a well, also from a spring.

No farm.

This school was opened as a Government day school December 10, 1897, with an enrollment of 21 pupils. Before this it had been a contract day school for a number of years, under the charge of the Archbishop of Santa Fe, N. Mex.

Santa Clara Day School.

Located 1½ miles south of Espanola, N. Mex., on Denver and Rio Grande Railroad. Site well suited for school purposes. Climate, dry with almost constant sunshine and a uniform temperature. Soil, a sandy loam.

Schoolhouse, rented by Government.—Character, one-story adobe. Use, schoolroom and teacher's quarters. Capacity, 30 pupils. Erected in 1895. Cost, $250. Present value, $225. Present condition, fair.

Lighted by kerosene lamps and heated by wood stoves. Ventilated by windows and a ventilator in ceiling. Good water is supplied from a well near schoolhouse. No sewerage. No bathing facilities. No fire protection.

No school farm.

School was opened about March, 1891, with enrollment of 28 pupils.

Santo Domingo Day School.

Located 2 miles southwest of Thornton, N. Mex., on the Atchison, Topeka and Santa Fe Railroad. Site satisfactory for school purposes. Climate, dry without extreme changes. Soil, sandy loam.

Schoolhouse, rented by Government.—Character, one-story wood frame, 20 by 46 feet. Use, class room, wood room, and sewing room. Capacity, 40 pupils. Erected in 1885. Cost, about $2,000. Present value, about $500. Present condition, poor.

Lighted by kerosene-oil lamps, and heated by wood and coal stoves. Ventilated by windows. Water is supplied from a well near schoolhouse. No sewerage. No bathing facilities. No fire protection.

No school farm.

This school was opened under Government management in 1897.

Sia Day School, Sia, N. Mex.

Located about 38 miles northeast of Albuquerque, N. Mex., on the Jemez River which is nearly dry for about four months each year. Site, the rock upon which Sia pueblo is built. Climate, fine, scarcely any rainfall, and no extreme changes. Soil of school site, sand and bowlders.

Sia Day School, Galban property, rented by Government.—Character, one-story, stone and adobe, mud floors, small windows. Use, schoolroom, teacher's quarters. Capacity, 30 pupils. Present condition, fair.

Lighted by oil lamps and heated by wood stove and open fire. Ventilation secured by opening doors and windows—when they can be opened. Water supply, none. Water is brought to school building from a mudhole about a quarter of a mile away, in ollas, at a cost of 5 cents for each olla of water.

This school was opened by the United States Government about September 1, 1892.

Taos Day School, Taos, N. Mex.

Located at Taos, N. Mex., 3½ miles northeast of the village of Taos. The altitude is 7,000 feet. Climate, dry and healthful but cold in winter.

The pueblo schoolhouse, rented by Government.—Character of material, adobe. Use, schoolroom and teacher's quarters. Capacity, 32 day pupils. Date of erection, 1886. Present value, $1,000. Present condition, good.

Lighted by kerosene lamps and heated by wood stoves and fireplace. Ventilated by fireplace and windows. Pure soft water from mountain stream. Sewerage, none. Bathing facilities, none. Fire protection, none.

No school farm.

Taos Day School was opened December 15, 1896.

Tesuque Day School.

Located 8 miles northwest of Santa Fe, N. Mex., near a small stream called Tesuque River. The region is mountainous. Climate is rather mild and without extreme changes. Soil is sandy, but rather rocky.

Schoolhouse rented by Government.—Character, one-story adobe. Use, class rooms. Capacity, 20 pupils. Erected in 1901. Present condition, good.

Teacher's quarters, rented by Government.—Character, one-story adobe. Use, teacher's dwelling. Capacity, 2 rooms. Present condition, good.

Lighted by kerosene lamps and heated by wood stoves. Ventilated by windows. The water supply is from well near school. No sewerage. No bathing facilities. No fire protection.

The school was opened in September, 1899.

PUYALLUP AGENCY, WASH.

(Under School Superintendent.)

Tribes.	Population.	Tribes.	Population.
Puyallup	533	Quinaielt	137
Chehalis	149	Quaitso	60
Nisqually	153	Georgetown	115
Squaxon	85	Humptulip	19
S'Klallam	305		
S'Kokomish	178	Total	1,734

STATISTICS OF INDIAN TRIBES, AGENCIES, AND SCHOOLS. 87

Area: Acres.
    Allotted 32,142
    Unallotted 225,681

Railroad station: Tacoma, on Northern Pacific Railroad.
Post-office address: Tacoma, Wash. Telegraphic address: Tacoma, Wash.

Puyallup School, Tacoma, Wash.

Located adjoining the city limits of Tacoma, about 3 miles from center of the city, on Northern Pacific Railroad. The farm is crossed by the main county road into the city and by the Interurban Electric line to Seattle. The Puyallup River forms the northern boundary of the farm. The buildings are beautifully situated on a side hill overlooking the city of Tacoma, and giving a superb view of Puget Sound and the Olympic Mountains. The climate is mild, with dry summers and wet winters. The soil in the low ground is rich valley land; on the upland gravel and clay.

Main school building.—Character, two-story frame with 2 two-story frame wings. Use, schoolrooms and chapel, girls' dormitory, employees' rooms, and assistant superintendent's office. Capacity, 100 girls. Erected in 1889. Cost, $11,000. Present value, $5,000. Present condition, fair.

Mess dining room.—Character, 1½-story frame. Not at present in use; to be fitted up for mess house. Dimensions, 25 by 36 feet. Erected in 1889. Cost, $575. Present value, $150. Present condition, poor.

Tailor shop.—Character, 1½-story frame. Use, tailor shop. Dimensions, 16 by 34 feet. Erected in 1883. Cost, $150. Present value, $50. Present condition, poor.

Guardhouse.—Character, one-story frame. Use, as a tool room. Dimensions, 20 by 25 feet. Erected in 1885. Cost, $200. Present condition, bad.

Carpenter shop.—Character, 1½-story frame. Use, carpenter shop. Dimensions, 20 by 40 feet. Erected in 1881. Cost, $200. Present value, $20. Present condition, bad.

Barn.—Character, 1½-story frame. Use, barn. Dimensions, 100 by 112 feet. Erected in 1879, one wing; 1885, one wing, 1899. Cost, $800. Present value, $250. Present condition, poor.

Cottage No. 1.—Character, one-story frame. Use, occupied by blacksmith and family. Dimensions, 31 by 37 feet. Erected in 1874. Cost, $1,000. Present value, $100. Present condition, very poor.

Cottage No. 2.—Character, 1½-story frame. Use, residence of employees' family. Dimensions, 24 by 42 feet. Erected in 1880. Cost, $1,000. Present value, $200. Present condition, poor.

Stove house.—Character, one-story frame. Use, storing stoves. Dimensions, 14 by 20 feet. Erected in 1894. Cost, $40. Present value, $25. Present condition, bad.

Shoe and harness shop.—Character, one-story frame. Use, shoe and harness shop. Dimensions, 18 by 30 feet. Erected in 1886. Cost, $225. Present value, $100. Present condition, fair.

Cottage No. 4.—Character, one-story frame. Use, residence of tailor and family. Dimensions, 24 by 30 feet. Erected in 1896. Cost, $300. Present value, $200. Present condition, good.

Boys' quarters No. 1.—Character, two-story frame with stone basement. Use, rooms for large boys. Dimensions, 52 by 45 feet. Erected in 1899. Cost, $5,800. Present value, $5,500. Present condition, good.

Boys' quarters No. 2.—Character, two-story frame. Use, home of small boys. Dimensions, 60 by 65 feet. Erected, part 1873, part 1882, part 1894. Cost, $3,100. Present value, $800. Present condition, poor.

Dining room and kitchen.—Character, one-story frame on stone foundation. Use, dining room and kitchen. Dimensions, 74 by 88 feet. Erected in 1899. Cost, $4,000. Present value, $4,000. Present condition, good.

Cottage No. 3.—Character, 1½-story frame. Use, residence of clerk. Dimensions, 30 by 34 feet. Erected in 1886. Cost, $1,000. Present value, $400. Present condition, fair.

Agent's office.—Character, one-story frame. Use, office of agent and clerk. Dimensions, 22 by 30 feet. Erected in 1885. Cost, $500. Present value, $150. Present condition, fair.

Cottage No. 5.—Character, one-story frame. Use, occupied by carpenter and family. Dimensions, 18 by 24 feet. Erected in 1897. Cost, $200. Present value, $150. Present condition, good.

Warehouse.—Character, two-story frame on stone foundation. Use, storing supplies. Dimensions, 30 by 50 feet. Erected in 1898. Cost, $850. Present value, $800. Present condition, good.

Employees' building.—Character, two-story frame on brick foundation. Use, residence of superintendent and of storekeeper. Erected in 1898. Dimensions, 40 by 42 feet. Cost, $1,300. Present value, $1,300. Present condition, good.

Cottage No. 6.—Character, 1½-story frame on brick foundation. Use, residence of assistant superintendent. Dimensions, 12 by 24 feet, with 14 by 14 foot wing. Erected in 1898. Cost, $575. Present value, $575. Present condition, good.

Laundry.—Character, two-story frame on stone foundation. Use, as laundry and sewing room. Dimensions, 28 by 60 feet. Erected in 1873. Cost, $800. Present value, $500. Present condition, fair.

Blacksmith building.—Character, two-story frame on stone foundation. Use, blacksmith shop. Dimensions, 28 by 50 feet. Erected in 1901. Cost, $800. Present value, $800. Present condition, good.

Lighted by lamps, hand and bracket. Heated by stoves, burning coal. Schoolrooms, chapel, and dormitories ventilated by means of boards placed at top of windows. Dormitory No. 1 has ventilating registers. The other buildings have no facilities.

The water supply is abundant, pure, and soft. Its source is a large spring from the side of a bluff, distance of 1¾ miles from the school, and at an elevation of 110 feet above tops of buildings. It is piped to the school through 7-inch pipe and distributed to the buildings by gravity. The land around the spring and the pipe line belongs to the Government, including the right of way. The system furnishes sufficient pressure for fire protection and is entirely satisfactory. Most of the buildings are connected by 5-inch laterals with an 8-inch terra-cotta main which empties into the Puyallup River at a distance of about 1,200 feet from the school grounds. Dormitory No. 1 has 5 ring baths and 1 tub; dormitory No. 2 has 5 tubs, and the girls' building has 6 tubs. Filled buckets in all the large buildings, with standpipes and hose connected in main building. Fire hydrants at accessible places throughout the grounds, and ample supply of hose and a well-drilled fire company.

The school has 62 acres of ground about equally divided between gravelly upland and rich valley land. Its value is about $15,000, all inclosed by fence. Thirty-one acres under cultivation; about 15 acres to fruit. Balance of ground occupied by school plant.

School was authorized by Medicine Creek treaty of 1854, but it was three years later before it was finally established, in a small way, on Squaxin Island. It proved a failure there on account of lack of attendance, and was moved to the Puyallup Reservation in the early sixties and located near the mouth of the Puyallup River. On account of the school being in low ground, frequently covered by the high tides, it was again moved in 1873 to near its present site. In 1876, owing to lack of appropriation, the school was discontinued for a year, but from 1877 to the present time it has continued to prosper. The school farm at that time consisted of 580 acres, only about 30 of which were under cultivation.

Chehalis Day School.

Located 4 miles southwest of Gate, Wash., on the Northern Pacific Railway. Excellent site for school, with mild, uniform climate, but copious rain during winter. Soil is fertile, the school farm being situated in the productive Chehalis Valley.

Teacher's cottage.—Character, 1½-story frame. Use, office and dwelling. Capacity, 1 office room, 2 kitchen rooms, 1 drug room, 3 dwelling rooms. Erected in 1870. Cost, $1,200. Present value, $200. Present condition, poor.

Schoolhouse.—Character, one-story frame. Use, used for day school. Capacity, 40 pupils in room in use. Erected about 1870. Cost, $2,400. Present value, $100. Present condition, poor.

Barn (formerly boarding hall).—Character, two-story frame. Present use, barn. Capacity, 20 head cows, 2 horses. Erected about 1872. Cost, $4,300. Present value, $800. Present condition, poor.

Physician's house.—Character, one-story frame. Use, not now used. Capacity, 3 rooms. Erected in 1870. Cost, $800. Present value, $100. Present condition, poor.

Jail.—Character, frame. Present use, storeroom for grain. Dimensions, 15 by 15 feet. Erected in 1884. Cost, $100. Present value, $25. Present condition, fair.

Commissary.—Character, 1½-story frame. Use, storing supplies and machinery. Dimensions, 20 by 30 feet. Erected in 1884. Cost, $125. Present value, $50. Present condition, poor.

Lighted by kerosene lamps and heated by wood stoves. There is no modern ventilation. Water supply for school is secured from windmill and piped to the respective buildings from the well. The windmill is situated about 50 yards from the school building. The water is soft, pure, and abundant. The school farm is well watered by Chehalis River and Willamette Creek. There is no sewerage system. There are no baths. The buildings are provided in part with chemical fire extinguishers (hand grenades).

The Chehalis school farm comprises 471 acres, 250 of which are of choice river bottom land. This land was set aside by Executive order, and is estimated to be worth $10,000. There are 471 acres under fence. There are 60 acres under cultivation, being used for meadow, grain and orchard. The remaining 421 acres can be cultivated when cleared properly. Four hundred and twenty-one acres are in pasturage and timber. There is no artificial irrigation, as it is not needed.

This school was probably instituted about 1864, and was at various times a boarding and day school. In 1896 it was changed from a boarding to a day school

Jamestown Day School.

Located 2½ miles south of Dungeness, Clallam County, Wash. It is well situated for a day school. The climate is mild and damp, without extreme changes in temperature.

Schoolhouse.—Character, one-story frame. Use, class-room. Capacity, 24 pupils. Erected about 1875. Cost, unknown. It was erected and is owned by the Indians. Present value about $150. Present condition, good.

Lighted by kerosene lamps and heated by wood stove; satisfactory. Ventilated by lowering windows. No water supply. No sewerage.

There is no school farm and no pasture.

This school was opened in 1878, at the request of the Indians, in a house which had been built for a church, with 1 teacher and about 20 pupils. Said building belongs to the Indians.

Port Gamble Day School.

Located one-half mile east of Port Gamble, Wash., on a sand spit and in the Indian village of Boston, the channel or entrance to Gamble Bay lying between school and Port Gamble. School site is submerged periodically by high tides. Climate is mild and uniform, temperature seldom falling below freezing point or rising above 70° F. Practically no opportunity for agriculture.

Schoolhouse.—Character, one story frame, 20 by 30 feet. Use, schoolroom. Capacity, 26 pupils. Erected in 1901. Cost, $350. Present condition, excellent. This building does not belong to the Government, but was built by the teacher, assisted by Indians. Lumber was donated by the Puget Mill Company, Port Gamble, Wash.; doors, windows, etc., purchased by teacher and Indians; paint and furniture supplied from agency. Government pays no rent.

Teacher's residence.—Character, 1½ story frame. Capacity, 5 rooms. Erected in 1896–97. Cost, $200. Present value, $175. Present condition, fair.

Lighted by kerosene lamps and heated by wood stoves. Ventilated by opening windows. Water obtained from small stream; stream is dammed and water conveyed through the village by elevated wooden trough. No sewerage. No bathing facilities. No fire protection.

Have no school farm. This school is situated in the midst of an Indian village on tidelands owned by the Puget Mill Company.

This school was opened October, 1889.

Quinaielt Day School.

Located at the mouth of the Quinaielt River in the Indian village of Granville. Climate, temperate; very rainy during winter months; seldom have snow or ice.

Boarding house.—Character, 1½ stories, rough boards, shingled. Use, leased to trader for dwelling. Capacity, 50 pupils. Erected in 1868. Present value, $200. Present condition, poor.

Barn and stable combined.—Character, 1½ stories, rough boards. Use, cow stable. Capacity, 50 tons hay, 15 head cattle or horses. Erected in 1887; repaired, 1890. Present value, $150. Present condition, fair.

Dwelling.—Character, one story, rough boards and shakes. Use, warehouse. Capacity, 4 rooms. Erected in 1881. Present condition, very poor.

Dwelling.—Character, 1½ stories, rough boards and shakes. Use, physician's residence and dispensary. Capacity, 5 rooms. Erected in 1881. Cost, $400. Present value, $100; Present condition, very poor.

Kitchen.—Character, one-story, rough boards. Use, store for trader. Capacity, 2 rooms. Erected in 1893. Present value, $50. Present condition, very poor.

Office and store combined.—Character, one-story weather-boarded. Use, physician's office. Capacity, 4 rooms. Erected in 1870. Present value, $50. Present condition, poor.

Schoolhouse.—Character, 1½-stories, rough boards, shingled. Use, day school. Capacity, 30 pupils. Erected in 1881. Cost, $400. Present value, $50. Condition, very poor.

Smith and carpenter shop combined.—Character, one-story, rough boards. Use, blacksmith shop. Capacity, one forge and one carpenter bench. Erected in 1870. Present value, $30. Present condition, very poor.

Dwelling, office, and schoolhouse lighted by kerosene and heated by wood stoves. No modern system of ventilation. Well water very poor; during rainy season rain water is used. No system of sewers. No baths. Water buckets and a few hand grenades.

This school has never had a reserve set aside for its use, although during boarding school days there was probably 20 acres used for garden and meadow.

Skokomish Day School.

Location, on Skokomish Indian Reservation, 12 miles northwest of Shelton, Wash. Present site, very poor.

Schoolhouse.—Character, a box building. Use, unoccupied at present. Capacity, 40 pupils. Dimensions, 20 by 60 feet. Erected in 1873. Cost, $850. Present value, $200. Present condition, fair.

Boys' quarters.—Character, two-story frame, 20 by 40 feet. Use, unoccupied. Capacity, 4 rooms. Erected in 1892. Cost, $1,515. Present value, $500. Present condition, fair.

Root house.—Character, box, lined with brick. Dimensions, 24 by 40 feet. Erected in 1880. Cost, $400. Present value, $50. Present condition, fair. Lighted by kerosene lamps and heated by wood stoves. Ventilated by means of raising windows. Water supply taken from Skokomish River in pails, which is salty oftentimes, owing to high tides. Has no sewer. Has no baths. Has no fire protection.

This school has 10 acres of good land partly cleared, situated near the center of the reservation, and if needed buildings were placed thereon would make an admirable site for school. The fencing is very poor. There are a few fruit trees growing thereon.

The reservation boarding school at this place was discontinued on June 30, 1896. September,. 1896, a day school was opened in the old boarding-school buildings. Being situated on low ground subject to tide overflow, and a long way from the Indians, attendance until this year has been very small. So far the present year the attendance has been considerably increased, owing to the adoption of the Indian Shaker Church (more centrally located) as a schoolroom.

QUAPAW AGENCY, IND. T.

(Under School Superintendent.)

Tribes.	Population.	Tribes.	Population.
Peoria	185	Eastern Shawnee	100
Ottawa	167	Miami	110
Quapaw	271	Wyandotte	354
Modoc	47		
Seneca	351	Total	1,585

Area:	Acres.
Unallotted	37,602
Allotted	173,387
Authorized to be sold	557
Reserved	680

Railroad station: Wyandotte, Ind. T., on St. Louis and San Francisco Railway. By private team three-fourth mile to agency.

Nearest military post: Fort Reno, Okla. Post-office address: Wyandotte, Ind. T. Telegraphic address: Wyandotte, Ind. T.

Seneca Indian Training School.

Located one-fourth mile north of Wyandotte, Ind. T., on the St. Louis and San Francisco Railway; a beautiful and healthful location for a school, well shaded, good drainage, and good water. The buildings are located on a high bluff, along a large spring-water creek. Climate, mild winters and pleasant summers. Soil, the greater part ashy, thin, and wet, with a small tract of bottom loam.

STATISTICS OF INDIAN TRIBES, AGENCIES, AND SCHOOLS. 91

Girls' building.—Character, two-story frame, of dressed clapboards, ceiled. Main building 82 by 30 feet, with two additions 36 by 60 and 30 by 24 feet. Use, dormitories, dining room, kitchen, and sitting room for girls. Capacity, 65 pupils. Erected in 1892. Cost, $3,661. Present value, $3,500. Present condition, good.

Small boys' building.—Character, two-story frame, of dressed clapboards, lathed and plastered. Main building 45 by 24 feet, with addition 40 by 20 feet. Use, dormitories, sewing room, and sitting room. Capacity, 35 pupils. Erected in 1895. Cost, $1,800. Present value, $1,700. Present condition, good.

Large boys' building.—Character, two-story frame, of dressed clapboards, ceiled, Use, dormitory and sitting room. Capacity, 30 pupils. Erected in 1895. Cost. $1,700. Present value, $1,200. Present condition, fair.

Schoolhouse.—Character, one-story frame, lathed and plastered, 3 rooms. Main building, 68 by 37 feet; addition, 31 by 29 feet. Use, 2 class rooms and 1 assembly and class room combined. Capacity, 130 pupils. Erected in 1895. Cost, $4,250. Present value, $4,000. Present condition, excellent.

Employees' quarters.—Character, two-story frame, dressed clapboards, lathed and plastered. Use, agency and school offices and school employees' quarters. Erected in 1892. Cost, $2,525. Present value, $2,000. Present condition, good.

Agents' residence (brought from old Quapaw agency).—Character, two-story frame, dressed clapboards, lathed and plastered. Use, employees' mess dining room, kitchen and employees' quarters. Erected in 1878. Cost, $4,000. Present value, $3,500. Present condition, excellent. (NOTE.—Moved from old agency site in 1901 to school, and reconstructed, replastered, etc., at cost of $900.)

Laundry.—Character, two-story frame of dressed clapboards. Use, laundry purposes. Erected in 1892. Cost, $1,224. Present value, $800. Present condition, fair.

Farmer's house.—Character, one story, two-room frame boxed house. Erected in 1892. Cost, $190. Present value, $125. Present condition, good.

Superintendent's cottage.—Character, one-story frame, dressed clapboards, lathed and plastered. Erected in 1901-2. Cost, $1,400. Present value, $1,400. Present condition, excellent.

Bath house.—Character, one-story frame, dressed clapboards, ceiled, 30 by 20 feet. Use, bakery. Erected in 1892. Cost, $800. Present value, $400. Present condition, fair.

Carpenter shop.—Character, one-story frame, clapboards, 45 by 17 feet. Erected in 1892. Cost, $250. Present value, $150. Present condition, poor.

Barn.—Character, 1½-story frame. Main building, 60 by 32 feet; two wings each, 60 by 14 feet. Use, housing live stock and storing feed and hay. Erected in 1893. Cost, $1,500. Present value, $1,300. Present condition, good. Capacity, 10 horses, 6 milch cows, 35 tons hay, 600 bushels feed.

Warehouse.—Character, one-story frame, dressed clapboards, ceiled. Use, storing clothing and supplies. Dimensions, 40 by 16 feet. Erected in 1892. Cost, $425. Present value, $400. Present condition, good.

Fruit house and cellar.—Character, one-story frame, dressed clapboards. Use, storing groceries and subsistence. Dimensions, 30 by 20 feet. Erected in 1892. Cost, $333. Present value, $200. Present condition, fair.

Buildings lighted by kerosene-oil lamps, and heated throughout by box stoves in which wood is used as fuel. Ventilation of schoolrooms and dormitories is by system devised by Indian Office. Other buildings have no modern system.

Water supply is furnished from a basin formed by enlarging the basin of a natural spring. Good, pure water; but the supply is insufficient, since the tank can not be filled from the basin. Barely enough is supplied for domestic purposes, with none for protection from fire. Location is well adapted for good sewerage, but the system is not perfect; condition, fair. Tub and ring bath system in each of the dormitory buildings, but lack of space in these buildings makes the system inconvenient, it having been necessary to use what should have been dormitory space for bathrooms. Fire hydrants are in the yards, with fire hose. Fire buckets are placed in the halls and dormitories; but the supply of water is inadequate and does not furnish the protection that it should. There are no fire hose in any of the buildings.

School farm contains 160 acres; 40 acres good hay land, 60 acres fair farming land, 20 acres pasture, 5 acres garden, 25 acres good farming land, and 10 acres timber and school grounds. Reserved for school purposes from Wyandotte Reserve. Estimated value, $5,000. One hundred and sixty acres under fence; 70 acres in cultivation; 20 acres in pasture.

This school began in 1871 or 1872 as a mission school under the patronage of the Friends or Quakers. For a time it received a partial support from the Government, and finally the Friends withdrew their support and it became wholly a Government institution. When the allotment of lands in severalty took place, 160 acres of land was reserved for school purposes, confirming the occupancy of land that had been set aside by the Wyandotte tribe of Indians.

ROSEBUD AGENCY, S. DAK.

Tribes.	Population.
Brule Sioux	
Loafer Sioux	
Waziaziah Sioux	4,923
Two Kettle Sioux	
Northern Sioux	

Area:	Acres.
Allotted	972,059.52
Unallotted	2,256,100.00

Railroad station: Valentine, Nebr., on Fremont, Elkhorn and Missouri Valley Railroad. Thirty-five miles to agency.
Nearest military post: Fort Niobrara, Nebr. Post-office address: Rosebud, S. Dak. Telegraphic address: Rosebud, S. Dak., via Valentine, Nebr.

Rosebud Agency School.

Located 12 miles east and 5 miles north of Rosebud Agency, and 30 miles north of Valentine, on the Fremont, Elkhorn and Missouri Valley Railroad. An ideal site for a school. It is situated on the table-land on the north bank of Antelope Creek. There is natural drainage to the north, east, and south. On the north is a ridge of low hills, while a fine view is had to the south and east. The climate is delightful, but subject to sudden extreme changes in temperature. Soil on the creek is sandy, mixed with loam. On the table-land a rich, dark loam, with just enough sand to make it productive.

Girls' home.—Character, two-story brick, with basement. Use, dormitories, reception room, sitting rooms, hospital for girls, employees' quarters, and a basement for play room and trunk rooms. Capacity, 100 pupils. Erected in 1897. Cost, $9,910. Present value, $9,910. Present condition, excellent.

Boys' home.—Character, two-story brick with basement; basement one-half above ground. Use, dormitories, sitting rooms, dispensary, hospital for boys, employees' quarters, and the basement for play rooms. Capacity, 100 pupils. Erected in 1897. Cost, $9,910. Present value, $9,910. Present condition, good.

School and assembly rooms.—Character, two-story brick with basement. Basement one-half above ground. Use, class rooms, assembly hall, sewing room, and the basement for a storeroom. Capacity, 200 pupils. Erected in 1897. Cost, $11,060. Present value, $11,060. Present condition, good.

Kitchen and dining room.—Character, one-story brick with cellar. Use, kitchen and dining room, the cellar to store vegetables and coal, two employees' rooms over the kitchen. Capacity, 168 in dining room. Erected in 1897. Cost, $4,055. Present value, $4,055. Present condition, good.

Two employees' cottages.—Character, 1½-story brick. Use, superintendent's cottage, employees' quarters, and employees' mess kitchen and dining room. Capacity, 10 employees. Erected in 1897. Cost, $3,880 each. Present value, $3,880 each. Present condition, good.

Warehouse.—Character, one-story brick. Use, storing supplies. Dimensions, 21 by 61 feet. Erected in 1897. Cost, $1,150. Present value, $1,150. Present condition, excellent.

Boiler house.—Character, two-story with two ells, all of brick. Use, the back part is used for boiler and dynamo, the main part is used for laundry and drying room, and the basement to store coal. Erected in 1897. Cost, $4,575. Present value, $4,575. Present condition, good.

Workshops.—Character, one-story brick, 22 by 104 feet. Use, blacksmith, carpenter, shoe, and harness shops. Capacity, 20 boys. Erected in 1897. Cost, $1,985. Present value, $1,985. Present condition, good.

Ice house.—Character, one-story frame, veneered with brick. Use, ice house, bake shop, cold storage for meat and butter, and tool room. Dimensions, 31 by 61 feet. Erected in 1898. Cost, $950. Present value, $950. Present condition, good.

Barn.—Character, two-story brick with basement. Use, storing hay and housing live stock. Capacity, 18 horses and 24 cows and 42 tons of hay. Erected in 1897. Cost, $3,840. Present value, $3,840. Present condition, good.

New barn.—Character, frame, 24 by 75 feet, with 14-foot posts. Use, housing live stock and storing hay. Capacity, 60 cows and 34 tons of hay. Erected in 1901. Cost, $900. Present value, $900. Present condition, excellent.

Piggery.—Character, one-story frame. Use, housing pigs. Dimensions, 16 by 32 feet. Erected in 1898. Cost, $450. Present value, $450. Present condition, good.

STATISTICS OF INDIAN TRIBES, AGENCIES, AND SCHOOLS. 93

Poultry house.—Character, one-story frame. Use, housing poultry. Dimensions, 16 by 40 feet, with 8-foot posts. Erected in 1898. Cost, $400. Present value, $400. Present condition, good.

Slaughterhouse.—Character, frame. Use, slaughtering beef. Dimensions, 16 by 20 feet, with 12-foot posts. Erected in 1897. Cost, $500. Present value, $500. Present condition, good.

Pump house.—Character, one-story brick, with ell. Use, to house boiler and pump. Dimensions, 33 by 14 feet; ell, 12 by 14 feet. Erected in 1897. Cost, $560. Present value, $560. Present condition, good.

Lighted by electricity furnished by a dynamo in the boiler house. There are 200 incandescent lights of 16 candlepower and 2 arc lights. The plant was installed at a cost of $9,262. It is in good condition. The whole plant is heated by steam from the boiler house. The steam plant was also put in at a cost of $9,262. It has not always given the best of satisfaction. The ventilation of the school and dormitories is the system devised by the Indian Office. It is entirely satisfactory. The other buildings have no modern system.

The water supply is ample and from a good, pure, spring brook. It is filtered and pumped to a standpipe 60 feet high, which stands on a slight elevation above the school buildings. The capacity of this pipe is 50,700 gallons. The water is carried to all the main buildings. This system was put in at a cost of $4,000. Since then the water supply has been extended to the barns. The buildings are connected with the main sewer with a 4-inch pipe except the outside buildings. The main sewer pipe is 10 inches and leads off about 160 rods from the building and empties into the creek below our water supply. The sewer has about 30 feet fall. There are 10 ring baths, and under each is a tub of homemake in each of the homes. They are supplied with both hot and cold water. Each cottage is supplied with two bath tubs, with both hot and cold water.

There are two standpipes in each home, on either side of the hall, and a hose connected ready for use. These pipe are connected with the mains. Fire hydrants are placed at convenient points, and a fire hose is attached. In case of fire water is used from the standpipe till it can be pumped direct into the mains.

This school has 6,600 acres of good land in its reserve, all of which it expects to use in the near future. The value is about $24,000. About 60 acres are under cultivation; 200 acres additional can be irrigated and cultivated; 2,760 acres are not fenced. A fire guard extends around all that is fenced.

This school was opened in 1897, with an enrollment of 177 pupils. The capacity is 200 pupils.

Little White River Day School.

Located 37 miles north of the agency on Little White River. Site favorably situated for school purposes. Climate, subject to extreme changes in temperature. The soil is a white sand overlying a stratum of gravel.

Schoolhouse and teacher's residence.—Character, one-story frame. Use, school and employees' quarters. Capacity, 30 pupils. Erected in 1885. Cost, $800. Present value, $800. Present condition, good.

Carpenter and blacksmith shop.—Character, one-story frame. Use, general workshop. Capacity, 7 boys. Erected in 1887. Cost, $150. Present value, $100. Present condition, good.

Barn.—Character, one-story log. Use, housing live stock. Capacity, 4 horses. Erected in 1892. Cost, $15. Present value, $10. Present condition, poor.

Lighted by kerosene lamps and heated by wood stoves. Ventilation of schoolroom is secured through two ventilating shafts at one end of the room and a register under the stove through which the fresh air enters the room. Water supply obtained from the river, carried by hand. Sewage refuse carried 200 feet from the house, and in no way affects water or health. Bathing facilities, washtubs and basins. Fire protection, water buckets, etc.

There has been allotted 40 acres of land for use at this school; 40 acres under fence; 5 acres under cultivation; 34 acres in pasture. None of the land is irrigated.

This school was opened in 1885 with an enrollment of about 25 pupils.

Ring Thunder Day School.

Located 13½ miles north of Rosebud, S. Dak. Site good; well drained and healthful. Climate, dry, healthful, but subject to sudden and extreme changes. Soil is a black, sandy loam on a substratum of white sand.

Schoolhouse and employees' cottage.—Owned by missionary society of Protestant Episcopal Church. Character, one-story frame. Use, class room, sewing room, and employees' quarters. Capacity, 29 pupils, sewing room and 3 dwelling rooms. Erected in 1885. Present condition, school and sewing room, poor; quarters, excellent.

Lighted by coal-oil lamps and heated by wood stoves. Ventilation, no system provided. The water supply is pure and almost soft. Its source is a spring located at the foot of a hill 200 yards east and 60 feet below the schoolhouse. The water from the spring is conducted by pipes into a trough, from whence it flows into a reservoir for irrigation and ice. Natural drainage employed. Bathing facilities, none provided. Fire protection, water buckets, hand grenades, and ladder.

This school has 50 acres of good, level upland, 40 acres having been set aside for the Protestant Episcopal Church, with 10 acres additional for the school to include the spring. Thirty acres under fence; 4 acres under cultivation; 30 acres additional can be cultivated; 25 acres in pasture; one-fourth acre irrigated.

This school was opened in 1885.

Spring Creek Day School.

Located 17 miles southwest of agency. Site fair. The school buildings are located down near the creek on a bench of less than 1½ acres. Soil, light, sandy. Climate, dry, with extreme changes.

Schoolhouse and teacher's dwelling house.—Character, one-story frame. Use, school and living rooms for teachers. Capacity, 29 pupils. Erected in 1893. Cost, $1,200. Present value, $1,000. Condition, good.

Carpenter and blacksmith shop.—Character, one-story frame. Use, workshop and storeroom. Dimensions, 16 by 20 feet. Erected in 1895. Cost, $75. Present value, $60. Condition, good.

Barn.—Character, frame. Use, housing stock. Capacity, 2 horses and 2 cows. Erected in 1893. Cost, $50. Present value, $40. Condition, good.

Lighted by kerosene lamps and heated by wood stoves. Ventilated through open windows. Water supply, a good well near the house. Sewerage, natural drainage. Bathing facilities, washtubs. Fire protection, water pails.

Number of acres under fence, 40. Number of acres under cultivation, 1. No additional land can be cultivated. Number of acres in pasture, 40. None of the land at this school can be irrigated.

This school was opened in 1893 with an enrollment of 32 pupils.

Red Leaf Camp Day School.

Located 25 miles northwest of Rosebud Agency, S. Dak. Climate, subject to extreme changes. Soil, sandy; clay subsoil on hilly portions.

Schoolhouse and cottage.—Character, one-story frame. Use, school and sewing room and teacher's dwelling. Capacity, 25 pupils. Erected in 1866. Cost, $1,250. Present value, $1,000. Present condition, good.

Workshop.—Character, one-story frame. Use, carpenter shop and storeroom. Capacity, 4 pupils. Erected in 1886. Cost, $75. Present value, $30. Present condition, poor.

Lighted by kerosene lamps and heated by wood-burning stove. Ventilated by cold-air shaft under stove and warm-air exit near ceiling connecting with flues leading to ventilator on the roof. Water supply derived from creek, spring, and well. The school is also supplied with a cistern, but it is not in use. Sewerage, natural drainage. Bathing facilities, washtubs and basins. Fire protection, water pails.

This school has 40 acres allotted for its use, the present value of which is estimated at $100. Forty acres under fence; 2 acres under cultivation; 5 additional acres can be cultivated; 38 acres pasturage. None of the land is irrigated.

This school was opened in 1886 with an enrollment of 31 pupils.

Whirlwind Soldier Day School.

Located on Oak Creek, 4 miles south of White River, 52 miles northeast of agency, and about 55 miles south of Pierre. Climate is healthful, but subject to extreme changes of temperature. Soil is a black prairie loam overlying a stratum of yellow clay.

Schoolhouse and teacher's residence.—Character, one-story frame. Use, schoolroom, sewing room, and employees' dwelling. Capacity, 30 pupils and 2 employees. Erected in 1893. Cost, $2,500. Present value, $2,000. Present condition, excellent.

Barn.—Character, one-story frame. Use, housing live stock. Capacity, 4 head of stock. Erected in 1893. Cost, $125. Present value, $100. Present condition, excellent.

Workshop.—Character, one-story frame, 16 by 20 feet. Use, workshop, tool room, and lumber shed. Capacity, 5 pupils. Erected in 1893. Cost, $125. Present value, $100. Present condition, good.

Outhouses.—Character, frame. Use, water-closets, etc. Erected in 1896–1899. Cost, $25. Present value, $20. Present condition, fair to excellent.

Lighted by kerosene lamps and heated by wood stoves. Ventilation is secured by 4-inch strips under windows and lowering upper sashes in winter, and by windows in summer.

Water supply is abundant and of fine quality. The cistern affords plenty for drinking and cooking, and a dam was built by the schoolboys that forms a reservoir in which is stored the water from a distant spring, the stream of which flows for a part of the year past the school. This reservoir affords more than is needed for bathing, scrubbing, etc., and plenty for irrigation. The water is raised from the reservoir to the table-land by means of a cistern pump attached to a home-made windmill of good efficiency constructed here by the schoolboys. Sewerage, natural drainage. Necessary bathing is accomplished by means of washtubs and a wash boiler. Protection from fire is afforded by a barrel of water standing constantly in the house and by the easy accessibility of a cistern near the house.

The school farm contains 40 acres; 13 acres are in creek bottom. Value of farm; estimated at about $300. Twenty-five acres under fence; 1½ acres under cultivation; about 12 additional acres can be cultivated; 18 acres are used for pasturage. About one-half acre has been irrigated, and 1-acre more will soon be irrigated.

This school was opened in 1894 with an enrollment of 25 pupils.

Corn Creek Day School.

Located about 37 miles northwest of agency, at the junction of Corn Creek with Black Pipe Creek. The site is fairly well suited for school purposes. Climate, subject to extreme changes in temperature, and usually dry. The soil is sandy, on a substratum of gravel. Subsoil in some parts is alkali clay.

Schoolroom and teacher's residence.—Character, one-story frame. Use, schoolroom, industrial room, and teacher's residence. Capacity, 23 pupils. Erected in 1885. Cost, $800. Present value, estimated at $800. Present condition, good.

Workshop.—Character, one-story frame. Use, general repair shop. Capacity, 5 boys. Erected in 1899. Cost, $150. Present value, $125. Present condition, good.

Outbuilding.—Character, frame. Use, water-closet. Erected in 1898. Cost, $20. Present value, $10. Present condition, fair.

Lighted by kerosene lamps and heated by wood stoves. Ventilation of schoolroom is by direct draft, by ingress through a ventilator in the floor and by egress through air shafts at one end of the room. There is no water at the school suitable for house use. A spring about 1 mile from the school affords a limited supply of water. Sewerage, natural drainage. Bathing facilities, washtubs and basins. Fire protection, hand grenades and pails.

There are 40 acres of land reserved for the use of the school. There are about 35 acres under fence; about 1 acre under cultivation; no more is suitable for cultivation. About 30 acres are used for pasturage. No land is irrigated.

This school was opened in 1886 with an enrollment of 29 pupils.

White Thunder Day School.

Located 25 miles northeast of Rosebud and 45 miles north of Valentine, Nebr., on the Fremont, Elkhorn and Missouri Valley Railroad. Site very well suited for day-school purposes. Climate, subject to extreme changes of temperature. Soil of immediate site, sandy loam with a substratum of clay and gravel.

School building and teacher's residence.—Character, one-story frame. Use, schoolroom, sewing room, and living room. Capacity, 27 pupils and 2 employees. Erected in 1885. Cost, $2,000. Present value, $1,500. Present condition, fair.

Workshop.—Character, one-story frame, 16 by 20 feet. Use, general workshop. Capacity, 7 boys. Erected in 1898. Cost, $100. Present value, $75. Present condition, fair.

Miscellaneous outbuildings.—Character, all frame. Use, henhouse, woodhouse, stable, etc. Capacity, 3 animals. Erected in 1897–1901. Cost, $35. Present value, $25. Present condition, fair.

Lighted by kerosene lamps and heated by wood stoves. Ventilation of schoolroom is by means of ventilator in the floor and an air shaft. The water supply is of fair quality; the source is from wells and a cistern near the house. The means of procuring it is by buckets and hand pump. There is no sewerage system except surface drainage, but as the buildings stand on high ground the drainage is good.

The bathing is done in common washtubs. The only fire protection is by means of water pails.

The school occupies 40 acres of an Indian allotment, 8 or 10 acres of which are suitable for farming. Of this amount about 5 acres could be irrigated, and a dam has just been constructed with that end in view. There are at present about 2 acres under cultivation.

This school was opened in 1885 with an enrollment of 27 pupils.

Pine Creek Day School.

Located on Little White River, 28 miles northeast of Rosebud Agency. Site very favorable for school purposes. Climate subject to extremes of temperature.

Schoolhouse and teacher's residence.—Character, one-story frame. Use, schoolroom, industrial room, and teacher's residence. Capacity, 22 pupils. Erected in 1886. Cost, $800. Present value, $800. Present condition, excellent.

Workshop.—Character, one-story frame. Use, blacksmith and carpenter shops. Capacity, 10 pupils. Erected in 1896. Cost, $200. Present value, $150. Present condition, good.

Barn.—Character, one-story frame. Use, housing live stock. Capacity, 4 horses. Erected in 1901. Cost, $40. Present value, $40. Present condition, good.

Lighted by kerosene lamps, heated by wood stoves, and ventilated through open windows. Water is supplied by a river and cistern. Sewerage is the natural drainage of surrounding country. The only bathing facilities are common washtubs. Water pails afford fire protection.

This school has 40 acres of valley land which was allotted to the school for its use. Present value estimated at $80. There are 40 acres under fence. About 4 acres are under cultivation. The entire 40 acres can be cultivated. About 30 acres in pasture. No land irrigated.

This school was opened in 1886 with an enrollment of about 20 pupils.

Butte Creek Day School.

Located 35 miles northeast of Rosebud. The site is well suited for the location of the school. The climate is subject to sudden extreme changes of temperature. The soil is a black prairie loam with a substratum of clay.

Schoolhouse and teacher's residence.—Character, one-story frame. Use, school and teacher's quarters. Capacity, 29 pupils. Erected in 1894. Cost, $2,500. Present value, $2,000. Present condition, good.

Workshop.—Character, one-story frame. Use, carpenter shop and storage room. Capacity, 4 pupils. Erected in 1894. Cost, $250. Present value, $200. Present condition, good.

Outbuildings.—Character, all frame. Use, stable for stock and closet. Capacity, 4 head of stock. Erected in 1890 and 1898. Cost, $35. Present value, $25. Present condition, good.

Lighted by kerosene lamps and heated by wood stoves. Ventilated by means of windows and doors. Water supply, very poor. No water obtainable on school premises. Rain water is carried from the roof of building into two cisterns. Well water has to be hauled 3½ miles and is not very good. Sewerage, natural drainage. Bathing facilities, washtubs and basins. Fire protection, practically none.

There are about 25 acres under fence; about 1 acre under cultivation; 5 additional acres can be cultivated. There are about 20 acres in pasture. No land is irrigated.

This school was opened in 1894 with an enrollment of about 30 pupils.

Little Crow's Camp School.

Located 40 miles northeast of Rosebud Agency, 60 miles north of Valentine, Nebr., and 75 miles southwest of Chamberlain, S. Dak. Site admirably suited for school purposes. Climate has some extreme changes. Soil is deep, rich, black prairie loam.

School building and cottage.—Character, one-story frame. Use, school and teacher's living rooms. Capacity, 28 pupils, 2 employees. Erected in 1894. Cost, $2,000. Present value, $1,900. Present condition, excellent.

Barn.—Character, one-story frame. Use, housing horses. Capacity, 4 horses. Erected in 1894. Cost, $100. Present value, $80. Present condition, good.

Workshop.—Character, one-story frame 18 by 36 feet. Use, blacksmith and carpenter shops. Capacity, 10 pupils. Erected in 1896. Cost, $125. Present value, $100. Present condition, excellent.

STATISTICS OF INDIAN TRIBES, AGENCIES, AND SCHOOLS. 97

Miscellaneous outbuildings.—Character, all frame and sod. Use, henhouse, outhouses, etc. Erected in 1894-1898. Cost, $25. Present value, $15. Present condition, good.

Lighted by kerosene lamps and heated by wood stoves. Ventilated through open windows. The water supplied is pure and soft. Its source is a good spring located about 400 yards southwest of schoolhouse. We also have a good cistern with a capacity of about 100 barrels. Sewerage, natural drainage. Bathing facilities, washtubs and basins. For fire protection water pails filled with water are kept in the school and other rooms.

This school has 40 acres of fine land allotted for its use, all under fence, the estimated value of which is about $100. About 10 acres under cultivation; 20 additional acres can be cultivated; 30 acres are used for pasturage.

This school was opened January 14, 1895, with an enrollment of 16 pupils.

Oak Creek Day School.

Located 30 miles northeast of Rosebud and 45 miles north of Valentine, Nebr. Site is on a small creek surrounded by Indian huts. The climate is mild but subject to high winds and extremes of temperature.

School and teacher's dwelling.—Character, one-story frame. Use, school and sewing room and teacher's living room. Capacity, 30 pupils and 2 employees. Erected in 1884. Cost, about $1,000. Present value, $700. Present condition, good.

Workshop.—Character, one-story frame. Use, carpenter shop and buggy shed. Capacity, 6 pupils. Erected, about 1884. Cost, $100. Present value, $80. Present condition, good.

Outbuildings.—Character, frame and sod. Use, cellar, closet, stable, and henhouse. Erected in 1884-1901. Cost, $50. Present value, $35. Present condition, good.

Lighted by kerosene lamps and heated by wood stoves. Ventilation, by windows. Water supply, a 20-foot well and a 100-barrel cistern, both within 10 feet of the house. The well water is abundant and pure and the cistern catches nearly all the water that falls from the roof. The buildings are situated on a bluff 15 feet high and the natural drainage is excellent. Bathing facilities, washtubs and basins. Fire protection, well and cistern and near-by creek.

This school has 40 acres of grazing land allotted for its use. Present value, estimated at $100. Fifteen acres under fence; 2 acres under cultivation; 15 additional acres can be cultivated; 13 acres in pasture. No irrigated land.

This day school was opened in 1884 with an enrollment of about 30 pupils.

Black Pipe Creek Day School.

Located about 30 miles northwest of Rosebud Agency.

School building and teacher's dwelling.—Character, one-story frame, ceiled. Use, school and teacher's residence. Capacity, 23 pupils, and 2 employees. Erected in 1885. Cost, $800. Present value, $750. Present condition, good.

Workshop.—Character, one-story frame. Use, carpenter and blacksmith shops. Dimensions, 16 by 34 feet. Erected in 1885. Cost, $100. Present value, $75. Present condition, good.

Barn.—Character, frame and log. Use, housing live-stock. Capacity, 2 horses, 1 cow and calf. Erected in 1886. Cost $50. Present value, $12. Present condition, poor.

Henhouse.—Character, frame. Use, chicken house. Dimensions, 11 by 13 feet. Erected in 1888. Present value, about $9. Present condition, fair.

Lighted by kerosene lamps and heated by wood stoves. In the schoolroom fresh air enters through a register under the stove and the foul air escapes in the front of the room through a ventilating shaft. A good well with common hand pump furnishes abundance of water. The water contains much alkali. Black Pipe Creek furnishes water all the year for stock. Sewerage, natural drainage. Common washtubs are used for bathing. Buckets filled with water and ladder hung at side of shop furnish fire protection.

The school farm contains 40 acres. There are only 10 acres under fence. To fence the school land would interfere with some roads, and especially with a good watering place for the Indian stock. One acre is cultivated; 10 additional acres can be cultivated; 8 acres are used for pasture. None of the land is irrigated.

This school was opened in 1885 with an enrollment of about 25 pupils.

8193—03——7

Upper Pine Creek Day School.

Located 20 miles northwest of Rosebud, at the head of Pine Creek. Site fairly well suited for school purposes. The climate is very agreeable most of the year, but is subject to extreme changes.

Teacher's dwelling and schoolhouse.—Character, one-story frame. Use, teacher's quarters, school and sewing room. Capacity, 28 pupils. Erected in 1894. Cost, $2,500. Present value, $2,000. Present condition, good.

Workshop.—Character, one-room, frame building. Use, carpenter shop and tool house. Capacity, 4 pupils. Erected in 1900. Cost, $40. Present value, $40. Present condition, excellent.

Barn.—Character, two-story frame building. Use, stable for horses and cows. Capacity, 4 head of stock. Erected in 1894. Cost, $150. Present value, $125. Present condition, excellent.

Lighted by kerosene lamps and heated by wood stoves. Ventilated through open windows. Water supply is very poor. The well is dry about half the year and the creek is nearly always dry. The water is impregnated with alkali and the stock will not drink it until they are starved to it. The house has waterspouts about one-third the way around that carries enough water into the cistern to furnish drinking water most of the time. The rest of the water is hauled from a distance of 8 miles. The buildings are all situated on a gentle slope and are well drained. We have poor facilities for bathing. The water supply is scarce and the bathing is done in washtubs in the schoolroom. The fire protection is poor. We have regular fire drills, but on account of scarcity of water we are poorly protected from fire.

This school has a 40-acre allotment. Its present value is $200. There are 40 acres under fence and 1 acre under cultivation. No more land could be cultivated. There are 35 acres in pasturage. No land is irrigated.

This school was opened December 20, 1894, with an enrollment of 21 pupils.

Ironwood Creek Day School.

Located 8 miles west of Rosebud Agency. Site well suited for school purposes. Climate is one of extreme changes and very dry. Soil is black sand on a subsoil of quicksand.

School building.—Character, one-story frame. Use, schoolroom, girls' industrial room, and employees' living room. Capacity, 30 pupils. Erected in 1893. Cost, $1,300. Present value, $1,000. Present condition, excellent.

Workshop.—Character, one-story frame, 16 by 20 feet, with 12 by 16 feet addition. Use, carpenter shop, blacksmith shop, and warehouse. Capacity, 15 pupils. Erected in 1893. Cost, $125. Present value, $100. Present condition, good.

Miscellaneous outbuildings.—Character, made of logs and frame. Use, barn, wood shed, cellar, spring house, etc. Capacity, sufficient for the required needs. Erected all in 1900–1901. Cost, about $15. Present value, $15. Present condition, excellent.

Lighted by kerosene lamps and heated by wood stoves. Ventilation, 2 air shafts. Water supply, good, pure well water within 15 feet of kitchen door. Sewerage, natural drainage. Bathing facilities, washtubs. Fire protection, water pails.

This school has 40 acres allotted to its use by the Government. Its present value is estimated to be about $100. There are 40 acres under fence and 3 acres under cultivation. About 20 additional acres can be cultivated. There are about 34 acres in pasturage. One-half acre is subirrigated.

This school was opened in 1893 with an enrollment of about 30 pupils.

Lower Cut Meat Creek Day School.

Located 15 miles west of Rosebud Agency on a creek of the same name, and 50 miles from a railroad. Site fairly well suited for school purposes. Climate extremely changeable. School has 1 acre of irrigated land—very rich creek bottom (alluvial composition).

School and dwelling house.—Character, one-story frame, ceiled inside. Use, schoolroom, sewing room, and teacher's living rooms. Capacity, 28 pupils. Erected in 1891. Cost, $2,500. Present value, $1,000. Present condition, good.

Workshop.—Character, one-story frame, 16 by 20 feet, with 12 by 16-foot addition. Use, blacksmith and carpenter shops. Capacity, 7 boys. Erected in 1896. Cost, $250. Present value, $200. Present condition, excellent.

Barn.—Character, one-story frame. Use, 2 horses and 2 cows housed. Capacity, 5 head of stock. Erected in 1892. Cost, $50. Present value, $40. Present condition, fair.

STATISTICS OF INDIAN TRIBES, AGENCIES, AND SCHOOLS. 99

Miscellaneous outbuildings.—Character, all frame. Use, water-closets. Erected in 1895-96. Cost, $30. Present value, $20. Present condition, fair.

Lighted by kerosene lamps. Heated by stoves, using wood for fuel. Ventilation is secured through windows. Water supply is from the well, located about 150 yards from the house, and a cistern about 10 feet from the kitchen door. Sewerage, natural drainage. Bathing facilities, washtubs, using water from the well or cistern. Fire protection, water pails.

There are 40 acres allowed for school purposes, estimated at about $2.50 per acre, all under fence. There are 5 acres under cultivation; no more can be cultivated. Thirty-five acres are in pasture.

This school has been running since 1891. It was opened with an enrollment of 33 pupils.

Big White River Day School.

Located about 70 miles northeast of agency, on the south side of Big White River. Soil, sand. Climate subject to extreme changes in temperature.

School building.—Character, one-story frame, 3 rooms. Use, schoolroom, sewing room, and small storeroom. Capacity, 30 pupils. Erected in 1897-98. Cost, $2,500 (for school building and residence). Present value, $2,500. Present condition, good.

Teacher's residence.—Character, one-story frame, 4 rooms. Use, teacher's living rooms. Capacity, teacher's family. Erected in 1897-98. Cost, $2,500 (for school building and residence. Present value, $2,000. Present condition, good.

Outbuilding.—Character, frame. Use, water-closet. Capacity, 2. Erected in 1899. Cost, $30. Present value, $30. Present condition, good.

Workshop.—Character, frame. Use, carpenter and blacksmith shop. Capacity, 7 pupils. Erected in 1899. Cost, $175. Present value, $175. Present condition, good.

Stable of logs, built by teacher at no expense to the Government.

Lighted by kerosene lamps and heated by wood stoves. Ventilation through windows. Cistern and well; also Big White River about 40 yards from school. Sewerage, natural drainage. Bathing facilities, washtubs and basins. Fire protection, water buckets.

This school has 40 acres allotted for its use, all under fence. One acre under cultivation; no more land can be cultivated. Thirty-five acres in pasture. No land is irrigated.

This school was opened in September, 1899, with an enrollment of 32 pupils.

Upper Cut Meat Day School

Located 16 miles northwest of Rosebud on Cut Meat Creek. Site well suited for school purposes. Soil of immediate site, sand overlying a substratum of clay. Climate subject to extremes in temperature.

School building and teacher's residence.—Character, one-story frame. Use, for school purposes and teacher's quarters. Capacity, 28 pupils. Erected in 1892. Cost, $2,500. Present value, $2,000. Present condition, good.

Workshop.—Character, one-story frame. Use, carpenter shop. Capacity, 4 pupils. Erected in 1894. Cost, $150. Present value, $125. Present condition, good.

Miscellaneous outbuildings.—Character, all frame. Use, ice house, hen house, and cattle shed, etc. Capacity, of stable, 4 head of cattle. Erected, 1891 to 1901. Cost, $50. Present value, $50. Present condition, good.

Lighted by kerosene lamps and heated by wood stoves. Ventilated through windows and doors. Water supply secured from a well, cistern, and creek. Sewerage, natural drainage. Bathing facilities, washtubs and basins. Fire protection, pails of water.

Forty acres of land has been allotted for school purposes; all under fence. About 2 acres under cultivation; about 25 more could be cultivated. Thirty-eight acres in pasture. No land is irrigated. This school was opened in 1892 with an enrollment of 34 pupils.

Milk's Camp Day School.

Located 100 miles east of the agency, on Ponca Creek. Soil is good. Climate is subject to extreme changes in temperature.

School building and teacher's residence.—Character, one-story frame. Use, school and teacher's quarters. Capacity, 30 pupils. Erected in 1891. Cost, $2,500. Present value, $2,000. Present condition, good.

Workshop.—Character, frame. Use, carpenter and blacksmith shops. Capacity, 7 pupils. Erected in 1897. Cost, $150. Present value, $125. Present condition, good.

Outbuilding.—Character, frame. Use, water-closet. Capacity, 2. Erected in 1897. Cost, $25. Present value, $20. Present condition, good.

Stable for 4 horses, of poles and hay; built by the teacher, without cost to Government.

Lighted by a kerosene lamp and heated by wood stoves. Ventilated through windows. Water is secured from a spring, which furnishes abundant supply. Sewerage is natural drainage. Bathing facilities are washtubs. Fire protection is water buckets.

This school has 40 acres on an Indian allotment, all under fence. About 1 acre under cultivation. No more additional land can be cultivated. Thirty-five acres in pasture. No land irrigated.

This school was opened in 1891 with an enrollment of about 25 pupils.

Bull Creek Day School.

Located about 75 miles northeast of agency, on the east side of Bull Creek. Soil, "gumbo." Climate, subject to extreme changes in temperature.

School building.—Character, one-story frame, 3 rooms. Use, schoolroom, sewing room, and small storeroom. Capacity, 30 pupils. Erected in 1897–98. Cost, $2,500 (for school building and residence). Present value, $2,500. Present condition, good.

Teacher's residence.—One-story frame, 4 rooms. Use, teacher's living rooms. Capacity, teacher's family. Erected in 1897–98. Cost, $2,500 (for school building and residence). Present value, $2,500. Present condition, good.

Outbuilding.—Character, frame. Use, water-closet. Capacity, 2. Erected in 1899. Cost, $30. Present value, $30. Present condition, good.

Workshop.—Character, frame. Use, carpenter and blacksmith shops. Capacity, 7 pupils. Erected in 1899. Cost, $175. Present value, $175. Present condition, good.

Stable of stone, built by teacher at no expense to Government.

Lighted by kerosene lamps and heated by wood stoves. Ventilation through windows. Water supply, cistern, and fine spring about 150 yards from school. Sewerage, natural drainage. Bathing facilities, washtubs and basins. Fire protection, water buckets.

This school has 40 acres of an Indian allotment, all under fence. One and one-half acres under cultivation. No more land can be cultivated. Thirty-five acres in pasture. No land is irrigated.

This school was opened in September, 1899, with an enrollment of 29 pupils.

He Dog's Camp Day School.

Located 18 miles northwest of Rosebud Agency, on a branch of Cut Meat Creek. Site admirably suited for school purposes. Climate subject to sudden extreme changes in temperature. Soil is black sand overlying a stratum of clay.

School building and teacher's residence.—Character, one-story frame. Use, schoolroom, girls' industrial room, and employees' living rooms. Capacity, 29 pupils. Erected in 1893. Cost, $2,500. Present value, $2,000. Present condition, good.

Workshop.—Character, one-story frame. Use, carpenter and blacksmith shops. Capacity, 7 pupils. Erected in 1895. Cost, $150. Present value, $150. Present condition, excellent.

Buggy shed.—Character, one-story frame. Use, housing buggies, and storeroom. Dimensions, 14 by 18 feet. Erected in 1893. Cost, $25. Present value, $15. Present condition, fair.

Barn.—Character, one-story frame. Use, housing horses. Capacity, 4 horses. Erected in 1893. Cost, $50. Present value, $25. Present condition, fair.

Outbuildings.—Character, frame. Use, water-closets. Capacity, 2 each. Erected in 1895. Cost, $15 each. Present value, $10 each. Present condition, good.

Henhouse.—Character, frame. Use, housing poultry. Dimensions, 12 by 16 feet. Erected in 1896. Cost, $25. Present value, $20. Present condition, good.

Lighted by kerosene lamps and heated by wood stoves. Ventilated through windows. A well near the house furnishes an abundant supply of pure water. The house stands on a gentle slope, and the natural drainage is excellent. Bathing facilities, washtubs and basins. Fire protection, pails of water kept in house.

Forty acres of land has been allotted for school purposes, all under fence. About 2½ acres under cultivation; 2 additional acres can be cultivated. Thirty acres in pasture. No land is irrigated.

This school was opened in 1893 with an enrollment of 31 pupils.

Cut Meat Day School.

Located 13 miles northeast of agency on Cut Meat Creek. Site well suited for location of school. Climate subject to extremes of temperature. Soil, sand.

School building and teachers' residence. Character, one-story frame. Use, schoolroom, industrial room, and teachers' quarters. Capacity, 30 pupils. Erected in 1885. Cost, $2,500. Present value, $2,000. Present condition, good.

Workshop.—Character, frame. Use, carpenter shop and storeroom. Capacity, 5 pupils. Erected in 1895. Cost, $150. Present value, $150. Present condition, good.

Woodshed.—Character, frame. Use, storing wood. Dimensions, 12 by 16 feet. Erected in 1900, by teacher, of refuse material. Cost, no expense to Government. Present value, $10. Present condition, fair.

Outbuilding.—Character, frame. Use, closet. Capacity, 2. Erected in 1892. Cost, $20. Present value, $10. Present condition, fair.

Lighted by kerosene lamps and heated by wood stoves. Ventilated through air shafts. A spring about 100 yards from the house furnishes an abundance of pure water. Sewerage, natural drainage. Bathing facilities, washtubs and basins. Fire protection, water pails and hand grenades.

This school stands on 40 acres of an Indian allotment, all under fence. About 2 acres under cultivation and about 4 additional acres can be cultivated. Thirty-five acres in pasture. No land is irrigated.

This school was opened in 1885, with an enrollment of about 30 pupils.

ROUND VALLEY AGENCY, CAL.

Under School Superintendent.

Tribes.	Population.
Concow	173
Little Lake and Redwood	108
Ukie and Wylackie	263
Pitt River and Nomelackie	77
Total	621

Area:	Acres.
Allotted	5,408
Unallotted	32,282
Reserved for school, mission, and cemetery	190
Reserved for agency	180

Railroad station: Ukiah, on San Francisco and Northern Pacific Railroad. Sixty-five miles to school.

Post-office address: Covelo, Cal. Telegraphic address: Covelo, via Cahto, Cal.

Round Valley School.

Located 4 miles north of Covelo, Cal. Site fair for school purposes. Climate without extreme changes. Soil adobe.

Schoolhouse.—Character, two-story frame. Use, dormitories, employees' quarters, sewing room, schoolrooms and chapel. Capacity, 63 pupils. Erected in 1892. Cost, $8,000. Present value, $8,000. Present condition, good.

Dining room, etc.—Character, two-story frame. Use, boys' dormitory, employees' quarters, dining room, and kitchen. Capacity, 62 pupils. Erected in 1900. Cost, $3,546.21. Present value, $3,546.21. Present condition, excellent.

Commissary.—Character, one-story frame. Use, storing supplies. Dimensions, 18 by 37 feet. Erected in 1893. Present value, $250. Present condition, fair.

Superintendent's dwelling.—Character, one-story frame. Use, superintendent's dwelling and office. Capacity, 1 office room, 6 dwelling rooms. Erected in 1893. Cost, $1,500. Present value, $1,200. Present condition, good.

Barn.—Character, two-story frame. Use, housing live stock and storing hay. Capacity, 13 horses, 20 cows, 100 tons hay. Erected in 1900. Cost, $898.50. Present value, $898.50. Present condition, excellent.

Tank house.—Character, one-story frame. Use, housing tank. Dimensions, 20 by 20. Erected in 1895. Cost, $57. Present value, $50. Present condition, fair.

Lighted by coal oil and heated by wood stoves. Ventilation of schoolrooms and dormitories is by the system devised by the Indian Office. Other buildings have no modern system.

The water supplied is pure and soft. Its source is a number of springs located on a mountain 1 mile north of the buildings and 900 feet higher than plant. The water from these springs is assembled into a 20,000-gallon tank, situated on the side of the mountain, 100 feet high. The pressure is ample to force the water wherever required.

None of the water is used for irrigation. Water system was installed when plant was constructed. Boys' dormitory and kitchen are connected with a 4-inch sewer pipe which empties into a small ravine about 200 feet from building; schoolhouse connected by 6-inch pipe with same. There are no bathing facilities whatever. There are standpipes in the large buildings, with hose on each floor. Water buckets in other buildings and hydrants on grounds.

This school has 180 acres under fence; nearly 110 acres under cultivation; 80 additional acres can be cultivated. Fifty acres are used for pasture, while 20 acres are worthless.

The main school building was erected in 1892 and was opened as a day school September 6, 1893, with an attendance of 50 pupils. It was continued as such until May 10, 1897, at which time it was reopened as a boarding school with an attendance of 60.

SAUK AND FOX AGENCY, IOWA.

Tribe.	Population.
Sauk and Fox of Mississippi	338

Area, 2,965 acres, unallotted.

Railroad station: Toledo, Iowa, on Toledo and Northern Iowa Railroad, and Chicago, Milwaukee and St. Paul Railway.

Nearest military post: Fort Omaha, Nebr. Post-office address: Toledo, Iowa. Telegraphic address: Toledo, Iowa.

Sauk and Fox Agency School.

Located 1 mile west of the business center of Toledo, Iowa, and three-fourths of a mile west of the depot of the Chicago and Northwestern Railroad. Site of the buildings is on high land, sloping gently to the east, the main building or dormitory standing directly in line with and on about the same elevation with the main street of Toledo, and affords an excellent view of the city and is admirably adapted for school purposes. Climate is equable, very healthful, and without sudden or extreme changes. Soil of the immediate site of the buildings, a rich loam, with clay subsoil. A beautiful grove of native timber stands immediately in the rear, to the west of the buildings, affording protection from wind and storms, and forms a magnificent background for the entire school plant when viewed from the public square of Toledo.

Dormitory or main building.—Character, two-story, pressed brick; basement, stone. Size, 159 by 80 feet. Use, boys' and girls' dormitories, assembly room, schoolroom, dining room, kitchen, sewing room, boys' parlor, girls' parlor, employees' parlor, superintendent's office, employees' rooms, lavatories, and closets. Basement is used for boiler room, coal bins, lighting plant, play rooms, and storage rooms. Capacity, 80 pupils. Erected in 1897. Cost, $19,130. Present value, $19,130. Present condition, good.

Barn.—Character, two-story frame, with stone basement. Size, 35 by 55 feet. Use, housing live stock, storing hay and grain, and room for storing farm implements when not in use. Capacity, 6 horses, 10 cows, 20 head young stock, 35 tons hay, 1,000 bushels grain, and all farm implements, wagons, etc. Erected in 1898. Cost, $1,623. Present value, $1,623. Present condition, excellent.

Warehouse and carpenter shop.—Character, two-story brick. Use, carpenter shop and warehouse. Capacity—workshop, 10 pupils; warehouse, all necessary stores. Erected in 1898. Cost, $1,100. Present value, $1,100. Present condition, excellent.

Laundry.—Character, brick; two-story. Size, 20 by 36 feet. Use, laundry purposes. Capacity, 80 pupils. Erected in 1898. Cost, $950. Present value, $950. Present condition, good.

Ice house.—Character, frame, 16 by 24 feet; one-story. Use, storing ice for school. Capacity, 30 tons. Erected in 1899. Cost, $225. Present value, $225. Present condition, excellent.

Poultry house.—Character, frame, 12 by 24 feet; one-story. Use, raising and housing poultry. Capacity, 200 fowls. Erected in 1899. Cost, $240. Present value, $240. Present condition, excellent.

Hog house.—Character, frame, 12 by 24 feet; one-story. Use, raising and housing hogs. Capacity, 25 hogs. Erected in 1899. Cost, $125. Present value, $125. Present condition, excellent.

Coal house.—Character, frame, 12 by 30 feet; one story. Use, storing coal supply. Capacity, 60 tons. Erected in 1899. Cost, $95. Present value, $95. Present condition, excellent.

Lighted by gasoline gas. Generator located in basement of the building and is of 100-light capacity. There are 100 burners in and around the buildings, including warehouse and laundry, lighting satisfactory. Plant installed when the building was erected. Dormitory heated with steam supplied from an American boiler located in the basement, and is very satisfactory. Laundry and workshop heated with hard-coal stoves. Ventilation of dormitory is effected by means of a system devised by the Indian Department or architect who erected the building. Ventilation may also be had by means of the windows, devices having been placed therein to prevent direct drafts.

The water supply is pure and abundant for all purposes, including fire protection. It is supplied from the Toledo city waterworks, the pressure of which is sufficient to afford protection from fire to every building constituting the school plant. The original source of supply is from wells constructed for the express purpose of supplying the said city with an abundant supply of good, pure water, and is conducted to the school plant by means of mains laid for that purpose. Water faucets are conveniently arranged in the different parts of the building where needed. The lavatories, bathrooms, and closets are all in the second story, very conveniently arranged for the accommodation of the pupils. The main sewer is constructed of 10-inch sewer pipe, laid in cement, and is connected with the laundry, kitchen, closets, and down spouts of the dormitory with 6-inch tile, and discharges into Deer Creek, a running stream, more than 2,000 feet from the buildings, and is very satisfactory. Four 50-foot lengths of hose are on the inside of the dormitory, two on each story, attached to the main water supply and always ready for any emergency. There are also two fire hydrants on the outside of the building, conveniently located, and a sufficiency of 2½-inch hose to reach every building constituting the school plant. There is also a deep well, equipped with windmill, cistern, and water tank, conveniently located for stock water for the stock on the school farm.

There are 70 acres of excellent land in the school farm, all of which is under fence. Forty acres of the farm is creek bottom and the remainder slopes gently to the east, and is all first-class land, being a rich dark loam. The purchase price of the farm was $70 per acre, and it is fairly worth $90 per acre, independent of the buildings. There are 44 acres under cultivation in the various crops, including garden. Additional acres that can be cultivated, 16. Acres in pasture, 11; meadow, 9; grove, 3; grounds about the buildings, including lawn, yards, etc., 3. None irrigated.

The school was nominally opened September 1, 1898, with a capacity of 80 pupils, but without one pupil. On February 1, 1899, there were 35 pupils enrolled, and at the end of the school year, June 30, 1899, there were 48 pupils enrolled. Enrollment December, 1902, 88.

SAUK AND FOX AGENCY, OKLA.

(Under School Superintendent.)

Tribes.	Population.
Sauk and Fox of Mississippi	479
Iowa	91
Mexican Kickapoo	247
Citizen Pottawatomie	1,686
Total	2,503

Area:	Acres.
Allotted	334,577.51
Reserved	1,299.72

Railroad station: Stroud, on St. Louis and San Francisco Railway. Five miles to agency.

Nearest military post: Fort Reno, Okla. Post-office address: Sac and Fox Agency, Okla. Telegraphic address: Stroud, Okla.; telephone to agency.

Sauk and Fox Agency School.

Located at Sauk and Fox Agency, Okla., 5 miles south of Stroud, Okla., on the St. Louis and San Francisco Railway. Site well suited for school purposes. Climate very warm in summer and mild in winter. Immediate site sparcely timbered rolling upland, underlain with rock that crops out frequently on slopes.

Girls' building—Character, two-story frame. Use, girls' dormitory, hospital, sitting rooms, and wash room, employees' quarters, dining rooms and kitchens. Capacity, 50 pupils and 4 employees. Erected in 1892. Cost, $7,944. Present value, $7,000. Present condition, good.

Schoolhouse.—Character, two-story frame. Use, schoolroom purposes and chapel. Capacity, 70 pupils. Erected in 1892. Cost, $4,412. Present value, $4,000. Present condition, good.

Schoolhouse.—Character, one-story brick. Use, schoolroom purposes. Capacity, 40 pupils. Cost, $1,900. Present value, $500. Present condition, good.

Boys' building.—Character, three-story brick. Use, boys' dormitories, sitting rooms, and wash room, employees' quarters, and commissary. Capacity, 40 pupils and 4 employees. Cost, $4,500. Present value, $2,000. Present condition, fair.

Additional boarding.—Character, two-story frame. Use, boys' hospital and dormitory and employees' quarters. Capacity, 10 pupils and 4 employees. Erected in 1886. Cost, $2,200. Present value, $2,000. Present condition, fair.

Barn.—Character, 1½-story frame. Use, housing live stock, feed, farming implements, etc. Capacity, 6 horses, 10 cows, 70 tons feed, and farm machinery. Cost, $1,800. Present value, $500. Present condition, fair.

Washhouse.—Character, one-story frame. Use, laundering. Capacity, 100 pupils. Erected in 1891. Cost, $700. Present value, $500. Present condition, good.

Smokehouse.—Character, one-story brick. Use, not used. Present value, nothing. Present condition, poor.

Wood shed.—Character, one-story frame. Use, carpenter shop and storage room. Capacity, 16 by 30 feet. Erected in 1891. Cost, $140. Present value, $100. Present condition, fair.

Additional boarding.—Character, one-story frame, 12 by 46 feet. Use, wash room and employee quarters. Capacity, one employee. Present value, $100. Present condition, fair.

Lighted by kerosene lamps. Heated by wood stoves. Not entirely satisfactory. No modern method of ventilation. The water is supplied from an open well. It is pumped from this to a reservoir of about 200 barrels capacity, set upon a steel tower 30 feet high, and from thence piped into the houses and to the barn and pastures. It is entirely seepage water, but is of good quality, though somewhat hard. Not sufficient for fire protection. Two lines of crocks, one from boys' building and one from girls' building, convey the waste matter, not slops, to dry ravines at some distances from the houses. Other refuse is disposed of in the open fields. Sufficient. No bathing facilities other than tubs (wash). Fire protection, none except buckets and tubs of water about the buildings. Also hand grenades.

This school has 640 acres of fairly good land in its farm that was reserved, at no cost to the Government, when the allotments were taken. Present value, about $6,400. About 100 acres of it are first-class bottom lands, partially covered with small timber, uncultivated. Forty acres of wild hay land, 70 acres of cultivated land, and the balance covered with small timber. There are 560 acres under fence; 70 acres under cultivation. Eighty acres might be added at very little expense. Four hundred acres in pasture and no irrigated land.

This school was originally a mission under the control of the Quakers. According to the report of the Commissioner of Indian Affairs it was established in 1868, being thus the fourth oldest in the service. It had an attendance of 90, the largest in its history, during 1900–1901.

SAN CARLOS AGENCY, ARIZ.

Tribes.	Population.
Coyotero Apache	
San Carlos Apache	3,178
Tonto Apache	
Mohave	
Yuma	473
Total	3,651

Area, 1,834,240 acres; unallotted.
Railroad station, San Carlos, on Gila Valley, Globe and Northern Railway.
Nearest military post, Fort Apache, Ariz. Post-office address, San Carlos, Ariz. Telegraphic address, San Carlos, Ariz.

San Carlos Agency School.

Located at San Carlos, Ariz., 1 mile south of Gila Valley, Globe and Northern Railway station. Site poorly located for school purposes. Climate, mild in winter but very hot in summer. Sandy soil where farm is; school buildings are on a rocky mesa.

STATISTICS OF INDIAN TRIBES, AGENCIES, AND SCHOOLS. 105

School building.—Character, two-story stone. Use, class rooms and dormitory. Capacity, 150 pupils. Erected in 1894. Cost, $7,696.96. Present value, $5,000. Present condition, good.

Boys' dormitory.—Character, one-story adobe. Use, dormitory. Capacity, 40 pupils. Present condition, very poor; unfit for use.

Large girls' dormitory.—Character, two-story adobe. Use, dormitory, sewing room, employees' quarters. Capacity, 40 pupils. Present condition, very poor.

Small girls' dormitory.—Character, one-story adobe. Use, dormitory. Capacity, 15 pupils. Present condition, very poor.

Laundry.—Character, one-story frame. Use, laundry. Capacity, 12 pupils. Present condition, very poor.

Mess building.—Character, one-story adobe. Use, kitchen and dining room. Capacity, 100 pupils. Present condition, very poor.

Employees' cottages.—Character, one-story adobe. Use, employees' quarters and shops. Capacity, 11 employees and 6 pupils in shops. Erected in 1894. Cost, $4,510.90. Present value, $3,000. Present condition, fair to good.

Miscellaneous outbuildings.—Character, all frame. Use, henhouse, barn, hay shed, etc. Capacity, all small. Present condition, very poor.

Lighted by kerosene-oil lamps. Heated by wood stoves. Ventilation, poor; no modern system. Water supply, pumped by steam pump into tanks; from thence by gravity pressure through pipes into buildings. Sewerage, poor; only open wooden sewers. Bathing facilities, poor; have only two good bath tubs for entire school; most of the pupils use washtubs instead. Fire protection, fair; there are hydrants in the school yard, but water pressure is not good.

This school has very little land under cultivation and it is very poor. The scarcity of water is the greatest drawback, though. Present value of school farm, about $200. There are 16 acres under fence; 8 acres under cultivation. Much more could be cultivated, but have no water for irrigating it. There are 8 acres used for pasturage and 8 acres irrigated.

This school was organized about twenty years ago with a capacity of about 50 pupils. The present enrollment is 108 pupils.

The following school, although situated on the San Carlos Reservation, is under a bonded superintendent.

Rice Station School, Rice Station, Ariz. (Talklai post-office).

Located three-fourths of a mile northwest of Rice Station, Arizona, on the Gila Valley, Globe and Northern Railway. Site admirably suited for school purposes. The climate is without extreme changes. Soil is sandy.

School building.—Character, one-story adobe; interior and exterior plastered. Use, class rooms and assembly hall. Capacity, 200 pupils. Erected in 1899. Cost, $7,820.42. Present value, $7,820.42. Present condition, good.

Girls' building.—Character, one-story adobe; interior and exterior plastered. Use, dormitory and sewing room. Capacity, 100 pupils. Erected in 1899. Cost, $12,424.665. Present value, $12,424.665. Present condition, good.

Boys' building.—Character, one-story adobe; interior and exterior plastered. Use, dormitory. Capacity, 100 pupils. Erected in 1899. Cost, $12,424.665. Present value, $12,424.665. Present condition, good.

Mess hall and kitchen.—Character, one-story adobe; interior and exterior plastered. Use, dining room, kitchen, bakery, and laundry. Capacity, 250 pupils. Erected in 1899. Cost, $10,254.85. Present value, $10,254.85. Present condition, good.

Employees' building.—Character, one-story white stone. Use, employees' quarters. Capacity, 10 employees. Erected in 1901. Cost, $7,669.35. Present value, $7,669.35. Present condition, excellent.

Warehouse.—Character, one-story white stone. Use, storing supplies and carpenter shop. Dimensions, 100 by 30 feet. Erected in 1901. Cost, $3,597.35. Present value, $3,597.35. Present condition, excellent.

Ice-plant building.—Character, one-story white stone. Use, cold-storage room for meats, vegetables, etc., and in which ice-plant machinery is installed. Dimensions, 28 by 30 feet. Erected in 1901. Cost, building, $1,498.05; ice-plant machinery, $4,000. Present value, building, $1,498.05; machinery, $4,000. Present condition, excellent.

Blacksmith shop (formerly pump house).—Character, one-story frame. Use, blacksmith shop. Dimensions, 25 by 15 feet. Erected in 1900. Cost, $125. Present value, $125. Present condition, good.

Barn and granary.—Character, one-story frame. Use, housing live stock and storing grain. Capacity, 11 horses and 200,000 pounds grain. Erected in 1900 and 1901.

Cost, barn, $1,000; granary, $250. Present value, barn, $1,000; granary, $250. Present condition, excellent and good.

Outhouses.—Character, one-story adobe, interior and exterior plastered. Use, water-closets. Erected in 1899. Cost, $1,957. Present value, $1,957. Present condition, good.

Boiler house.—Character, one-story white stone. Use, power house. Dimensions, 35 by 28 feet. Erected in 1902. Cost, $781. Present value, $781. Present condition, excellent.

Lighted by gasoline gas furnished by a gasoline-gas machine in school building. Plant was installed in 1899 at a cost of $2,008.50. It is in poor working condition. Heated by box-wood stoves. Ventilation of schoolrooms and dormitories is by the system devised by the Indian Office.

Water is supplied from a well 35 feet deep, which appears to be inexhaustible and is good for all purposes. It is forced into two tanks of 20,000 gallons capacity each, on the side of a hill 90 feet high, by a steam boiler and pump. The pressure is ample to force the water wherever required. Water system was installed in 1899 at a cost of $5,300. The buildings are connected with an 8-inch main sewer pipe which empties into the San Carlos River three-fourths of a mile from the buildings. The outfall is 22 feet. There are six ring baths and one tub in each of the dormitories for use of pupils and two tubs in employees' quarters for employees' use. Fire hydrants are situated in several places in the grounds with hose for each and drilled fire companies appointed to take charge of each hydrant and hose cart.

This school is situated on the San Carlos Reservation, and has about 150 acres of good land for its use, valued at about $15,000. In 1899 an irrigation ditch was put in at a cost of $6,500. There are 150 acres under fence; 40 acres under cultivation. Ninety-six acres additional can be cultivated. Fourteen acres are used for pasturage; 54 acres irrigated.

This school was opened December 1, 1901, with a capacity of 200 pupils.

SANTEE AGENCY, NEBR.

(Under School Superintendent.)

Tribes.	Population.
Santee Sioux of Flandreau	283
Santee Sioux	1,047
Ponca of Nebraska	232
Total	1,562

Area:	Acres.
Homesteads	32,875.75
Allotted	66,110.09
Reserved	1,290.70

Railroad station: Springfield, S. Dak., on Chicago, Milwaukee and St. Paul Railway. Three and one-half miles to agency.

Nearest military post: Fort Crook, Nebr. Post-office address: Santee Agency, Nebr. Telegraphic address: Springfield, S. Dak.

Santee Training School.

Located 3½ miles southeast of Springfield, S. Dak., across the Missouri River, at Santee Agency, Nebr., and 25 miles northwest of Bloomfield, Nebr., a station on the St. Paul, Minneapolis and Omaha Railway. The school is situated on the first bench above the Missouri River bottoms. The soil of the vicinity is sandy, and the climate is subject to sudden changes.

Dormitory and school.—Character, two-story brick, with one-story brick addition. Use, dormitories, dining room, play rooms, employees' quarters, kindergarten department, kitchen. Capacity, 80 pupils. Erected in 1898. Cost, $20,000. Present value, $20,000. Present condition, excellent.

School.—Character, one-story frame. Use, class rooms. Capacity, 51 pupils. Erected in 1891. Cost, $1,300. Present value, $800. Present condition, good.

Dwelling.—Character, one-story frame. Use, sewing room and employees' quarters. Capacity, 6 rooms. Erected in 1880; remodeled in 1900. Cost, $300. Present value, $300. Present condition, good.

Dwelling.—Character, one-story frame. Use, laborers' quarters. Capacity, 3 rooms. Erected in 1884. Cost, $225. Present value, $200. Present condition, fair.

Dormitory, girls.—Character, one-story frame. Use, warehouse. Capacity, 18 by

60 feet. Erected in 1895. Cost, $600. Present value, $600. Present condition, good.

Cook houses.—Character, one-story frame. Use, laundry and employees' mess. Dimensions, 20 by 46 and 10 by 16 feet. Erected in 1895 and 1896. Cost, $50 and $500. Present value, $25 and $250. Present condition, fair.

Stable.—Character, one-story frame. Use, housing live stock and storing hay. Capacity, 4 horses, 11 cattle, 48 tons hay. Erected in 1893. Cost, $500. Present value, $500. Present condition, good.

Miscellaneous outbuildings.—Character, two brick, others frame. Use, ice house, closets, hennery, etc. Erected in 1888–1898. Cost, $20 to $487. Present value, $5 to $487. Present condition, poor to good.

Lighted by kerosene oil lamps. Heated by steam from plant installed when the main building was erected in 1898. Dwellings and schoolhouse are heated by coal stoves. System of ventilation installed in main building. Other buildings have no system. Water supply is abundant. It is supplied from an artesian well on the school premises and distributed by direct pressure throughout the main building. The school plant being located on a terrace, the sewerage is conducted through a system of 4-inch iron pipes to the edge of the bluff overhanging the bottom lands of the Missouri River. Distance from the school buildings to the edge of the bluff is about 150 yards. Water from the artesian well flows constantly through the sewer pipes, eventually reaching the Missouri River, about 3 miles distant. Shower baths are provided for both the boys and girls. Fire hose is provided. Direct pressure from the artesian well makes it an easy matter to throw a stream of water on any of the buildings in case of fire. Fire hydrants in the grounds, and fire escapes provided for the main building.

This school has about 320 acres of land which is estimated to be worth about $4,000. There are 160 acres under fence; 15 acres are in cultivation; 130 acres are used for pasture; none of the land is irrigated.

This school was opened about 1874. No data obtainable showing the capacity of the school at that time. The attendance during the fiscal year 1901 was 126, which is thought to be the largest in the history of the school.

Ponca Day School.

Located at Ponca subagency, 5 miles from Niobrara, Nebr., a station on the Fremont, Elkhorn and Missouri Valley Railway. Site of school is a good one. Soil of vicinity is a good prairie loam. Climate subject to sudden changes.

School.—Character, one-story frame. Use, class room for pupils. Capacity, 35 pupils. Erected in 1884. Cost, $1,100. Present value, $800. Present condition, good.

Miscellaneous outbuildings.—Character, all frame. Use, coal house, etc. Erected in 1901 and 1897. Cost, $39 and $75. Present value, $39 and $75. Present condition, good.

Lighted by kerosene oil lamps. Heated by coal stove. No modern system of ventilation. Water obtained from neighboring well. No sewer system. Earth vaults for closets. No bathing facilities. No system of fire protection.

No farm.

This school was opened about 1884 with less than a dozen pupils.

The following school, formerly under the jurisdiction of Santee Agency, is now under a bonded superintendent:

Springfield Indian Training School.

Located at Springfield, S. Dak., on the Chicago, Milwaukee and St. Paul Railway on bluff overlooking the Missouri River. Winter is long, with usually three or four weeks severe weather; summer short and hot. The dryness of the atmosphere renders it a very healthful location.

Stone building.—Character, two-story and basement, stone, with 1½ story and one-story stone additions. Use, dormitory, dining room, kitchen, schoolrooms, sewing room, and storerooms. Capacity, 40 pupils and 4 employees. Erected in 1884. Cost, $12,500. Present value, $6,500. Present condition, good.

Frame building.—Character, two-story frame with one-story addition. Use, dormitory and one schoolroom. Capacity, 14 pupils and 3 employees. Erected about 1875. Cost, $2,500. Present value, $300. Present condition, fair.

Barn.—Character, one-story frame with concrete basement. Use, housing live stock and storing grain and hay. Capacity, 3 horses and 4 cows; 5 tons hay and 300 bushels grain. Erected in 1889. Cost, $250. Present value, $150. Present condition, fair.

Laundry.—Character, one-story frame. Use, school laundering. Erected in 1884 and enlarged in 1892. Cost, $500. Present value, $100. Present condition, good.

Miscellaneous outbuildings.—Character, all frame. Use, ice house, woodshed, etc. Erected in 1880–1884. Present value, $50. Present condition, poor to good.

Lighted by kerosene oil lamps. Heated by hard coal stoves. Main building has old system of ventilation; register opening into ventilating flue near floor. Cottage ventilated only through windows.

Artesian water supplied from city mains for stock and out-door purposes. For domestic purposes rain water is used, there being four large cisterns on the premises. When rain water fails the cisterns are filled by hauling water with team from the Missouri River. All sewage is thrown into an open drain through which a constant stream of artesian water flows, carrying sewage to ravine and thence to Missouri River. About 700 feet from main building to river, with fall of 80 feet, giving excellent opportunity for improved sewer system. No improved bathing facilities. Bathing done in the laundry. City fire hydrant about 350 feet from main building, 100 feet from cottage, and both buildings within three blocks of city fire department. Fire buckets in buildings and one extinguisher on place.

A contract was made in July, 1903, for an addition to the main building (brick), $10,630; laundry, $2,300; moving and converting old laundry into cottages, etc., $500; extending sewer, $900; and new water plant, $1,800.

The school premises contain about 6 acres besides a detached block in another part of the city containing 2 acres. About 3½ acres are broken up and available for gardening. Estimated value of the land attached to the school, $1,000.

This school was opened about 1880 as a mission school of the Protestant Episcopal Church, and known as Hope school. The real property of the school was leased and the equipment purchased by the Government in 1895, and the school was maintained under the name of the Hope Boarding School. In 1901 the Government purchased the real estate of the school.

SEMINOLE IN FLORIDA.

Tribe.	Population.
Seminole	358

Area, 8,960 acres; unallotted.

Steamboat landing: Myers, Fla. Forty miles southeast by private conveyance to headquarters.

Post-office address: Myers, Fla. Telegraphic address: Myers, Fla.

No school.

SHEBIT AND KAIBAB INDIANS, UTAH.

(Under Superintendent of Southern Utah School.)

Tribes.	Population.
Shewits band, Pah-utes	129
Pahranagat band, Pah-utes	53
Cedar band, Pah-utes	30
Kaibabs band, Pah-utes	185
Grass Valley band, Pah-utes	25
Rabbit Valley band, Pah-utes	100
Kanash band, Pah-utes	100
San Juan band, Pah-utes	120
Total	742

Located at St. George, Cedar City, Muddy, Panaca, Santa Clara, and vicinity. Congress has provided for these Indians as the "Shebit, Cedar City, Muddy, Panaca, and other Indians in the southern part of Utah."

Railroad station: Modena, on Utah and Pacific Railroad; thence by team 55 miles to school.

Post-office address: St. George, Utah. Telegraphic address: St. George, Utah.

Shebit Indian School, Southern Utah.

Work is carried on at the Indian farms, 13 miles from St. George, the county seat of Washington County, and 55 miles from Modena, on the Oregon Short Line Railway. The climate is semitropical and the soil excellent in the region, but water is a scarce commodity at times.

Schoolhouse.—Character, one-story stone building, unfinished, in one room, end partitioned off. Use, dormitory, dining room and kitchen, schoolroom and chapel; cellar used as storeroom. Capacity, schoolroom, 30 pupils; kitchen and dining room, about 20 pupils. Dormitory limited by floor capacity outside desks and tables. Erected in 1885. Present condition, poor.

Office.—Character, two tents, with lumber floors and walls, 4 feet and chimney between. Use, superintendent's office, drug room, and bedroom. Capacity, 14 by 18 and 12 by 14 feet. Erected in 1900. Present condition, poor; partially destroyed by fire December 31, 1901.

Boys' quarters.—Character, a wooden shack, old. Use, boys' dormitory. Capacity, size, 8 by 18 feet. Erected, moved up from old Conger house when school opened in 1898. Present condition, last stage of dilapidation.

Lighted by kerosene lamps. Heated by wood stoves. No system of ventilation needed; the winds blow right through all our buildings, carrying away all disease germs, and depositing clean sand and dust instead. Water is obtained from the irrigating ditch near by, and when the ditch breaks must be carried from the creek. A washtub or hand basin used for bathing. Tubs and barrels of water are kept always ready for use, and our bucket brigade of the schoolboys are quick and efficient workers.

There is no farm, and no land available here for the use of the school, the buildings standing on the farm of one of the Indians.

The school was opened as the Shebit Day School, independent, and continued as such until May, 1901.

The Haycock farm at Panquitch, Garfield County, Utah, has been purchased, October, 1903, and school will be moved to that point and old one abandoned.

SHOSHONI AGENCY, WYO.

Tribes.	Population.
Shoshoni (or Snake)	800
Northern Arapaho	828
Total	1,628

Area, 1,754,960 acres; unallotted.

Railroad station: Rawlins, on Union Pacific Railway. One hundred and forty-five miles to agency.

Nearest military post: Fort Washakie, Wyo. Post-office address: Shoshoni Agency, Fremont County, Wyo. Telegraphic address: Shoshoni Agency, Wyo.

Shoshoni Indian School.

Located 1½ miles east of Fort Washakie, 1½ miles northeast of agency, 15 miles northwest of Lander, and 150 miles north of Rawlins, on the Union Pacific Railroad, and 150 miles west of Casper on Fremont, Elkhorn and Missouri Valley Railroad, situated in the fertile valley of Little Wind River, on an alkali flat.

Main building.—Character, two stories with basement, brick, with one-story addition, wall of basement, stone. Use, girls' dormitory, dining room and kitchen, employees' dining room and kitchen, nine rooms for employees, sewing room, sitting room, and wash room for girls, one room for the sick, an office and a parlor, two pantries for kitchen, a reading room, and two clothes rooms, basement is used for power house, baking, one storeroom. Capacity, dormitory, 50 pupils; dining room, 160 pupils. Erected in 1892. Cost, $51,700, including boys' building and school building. Present value, probably $20,000, including boys' building and school building. Present condition, very poor.

Boys' building.—Character, two stories with basement, brick, wall of basement stone. Use, dormitory, sitting room for little boys, two rooms for employees, one clothing room, one room for the sick; the basement is used for sitting room, wash room, and clothes room. Capacity, 75 pupils. Erected in 1892. Present condition, very poor.

School building.—Character, two stories with basement. Use, class room and assembly hall, basement for supplies. Capacity, 180 pupils. Erected in 1895. Present condition, fair.

Hospital.—Character, one story, two wards, one room for nurse, one room for medicine. Use, isolation and care of the sick. Capacity, 20 pupils. Erected in 1900. Cost, $2,500. Present value, $2,500. Present condition, excellent.

Employees' cottage.—Character, 1½ stories, stone. Use, employees' quarters. Capacity, 4 employees. Erected in 1900; moved to present site. Cost, $750 for tearing down, moving, and rebuilding. Present value, $2,000. Present condition, excellent.

Workshops.—Character, one story, stone. Use, blacksmith, carpenter, shoe shop. Dimensions, 23 by 85 feet. Erected in 1899. Cost, $2,490. Present value, $2,490. Present condition, excellent.

Barn.—Character, 1½ stories, frame, 30 by 104 feet. Use, sheltering horses and cattle and storing grain and hay. Capacity, 10 horses, 16 cows, 20 calves, 50 tons hay, 800 bushels grain. Erected in 1896. Cost, $1,100. Present value, $1,000. Present condition, good.

Laundry.—Character, one-story, stone, 20 by 48 feet. Use, laundering. Capacity, 150 pupils. Erected in 1899. Cost, $1,598. Present value, $1,598. Present condition, excellent.

Miscellaneous outbuildings.—Character, log and frame. Use, hog house, henhouse, cattle sheds, root house, etc. Erected in 1892–1901. Present condition, fair.

Lighted by electricity, dynamo in the basement of main building; there are 250 incandescent lights; plant was installed June, 1899, at a cost of $2,400; engine, dynamo, and wiring in good condition and satisfactory; power boiler very poor. Heated by steam from low-pressure boiler in basement of main building which was installed when buildings were erected in 1892. To this has been added the exhaust steam from power boiler; cottage and shops are heated by coal stoves. Ventilation of schoolrooms and dormitories by adjustment of windows.

The water supplied is hard, being surface water or seepage through alkaline soils, from a well located near school building; the water is forced by steam pump into a wooden tank of 8,000-gallons capacity, elevated 40 feet on wooden trestle; water supply sufficient. Kitchen and wash rooms are connected with a 6-inch sewer pipe, which empties into an irrigating ditch 500 feet from school building. The fall in the ditch below outlet of sewer is so slight that it fills with sand during spring freshets. Bathing is done in the hot spring, 1½ miles from the school; excellent during favorable weather.

There are stand pipes in main buildings with hose connections, well supplied with fire buckets and a few chemical fire extinguishers. Fire buckets in other buildings.

This school has a very fine and productive farm of 620 acres, well watered, and very easily irrigated. The whole farm is under fence. About 120 acres under cultivation. All could be cultivated. Five hundred acres in pasturage.

In 1879 two day schools were started, one for the Shoshoni, the other for the Arapaho tribe. In 1881 a boarding school was organized at the agency. In 1892 the school was transferred to the present site.

SILETZ AGENCY, OREG.

(Under School Superintendent.)

Tribe.	Population.
Siletz	463

Area, 47,716 acres, allotted.

Railroad station: Toledo, Oreg., on Oregon Central and Eastern Railroad. Nine miles to agency.

Nearest military post: Boise Barracks, Idaho. Post-office address: Siletz, Lincoln County, Oreg. Telegraphic address: Toledo, Oreg.

Siletz Training School.

Located 9 miles north of Toledo, Oreg., on the Corvallis and Eastern Railroad; site admirably suited for school purposes; climate mild, but extremely wet; soil, volcanic ash and vegetable loam on a substratum of rock.

Boarding house.—Character, two-story frame. Use, dormitories, clothing rooms, lavatories, play rooms, and sitting rooms for boys and girls; eight employees' rooms; kitchen, dining room, and quarters for employees' mess. Capacity, 80 pupils. Erected in 1883. Cost, $4,000. Present value, $2,500. Present condition, fair.

Dining room and kitchen.—Character, two-story frame. Use, dining room and kitchen; sewing room; three rooms for employees. Capacity, 80 pupils. Erected in 1899. Cost, $4,797. Present value, $4,000. Present condition, good.

Schoolhouse.—Character, one-story frame. Use, class rooms (also used for assembly hall). Capacity, 80 pupils. Erected in 1883. Cost, $1,000. Present value, $500. Present condition, fair.

Hospital.—Character, one-story frame. Use, isolation and care of sick, and nurse's room. Capacity, 8. Erected in 1898. Cost, $2,150. Present value, $1,800. Present condition, good.

Laundry.—Character, 1½-story frame. Use, washing, ironing, drying clothes, etc. Dimensions, 18 by 32 feet. Erected in 1890. Cost, $500. Present value, $300. Present condition, fair.

Commissary.—Character, 1½-story frame. Use, storing supplies. Dimensions, 24 by 40 feet. Erected in 1894. Cost, $571. Present value, $450. Present condition, good.

Wood shed.—Character, one-story frame. Use, storing firewood. Dimensions, 24 by 60 feet. Erected in 1901. Cost, $223. Present value, $223. Present condition, excellent.

Vegetable house.—Character, one-story frame. Use, storing vegetables. Dimensions, 24 by 30 feet. Erected in 1899. Cost, $130. Present value, $100. Present condition, good.

Barn.—Character, one-story frame. Use, stabling cows and calves, and storing hay. Capacity, 20 cows and 10 calves. Erected in 1884. Cost, $250. Present value, nothing. Present condition, very poor.

Dwelling.—Character, one-story frame. Use, one employee (Indian). Cost, about $150. Present value, $50. Present condition, poor.

Henhouse.—Character, one-story frame. Use, housing of chickens. Dimensions, 14 by 18 feet. Cost, about $50. Present value, nothing. Present condition, very poor.

The plant is lighted by kerosene oil lamps. The plant is heated by wood stoves. The ventilation of dining room and kitchen and the hospital is by the system devised by the Indian Office. Other buildings have no modern system.

The water supplied is pure and soft. Its source is two springs located in the mountains about 1¼ miles east of the school site. Instead of assembling the water of these springs in a reservoir located at a lower level than the lower spring, a reservoir with an incomplete bottom was built over the lower spring under the erroneous notion that the water would rise and keep the reservoir filled, whereas it is a demonstrated fact that the water rises and falls in the reservoir in accordance with its rise or fall in the surrounding earth, as the weather is wet or dry. There is never a reservoir full of water (its capacity is about 3,500 gallons), and during the summer months the supply is inadequate to the ordinary needs of the house service of the school.

This water system affords practically no fire protection to the school plant. All the main buildings are connected with a 12-inch sewer pipe, which empties into the Siletz River about 20 rods from the buildings and far below the source of the water supply. The outflow is about 70 feet below the buildings. There are two bath tubs in the hospital building, but aside from this there are no facilities for bathing pupils, and bathing is being done in ordinary wash tubs. Water buckets, chemical fire extinguishers, and fire hose are located in buildings; the fire hydrants in grounds are of little value.

This school and agency has 184 acres of land in its reserve. Its present value is estimated to be about $1,840. It is all under fence. Nearly all of this land has been under cultivation. No irrigation is required. The greater portion of this land is chiefly valuable for hay and pasture for the subsistence of a dairy herd. A few acres can be profitably used by the school for the raising of vegetables.

This school was opened in 1878 with a capacity of 50 pupils.

SISSETON AGENCY, S. DAK.

Tribe.	Population.
Sisseton and Wahpeton Sioux	1,923

Area:	Acres.
Allotted	309,904.92
Reserved (schools)	32,840.25
Reserved (churches and agency)	1,347.01

Railroad station: Sisseton, on Chicago, Milwaukee and St. Paul Railway. Ten miles to agency.

Nearest military post: Fort Niobrara, Nebr. Post-office address: Sisseton Agency, S. Dak. Telegraphic address: Sisseton, S. Dak.

Sisseton Training School.

Located 10 miles south of Sisseton on the Chicago, Milwaukee and St. Paul Railway. Site well suited for school purposes, climate cold with frequent and extreme changes, very windy. Soil of immediate site dark loam, admirably adapted to the production of vegetables and all kinds of cereals.

Girls' building.—Character, two-story frame, with two-story addition. Use, dormitory, dinning room, and kitchen, schoolrooms, office, and employees' quarters. Capacity, 50 pupils. Erected in 1872, addition in 1888. Cost, $21,000. Present value, $6,500. Present condition, frame is good.

Boys' building.—Character, two-story frame. Use, dormitory and sitting rooms. Capacity, 50 pupils. Erected in 1872. Cost, $2,000. Present value, $600. Present condition, poor.

Bakery and laundry.—Character, two-story frame. Use, laundry and bath rooms. Dimensions, 32 by 60 feet. Erected in 1888. Cost, $1,200. Present value, $800. Present condition, good.

Carpenter shop.—Character, 1½-story frame, 26 by 40 feet. Use, carpenter shop. Capacity, 30 pupils. Erected in 1896. Cost, $436. Present value, $375. Present condition, good.

Barn.—Character, 1½-story frame, and one shed 24 by 108 feet. Use, housing live stock and storing hay. Capacity, 12 horses, 20 cows, and 15 tons of hay. Erected in 1881, 1882. Cost, $1,375. Present value, $500. Present condition, poor.

Cottage.—Character, 1½-story frame. Use, Dormitory. Capacity, 12 pupils and 1 employee. Erected in 1888. Cost, $400. Present value, $200. Present condition, poor.

Miscellaneous outbuildings.—Character, all frame. Use, henhouse, oil house, spring house, and wagon shed. Erected in 1882–1896. Cost, $440. Present value, $125. Present condition, poor.

Lighted by coal-oil lamps Main part of girls' building heated by steam, the addition and other buildings heated by coal stoves. No modern system of ventilation. Water supply, hard. Its source is a spring located about 200 feet from girls' building. Water is forced into iron tank in girls' building by means of a hydraulic ram. No system of sewerage. There are 4 bath tubs located in the laundry building for the use of the school. No fire protection.

This school has 480 acres of good land. This land was set aside by Executive order and its present value is estimated to be about $7,000. There are 320 acres under fence. Nearly 160 acres under cultivation. Nearly 160 additional acres can be cultivated; 320 acres are used for pasturage and hay.

School was established in 1872.

SOUTHERN UTE AGENCY, COLO.

(Under School Superintendent.)

Tribe.	Population.
Moache, Capote, and Wiminuchie Ute	955

Area:	Acres.
Unallotted	483,750.00
Allotted	72,810.65
Reserved	360.00

Railroad station: Ignacio, on Denver and Rio Grande Railroad. One and three-fourth miles to agency.

Nearest military post: Fort Logan, Colo. Post-office address: Ignacio, La Plata County, Colo. Telegraphic address: Ignacio, Colo.

Southern Ute School.

Located 1¾ miles north of Ignacio, Colo., on the Denver and Rio Grande Railway. The school is nicely located, climate free from extreme changes, altitude 6,300 feet. Soil of immediate site very fertile.

Dormitory.—Character, two-story brick with basement and with one-story addition with basement. Use, dormitory, dining room and kitchen, schoolrooms, bathrooms, and laundry. Capacity, 60 pupils. Erected in 1902. Present estimated value, $23,000. Present condition, excellent.

Warehouse.—Character, one-story brick. Use, storing supplies. Dimensions, 20 by 50 feet. Erected in 1902. Present estimated value, $1,700. Present condition, excellent.

Gas house.—Character, one-story frame. Use, housing gas generator and carbide. Dimensions, 22 by 14 feet. Erected in 1902. Present value, $400. Present condition, excellent.

Pump house.—Character, one-story brick. Use, engine house. Dimensions, 14 by 16 feet. Erected in 1902. Present value, $800. Present condition, excellent.

The cost of each building taken separately is unknown, but the cost of the entire plant, including water and sewer systems, is $35,500.

STATISTICS OF INDIAN TRIBES, AGENCIES, AND SCHOOLS. 113

Lighted by acetylene gas; there are 100 lights. The plant was installed when the buildings were constructed. The system is in good condition and satisfactory. Heated by steam from a low-pressure boiler, which was installed in the construction of the building. The heating system is in good condition and very satisfactory. The ventilation of dormitory is by the system devised by the Indian Office.

Water, quality excellent, quantity abundant except in midsummer. The water is pumped from the Pine River by a gasoline engine and windmill into a wooden tank of 12,600 gallons capacity, on a steel tower standing 50 feet high. The pressure is very good. The entire elevation to which the water must be raised is 110 feet above the supply, and it is a question yet to be determined whether the present gasoline engine has sufficient power to raise the water to this elevation successfully. The dormitory is connected with an 8-inch sewer pipe which empties into the Pine River about 450 yards from the building and below the water supply. The outfall of the sewer is 35 feet below the building. There are 10 ring baths and 2 tubs. They are located in the basement. There are standpipes on the first and second floors with two-inch hose attached. Fire hydrants on the outside.

This school it on the agency reserve and there are about 50 acres of very fertile land adjoining the school which can be easily irrigated. The school has not any land fenced yet. None under cultivation.

This school was opened November 19, 1902, with a capacity of 60 pupils.

STANDING ROCK AGENCY, N. DAK.

Tribes.	Population.
Yanktonai Sioux	
Hunkpapa Sioux	3,564
Blackfeet Sioux	

Area, 2,672,640 acres; unallotted.

Railroad station: Bismarck, on Northern Pacific Railway. Sixty-five miles to agency.

Nearest military post: Fort Yates, N. Dak. Post-office address: Fort Yates, Boreman County, N. Dak. Telegraphic address: Fort Yates, via Bismarck, N. Dak.

Standing Rock School.

Located at Standing Rock Agency, N. Dak., adjoining the Fort Yates military garrison, about 25 miles northwest of Pollock, S. Dak., which is now the nearest railroad point. Site well suited for school purposes. Climate dry and very healthful. Soil sandy and not very productive, on account of lack of moisture.

Main building.—Character, two-story frame, consisting of a front building and two wings. Use, dormitories for boys, dormitories for girls, employees' rooms, superintendent's rooms, class rooms, kitchen, dining room, boys' assembly rooms, girls' assembly rooms, sewing room, mess dining room, bakery, ironing room, and office. Capacity, dormitory, 136; dining room, 123; class room, 167. Erected, from 1883 to 1897, different additions. Cost, about $35,000. Present value, $20,000. Present condition fair.

Agency hospital.—Character, one-story frame, on a stone foundation. Use, for sick pupils and sick Indians. Capacity, 5 beds for male and 5 beds for female patients. Erected in 1887. Cost, $3,000. Present value, $2,000. Present condition, good.

Refrigerator.—Character, stone basement and frame. Use, storing meat, vegetables, and milk. Capacity, 8 quarters of beef and 100 bushels vegetables. Erected in 1895. Cost, about $250. Present value, none. Present condition, good, but of no utility.

Laundry.—Character, one-story frame. Use, washing clothes. Capacity, 5 hand washing machines. Erected in 1883 for a day school. Since 1895 used as a laundry. Cost, about $550. Present value, $400. Present condition, good.

Wood shed.—Character, frame. Use, wood sawing and storing coal. Capacity, 60 cords of wood or 300 tons of coal. Erected in 1893. Cost, $750. Present value, $600. Present condition, fair.

Carpenter shop and engine room.—Character, two-story frame. Use, carpenter shop and pumping station and carpenter's quarters. Capacity, 5 pupils. Erected in 1899. Cost, about $1,000. Present value, $1,000. Present condition, good.

Industrial teachers' quarters.—Character, frame cottage. Use, living quarters for industrial teacher and family. Capacity, one family. Erected in 1901. Cost, $395. Present value, $600. Present condition, good.

Tank house.—Character, frame structure of one room below, and a trestle with tank on top. Use, room used by an employee. Tank for water supply. Capacity, tank, 420 barrels. Erected in 1896. Cost, $800. Present value, $375. Present condition, poor.

Chicken house.—Character, one-story frame. Use, for school fowl. Capacity, 600 chickens. Erected in 1895. Cost, $550. Present value, $500. Present condition, good.

Barn.—Character, two-story frame. Use, housing live stock and storing hay. Capacity, 2 horses, 8 cows, and 20 tons of hay. Erected in 1893. Cost, $1,200. Present value, $1,000. Present condition, good.

Outhouse.—Character, frame with cemented vault. Use, water-closet. Capacity, 8 stools. Erected in 1896. Cost, about $150. Present value, $90. Present condition, fair.

Lighted by kerosene lamps. Heated by steam from a boiler in the basement of the building. Plant installed in 1897 at a cost of about $3,000. In good condition and satisfactory. The dormitories and class rooms are ventilated by shafts conducted through the roof. Ventilation not satisfactory in cold season; in fact, not sufficient at any time.

Water supply pure but insufficient. Its source is 5 wells located in the school yard. The water from these wells is pumped into a wooden tank. The cost of the water system, about $1,800. The main building and hospital are connected with a 6-inch general sewer pipe, which empties below the elevation upon which the school is situated, at a distance of about 2,000 feet from the main building. Not satisfactory. New water and sewer systems installed during 1902 at a cost of $7,653. There are 4 bath tubs for the boys and 4 for the girls. They are located in the basement of the building. There is a hose on the top floor of the main building. Fire pails are placed in different portions of the building.

This school has about 25 acres of land for its use. The value unknown. Estimated at $2.50 per acre. There are 22⅓ acres under fence; 10.7 acres are cultivated. One section of land should be set aside for cultivation and pasture. There are 11.63 acres now used for pasture. No land irrigated.

This school was opened in 1878 in a log building, still standing. In 1883 a part of the present plant was occupied.

Agricultural Boarding School.

It is located 16 miles south of Standing Rock Agency, on the west bank of the Missouri River. Climate, moderate, healthy.

Original cost, etc., of each building could not be ascertained, but only the total amount of the cost of all, which is $16,450. Present value, $10,000.

Boys' building.—Character, two-story frame. Use, two sitting rooms, one clothes room, and one dormitory. Capacity, 50 pupils. Erected in 1888. Present condition, good.

Superintendent's building.—Character, one-story frame. Use, superintendent's office and dwelling room, one employee's room, and infirmary. Dimensions, 20 by 50 feet. Erected in 1879. Present condition, good.

Employees' building.—Character, one-story frame. Use, four dwelling rooms, mess dining room, bakery, and kitchen. Dimensions, 26 by 100 feet. Erected in 1879. Present condition, good.

Girls' building.—Character, two-story frame. Use, pupils' dining room and two girls' sitting or assembly rooms. Capacity, 50 pupils. Erected in 1887. Present condition, good.

Schoolhouse.—Character, two-story frame structure. Use, two schoolrooms and one girls' dormitory. Capacity, 100 pupils. Erected in 1890. Present condition, good.

Laundry.—Character, 1½-story frame. Use, washing and ironing, drying and sewing rooms. Dimensions, 24 by 48 feet. Erected in 1890. Present condition, good.

Workshop.—Character, 1½-story frame. Use, blacksmith and carpenter shop. Upstairs for storing lumber and other articles belonging to shop. Dimensions, 16 by 46 feet. Erected in 1888. Present condition, good.

Barn.—Character, one-story frame with hay loft. Use, housing live stock and storing hay. Capacity, 14 animals and 20 tons of hay. Erected in 1893. Present condition, good.

Woodhouse.—Character, one-story frame. Use, storing split and sawed wood. Dimensions, 30 by 50 feet. Erected in 1895. Present condition, good.

Miscellaneous outbuildings.—Character, all log. Use, henhouse, ice house, cattle sheds, etc. Erected in 1879–1890. Present condition, fair to poor.

All buildings are lighted by kerosene lamps. Heated by wood and a few coal stoves. Ventilated by windows provided with boards at bottom to regulate draft and by chimneys provided with registers, etc. No modern device or system.

The water supply is good. Its source is the Missouri River, from which it is forced by a 16-foot windmill and a 3 by 10 R. R. D. A. pump into a tank of 12,400 gallons capacity. Main pipe, 2-inch; water system practically only extends to first story of buildings. Established in 1889. Cost, $2,000. There is no sewerage system in connection with the school. There being no sewerage, there are also no proper bathing facilities. Fire protection is very limited, and consists of the regulation water buckets placed at different places in the building—3 hydrants on first floor of buildings and 1 outside of buildings.

The school farm comprises 100 and the school garden 4 acres of level land of sandy character, which is good and productive, provided there is a sufficient supply of rain and moisture at the proper season of the year. There are 100 acres under fence; 100 acres under cultivation, plus 4 acres of school garden. No additional land for cultivation. No pasture; stock runs over the neighboring prairies. No irrigation. Original cost may be called $1.25 per acre. Present value, $10 per acre.

The school was originally established in 1879 as the first boarding school of this reservation. In 1882 all the girls and the smaller boys were transferred to the newly erected agency boarding school. From 1882 to 1886 it was a farm school for larger boys only. In 1886 it was reorganized as a boarding school for boys and girls, with literary, domestic, and industrial departments.

Grand River Boarding School.

Located 32 miles southwest of Standing Rock Agency, near the Grand River. Surrounding country best adapted to stock raising. Extremely cold in winters, with hot, dry summers.

Dormitory building.—Character, three-story frame with a one-story addition. Basement under entire building. Use, dormitory, dining rooms and kitchens, employees' quarters. Capacity, 130 pupils and 15 employees. Erected in 1893; one-story addition erected in 1901. Cost, $17,906; several thousand dollars were expended in 1901 for the erection of the one-story addition. Present value, $25,000. Present condition, excellent.

Schoolroom building.—Character, one-story frame. Basement under ell. Use, class rooms and assembly hall. Capacity, 130 pupils. Erected in 1901. Present condition, excellent.

Physician's quarters.—Character, one-story frame building. Use, office and dwelling. Capacity, one office room, three dwelling rooms. Erected in 1891. Cost, $1,000; present value, $800. Present condition, good.

Laundry.—Character, one-story frame. Use, laundering. Capacity, one washing room and one drying room. Erected in 1901. Present condition, excellent.

Warehouse.—Character, one-story frame with basement under. Use, storing supplies. Dimensions, 20 by 38 feet. Erected in 1891. Cost, $2,000. Present value, $1,600. Present condition, good.

Ice house.—Character, one-story frame. Use, storing beef. Dimensions, 15 by 17 feet. Erected in 1895. Cost, $650. Present value, $400. Present condition, good.

Pump house and shop.—Character, one-story frame. Use, carpenter shop, pumping room, and carpenter's quarters. Dimensions, 30 by 50 feet. Erected in 1901. Present condition, excellent.

Horse barn.—Character, 1½-story frame. Use, housing horses and storing hay. Capacity, 6 horses and 8 tons of hay. Erected in 1893. Cost, $1,696. Preent value, $1,200. Present condition, fair.

Cow barn and wagon shed.—Character, one-story frame. Use, housing cattle and farm machinery. Dimensions, 24 by 32 feet. Erected in 1895. Cost, $701. Present value, $650. Present condition, good.

Tool house (formerly a water-closet).—Character, one-story frame. Use, housing small farm tools. Dimensions, 12 by 20 feet. Erected in 1893. Cost (included in original cost of dormitory). Present value, $300. Present condition, good.

Cow barn.—Character, one-story log. Use, housing cattle. Capacity, 17 head of cattle. Erected in 1899. Cost, $100; built by the schoolboys. Present value, $150. Present condition, good.

Ice houses (2).—Character, one-story log. Use, storing ice. Dimensions, 14 by 14 and 13 by 18 feet. Erected, No. 1 in 1898 and No. 2 in 1901. Cost, built entirely by the schoolboys. Present value, $125. Present condition, excellent.

Root house.—Character, one-story log. Use, storing vegetables, etc. Dimensions,

18 by 18 feet. Erected in 1901. Cost, built by the schoolboys. Present value, $60. Present condition, excellent.

Water-closets (2).—Character, frame. Use, water-closets. Dimensions, 6 by 10 feet. Present value, $100. Present condition, fair.

Lighted by gasoline gas furnished by a Matthews gas machine, 200-light capacity. There are 162 single lights, the No. 95 adjustable incandescent burners with mantle chimney and porcelain shade being used. Plant was installed November, 1901, at cost of $1,905. Dormitory building heated by steam furnished by a No. 7 E American boiler. Fifty-four direct radiators and 10 coils are distributed throughout the building. This plant is not completely successful with lignite coal. The schoolroom building is heated by steam furnished by a No. 603 American boiler. Eight direct-indirect radiators, 2 direct radiators, and 3 coils are in this building. Very satisfactory. The other buildings are heated by wood stoves. Heating plant installed 1901. Ventilation in schoolrooms by system devised by the Indian Office. Other buildings have no modern system.

The water supply was insufficient and of a poor quality, when its only source was from two wells about 600 feet from the dormitory building and under the pump house and shop building. The water from these wells is pumped by a 4-horse gasoline engine, and pumped into a tank of 12,000 gallons capacity, on a 60-foot steel trestle. The pressure thus obtained is ample to force the water to any desired place. Plant installed 1901. In 1902 the source of supply was extended to the river, at a cost of $850. Supply now sufficient. The laundry, dormitory, and schoolroom buildings are connected with an 8-inch sewer main which empties into the Grand River, a distance of 1,700 feet from the school. The outfall is nearly 34 feet. There are 5 ring baths and 2 tubs for the boys, and the same number for the girls. They are located in the basement of the dormitory building. A standpipe extends from the basement to the attic floor in the dormitory building, with hose attached on each floor. Fire hydrants on grounds.

No definite quantity of land has been set aside as a school farm. However, 15 acres are under fence, which is suitable for garden truck. Unless some of the Indians that now live in close proximity to the school were removed, very few additional acres could be added to that already under cultivation. The school herd now pasture out on the range. Irrigation is not used.

This school was opened November 6, 1893; capacity, 80, and an enrollment of 69. During 1901, $41,355.70 were expended on the plant for additions, repairs, and improvements, increasing the capacity to 130 pupils.

No. 1. Day School.

Located 18 miles north of Standing Rock Agency, N. Dak., under bluffs of the Missouri River Valley, consequently the soil, washed down from the bluffs, is rich and well suited for a garden.

Day school.—Character, one-story frame building. Use, class room, storeroom, kitchen, and teacher's and housekeeper's quarters. Capacity, 30 pupils. Erected in 1885. Cost, $750. Present value, $350. Present condition, good.

Water-closet.—Character, frame. Present condition, good.

The school is lighted by lamps burning kerosene oil. It is heated by stoves burning wood and lignite coal. No modern system of ventilation. Water is hauled to the school from the Missouri River, a distance of about 1½ miles. The school has no sewerage system. Bathing facilities, none. There is no adequate protection against fire.

The school farm consists of about 4 acres. The land is rich and well located. Six acres are under fence. Four acres are under cultivation. There are no acres in pasture and none irrigated.

This school was organized with about 25 or 30 pupils.

No. 2. Day School.

Located 3 miles northwest of the agency, in Siaka's camp, the site being well adapted for day-school purposes. Climate subject to extreme variations; soil is a sandy loam.

School building.—Character, one-story frame. Use, schoolroom. Capacity, 30 pupils. Erected in 1885. Cost, $750. Present value, $500. Condition, fair.

Teacher's cottage.—Character, one-story frame, three rooms. Use, teacher's quar-

ters. Erected about 1890. Cost, about $750. Present value, about $500. Condition, poor.
No lighting system. Heated by stoves. No system of ventilation. Water is hauled in barrels from Missouri River. No sewerage system. No bathing facilities. No fire protection except water in pails and barrels.
No school farm.
Erected in 1885, and has been in use as a day school since that time.

Bullhead Day School.

Located at Bullhead Station, S. Dak., 40 miles southwest of Standing Rock Agency, N. Dak. Site suited for school purposes. Climate, mild and dry. Soil uneven, gumbo and sandy. Not adapted for farming.
Schoolhouse.—Character, one-story frame building. Use, class room. Capacity, 30 pupils. Erected in 1891. Cost, $1,000. Present value, $500. Present condition, fair.
Teacher's quarters.—Character, one-story frame building. Use, teacher's dwelling and cooking midday meal for pupils. Capacity, one male teacher with small family. Erected in 1891. Cost, $1,000. Present value, $500. Present condition, fair.
No light plant in schoolhouse or teacher's quarters. Buildings heated by coal stoves. No special ventilating system created for school. The water supplied is fair; contains alkali, and it is hard. It is obtained from the only well at the school. No sewerage system connected with the school. No bathing facilities created for school; only tubs. Water in buckets are constantly on hand for fire protection.
This school has no fencing on any part of the school grounds. All gardening was carried on in the 5 acres allowed in the farmer's garden.
Erected in 1891, and has been continued in use since that time as day school. Has been closed at times for lack of attendance, but is fairly well attended at the present time.

Cannon Ball Day School.

Located about 25 miles north of Standing Rock Agency, at Cannon Ball subissue station.
School building.—Character, one-story log building. Use, schoolrooms, kitchen, and employees' rooms. Capacity, 40 pupils. Erected in 1884. Cost, $1,250. Present value, $500. Present condition, very poor.
Lighted by lamps. Heated by wood stoves. Water is obtained from a spring close by, and is brought to the school in barrels. No sewerage. No bathing facilities. There is no fire protection.
The school has a garden of 3 acres.
Erected in 1884, and used as day school since that time.

Porcupine Day School, Porcupine Subagency.

Located 30 miles west by north of Fort Yates, N. Dak., on bank of Cannon Ball River. Site well suited for school purposes. Climate, severe, continued cold in winter. Summers usually hot, and not always sufficient rain to insure successful farming. Soil of immediate site, light sandy loam.
School building.—Character, 1½-story frame with one-story frame addition. Use, schoolroom, dining room, and kitchen, two halls. Capacity, 40 pupils. Erected in 1895. Cost, $1,000. Present value, $750. Present condition, very good.
Teacher's cottage.—Character, 1½-story frame with ½-story frame shed attached, one outbuilding, frame.. Use, teacher's dwelling. Capacity, four dwelling rooms and wood shed or storm shed. Erected in 1895. Cost, $1,000. Present value, $750. Present condition, excellent.
Heating, by stoves—wood burners. Ventilation, by transom above boys' hallway, and by lowering windows. Water supply, from the Cannon Ball River. Fire protection, wash boiler full of water, also pails of water on hand in kitchen.
This school was opened in 1895 with attendence of about 18 pupils.

TONGUE RIVER AGENCY, MONT.

Tribe.	Population.
Northern Cheyenne	1,402

Area, 489,400 acres; unallotted.
Railroad station: Forsyth, on Northern Pacific Railway. Sixty-five miles to agency.

Nearest military post: Camp Merritt, Mont. Post-office address: Lamedeer, Custer County, Mont. Telegraphic address: Forsyth, Mont.

Tongue River Day School.

Located at Tongue River Agency, Mont., 65 miles south of Forsyth, on the Northern Pacific Railway, and 55 miles east of Crow Agency, on the Burlington route. Good site for day school. Very little land available for garden. Extremely cold in winter.

School building.—Character, one-story log. Use, schoolroom, sewing room, and kitchen. Capacity, 32 pupils. Erected in 1888. Cost $500. Present value, $200. Present condition, poor.

Lighted with kerosene lamps. Heated with stoves. Ventilated by doors and windows. Water is supplied from a well; good; drawn with buckets. No sewerage system. Bathing is done in washtubs. Fire protection, buckets filled with water.

This school has no farm. There are about 2 acres under fence. No school land under cultivation. No land irrigated.

This school was opened in 1888, but the attendance was very poor until 1895, when it began to increase. During the last three years it has been from 28 to over 31.

Tongue River Boarding School.

Located 20 miles from the agency, and about 30 east of the Crow Agency, on Busby Ranch, the greater part of which is a sandy loam, very fertile with irrigation.

School plant now under construction. School to be opened September, 1904. Cost of plant and improvements to date of opening, $48,158. Buildings, etc., to consist of the following:

Dormitory building.—Character, 2½-story brick. Use, living quarters, dining room, kitchen, play rooms and schoolrooms for pupils. Capacity, 75 pupils.

Employees' quarters.—Character, two-story brick. Use, living quarters, mess dining room and kitchen. Capacity, 8 employees.

Laundry.—Character, one-story brick. Use, general laundry purposes. Dimensions, 42 by 38 feet.

Warehouse.—Character, one-story brick. Use, storing school supplies. Dimensions, 50 by 20 feet.

Gas house.—Character, one-story frame. Use, housing gas machine. Dimensions, 23 by 13 feet.

Water and sewer systems.

TULALIP AGENCY, WASH.

(Under School Superintendent.)

Tribes.	Population.
D'Wamish (absorbed in the tribes below).	
Tulalip	465
Madison	160
Lummi	354
Muckleshoot	150
Swinomish	287
Total	1,416

Area:	Acres.
Allotted	34,717
Unalloted	17,906

Railroad station: Marysville (via Seattle), on Marysville and Seattle Railway. Eight miles to agency.

Nearest military post: Fort Walla Walla, Wash. Post-office address: Tulalip, Snohomish County, Wash. Telegraphic address: Marysville, Wash.

Tulalip Boarding School.

This school was partially destroyed by fire in March, 1902, and had to be closed. A modern plant has been contracted for, Congress having appropriated $30,000 therefor. Upon its completion this school will be reopened.

Lummi Day School, Lummi Reservation.

Located 7 miles west of Whatcom, Wash., at the mouth of the Nooksack River. Site poorly suited for school purposes. Climate without extreme changes. Soil of immediate site, alluvium on a substratum of gravel.

Schoolhouse.—Character, one-story frame. Use, class room. Capacity, 32 pupils. Erected in 1880. Present value, $300. Present condition, poor.

School dining room and kitchen.—Character, one-story frame. Use, dining room, kitchen, commissary and sewing room. Capacity, 32 pupils. Erected in 1880. Present value, $200. Present condition, poor.

Lighted by oil lamps. Heated by wood stoves except the room used as a dining room and sewing room, which contains a fireplace. Ventilation, no modern system. The water supply is pure and soft, its source is the glaciers of the Cascade Mountains. It is conveyed from the Nooksack River (which flows about 200 yards east of the school) to the school in buckets. The sewage is deposited in the vaults of two good water closets (privies) near the schoolhouse. No bathing facilities exist, save three washtubs at the school kitchen. There are water buckets and ladders at each building for fire protection.

There is no farm or garden at this school.

This school was opened October 1, 1891, with a capacity of 32 pupils.

Port Madison Day School, Port Madison Reservation.

Located 12 miles northwest of Seattle, Wash., on the west shore of Puget Sound. Site well chosen, near shore on low hill. Climate very equable as to temperature, with moist winters and dry summers. Soil, gravelly loam.

Court-house and jail.—Character, one-story frame structure. Use, school room, court room, and prison. Capacity, 30 pupils. Erected about 1891. Present value, about $300. Present condition, poor.

Farmer's residence.—Character, one-story frame structure. Use, residence of teacher and acting farmer and of his wife, the housekeeper. Capacity, five rooms. Erected about 1892. Present value, about $200. Present condition, poor.

Lunch house.—Three-room, one-story, frame building, worth perhaps $25. It is rented from an Indian.

Lighting, by means of kerosene lamps. Heating, box stoves burning wood; cooking, the same. Ventilation, effected in school room by means of baffle boards under the windows. A boxed and curbed spring near the lunch house affords an ample supply of soft water of good quality. This water is piped to the farmer's residence. Sewage, flows past the lunch house and the farmer's residence in an open "run" to the Sound. No facilities for bathing save tubs.

The school has no land, but is located on a Government reserve strip of the Port Madison Reservation containing about 75 acres.

This school opened October 15, 1900, with a capacity for 30 pupils. On that day it enrolled 13, but increased to 42 during the year.

Swinomish Day School, Swinomish Reservation.

Located on the east coast of Fidalgo Island, directly opposite the town of La Conner (on the mainland) from which it is separated by Swinomish Slough (about one-eighth of a mile in width). Location for a school, good. Climate without extreme changes, but very moist. Soil extremely poor and rocky.

Schoolhouse.—Character, one-story frame. Use, class rooms and sewing room. Capacity, 50 pupils. Erected, main building, 1897; addition, 1898. Cost, main building, $400; addition, $350. Present value, main building, $400; addition, $350. Present condition, good.

Cook house.—Character, one-story frame. Use, kitchen, dining room, and store room. Capacity, 37 pupils. Erected, main building, 1898; addition, 1898. Cost, main building, $260; addition, $50. Present value, main building, $260; addition, $50. Present condition, good.

Miscellaneous buildings (2).—Character, sheds (2) of rough lumber. Use, wood sheds (2) for school and for teacher. Capacity, about 25 cords of wood. Erected in 1898 and 1900. Cost, school shed, $50; teacher's shed, $31. Present value, school shed, $50; teacher's shed, $31. Present condition, good.

Lighted by coal-oil lamps. Heated by wood stoves. Schoolroom and cook house ventilated by system recommended by Indian Office. Water supply derived from shallow well affording practically little else than surface water. Water is drawn up by hand by means of bucket, rope, and well wheel. No sewerage system. Water thrown on ground. No bathing facilities. Galvanized pails (fire buckets) filled with water drawn from the well.

School yard and teacher's yard embrace about 1 acre of rocky land. This school was opened April 26, 1897, with a capacity of 42 pupils.

UINTA AND OURAY AGENCY, UTAH.

Tribes.	Population.
Uinta Ute at Uinta	472
White River Ute at Uinta	370
Uncompahgre Ute at Ouray	795
White River Ute at Ouray	24
Total	1,661

Area:	Acres.
Unallotted	2,039,040
Allotted (estimated)	15,000

Railroad station: Price, on Rio Grande Western Railway. One hundred and five miles to agency by stage.

Nearest military post: Fort Duchesne, Utah. Post-office address: Whiterocks, Utah. Telegraphic address: Fort Duchesne, Utah.

Uinta Boarding School.

Location at Uinta and Ouray Agency, 110 miles northeast of Price, Utah, the nearest railway point, being on the Rio Grande Western Railway. Site, a subirrigated meadow, naturally too wet to be a good location; climate mild, with no extremes of heat and cold; on a southern slope, 8 miles south of the base of the Uinta Mountains. Whiterocks River skirts the grounds on the east.

Apartment building.—Character, two-story frame with one-story frame kitchen added. Use, employees' quarters, mess hall and kitchen, reception room, and office. Capacity, 10. Erected in 1894. Cost, $7,500. Present value, $7,000. Present condition, fair.

Boys' building and school building.—Character, frame, two story, with 2 one-story additions. Use, boys' dormitories, clothes rooms, and play room, with bath room. Schoolrooms. One employee's room. Capacity, dormitories, 36; schoolrooms, 90. Erected in 1891. Cost, $5,300. Present value, $4,500. Present condition, poor.

Girls' building.—Character, two-story brick. Use, girls' dormitories, clothes rooms, sewing room, play room, bathroom, kitchen, dining room, and pantry, and three employees' rooms. Capacity, dormitories, 49; dining room, 90. Erected in 1891. Cost, $10,950. Present value, $10,000. Present condition, poor.

Laundry.—Character, two-story frame, ceiled. Use, accommodation of school laundry work. Dimensions, 15 by 25 feet. Erected in 1895. Cost, $4,776. Present value, $4,500. Present condition, good.

Storehouse and hall.—Character, two-story frame. Use, storing supplies and assembly hall. Capacity, assembly hall, 82. Erected in 1899. Present condition, good.

Industrial building.—Character, 1½ story frame, neither plastered nor ceiled. Use, work shop and oil room. Capacity, 12 pupils. Erected in 1893. Cost, $400. Present value, $300. Present condition, good.

Ice house.—Character, frame. Use, storing ice; also contains meat room and refrigerator. Dimensions, 16 by 24 feet. Erected in 1896. Cost, $150. Present value, $125. Present condition, good.

Stable.—Character, 1½ story frame. Use, sheltering stock and storing hay, etc. Capacity, 8 head of stock. Erected in 1892. Cost, $200. Present value, $150. Present condition, poor.

Lighted by kerosene lamps. Heated by wood and coal stoves. Ventilation currents through class rooms and dormitories are induced by the heat of kerosene lamps in shafts and jacketed stoves over inlets.

Water supplied by open ditches from mountain stream of the purest and best of water and in unlimited supply. Sewerage by open ditch, constantly flushed by canal from the river, and leading back into the same stream. This canal is closed by freezing about three months in the year, when refuse must be hauled away. Satisfactory as to results when not frozen, but unsightly. Each bathroom is supplied with a long galvanized tank fitted with 6 faucets. The bath is taken in running water under these faucets. These tanks are filled with buckets. Results satisfactory from a sanitary standpoint, but the system is unhandy. Fire protection consists of fire pails in dormitories and halls and fire escapes.

There are 65 acres under fence; about 20 acres under cultivation. Thirty acres more might be put under cultivation. The school has no pasture of its own, but keeps its few milch cows in a pasture belonging to the agency. Twenty acres are under irrigation. Water is plentiful and might be run over all the school land.

The old school building was erected in 1880. The present boys' and girls' buildings were erected in 1891, having a capacity of 80. By the erection of an apartment or employees' building in 1894 the capacity was increased to 85.

Ouray Boarding School.

Located 5 miles southeast of Fort Duchesne and 100 miles northeast of Price, on the Rio Grande Western, the nearest railroad point. Site well suited for school purposes. Climate dry and healthy and almost entirely free from sudden changes. Soil in immediate vicinity is a mixture of sand, clay, and cobble stone, strongly impregnated with alkali. This is underlaid by a substratum of cobble stone and solid rock.

Girls' building.—Character, two-story brick with one one-story frame addition. Use, dormitory, dining room and kitchen, mess dining room and kitchen, office, sitting room, employees' rooms. Capacity, 35 pupils; 5 employees. Erected in 1893. Cost, $12,100. Present value, $11,000. Present condition, good.

Boys' building.—Character, two-story brick, with one one-story addition. Use, dormitory, sitting room, bathroom, employees' rooms. Capacity, 40 pupils, 3 employees. Erected in 1893. Cost, $7,700. Present value, $7,000. Present condition, good.

Schoolhouse.—Character, two-story brick. Use, class rooms and assembly hall. Capacity, 120 pupils. Erected in 1893. Cost, $8,525. Present value, $8,000. Present condition, excellent.

Physician's residence.—Character, 1½ story frame. Use, physician's office and dwelling. Capacity, 1 office room, 5 dwelling rooms. Erected in 1895. Cost, $2,000. Present value, $1,800. Present condition, good.

Laundry building.—Character, two-story frame. Use, laundry. Dimensions, 20 by 40 feet. Erected in 1895. Cost, $2,000. Present value, $1,800. Present condition, good.

Barn.—Character, 1½-story frame. Use, housing live stock and storing hay and grain. Capacity, 4 horses, 200 bushels grain, 5 tons hay. Erected in 1895. Cost, $1,030. Present value, $900. Present condition, good.

Storehouse.—Character, one-story frame. Use, storing supplies. Dimensions, 30 by 46 feet. Erected in 1895. Cost, $1,515. Present value, $1,400. Present condition, good.

Gymnasium.—Character, one-story frame. Use, storing supplies and unserviceable property. Dimensions, 28 by 36 feet. Erected in 1895. Cost, $1,440. Present value, $1,300. Present condition, good.

Miscellaneous outbuildings.—Character, all frame. Use, ice house, cattle sheds, etc. Erected in 1893–1897. Present condition, fair to good.

Lighted by kerosene oil lamps. Heated by wood and coal stoves. Ventilation of all buildings by windows only. No modern system. During about half the year the water supply is obtained from the Uinta River, 200 yards distant, by hauling in barrels. During the remainder of the year the supply is taken from an irrigating ditch flowing through the yard near the buildings. Bathrooms and laundry are provided with drain pipes made of lumber and placed 18 inches under ground. Closets are provided with open vaults. The boys' building is provided with four and the girls' building with two bath tubs, all on the ground floor. The water for bathing and laundry purposes is heated in open caldrons. Water buckets are kept in convenient places in the dormitories. This is our only fire protection.

The school farm consists of 312 acres of land. The land is all poor, and some of it is utterly worthless for farming or grazing. The land was selected from the Uinta Reservation in 1897, by authority of the Indian Office. The Uinta River flows in a southeasterly direction entirely across the farm. There is but little timber along this stream. The present value of the farm is unknown. About 240 acres are under fence. About 100 acres in cultivation, mostly in alfalfa. Nearly 100 acres more can be cultivated. Forty acres are used for pasture. The remaining 100 acres under fence does not produce anything. One hundred acres are irrigated. All the land can be irrigated.

This school was opened in January, 1893. The attendance has always been small, irregular, and unsatisfactory.

UMATILLA AGENCY, OREG.

Under School Superintendent.

Tribes.	Population.
Cayuse	391
Walla Walla	569
Umatilla	184
Total	1,144

Area:

	Acres.
Allotted	76,933
Reserved for school and mission	980
Unallotted	79,820

Railroad station: At agency, on Oregon Railway and Navigation Company Railway.

Nearest military post, Fort Walla Walla, Wash. Post-office address, Pendleton, Oreg. Telegraphic address, Pendleton, Oreg.

Umatilla Training School.

Located 5½ miles east of Pendleton, Oreg., and 1 mile east of Umatilla Agency, on the Oregon Railway and Navigation Company's railway line. Site admirably suited for school purposes. Climate without extreme change. School buildings are located on a gravel bar covered with 18 inches of loam, well adapted for gardening.

Girls' building.—Character, two-story brick. Use, dormitory, dining room, and kitchen. Capacity, 50 pupils. Erected in 1892. Cost, $7,000. Present value, $6,000. Present condition, fair.

Boys' building.—Character, two-story brick with basement. Use, dormitory, carpenter shop, and play rooms. Capacity, 60 pupils. Erected in 1901. Cost, $9,387. Present value, $9,387. Present condition, excellent.

School building.—Character, two-story brick. Use, 3 schoolrooms and assembly hall. Capacity, schoolrooms, 120; assembly hall, 400. Erected in 1902. Cost, $7,982. Present value, $7,982. Present condition, excellent.

Employees' building, formerly boys' dormitory.—Character, two-story frame. Use, residence of superintendent, teachers, etc., office, dining room, kitchen, etc. Capacity, 8 employees. Erected in 1892. Cost, $3,000. Present value, $1,500. Present condition, fair.

Laundry and dry room.—Character, one-story brick. Use, laundry. Capacity, 2 large rooms. Erected, laundry proper, 1892; dry room, 1894. Cost, $2,000. Present value, $2,000. Present condition, good.

Brick cellar.—Character, low one-story brick, partly below ground. Use, storing vegetables, etc. Capacity, 600 bushels. Erected in 1892. Cost, $500. Present value, $500. Present condition, good.

Miscellaneous outbuildings.—Character, all frame. Use, privies, cattle sheds, stables, wood houses, etc. Erected in 1892–1899. Cost, $1,654.25. Present value, $1,000. Present condition, poor to good.

Lighted with kerosene lamps. All except the boys' dormitory are heated by stoves burning wood. Boys' dormitory has a hot-air furnace burning coal or wood. Ventilation in boys' dormitory is by system devised by Indian Office. Other buildings have no modern system. The water supply is inadequate at present, but steps are being taken looking to a better source of supply. At present the supply is drawn from a well located in the campus. The water from this well is forced by a gasoline engine into a redwood tank having a capacity of 10,000 gallons, standing on a trestle 60 feet high. The water flows thence by gravity into the buildings, and is to be used also for irrigation on the campus. The pressure is ample to force the water wherever it is required. The waterworks system was installed in 1901 and cost $5,496. All principal buildings are connected with 8-inch general sewer pipe, which empties into a small stream about 200 yards below the school. The fall is ample. The children are bathed in tubs with water heated in caldrons. Hose plugs stand at convenient points about the grounds and campus, and 400 feet of 2½-inch fire hose have been provided. A supplemental gravity system from springs was installed in 1903 at a cost of $1,500.

The school has 640 acres, which were set apart at the time of the allotment of lands upon this reserve (1892), and its present value is about $15,000. A large part of it is excellent wheat land and the balance is fine pasture. All under fence. Four hundred and twenty acres are under cultivation. No more can be cultivated to advantage. Two hundred and twenty-five acres are in pasture. Only the campus, about an acre, is irrigated.

STATISTICS OF INDIAN TRIBES, AGENCIES, AND SCHOOLS. 123

In 1866 a day school with 16 scholars was opened. It was closed in 1881. A boarding-school plant was constructed in 1882, and the school was formally opened January 1, 1883, with about 40 pupils. The nucleus of the present school plant was constructed in 1892, but several additions have been made since.

UNION AGENCY, IND. T.

Tribes.	Population.
Cherokee	35,000
Chickasaw	11,500
Choctaw	20,250
Creek	15,000
Seminole	2,750
Total	84,500

Area, 19,456,614 acres; unallotted.
Railroad station: Muscogee, on Missouri, Kansas and Texas Railway.
Nearest military post: Fort Reno, Okla. Post-office address: Muscogee, Ind. T. Telegraphic address: Muscogee, Ind. T.

The schools of Indian Territory are conducted generally under the provisions of the tribal laws of the nation in which the same are situated, modified by agreements with the Secretary of the Interior. The schools in the Choctaw Nation are conducted by the Government with the assistance of the tribal authorities out of their pro rata share of royalties accruing from coal and asphalt mined. The Chickasaw schools are supported partly by tribal appropriations and their pro rata share of coal and asphalt royalties. The United States is represented in the management of schools by a superintendent of schools, assisted by four supervisors.

Cherokee Nation.—There are 2 seminaries, an orphan academy, a colored high school, and 140 day schools.

Creek Nation.—There are 6 boarding schools, an orphan home, 2 colored boarding schools, a colored orphan home, and 52 day schools.

Choctaw Nation.—There are 5 academies and 190 day schools.

Chickasaw Nation.—There are 3 boarding schools, an orphan home, and 16 day schools.

Seminole Nation.—No statistics of educational work among the people of this small nation are available, they having sole conduct of all such affairs.

No public appropriations are made for educational interests among the Five Civilized Tribes.

WALKER RIVER RESERVATION, NEV.

(Under Carson School Superintendent.)

Tribe.	Population.
Pah-Utes	427

Area, 318,815 acres; unallotted.

NOTE.—The Carson Boarding School and the Walker River Day School, in Nevada, and the day schools at Bishop, Big Pine, and Independence, in California, are under the control of the Carson school superintendent.

Walker River Day School.

Location, near the center of the Walker River Agency, on the Walker River, one-fourth mile from Schurz, Nev., on the Carson and Colorado Railroad. The climate is mild and dry, altitude about 5,000 feet above sea level. Agriculture carried on by means of irrigation, for which purpose the water of Walker River is used.

Schoolhouse.—Character, one-story frame. Use, schoolroom, kitchen, and dining room. Capacity, 30 pupils. Erected in 1894. Present value, $600. Present condition, good.

Teacher's quarters.—Character, 1½-story frame; one-story frame addition. Use, teacher and field matron's quarters. Capacity, 2. Erected in 1882; addition in 1882. Present value, $300. Present condition, good.

Lighted by kerosene lamps. Heated by wood stoves. Ventilation, no modern system; by means of doors and windows. Water supply for drinking purposes obtained from trader's well one-fourth mile away. Wells near schoolhouse unfit for cooking or drinking on account of alkaline. Sewerage, none. Bathing system, none. Children are bathed in washtubs. Fire protection, chemical fire extinguishers in all buildings.

The school is located on agency land; has no farm of its own.

Bishop Day School, Bishop, California.

Location, Bishop, Inyo County, Cal., on the Carson and Colorado Railroad, the school being 6 miles from Bishop station.

Schoolhouse.—Character, one-story frame. Use, 2 class rooms. Capacity, 60 pupils. Erected in 1900. Cost, $900. Present condition, good.

The building is lighted by kerosene lamps. The heating is done by heating stoves. It is ventilated by raising and lowering windows. The water supply is obtained from an irrigation ditch near at hand. Sewerage, none. Bathing system, none. Fire protection, none.

The school has $1\frac{1}{6}$ acres of land, value about $150, and owned by the young people's department of Women's National Indian Association.

This school was opened about March, 1882, with an enrollment of 25 pupils.

Independence Day School, Independence, Cal.

Located $2\frac{1}{2}$ miles northwest of Independence, Cal.; its site is on the mountain slope, with streams on both sides; the climate without extremes. The soil is very sandy.

Schoolhouse.—Character, one-story frame. Use, schoolroom. Capacity, 28 pupils. Erected in 1897. Cost, $300.26. Present value, $350. Present condition, good.

No modern system of lighting. Heating by stoves; wood fires. No modern system of ventilating, except by raising and lowering windows. The water supply is from the mountain streams, and is pure and soft. Sewerage, none. Bathing system, none. Fire protection, none.

The schoolhouse was built by the Indians; located on land belonging to one Mrs. Lewis.

The school opened March 14, 1898, with 16 pupils.

Big Pine Day School, California.

Location, about $2\frac{1}{2}$ miles west of Alvord station, on the Carson and Colorado Railroad.

Schoolhouse.—Character, one-story frame. Use, schoolroom. Capacity, 30 pupils. Erected in 1896. Cost, about $300. Present condition, very poor.

Heating, by wood stoves. Ventilation, by opening doors and windows. Water is obtained from an irrigation ditch outside of school grounds. Sewerage, none. Bathing system, none.

The school is built on a lot containing about $1\frac{1}{2}$ acres, which is level and very sandy. This land was deeded to the Government about one year ago.

The Indians built the schoolhouse. It was destroyed by fire in 1896 and rebuilt the same year by white people living in the vicinity.

WARM SPRINGS AGENCY, OREG.

(Under School Superintendent.)

Tribes.	Population.
Warm Springs	
Wasco	
Tenino	778
Piute	

Area: Acres.
Allotted 140,696
Reserved 1,195
Unallotted 322,108

Railroad station: The Dalles, on Oregon Railway and Navigation Company's Railroad. Seventy-five miles to agency.

Nearest military post: Vancouver Barracks, Wash. Post-office address: Warmspring, Crook County, Oreg. Telegraphic address: Shanico, Oreg.

Warm Springs Training School.

Located at Warm Springs Agency, 75 miles south from The Dalles, Oreg. Climate dry and without extreme changes. Soil gravelly on the uplands, black loam in the bottoms.

Dormitory.—Character, two-story frame. Use, dormitories, play room, and employees' quarters. Capacity, 150 pupils. Erected in 1896. Cost, $9,200. Present value, $9,000. Present condition, good.

Mess hall and kitchen.—Character, one-story frame. Use, dining room and kitchen. Capacity, 150 pupils. Erected in 1896. Cost, $2,964. Present value, $2,900. Present condition, excellent.

Schoolhouse.—Character, one-story frame. Use, classrooms and chapel. Capacity, 150 pupils. Erected in 1896. Cost, $2,600. Present value, $2,600. Present condition, excellent.

Hospital.—Character, two-story frame. Use, isolation and care of sick. Capacity, 12 pupils. Erected in 1896. Cost, $1,613. Present value, $1,600. Present condition, good.

Seamstress' building.—Character, two-story frame. Use, sewing rooms and seamstress' private rooms. Capacity, 10 pupils. Erected in 1900. Cost, $750. Present value, $750. Present condition, excellent.

Laundry.—Character, two-story frame. Use, washing and ironing. Capacity, 10 pupils. Erected in 1896. Cost, $1,063. Present value, $1,000. Present condition, good.

Employees' cottage.—Character, two-story frame. Use, quarters for employees. Capacity, dining room and kitchen and 4 private rooms. Erected in 1896. Cost, $1,437. Present value, $1,400. Present condition, excellent.

Miscellaneous outbuildings.—Character, all frame. Use, wood sheds, carpenter shop, oil house, etc. Erected in 1896–1901. Cost, $500. Present value, $500. Present condition, good.

Lighted by electricity, furnished by dynamo run by water power. There are 120 incandescent lamps. Plant installed in 1899, at a cost of about $1,650. All buildings heated by stoves. Ventilation of dormitory, mess hall and kitchen, and school rooms is by the system devised by Indian Office. Other buildings have no modern system.

The water supply is taken from the Shitike Creek and pumped into a reservoir of capacity of 90,000 gallons, located on a sidehill about 100 feet above the level of the buildings. The water is pure and soft, and the supply is adequate for all school purposes, including irrigation of lawn. All the school buildings, except seamstress' building, are connected with a 6-inch sewer, which has a good fall, and empties into the Shitike Creek about half a mile below the pumping plant. The water and sewer system was installed in 1897, at a cost of $6,243. The bathing facilities at present consist of 12 shower baths, the most of which are entirely unfit for use. Authority has been received for remodeling the bathrooms, installing 14 ring baths and 4 bath tubs in place of the shower baths. There are standpipes in each end of the dormitory, with hose on each floor; also 4-inch fire hydrants on the school grounds.

There are 720 acres in the reserve. Seventy acres are under fence. There are 35 acres under cultivation. Two hundred additional acres can be cultivated. There is no pasturage fenced. There are about 10 acres irrigated.

This school was opened July 1, 1897, with a capacity for 150 pupils.

WESTERN SHOSHONE AGENCY, NEV.

(Under School Superintendent.)

Tribes.	Population.
Shoshones	226
Paiutes	224
Shoshones and Paiutes not under the agency	3,701
Total	4,151

Area, 312,320 acres; unallotted.

Railroad station: Elko, on the Southern Pacific Railway. One hundred and twenty miles to agency by stage.

Nearest military post: Fort Douglas, Utah. Post-office address: Owyhee, Nev. Telegraphic address: Elko, Nev.

Western Shoshone Training School.

Located on the Duck Valley Reservation, 120 miles north of Elko, Nev., the shipping point on the Central Pacific Railway. The buildings being on a rocky slope, slightly elevated above the general level of the valley. Soil of the immediate site is barren and rocky. Climate is noted for long and severe winters.

Schoolhouse.—Character, two-story frame with stone foundation. Use, dormitories, schoolrooms, dining room and kitchen, girls' sitting room, and boys' wash room. Capacity, 40 pupils. Erected in 1893. Cost, $8,300. Present value, $7,500. Present condition, good.

Hospital.—Character, 1½-story frame with stone foundation. Use, sewing room, employees' quarters, and by cooking class. Capacity, 1 kitchen and dining room, 1 sewing room, and 3 employees' rooms. Erected in 1893. Cost, $3,300. Present value, $3,000. Present condition, good.

Washhouse.—Character, one-story frame. Use, laundry. Capacity, 24 by 30 feet floor space. Erected in 1893. Present value, $750. Present condition, good.

Woodhouse.—Character, 1½-story frame. Use, mess dining hall and woodshed. Capacity, 10 employees in dining hall, 25 cords wood in shed. Erected in 1896. Cost, $1,200. Present value, $1,000. Present condition, good.

Stable.—Character, rough stone and wood. Use, shelter for stock. Capacity, 5 horses, 4 tons of grain. Erected in 1893. Cost, $1,000. Present value, $700. Present condition, good.

Ice house.—Character, one-story frame with stone basement. Use, storing ice and keeping beef. Capacity, 50 tons of ice, one whole beef. Erected in 1898. Present value, $400. Present condition, good.

Miscellaneous outbuildings.—Character, frame. Use, cow sheds, wagon shed, henhouse, storehouse, etc. Erected in 1889–1894. Present value aggregates about $900. Present condition, poor to good.

Lighted by kerosene lamps. Heated by wood-burning stoves. Ventilation is by means of doors and windows. Water supply is good, pure, and sufficient for all domestic purposes. Its source is a number of springs assembled into a stone and concrete reservoir located one-half mile east of the school and at an elevation of about 220 feet, from thence to the buildings through a 2-inch iron pipe, which is about to be replaced by a 4-inch spiral riveted pipe. The system was installed soon after establishing the school. The main building and laundry have short iron pipe sewers, emptying into an open ditch a short distance from the buildings. The material is on the ground to connect these with a 4-inch general sewer pipe that will carry the sewerage to a safe distance. There are practically no bathing facilities, the laundry tubs being used for the purpose. There are standpipes in the main building with hose on both floors, a hydrant and hose at the hospital and at the woodhouse, also a hydrant and hose centrally located on the ground. When the 4-inch main is completed the fire protection will be ample.

There has been no specified amount of land set apart for school purposes, but about 50 acres of the reservation has been fenced and used for a school farm. Its present value, with clear title, would be about $250. There are about 50 acres under fence. About 30 acres under cultivation, including 25 acres of alfalfa and meadow. The remaining 20 acres could be cultivated. The entire range on the reservation is used for pasturage, besides about 20 acres that is fenced. The 30 acres under cultivation is irrigated. This school was opened as a boarding school February 11, 1893.

WHITE EARTH AGENCY, MINN.

Tribes.	Population.
Mississippi Chippewas, White Earth	1,615
Mississippi Chippewas, White Oak Point	87
Mississippi Chippewas, Gull Lake	340
Mississippi Chippewas, Mille Lac	1,193
Pembina	314
Leech Lake Chippewa	297
Cass Lake and Winnibigoshish Chippewa	56
Otter Tale Pillager Chippewa	717
Fond du Lac	100
Total	4,719

Area unallotted, 703,512 acres.

Railroad station: Detroit, Minn., on the Northern Pacific Railway. Twenty-two miles to agency.

Nearest military post: Fort Snelling, Minn. Post-office address: White Earth, Minn. Telegraphic address: Detroit, Minn.; telephone to agency.

White Earth Boarding School.

Located 22 miles north of Detroit, Minn., the nearest railroad point. Site almost an ideal location for a school plant. Climate, very long, cold winters; the summers are delightful. Soil, black loam with clay subsoil.

Dormitory.—Character, two-story stone and brick. Use, boys' and girls' dormitories, dining room, kitchen, bakery, playrooms, reading rooms, and employees' rooms. Capacity, 134 pupils, 67 boys and 67 girls. Erected in 1899. Cost, about $37,500. Present value, $36,000. Present condition, excellent.

Schoolhouse.—Character, 1½-story, stone and brick. Use, classrooms, assembly hall and teachers' rooms. Capacity, 150 pupils and 2 teachers' private rooms. Erected in 1899. Cost, about $10,000. Present value, $9,500. Present condition, excellent.

Employees' quarters.—Character, two-story brick. Use, living rooms for employees. Capacity, 8 employees. Erected in 1902. Cost, $4,800. Present value, $4,800. Present condition, excellent.

Warehouse.—Character, 1½-story brick. Use, storing supplies. Dimensions 20 by 40 feet. Erected in 1899. Cost, about $1,000. Present value, $1,000. Present condition, excellent.

Barn.—Character, 1½-story frame and stone. Use, housing live stock and storing hay. Capacity, 5 horses, 10 cows, 6 calves, and 5 tons hay. Erected in 1889. Cost, about $1,000. Present value, $700. Present condition, fair.

Laundry.—Character, one-story brick. Use, washing and ironing pupils' clothing. Capacity, wash room, drying room, and ironing room. Erected in 1899. Cost, about $1,000. Present value, $900. Present condition, excellent.

Well house.—Character, one-story brick. Use, for steam boiler, engine, pump and well covering. Capacity, one boiler, pump and engine room, and coal bin. Erected in 1899. Cost, about $500. Present value, $450. Present condition, good.

Miscellaneous temporary buildings.—Character, all frame. Use, carpenter's shop, employees' quarters, etc. Erected in 1899. (Moved from old school grounds.) Present value, nothing. Present condition, very poor.

Ice house.—Character, frame. Use, for storing ice for school. Capacity, 75 tons ice. Erected in 1901. Cost, $300. Present value, $300. Present condition, excellent.

At present lighted by kerosene lamps, but the buildings are piped for acetylene gas. Heated by steam from two cast-iron sectional low-pressure steam boilers located in basements of buildings. Cost of heating plant included in cost of buildings. Ventilation of the schoolhouse and dormitory building is by the system devised by the Indian Office.

The water is supplied from a well 300 feet deep and is pumped into a large wooden tank of about 15,000 gallons capacity, supported on a steel trestle 60 feet high. The water system was installed when the plant was constructed. The schoolhouse and dormitory building are connected with a 6-inch vitrified, salt-glazed sewer pipe, which empties into a lake about 500 yards east of the buildings; the outfall is 20 feet below the buildings. There are 6 ring baths and 1 bath tub for each of the two dormitories in the main building. They are located on the first floor of the building. There are standpipes in the dormitory building with hose attached on each floor. Water buckets and chemical fire extinguishers in other buildings. Fire hydrants in the grounds.

This school has 160 acres in its reserve, mostly in woods, lakes, and pasture. Only about 20 acres are under cultivation.

This school was opened in the present buildings in December, 1900, with a capacity of 134 pupils.

Pine Point School.

Located near the southeast corner of the White Earth Reservation, near Ponsford Post-office, 20 miles northwest of Park Rapids, Minn., on the Great Northern Railway. Site very low, only about 3 feet above level of a rice lake which adjoins the yard. Climate pleasant and very healthful. Soil a white sand, specially adapted to the growing of Norway pines.

School building.—Character, two-story frame. Use, class rooms, boys' dormitories, sewing room, superintendent's office, quarters for 6 employees, and storeroom for dry goods. Capacity, schoolrooms, 80 pupils; dormitories, 40 pupils. Erected in 1895. Cost, $3,824.80. Present value, $2,500. Present condition, fair.

Girls' building.—Character, two-story frame. Use, dormitory, kitchen, dining room, sitting room, and quarters for 2 employees. Capacity of dormitories, 25 pupils. Capacity of dining room, 50 pupils. Erected in 1889. Present value, $300. Condition, poor.

Boys' building.—Character, two-story frame. Use, mess kitchen and dining room, boys' playroom, washroom, and reading room. Capacity, 30 pupils. Present value, $150. Condition, poor.

Laundry.—Character, one-story log. Use, pupils' washing department. Dimensions, 15 by 30 feet. Present value, nothing. Condition, poor.

128 STATISTICS OF INDIAN TRIBES, AGENCIES, AND SCHOOLS.

Warehouse.—Character, one-story frame. Use, storing supplies. Dimensions, 14 by 22 feet. Present value, nothing. Present condition, poor.

Miscellaneous buildings.—Character, all log except frame wagon shed. Use, stables for horses and cows, ice house, and wagon shed. Capacity, 2 horses, 6 cows, and 2 wagons. Present value, $150. Present condition, fair.

Lighted by kerosene lamps. Heated by wood stoves. No modern system of ventilation. Water of good quality obtained by pumping by hand from shallow driven wells. Refuse carried out in buckets and thrown into pools. These pools are frequently filled up with sand and new ones dug. Washtubs used for bathing. Barrels of water and fire grenades kept ready in all buildings in case of fire.

The school farm consists of 240 acres of swamp and Norway pine. The land is of no value for farming purposes. Furthermore, the title to this land vests in the Episcopal Church; it is held by the church for missionary purposes, but is called Church and School Reservation. Number of acres under fence, 6; acres under cultivation, 2. Additional acres that can be cultivated, none. No fenced pasture. No irrigation.

This school was formerly owned and conducted by the Episcopal Church. In 1892 it was purchased by the United States Government. At that time the capacity was 50 pupils. In 1895 another building was constructed, increasing the capacity to 75 pupils.

Wild Rice River School.

Located 18 miles north of White Earth Agency, White Earth Reservation, Minn. Site is fairly good for school purposes, but is not owned by the Government, having been set aside for the Episcopal mission. Climate, good. Soil is prairie loam, with substratum of clay.

Girls' building.—Character, two-story frame. Use, dining room, kitchen, girls' sitting room, sewing room, dormitory, and employees' quarters. Capacity, 23 pupils. Erected in 1886. Cost, $3,200. Present value, $1,500. Present condition, poor.

Boys' building.—Character, two-story frame. Use, class rooms, boys' sitting room, dormitories, employees' rooms. Capacity, 25 pupils. Erected in 1892. Cost, $1,800. Present value, $1,000. Present condition, poor.

Laundry.—Character, 1½-story frame, with one-story addition. Use, laundry purposes. Capacity, 6 pupils. Erected in 1886. Cost, $800. Present value, $400. Present condition, poor.

Warehouse.—Character, one-story frame. Use, storing supplies. Dimensions, 22 by 57 feet. Erected in 1892. Present value, nothing. Present condition, very poor.

Barn.—Character, one-story frame. Use, housing live stock. Capacity, 5 cows and 4 horses. Erected in 1887. Present value, nothing. Present condition, poor.

Lighted by kerosene lamps. Heated by wood stoves. No modern system of ventilation. The water supply is poor; it is hauled in barrels from the river. There is no sewerage system. Natural drainage is good. Ordinary wash tubs are used for bath tubs. Sitting rooms have to be used for bathrooms. Chemical fire extinguishers, water pails, and barrels furnish fire protection.

The school is situated on mission land, so there is none that belongs to it exclusively. There are 10 acres under fence. About 4 acres under cultivation. There are 160 acres of land reserved for Government purposes half a mile from the present school site, and school cattle are pastured there. This land could be cultivated.

The school was at first under the charge of the Episcopal mission. In 1892 the buildings were purchased by the United States Government. It then had an enrollment of 60 pupils. Present enrollment, 96. The school has never been able to take in all who wish to come, yet is always overcrowded.

YAKIMA AGENCY, WASH.

Under School Superintendent.

Tribes.	Population.
Yakima, Wasco, and others	2,313
Wild Yakimas	366
Total	2,679

Area:	Acres.
Unallotted	587,009
Allotted	211,972
Reserved for agency, school, and church	1,020

Railroad station, North Yakima, on Northern Pacific Railway. Thirty-one miles to agency.

STATISTICS OF INDIAN TRIBES, AGENCIES, AND SCHOOLS. 129

Nearest military post, Fort Spokane, Wash. Post-office address, Fort Simcoe, Wash. Telegraphic address, North Yakima, Wash.

Yakima Indian Training School.

Located 34 miles southwest of North Yakima, Wash., which is on the Northern Pacific Railway. Site is located in the foot-hills of the Cascade Mountains. A small oak grove surrounds the buildings, making it a very pleasant location. The soil is a mixture of loam, clay, sand, volcanic ash, and rock.

Boys' dormitory.—Character, two-story frame. Use, dormitory, sitting room, and play room for boys. Capacity, 75 boys. Erected in 1897. Cost, $5,225. Present value, $4,000. Present condition, fair.

Girls' dormitory.—Character, two-story frame. Use, dormitory and sitting room for girls, dining room for school. Capacity, 75 girls. Erected in 1890. Cost, $7,968. Present value, $5,500. Present condition, fair.

Residences.—Character, 1½-story frame. Use, employees' quarters. Capacity, 3 families. Erected between 1880 and 1900. Present value, nothing. Present condition, poor.

Schoolhouse.—Character, two-story frame. Use, class and assembly rooms. Capacity, 150. Erected in 1881. Cost, $3,000. Present value, $450. Present condition, poor.

Miscellaneous outbuildings.—Character, all frame. Use, wood shed, coal shed. Present value, nothing. Present condition, poor.

Lighted by kerosene lamps. Heated by box stoves burning wood. Boys' and girls' dormitories ventilated by the system devised by the Indian Office; other buildings have no arrangements for ventilation. The water supply is ample except sometimes in the midst of the summer. The water is good and is supplied from springs about 1½ miles from the school, piped to a large reservoir about 120 feet above the buildings. Good pressure for fire protection. Buildings are connected with main sewer, which carries to an irrigation ditch in the field. Both dormitories are equipped with ring and tub baths. Water mains are laid so as to have hydrants within reach of all the buildings. The dormitories have stand pipes with hose attached on both floors.

There are 100 acres under fence. This land was reserved from tribal lands and has not cost the Department anything. There are 277 acres in reserve, 100 acres under fence, 70 acres under cultivation. There is no more land to be put into cultivation. Thirty acres in pasture. Practically 80 acres irrigated.

This school was established in 1860 at its present location as Yakima Agency Boarding School.

YANKTON AGENCY, S. DAK.

Under School Superintendent.

Tribe.	Population.
Yankton Sioux	1,680

Area:	Acres.
Allotted	268,568
Reserved for agency, school, and church	1,253

Railroad station: Wagner, on Chicago, Milwaukee and St. Paul Railway. Fourteen miles to school by stage.

Nearest military post, Fort Niobrara or Fort Crook, Nebr. Post-office address, Greenwood, S. Dak. Telegraphic address, Wagner, S. Dak.

Yankton Training School.

Located on the Missouri River, 13 miles south of Wagner on the Chicago, Milwaukee and St. Paul Railway. Site is finely located on slight elevation. Climate is usually mild, but subject to extremes in temperature.

Boys' building.—Character, three-story frame with stone basement. Use, boys' dormitory, two school rooms, sewing room, employees' quarters, lavatories, etc., in basement. Capacity, 50 boys. Erected in 1882. Cost, $13,000. Present value, $5,000. Present condition, fair.

Girls' building.—Character, two-story frame. Use, girls' dormitory, 2 schoolrooms, employees' quarters, lavatories, etc., in basement. Capacity, 50 girls. Erected in 1890. Cost, $9,700. Present value, $8,000. Present condition, good.

Dining hall and kitchen.—Character, one-story frame, stone foundation. Use, dining hall, kitchen, and bakery. Capacity, 200. Erected in 1895. Cost, $3,994. Present value, $3,500. Present condition, excellent.

Laundry.—Character, one-story frame. Use, laundry and ironing room. Capacity, 100. Erected in 1886. Cost, $900. Present value, $500. Present condition, fair.

Teachers' residence.—Character, 1½-story frame. Use, employees' dining hall and kitchen. Capacity, 12 employees. Erected in 1879. Cost, 350. Present value, $100. Present condition, bad.

Teachers' residence.—Character, one-story frame. Use, employees' quarters. Capacity, 2 employees. Erected in 1895. Cost, $300. Present value, $200. Present condition, fair.

Blacksmith and carpenter shop.—Character, one-story frame, 2 rooms. Use, carpenter and paint shop. Dimensions, 12 by 16 feet. Erected in 1896. Cost, $350. Present value, $200. Present condition, fair.

Coal house.—Character, one-story frame. Use, storing coal. Capacity, 50 tons coal. Erected in 1898. Cost, $250. Present value, $200. Present condition, good.

Coal house.—Character, one-story frame. Use, storing coal. Capacity, 60 tons coal. Erected in 1900. Cost, $425. Present value, $400. Present condition, good.

Meat house.—Character, one-story frame, one room, cement floor. Use, cold-storage building. Dimensions, 16 by 24 feet. Erected in 1901. Cost, $225. Present value, $225. Present condition, excellent.

School barn.—Character, 1½-story frame. Use, stabling horses and hay loft. Dimensions, 24 by 32 feet. Erected in 1884. Cost, $400. Present value, $200. Present condition, good.

School barn addition.—Character, 1½-story frame. Use, cattle barn. Dimensions, 18 by 20 feet. Erected in 1900. Cost, $225. Present value, $200. Present condition, good.

Cattle sheds.—Character, one-story frame. Use, shelter for cattle. Dimensions, 18 by 36 feet. Erected in 1887. Cost, $300. Present value, $100. Present condition, fair.

Cattle sheds.—Character, one-story frame. Use, shelter for cattle. Dimensions, 14 by 40 feet. Erected in 1900. Cost, $100. Present value, $75. Present condition, good.

Warehouse.—Character, 1½-story frame. Use, storing agricultural implements. Dimensions, 20 by 30 feet. Erected in 1887. Cost, $200. Present value, $100. Present condition, good.

Corn crib.—Character, one-story frame on piles. Use, storing corn. Dimensions, 18 by 24 feet. Erected in 1900. Cost, $125. Present value, $100. Present condition, good.

Lighted by kerosene lamps. Heated by hard-coal stoves. Ventilation: There is none except through windows and transoms.

Water supply is pure, coming from Missouri River through steam pumping plant and tank recently installed, at a cost of $4,225. System good except lack of storage capacity in tank. The three main buildings are connected by an 8-inch general sewer pipe emptying into the Missouri River about 300 yards from the buildings and 150 yards below the intake pipe of the water system. Bathing facilities consist of shower baths in both dormitories. Both plants are so badly out of repair that system is practically useless. Ordinary washtubs are used at present. Fire protection is furnished through the new water system, but the three fire hydrants located on school grounds are too remote from buildings and fire hose on hand is insufficient. The pressure is good.

School has 600 acres of farm and pasture land of black loam soil and good quality. The farm is located on the original agency reserve, and is probably worth $10 per acre. Under fence, 600 acres. Under cultivation, 55 acres. Can cultivate 50 additional acres. Pasture contains 495 acres. None of farm is irrigated.

Day schools opened by missionaries as early as 1874 were supplanted by what is now known as the boys' building at the Yankton Training School, which was built in 1882 and opened in that year, with an attendance of 32 boys and 31 girls. The plant has gradually grown until it is now a fairly well-equipped reservation school, with an attendance of 150 pupils, its full capacity.

YUMA RESERVATION, CAL.

(Under School Superintendent.)

Tribe.	Population.
Yuma	650

Area, 45,889 acres, unallotted.

Railroad station: Yuma, on Southern Pacific Railroad, one-half mile to school.

Nearest military post: Presidio, Cal. Post-office address: Yuma, Ariz. Telegraphic address: Yuma, Ariz.

STATISTICS OF INDIAN TRIBES, AGENCIES, AND SCHOOLS. 131

Fort Yuma School.

Located one-half mile north of Yuma, Ariz., on the Southern Pacific Railway. Site on rocky, barren knoll; good drainage, otherwise a poor site. Soil very fertile when wa ered.

Employees' cottage.—Character, one-story adobe, 5 rooms. Use, principal teacher's house. Capacity, one family. Erected about 1860. Present value, very little. Present condition, very poor.

Commissary.—Character, one-story adobe. Use, storing supplies. Dimensions, 21 by 27 feet. Erected about 1860. Present value, very little. Present condition, very poor.

Superintendent's cottage.—Character, one-story frame. Use, superintendent's office and dwelling. Capacity, 2 office rooms and 5 dwelling rooms. Erected in 1895. Cost, $5,000. Present value, $4,000. Present condition, fair.

Girls' dormitory.—Character, two-story frame. Use, 3 dormitory rooms, 1 bathroom, and 2 employees' quarters. Capacity, 80 pupils. Erected in 1900. Cost, $8,500. Present value, $8,000. Present condition, good.

Dining room.—Character, one-story adobe. Use, dining room, kitchen, and storeroom. Capacity, 200 pupils. Rebuilt in 1900, after fire. Cost, $3,500. Present value, $3,500. Present condition, good.

Schoolhouse.—Character, one-story adobe. Use, 3 class rooms. Capacity, 75 pupils. Erected about 1860. Present condition, poor.

Boys' dormitory.—Character, one-story adobe. Use, 2 dormitory rooms and one employees' quarters. Capacity, 100 pupils. Erected about 1860. Present condition, fair.

Sewing-room building.—Character, one-story adobe. Use, sewing room, 1 schoolroom, and 2 employees' quarters. Capacity, sewing room, 20 pupils; schoolroom, 25 pupils; 2 employees. Erected about 1860. Present condition, fair.

Three cottages.—Character, 3 one-story adobe cottages. Use, employees' quarters, mess dining room, and kitchen. Capacity, 9 employees. Erected about 1860. Present condition, fair.

Carpenter shop.—Character, one-story adobe and frame. Use, carpenter shop and guardhouse. Dimensions, 25 by 67 feet. Erected about 1860; frame part later. Present condition, poor; frame part, fair.

Doctor's office.—Character, one-story adobe. Use, doctor's office. Capacity, doctor's office and medicine room. Erected about 1860. Present condition, fair.

Laundry.—Character, one-story adobe. Use, school laundry. Dimensions, 22 by 35 feet. Erected about 1860. Present condition, very poor.

Stable.—Character, one-story adobe. Use, housing live stock and storing hay, etc., and carriage. Capacity, 6 horses and 5 tons of hay. Erected about 1860. Present condition, poor.

Bakery.—Character, one-story adobe and frame. Use, bakery and one employees' quarters. Dimensions, 33 by 18 feet. Erected about 1860. Present condition, poor.

Shoe shop.—Character, one-story adobe. Use, shoe and harness shop. Dimensions, 25½ by 15½ feet. Erected about 1860. Present value, very little. Present condition, very poor.

Pump house.—Character, frame building. Use, pump and engine house. Capacity, boiler and 2 pumps. Erected and added to at different times. Cost, $200. Present value, $200. Present condition, fair.

Bath house.—Character, one-story frame. Use, bath house. Capacity, 6 ring baths, 1 tub, and lavatory. Erected in 1901. Cost, $1,200. Present value, $1,200. Present condition, good.

Outhouses.—Character, frame. Use, closets. Erected at different times. Present condition, very poor.

Lighted by electricity furnished by the Yuma Water and Light Company, of Yuma, Ariz. There are 130 incandescent lights. Installed July 1, 1901. Only fairly satisfactory. Heated by wood stoves. No special means of ventilation is used. None is needed, as no room remains closed while in use.

Water supply is good. The source is the Colorado River. The water is first pumped into a 25,000-gallon settling tank at pump house near the river; after settling it is forced into two tanks on the hill near the school. The pressure is ample for most purposes, but will not carry water to the top of one building. This system has been put in a piece at a time, as needed, and is not yet complete. It is difficult to estimate cost or present worth. There are two sewers emptying into cesspools. Very unsatisfactory. There are 6 ring baths and 1 tub in girls' dormitory, and the same in bath house connected with boys' dormitory. The girls' dormitory contains stand pipe. Water buckets are in all buildings and 3 fire hydrants on the grounds.

Three hundred and twenty acres of land belong to the school. About 12 acres have recently been put under irrigation. The soil is found to be highly impregnated with alkali; until this can be overcome little can be raised.

This school was opened in April, 1884, at the abandoned army post at Fort Yuma.

ZUÑI INDIANS, NEW MEXICO.

(Under School Superintendent.)

Tribe.	Population.
Pueblo	1,540

Area, 215,040 acres, unallotted.
Railroad station: Gallup, Santa Fe Pacific Railroad.
Post-office address: Zuni, N. Mex. Telegraphic address: Gallup, N. Mex.

Zuni Boarding School, Zuni Pueblo, N. Mex.

Located 45 miles south of Gallup, N. Mex., in the valley of the upper Zuni River. Site, very poor. Climate, very dry, without extreme changes; windy. Soil, adobe clay mixed with sand.

Employees' building.—Character, one-story adobe with one-half story frame addition. Use, employees' quarters. Capacity, 4 rooms and shed. Erected in 1882. Present value, $500. Present condition, poor.

Schoolhouse—Character, one-story adobe with one-half story frame addition. Use, class rooms and domestic teaching. Capacity, 60 pupils. Erected in 1878. Present value, $400. Present condition, poor.

Laundry.—Character, one-story frame with one-half story addition. Use, laundry and storeroom. Capacity, 4 rooms. Erected in 1892. Cost, $300. Present value, $300. Present condition, fair.

Lighted by kerosene lamps; heated by wood stoves; no system of ventilation. The water is slightly alkaline. Its source is a well on the grounds. The water is pumped by windmill power into a wooden tank of 500 gallons' capacity and situated on a wooden platform standing 20 feet high. Water is carried to buildings in iron pipes. Cost of water system, about $300. No underground system of sewerage, simply waste pipes and surface drainage. There are two bath tubs, one porcelain lined, situated in laundry room, and the other a tin one situated in employees' building. No system of fire protection.

There are about 10 acres of land in connection with this school, but it is of no value for farming purposes.

This plant was organized as a mission, Presbyterian, about 1890. The Government took charge of this school and purchased the property in 1898. It has been conducted as a day school with a noonday lunch, with the specific object of teaching domestic subjects aside from literary subjects.

NONRESERVATION BOARDING SCHOOLS.

Each of the following schools is under the direction of a bonded superintendent, and receives pupils from reservations assigned each:

Albuquerque Indian School.

Located 2½ miles north of Albuquerque, N. Mex., on the Atchison, Topeka and Santa Fe Railway. Site very poor for school purposes. Climate without extreme changes, and very delightful. Soil very strongly alkaline adobe, underlaid by gravel and sand. Scarcely anything will grow upon the farm.

Assembly hall.—Character, 1½-story adobe. Use, carpenter shop and storeroom for boys' clothing. Capacity, 5 rooms, 30 by 110 feet. Erected about 1882. Cost, $800. Present value, nothing. Present condition, very poor.

Bakery.—Character, one-story frame. Use, school bake shop. Capacity, 2 rooms, 24 by 36 feet. Erected in 1890. Cost, $300. Present value, $300. Present condition, fair.

Barn.—Character, 1½-story frame. Use, housing live stock and storing hay. Capacity, 9 horses, 10 cows, and 35 tons baled hay. Erected in 1889. Cost, $1,000. Present value, $700. Present condition, fair.

Bath house.—Character, 1½-story frame. Use, boys' bathing facilities. Capacity, 4 rooms, 40 by 50 feet, 16 baths. Erected in 1893. Cost, $1,000. Present value, $900. Present condition, good.

Superintendent's cottage.—Character, one-story frame. Use, superintendent's dwelling. Capacity, 5 rooms. Erected in 1888. Cost, $350. Present value, $200. Present condition, good.

Employees' cottages (2).—Character, one-story frame. Use, employees' quarters. Capacity, 3 employees and guest room, 8 rooms. Erected in 1890 and 1900. Cost, $500 each. Present value, $300 and $500. Present condition, good.

Hospital.—Character, two-story frame. Use, isolation and care of sick. Capacity, 30 pupils. Erected in 1890. Cost, $1,500. Present value, $1,200. Present condition, good.

Boys' dormitory.—Character, two-story brick. Use, boys' dormitory, dining rooms, and employee's quarters. Capacity, 200. Erected in 1884. Cost, $30,000. Present value, $10,000. Present condition, fair.

Girls' dormitory.—Character, two-story brick. Use, girls' dormitory and sitting room and employees' quarters. Capacity, 150 pupils, 9 rooms. Erected in 1893. Cost, $10,000. Present value, $10,000. Present condition, good.

Girls' bath house.—Character, one-story brick. Use, girls' bathing house. Capacity, 2 rooms, 11 baths. Erected in 1898. Cost, $800. Present value, $800. Present condition, good.

Carriage house.—Character, 1½-story frame. Use, carriage and storehouse. Capacity, 10 vehicles. Erected in 1889. Cost, $100. Present value, $75. Present condition, fair.

Kitchen.—Character, one-story frame. Use, school kitchen. Capacity, 1 three-oven range and 2 dish-washing sinks. Erected in 1890. Cost, $2,500. Present value, $1,500. Present condition, fair.

Laundry.—Character, one-story frame. Use, laundry for pupils' clothing. Capacity, 12 ironers and 2 steam washers, 2 rooms. Erected in 1885. Cost, $900. Present value, $500. Present condition, bad.

Manual training room.—Character, two-story frame. Use, kindergarten and shoe shop. Capacity, 24 kindergarten pupils and 10 shoe benches. Erected in 1887. Cost, $600. Present value, $500. Present condition, fair.

Office and storeroom.—Character, one-story brick. Use, 2 rooms for office work and 2 for storerooms. Dimensions, 45 by 75 feet. Erected in 1884. Cost, $5,000. Present value, $2,000. Present condition, fair.

134 STATISTICS OF INDIAN TRIBES, AGENCIES, AND SCHOOLS.

Schoolhouse.—Character, two-story brick. Use, class rooms and assembly hall. Capacity, 300 pupils. Erected in 1888. Cost, $12,000. Present value, $10,000. Present condition, good.

Miscellaneous outbuildings.—Character, all frame. Use, blacksmith shop, 3 coal houses, corn crib, meat house, poultry house, and 2 storerooms. Erected in 1889 to 1899. Cost, $745. Present value, $475. Present condition, fair.

Lighted by electricity furnished by private party. There are 250 incandescent lights; light satisfactory. Heated by coal and wood stoves. No system for ventilaton.

The water supplied is pure and cool, but hard. Derived from a number of points driven 55 feet into the river bottom, the tops of the pipes being united into one large pipe. From this pipe it is forced by a steam pump into two steel tanks on steel trestles standing 60 feet high, and thence distributed to all parts of the school plant. The pressure is ample to throw the water over the highest building. The water is used for domestic and stock purposes and for irrigating the lawns. The system was first instituted with small tanks on low towers, and afterwards improved with the large tanks and high towers, and has cost, approximately, $5,000. System further improved by erection of pump house in 1902 at a cost of $2,436.

All the buildings are connected with an 8-inch general sewer pipe, which empties into the city sewer pipes and thence into the Rio Grande River below the city of Albuquerque. The outfall is but little below the buildings, which necessitated the laying the head of the sewers slightly above the natural surface of the ground, but the sewer was laid to an accurate scale, and exposed places have been properly protected and it works in a manner entirely satisfactory. There are 16 ring baths for the boys' lavatory, and 9 rings and 2 tubs for the girls' lavatory, located in buildings specially constructed for the purpose. There are water buckets and chemical fire extinguishers on all floors and in all halls, and fire hydrants over the ground.

This school has 66 acres of land, which was donated to the Government by the citizens of Albuquerque, N. Mex. It is so strongly alkaline as to make it wholly worthless for farming purposes. What little land has been made suitable for gardening and lawns has been made so at a tremendous expense. There are about 66 acres under fence, divided into smaller tracts by division fences. The whole 66 acres has been cultivated, and is all subject to irrigation, but only about 5 acres produce crops worth mentioning.

In 1882 the citizens of Albuquerque, N. Mex., donated 66 acres of land, 2 miles north of Albuquerque, to the United States Government for the use of an Indian school. In 1884 the Government erected two brick buildings. These two buildings were occupied by the Presbyterian Mission, under contract from the Government, from 1884 to 1886. In 1886 the Government assumed charge, and has run the school ever since, making improvements and enlarging it from time to time until now there is a capacity of 300.

Carlisle Indian Industrial School.

Located about three-fourths of a mile northeast of Carlisle, Pa., on the Cumberland Valley Railroad, 18 miles southwest of Harrisburg. Carlisle is also reached by a branch of the Philadelphia and Reading Railroad. Location admirably adapted for the purpose of an Indian industrial school, being in a rich agricultural region, surrounded by the best civilizing influences of the East. Climate healthy. Extremes of heat and cold rarely experienced.

Guardhouse.—Character, one-story stone. Use, confinement of incorrigible male pupils; built for confinement of prisoners during Revolutionary war. Dimensions, 71 by 32 feet. Erected in 1776. Present value, $500. Present condition, good.

School building.—Character, two-story brick. Use, class rooms and assembly hall. Capacity, 773 pupils. Erected in 1888 and 1899. Cost, $23,831.03. Present value, $29,364.55. Present condition, good.

Office building.—Character, two-story brick. Use, offices on first floor, employees' rooms on second floor. Capacity, 5 offices and 5 rooms for employees. Erected in 1891. Cost, $3,000. Present value, $3,000. Present condition, good.

Teachers' quarters.—Character, two-story brick. Use, quarters and dining room for employees. Capacity, 30 employees. Erected in 1866. Present value, $13,000. Present condition, fair.

Superintendent's quarters.—Character, two-story brick. Use, superintendent's dwelling. Capacity, 10 rooms. Erected in 1866. Present value, $7,000. Present condition, excellent.

Assistant superintendent's quarters.—Character, two-story frame. Use, assistant superintendent's dwelling. Capacity, 9 rooms. Erected in 1847. Present value, $1,100. Present condition, fair.

STATISTICS OF INDIAN TRIBES, AGENCIES, AND SCHOOLS. 135

Small boys' quarters.—Character, two-story brick. Use, dormitory for small boys. Capacity, 132 pupils. Erected in 1887. Present value, $10,000. Present condition, good.

Large boys' quarters.—Character, three-story brick. Use, dormitory for large boys. Capacity, 279 pupils. Erected in 1887. Present value, $18,000. Present condition, good.

Girls' quarters.—Character, three-story brick. Use, dormitory for girls. Capacity. 292 pupils. Erected, 1866 to 1891. Present value, $33,300. Present condition, good.

Hospital.—Character, two-story frame. Use, isolation and care of sick pupils. Capacity, 43 pupils. Erected, 1881 and 1891. Cost, $4,900. Present value, $4,900. Present condition, good.

Dining hall.—Character, two-story frame. Use, pupils' dining room, kitchen, domestic-science department, sewing room, and rooms for employees. Capacity—of dining room, 1,000; of sewing room, 160, half-day work each. Erected 1885 and 1901. Cost, $13,500. Present value, $13,500. Present condition, good.

Bakery.—Character, one-story brick. Use, baking bread, etc., for pupils. Dimensions, 32 by 39½ feet. Erected in 1888. Cost, $500. Present value, $500. Present condition, fair.

Warehouse.—Character, two-story brick. Use, storing school supplies. Dimensions, 100 by 60 feet. Erected, 1890 and 1901; Cost, $5,500. Present value, $5,500. Present condition, good.

Lumber storehouse.—Character, one-story stone. Use, storing dressed lumber. Dimensions, 54 by 29 feet. Erected in 1866. Present value, $1,000. Present condition, good.

Shops.—Character, two-story brick. Use, carpenter, tin, paint, blacksmith, carriage and wagon, tailor, harness and shoe shops, printing office, band room, storeroom, and sleeping apartments. Capacity of industrial shops, 236 pupils, each working half days. Erected in 1866 and 1896. Present value, $12,700. Present condition, fair.

Hostler's house.—Character, one-story frame. Use, teamster's dwelling. Capacity, 3 rooms. Erected in 1864. Present value, $300. Present condition, fair.

Stable.—Character, two-story frame. Use, housing horses, feed, and vehicles. Dimensions, 72 by 42 feet. Erected in 1889. Cost, $2,500. Present value, $2,500. Present condition; good.

Coal house.—Character, part one story, part two story, stone, brick, and frame. Use, storing coal, and engineer's supply and workshop. Capacity, 2,000 tons coal. Erected in 1864. Present value, $500. Present condition, fair.

Disciplinarian's quarters.—Character, two-story frame. Use, disciplinarian's dwelling. Capacity, 7 rooms. Erected in 1883. Cost, $800. Present value, $800. Present condition, good.

Engineer's quarters.—Character, one-story frame. Use, engineer's dwelling. Capacity, 6 rooms. Erected in 1880. Cost, $600. Present value, $600. Present condition, fair.

Coal house at siding.—Character, one-story frame. Use, house built over railroad siding for unloading and storing coal. Dimensions, 97 by 28 feet. Erected in 1887. Cost, $400. Present value, $400. Present condition, good.

Mansion house, Parker farm.—Character, two-story brick. Use, farmer's dwelling. Capacity, 10 rooms. Present value, $3,000. Present condition, good.

Tenant house, Parker farm.—Character, 1½-story frame. Use, dairyman's dwelling. Capacity, 6 rooms. Present value, $400. Present condition, fair.

Barn, Parker farm.—Character, two-story stone and frame. Use, housing live stock and storing crops. Dimensions, 120 by 65 feet. Erected in 1891. Cost, $5,841. Present value, $6,000. Present condition, good.

Boiler house and smokestack.—Character, one-story brick. Use, housing four 150-horsepower steam boilers. Dimensions, 65 by 45 feet. Erected, 1891 and 1900. Cost, $7,500. Present value, $7,500. Present condition, good.

Gymnasium and society hall.—Character, one and three story brick. Use, physical training, baths, reading, Y. M. C. A., and literary society rooms. Dimensions, 194 by 64 feet. Erected, 1887 and 1895. Cost $13,000. Present value, $13,000. Present condition, good.

Laundry.—Character, one-story brick. Use, washing and ironing pupils' clothing and bedding. Dimensions, 138 by 45 feet. Erected in 1896. Cost, $3,700. Present value, $3,700. Present condition, good.

Double dwelling.—Character, two-story frame. Use, occupied by employees with families. Capacity, 16 rooms. Erected in 1900. Cost, $3,500. Present value, $3,500. Present condition, good.

Farmhouse, Kutz farm.—Character, two-story brick. Use, assistant farmer's dwelling. Capacity, 11 rooms. Erected (rebuilt) in 1901. Cost, $2,500. Present value, $2,500. Present condition, excellent.

Barn, Kutz farm.—Character, first story stone, second story frame. Use, housing live stock and storing crops. Dimensions, 72 by 54 feet. Cost, $5,000. Present value, $2,000. Present condition, fair.

Barn and wagon shed, Kutz farm.—Character, frame. Use, storing crops, wagons, and implements. Dimensions, 51 by 31 feet. Cost, $2,000. Present value, $1,000. Present condition, poor.

Miscellaneous outbuildings.—Character, principally frame. Use, smokehouse, spring house, wagon shed, corn crib, etc. Present condition, poor to fair.

Lighted by electricity furnished by the Carlisle Gas and Water Company at a cost of $2,060 per year for the current. There are nearly 600 incandescent lights and a dozen arc lights, three of which are located outside of the buildings and burn all night. Heated by steam from a central plant which was renewed and enlarged in 1900 by installing four 150-horsepower boilers. Ventilation in general is by transoms. No modern system in use.

The water is generally pure but hard, this being a limestone region. It is supplied from the town reservoir, by gravity, at an annual cost of $240. Flushing closets are in use throughout the various buildings. Pipes ranging from 4 to 10 inches in diameter carry the sewage from the buildings into a 12-inch main pipe which empties into the Letort Creek about half a mile from the school. The fall is about 20 feet to the outlet. There are 58 bath tubs in the various dormitories and other buildings; also 27 shower baths in the gymnasium. In addition to a fire engine and hose carriage owned by the school, the borough of Carlisle has placed one of their fire engines here for use of the school. Six patent fire extinguishers are also on hand, and pails filled with water are placed throughout the buildings, as required by the Department. Fire hydrants are located at suitable places on the school grounds.

This school has two farms, containing 284 acres, valued at about $40,000, all under fence; 259 acres in various kinds of grain, vegetables and fruit, 15 acres meadow land, used for pasturage. Irrigation unnecessary.

This school was organized October 6, 1879, with 82 pupils. For the fiscal year 1903 the school had an enrollment of 1,033 pupils. The outing system is a prominent feature of this school.

Carson Indian School.

Located 3½ miles south of Carson, Nev. The site well suited for school purposes. Climate, excellent. Soil of immediate site poor, very sandy, and requires frequent fertilizing. Crops produced by irrigation; an insufficient quantity of water obtainable for extensive farming or gardening.

Main school building.—Character, two-story frame building with ell, one story. Use, dormitory, dining room and kitchen, school rooms, sewing room, chapel, bathrooms (small boys' and employees'), employees' quarters. Capacity, 150 pupils, 12 employees. Erected, 1890-1892; dining room enlarged, and kitchen added 1900; bakery under same roof. Cost, $32,500. Present value, $25,000. Present condition, excellent.

Storehouse and office and addition to storehouse and office.—Character, one-story frame building, 4 rooms. Use, superintendent and clerks' offices, printing office, and storeroom. Erected in 1891 and addition in 1900. Cost, $1,164. Present value, $1,000. Present condition, good.

Tank tower.—Character, three-story frame. Use, 12,000-gallon water tank, storage room, and refrigerator. Erected in 1891. Cost, $1,000. Present value, $800. Present condition, fair.

Engine house.—Character, one-story frame with ell. Use, engine and boiler and turning lathes. Erected in 1895. Cost, $178.72. Present value, $150. Present condition, fair.

Laundry and bath house.—Character, one-story frame building, contains laundry and ironing room, boys' clothing room, lavatory, and bathrooms. Erected in 1891. Cost, $1,232.57. Present value, $1,000. Present condition, fair.

Hennery.—Character, one-story frame, siding perpendicular, plank roof. Use, for fowls. Erected in 1896. Cost, $67.32. Present value, $50.

Warehouse.—Character, one-story frame building. Use, storehouse. Dimensions, 24 by 30 feet. Erected—converted from coal and wood house to warehouse, 1901. Cost, $400; additional cost, $300. Present value, $700. Present condition, excellent.

Privies (2).—Dimensions, one story, 8 by 14 feet each. Erected in 1891. Cost, $69.75. Present value, $5 each. Present condition, poor.

Stone root house.—Character, one-story stone, 18 by 24 feet. Use, storing vegetables. Capacity, 500 bushels. Erected in 1876. Cost, $900. Present value, $200. Present condition, fair.

Employees' cottages.—Character, two 1½-story frames, one one-story frame with stone basement. Use, employees' quarters. Capacity, 15. Erected, 1859, 1893, 1859. Cost, average, $600. Present value, $400. Present condition, good.

Barn.—Character, 1½-story frame. Use, housing horses and storing hay and grain. Capacity, 12 horses, 20 tons hay. Erected in 1859. Cost, $2,000. Present value, $1,500. Present condition, fair.

Girls' dormitory.—Character, two-story frame, 40 by 60 feet. Use, girls' home. Capacity, 80 pupils. Erected in 1900. Cost, $10,000. Present value, $10,000. Present condition, excellent.

Workshops.—Character, two-story frame building. Use, blacksmith, carpenter, shoe, and tailor shops. Capacity, 40 pupils. Erected in 1901. Cost, $2,500. Present value, $3,000. Present condition, excellent.

Bath and clothing room.—Character, one-story frame, 24 by 36 feet. Erected in 1900. Cost, $496. Present value, $496. Present condition, good.

Acetylene gas house. Character, frame. Use, acetylene gas machine. Erected in 1901. Cost, $400. Present value, $400. Present condition, excellent.

Miscellaneous outbuildings.—Character, all frame. Uses, cow barns, wagon sheds, tool house, cow sheds, old carpenter and blacksmith shops, ice house, two pesthouses, and annex. Erected, 1893-1900. Present condition, fairly good.

Lighted by acetylene gas and gasoline gas. Furnished by acetylene gas and gasoline gas machines. The acetylene machine is placed in a house erected therefor. The gasoline machine installed in the girls' home; 100 acetylene lights are in use. Plant installed 1901; cost, $1,200. Gasoline plant was installed under the contract for the erection of the girls' home in 1900, cost unknown; 14 lights are in use. The acetylene light is the more satisfactory. The girls' home heated by steam from a boiler located in basement installed with the erection of the building in 1900. All other buildings heated by coal and wood stoves. The ventilation of the girls' home is by the system devised by the Indian Office. Other buildings have no modern system except open shafts, recently placed in the halls of the main schol building, extending above the roof.

The water supply is pure and soft. It is pumped from wells into an elevated tank and distributed through the buildings. Its source is from a mountain stream and finds its way by seeping through the porous sand to the wells from Clear Creek. It is pumped by a steam engine into a wooden tank of 12,000 gallons capacity. The tank has an elevation of 48 feet. This system was installed when the plant was constructed and afterwards improved at a cost unknown. All the buildings are connected with an 8-inch general sewer pipe which empties into Clear Creek about one-half mile from the building and below the source of the water supply. The outfall is about 8 feet below the building. There are 4 ring baths and 1 tub for the girls' dormitory. They are located on the lower floor of this building. There are 7 bath tubs for the larger boys at this time located at one end of the laundry building. There are 2 bath tubs for the employees located in small rooms in the main building. There are 2 small bath tubs and 1 large bathing tank for the small boys located in the main building. There are standpipes in the two larger buildings with a hose on each floor and fire hydrants in the grounds.

This school has 279 acres of land. It is sandy and poor. Its estimated value is about $3,000. There are about 150 acres under fence. About 80 acres under cultivation and in pasture. The pasture of little value. The grounds around the buildings have a number of shade and fruit trees. The fruit trees have never borne and will not bear, the fruit being destroyed by frost due to the cold winds late in the spring from the canyon immediately on the west of the grounds. No additional acres can be cultivated without securing more water for irrigation.

This school was opened in 1890.

Chamberlain School.

Located 1 mile north of Chamberlain, S. Dak., on the Chicago, Milwaukee and St. Paul Railway. Site not very well adapted for farming purposes, therefore not well suited for an agricultural school. All right for an industrial school wherein trades are taught. Soil of sandy loam on substratum of hardpan.

Main building or dormitory.—Character, two-story brick with basement. Use, dormitory, dining room, and kitchen. Capacity, 100 pupils. Erected in 1897. Cost, $21,100. Present value, $19,000. Present condition, fair.

Addition to above building.—Character, one-story brick. Use, kitchen and pantry. Erected, under construction (1903). Cost, $9,600.

Dormitory building.—Character, 2½-story brick. Use, dormitory. Capacity, 100 pupils. Erected, under construction (1903). Cost, $15,506.65.

School building.—Character, 1½-story brick. Use, assembly hall and class rooms. Capacity, hall, 500; class rooms, 150. Erected, under construction (1903). Cost, $14,505.50.

Hospital.—Character, one-story frame. Use, isolation and care of sick. Capacity, 6 pupils. Erected in 1898. Cost, $1,500. Present value, $1,200. Present condition, good.

Laundry.—Character, one-story frame. Use, laundry purposes. Dimensions, 22 by 46 feet. Erected in 1898. Cost, $993. Present value, $850. Present condition, good.

Stable.—Character, 1½-story frame. Use, housing horses and storing hay. Capacity, 5 horses, 3 tons hay. Erected in 1898. Cost, $944. Present value, $800. Present condition, good.

Carpenter and blacksmith shop.—Character, one-story frame. Use, carpenter and blacksmith shop. Capacity, 5 pupils. Erected in 1898. Cost, $1,380. Present value, $1,200. Present condition, good.

Warehouse.—Character, one-story frame. Use, storing supplies. Dimensions, 20 by 50 feet. Erected in 1901. Cost, $1,435. Present value, $1,400. Present condition, excellent.

Shoe shop.—Character, one-story frame, 20 by 30 feet. Use, shoe shop. Capacity, 10 pupils. Erected in 1898. Cost, $327. Present value, $300. Present condition, good.

Pump house.—Character, one-story frame. Use, housing pumping machinery. Dimensions, 20 by 30 feet. Erected in 1898. Cost, $287. Present value, $200. Present condition, good.

Wagon shed.—Character, one-story frame. Use, housing vehicles and machinery. Dimensions, 20 by 50 feet. Erected in 1901. Cost, $400. Present value, $400. Present condition, excellent.

Miscellaneous outbuildings.—Character, all frame. Use, chicken house, cattle shed, coal house, ice house, root cellar, water-closets, and reel house. Erected, 1898 to 1901. Cost, $896. Present value, $600. Present condition, fair.

Gas house.—Character, one-story frame. Use, housing acetylene gas plant. Erected, under construction (1903). Cost, $918.75.

Dormitory lighted by acetylene gas. Hospital piped for gas, but connection not made yet. There are 94 one-half foot burners in use. Plant was installed October, 1901, at a cost of $1,200. Plant is in good condition, but lights give trouble on account of formation of carbon and soot. Dormitory heated by steam by plant located in basement. This steam plant was installed when building was erected. It is not satisfactory, and there is not enough radiation to keep all the rooms properly heated. The hospital, laundry, shops, and other small buildings are heated by coal stoves. Ventilation of schoolrooms and dormitories is by the system devised by the Indian Office. Hospital by same system.

The water supplied is pure and soft. It is taken from the Missouri River by means of a pump which is driven by an artesian well. The water is forced by pump to reservoirs located in a high hill east of the dormitory or main building. The pressure is ample to force the water to all parts of the building. This river water is not used for fire protection. The artesian water is used for fire protection and irrigation. The water system, artesian well, and sewer were installed in 1898 at a cost of $5,000.

All the buildings are connected with an 8-inch general sewer pipe which empties into the Missouri River below the source of our water supply. Extension of sewer and water systems now being constructed (1903) at a cost of $1,480. There are 8 shower baths, 4 in the boys' bathroom and 4 in the girls' bathroom. The bathrooms are located on the first floor of the dormitory. They have never been satisfactory. There are standpipes in the dormitory or main building. These are connected directly with artesian well, which has a running pressure of 65 pounds to the square inch. Fire main and hydrants connected with artesian well furnish ample fire protection at present.

This school has 160 acres of land. It was purchased in 1897 for $2,600. Very little of the land is level. What is not broken and rolling slopes toward the river. Present value of land is about $2,600. There are 130 acres under fence; about 20 acres under cultivation, mostly garden. Remaining portion too rolling and broken for cultivation, only suitable for pasture. One hundred and thirty acres are used for pasture.

This school was opened May 5, 1898, with a capacity of 80 pupils.

STATISTICS OF INDIAN TRIBES, AGENCIES, AND SCHOOLS.

Chilocco Industrial School.

Located 7 miles southwest of Arkansas City, Kans.; 1¾ miles from station of Chilocco on the Atchison, Topeka and Santa Fe Railway, and three-fourths mile southeast of station of Cale on the St. Louis and San Francisco Railway. Site admirably suited for school purposes, with climate without extreme changes. Soil, deep prairie loam on a substratum of rock.

Girls' home.—Character, three-story stone with basement. Use, dormitory for girls; employees' rooms on first floor. Capacity, dormitory, 150 pupils. Erected in 1893. Cost, about $21,000 (erected with chapel and domestic buildings for $61,725). Present value, $20,000. Present condition, good.

Boys' home.—Character, three-story and basement, stone, with two-story wing. Use, dormitory for boys; first floor and part of second floor, main building, taken up by employees' rooms and mess. Capacity, dormitory, 200 pupils. Erected in 1883. Cost, $15,000. Present value, $10,000. Present condition, fair.

Small boys' home.—Character, two-story stone with basement. Use, dormitory for small boys. Capacity, 100 pupils. Erected in 1899. Cost, $8,449. Present value, $8,449. Present condition, good.

Addition to above building.—Character, one-story stone with basement. Capacity, 25 pupils. Cost, $3,754. Now under contract.

Dormitory building.—Character, two-story stone with finished attic and basement. Capacity, 150 pupils. Cost, $29,800. Now under contract.

School and chapel building.—Character, two-story stone and two wings of 2 schoolrooms. Use, class rooms and assembly hall. Capacity—assembly room, 500; class rooms, 340. Erected, 1893 and 1902. Cost: About $21,000; addition, $7,541. Present value, $20,000; addition, $7,541. Present condition, good; addition, excellent.

Dining hall and kitchen.—Character, stone, mostly one story; front wing 1½-story, with basement under back wing. Use, dining hall and kitchen, laundry, sewing room, engine house. Capacity, dining hall, 450. Erected in 1893. Cost, about $19,725. Present value, $19,000. Present condition, good.

Shop building.—Character, two-story stone. Use, blacksmith, carpenter, shoe, tailor, and paint shops, printing office, and band room. Erected in 1890. Cost, $5,500. Present value, $5,000. Present condition, good.

Storehouse (new).—Character, 1½-story stone with basement. Use, storing goods. Dimensions, 34½ by 83 feet. Erected in 1901. Cost, $4,000. Present value, $4,000. Present condition, excellent.

Storehouse (old).—Character, 1½-story stone. Use, miscellaneous storage. Dimensions, 26 by 75 feet. Erected in 1888. Cost, $1,200. Present value, $500. Present condition, poor.

Superintendent's residence.—Character, two-story stone and frame. Use, superintendent's dwelling. Capacity, 10 small rooms. Erected in 1900. Cost, $4,000. Present value, $4,000. Present condition, excellent.

Cottages, 5.—Character, two 1½-story, 3 one-story. Use, occupied by employees with families. Capacity, 4 and 5 rooms. Erected 1885 and 1897. Cost about $500 each. Present value, about $300 each. Present condition, fair.

Employees' cottages.—Character, 2 one-story frames. Use, employees' quarters. Capacity, 5 rooms each. Erected in 1902. Cost, $500 each. Present value, $500 each. Present condition, good.

Hospital.—Use, isolation and care of sick. Character, two-story stone and two-story frame wing. Capacity, 50 pupils. Erected in 1897. Cost, $5,250. Present value, $4,500. Present condition, good.

Stock barn.—Character, one-story frame with four wings. Use, dairy barn and storage of hay. Dimensions, 24 by 258 feet, two wings each 37 by 34 feet, 1 wing 16 by 70 feet, 1 wing 16 by 62 feet. Erected in 1893. Cost, $6,998.40. Present value, $5,000. Present condition, fair.

Cattle shed.—Character, stone with shingle roof. Use, protection to cattle. Dimensions, 24 by 400 feet. Erected in 1892. Cost, $2,000. Present value, $1,800. Present condition, good.

Barn.—Character, 1½-story frame. Use, for horses and mules. Dimensions, 50 by 64 feet. Erected in 1887. Cost, $1,100. Present value, $200. Present condition, poor.

Implement house.—Character, one-story frame. Use, storing farm implements. Dimensions, 32 by 48 feet. Erected in 1892. Cost, $1,000. Present value, $700. Present condition, fair.

Office (old).—Character, one-story frame. Use, office. Dimensions, 32 by 20 feet, 2 rooms. Erected in 1896. Cost, $350. Present value, $300. Present condition, good.

Office building (new).—Character, two-story stone. Use, transacting all official business. Capacity, 8 rooms. Erected in 1902. Cost, $4,000. Present value, $4,000. Present condition, excellent.

Power house.—Character, one-story stone. Use, housing boilers and machinery and machine shops. Erected in 1903. Cost, $8,584.83. Present value, $8,584.83. Present condition, excellent.

Granary.—Character, one-story frame. Use, storing grain. Dimensions, 28 by 60 feet. Erected in 1891. Cost, $1,200. Present value, $800. Present condition, fair.

Corn crib.—Character, 1½-story frame. Use, storing grain. Dimensions, 50 by 30 feet. Erected in 1899. Cost, $500. Present value, $500. Present condition, good.

Outhouses, henhouse, slaughterhouse, guardhouse, and pump house.—Character, slaughterhouse, pump house, and guardhouse stone; the others frame. Use, miscellaneous. Erected, various dates. Present value, about $500. Present condition, fair to good.

Chilocco has its own electric-lighting plant, installed in 1901 at a cost of $4,500, consisting of one direct connected engine and dynamo and 750 incandescent lights; the plant is soon to be extended and enlarged by addition of one additional direct connected engine and dynamo, which will give an increased capacity of 500 lights, material for which is now on hand, having been purchased at a cost of $2,500. The main buildings are heated by steam from a central power, installed in 1893. The present value of plant is estimated at about $12,000. The hospital and superintendent's residence are heated by their own hot-water plants, while the shops and employees' cottages are heated by stoves. Ventilation of schoolrooms and dormitories is by ceiling, window, and side-wall ventilation. Only one building (small boys' dormitory) has a ventilating system that is modern.

The water is supplied by several springs situated on Chilocco Creek, about 200 yards, from buildings; the average output of 40,000 gallons per day is assembled into a reservoir from whence it is forced by a duplex steam pump into a tank of 40,000 gallons capacity erected on an 80-foot steel tower, which gives an average pressure of 50 pounds to the square inch, which is ample for all domestic purposes as well as fire protection. Present value of water system, including pumps, tank, and mains, about $7,000.

All of the principal buildings are connected with a good sewerage system, the principal main being 10 inches in diameter with feeders of 6 inches. Sewer empties into Chilocco Creek, three-fourths mile below buildings, and has a fall of about 14 feet. The large boys' home has 12 tubs; girls' home, 14 ring baths and 6 tubs; little boys' home, 6 ring baths, all of which are located in the basements of the respective buildings. There is a direct system of fire protection which consists of standpipes in the halls of the main buildings with hose in racks connected to valves; a water pressure of 50 pounds to square inch is on day and night, but in case of fire this pressure can be increased by means of a fire pump with a capacity of 200 gallons per minute, giving a pressure sufficient to throw water over any of the buildings. The barns and hospital have no fire protection excepting through small hose, chemical extinguishers, and barrels of water placed in position ready for use.

This school has 8,598 acres of fine land in its reserve. This land was set aside by Executive order and its present value is estimated to be about $270,000. There are 6,720 acres under fence; nearly 700 acres under cultivation, about 46 acres being in orchard and small fruit. Seven thousand five hundred additional acres can be cultivated. For pasturage, 2,500 acres are used, leaving about 5,000 acres meadow land which produces valuable hay.

This school was opened January 15, 1884, with a capacity of about 200 pupils. The present capacity is 450 pupils. Enrollment 1902-3 is 550 pupils.

Fort Bidwell School.

Located 88 miles north of Madaline, Cal., the terminal station of the Nevada, California and Oregon Railroad. Site excellent for school purposes. Climate pleasant. Soil black and gravelly.

Boys' building.—Character, two-story frame. Use, dormitory, sitting rooms, and class rooms. Capacity, 75 pupils. Erected in 1874. Present value, $4,475. Present condition, good.

Girls' building.—Character, two-story frame. Use, dormitory, sitting room, kitchen, and dining room. Capacity, 75 pupils. Erected in 1874. Present value, $4,550. Present condition, good.

Superintendent's residence.—Character, one-story frame. Use, superintendent's office and dwelling, guest's room, employees' dining room and kitchen. Capacity, 9 rooms. Erected in 1875. Present value, $1,600. Present condition, good.

Physician's office.—Character, one story frame. Use, physician's office and residence. Capacity, 9 rooms. Erected in 1875. Present value, $1,200. Present condition, good.

Sewing room.—Character, one-story frame. Use, sewing room and employees' dwelling. Capacity, 8 rooms. Erected in 1875. Present value, $1,500. Present condition, good.

Employees' dwelling.—Character, 1½-story frame. Use, employees' quarters. Capacity, 16 rooms. Erected in 1874. Present value, $3,000. Present condition, fair.

Employees' cottages.—Character, 2 one-story frame. Use, one employees' quarters; the other empty. Capacity, 10 rooms. Erected in 1879. Present value, $500 each. Present condition, fair.

Adjutant's office.—Character, one-story log, dressed siding outside and ceiled inside. Use, empty. Capacity, 4 rooms. Erected in 1868. Present value, $500. Present condition, fair.

Gymnasium.—Character, one-story frame. Use, empty. Dimensions, 40 by 100 feet. Erected in 1884. Present value, $500. Present condition, fair.

Carpenter shop.—Character, one-story frame. Use, workshop. Dimensions, 17 by 50 feet. Erected in 1879. Present value, $330. Present condition, good.

Commissary.—Character, one-story frame. Use, storing supplies, laundry, and drying room. Dimensions, 25 by 175 feet (6 rooms). Erected in 1881. Present value, $1,850. Present condition, good.

Bakery.—Character, one-story frame. Use, empty. Dimensions, 25 by 40 feet (2 rooms). Erected in 1880. Present value, $600. Present condition, fair.

Girls' bath house.—Character, one-story log, sided inside and out with dressed lumber. Use, bath, toilet, and lavatory. Dimensions, 24 by 38 feet (2 rooms). Erected in 1870. Present value, $600. Present condition, fair.

Hospital.—Character, one-story frame. Use, empty. Dimensions, 73 by 80 feet (10 rooms). Erected in 1880. Present value, $2,000. Present condition, fair.

Boys' bath house.—Character, one-story frame. Use, boys' bath. Dimensions, 10 by 22 feet. Erected in 1897. Cost, $400. Present value, $400. Present condition, good.

Stables.—Character, 2 one-story frame. Use, housing horses, storing hay and farm implements. Capacity, 10 horses, 50 tons hay, wagons, machines, etc. Dimensions, 30 by 215 feet each. Erected, 1884–1888. Present value, $500 each. Present condition, fair.

Dairy barn.—Character, one-story frame. Use, housing cows and storing hay. Capacity, 10 cows and 20 tons hay. Erected in 1880. Present value, $200. Present condition, fair.

Granary.—Character, one-story frame. Use, storing hay. Capacity, 30 tons hay. Erected in 1880. Present value, $200. Present condition, good.

Miscellaneous outbuildings.—Character, all frame. Use, blacksmith shop, meat shop, root house, cattle sheds, etc. Erected, 1874–1880. Present condition, poor to good.

All buildings are lighted by kerosene lamps and heated by wood stoves. Dormitories have ventilators in the ceiling. Other buildings are ventilated from the windows.

The water supplied is good except during a part of the summer months and after a rain or during the melting of the snow in the mountains. Its source is a number of springs located about a mile and a half west of the plant in a canyon. The water from these springs is stored in a reservoir 1,700 feet from the buildings, at an elevation 145 feet above the fire plug. The water is conducted through a 4-inch iron pipe to the fire plug. The buildings are supplied from 2-inch mains and smaller pipes. Cost of water system, unknown. Sewage is emptied into an open ditch of running water which carries it to the meadow half a mile from the buildings. The two bath houses are supplied with warm water from a warm spring located near the buildings. There are 5 ring baths for the girls and 6 ring baths for the boys. There are 500 feet of 2½-inch rubber-lined cotton hose connected with the fire plug, which will reach 12 of the larger buildings. There are also fire buckets and running water in each of the buildings.

This school has 3,078.85 acres in its reserve. This land was transferred to the Interior Department by a joint resolution of Congress approved January 30, 1897. There are 200 acres under fence and 60 acres under cultivation; 60 addditional acres can be cultivated and 120 acres are used for pasturage. About 20 acres are irrigated. The 200 acres under fence are valued at $50 per acre. The remainder is valueless, except 640 acres of timber land.

This school was opened April 4, 1898, with a capacity of 150 pupils. The plant is the abandoned military post of Fort Bidwell and was set aside about June, 1897.

Fort Lewis Indian School.

Located in the La Plata Mountains, Colo., on the La Plata River, at an elevation of about 6,800 feet above sea level. The nearest railroad station is Hesperus, Colo., which is 4 miles north, on the Rio Grande Southern Railroad. The climate is very good, dry, with not less than 300 cloudless days in the year. The soil is very fertile, but requires irrigation for cultivation.

Office and employees' quarters and employees' mess.—Character, three 1½-story frame and 3 two-story frame. Use, employees' quarters. Capacity, 36 employees. Erected in 1882–83. Cost, no record; built by War Department. Present value, $12,000. Present condition, good.

Small boys' dormitory.—Character, two-story frame. Use, dormitory. Capacity, 70 pupils. Erected in 1882 (for a hospital). Cost, no record; built by War Department. Present value, $1,200. Condition, poor.

Small girls' dormitory and hospital.—Character, two-story with wings on either side of one-story; all brick. Use: wings, dormitory for small girls; main building for hospital. Capacity, 80 pupils. Erected in 1887–88. Cost, no record; built by War Department. Present value, $5,000. Present condition, good.

Hospital (new).—Character, one-story frame. Use, employees' (married) quarters. Capacity, 6 beds. Erected in 1901. Cost, $2,644. Present value, $2,400. Present condition, very good.

Large girls' dormitory.—Character, two-story stone and brick; basement stone. Use, girls' dormitory. Capacity, 75 pupils. Erected in 1901. Cost, $12,609.80. Present value, $12,000. Present condition, very good.

Dining room and kitchen (new).—Character, one-story brick. Use, sewing room and tailor shop. Capacity, 150 pupils. Erected in 1901. Cost, $6,321.93. Present value, $6,000. Present condition, very good.

Dining room and kitchen (old).—Character, one-story frame. Use, pupils' dining room and kitchen. Capacity, 310 pupils. Erected in 1882–83. Cost, no record; built by War Department. Present value, $1,500. Present condition, fair.

Schoolrooms.—Character, one-story frame. Use, class rooms. Capacity, 300 pupils. Erected in 1882–83. Cost, no record; built by War Department. Present value, $1,200. Present condition, bad.

Chapel.—Character, one-story frame. Use, religious services, etc., and kindergarten class. Capacity, 300 pupils. Erected in 1882–83. Cost, no record; built by War Department. Present value, $1,200. Condition, poor.

Shoe and harness shop.—Character, two-story frame. Use, shoe and harness shop and rooms for night watchman and Indian assistants. Erected in 1882–83. Cost, no record; built by War Department. Present value, $800. Present condition, poor.

Large boys' dormitory.—Character, one-story frame. Use, dormitory, lavatory, and sitting rooms. Capacity, 100 pupils. Erected in 1882–83. Cost, no record; built by War Department. Present value, $500. Present condition, bad.

Storeroom.—Character, one-story stone, with cellar. Use, general storeroom. Capacity, sufficient for 500 pupils. Erected in 1883–84. Cost, no record; built by War Department. Present value, $2,500. Present condition, good.

Band room and meat house (old guardhouse). Character, one-story stone. Use, band practice and meat house. Capacity, sufficient for its use. Erected in 1882–83. Cost, no record; built by War Department. Present value, $2,000. Present condition, good.

Laundry, carpenter, and blacksmith shops.—Character, one-story frame. Use, laundry, carpenter, and blacksmith shop. Capacity, insufficient. Erected in 1882–83. Cost, no record; built by War Department. Present value, $200. Present condition, bad.

Barn.—Character, one-story frame. Use, horse and cow stables and hay storeroom. Capacity, 13 horses, 20 cows, 200 tons baled hay. Erected in 1882–83. Cost, no record; built by War Department. Present value, $500. Present condition, poor.

Barn for young stock.—Character, one-story frame. Use, housing young stock in winter. Capacity, 40 head of stock. Erected in 1882–83. Cost, no record; built by War Department. Present value, $400. Present condition, fair.

Pump house.—Character, one-story frame. Use, pumping station. Erected in 1899. Cost, $200. Present value, $200. Present condition, good.

Milk house and bath house.—Character, both one-story frame. Use, storing milk and bath house. Erected in 1893. Cost, built from material from sheds which had been torn down.

Lighting is by oil lamps. Heating is by stoves, excepting the two new buildings, which are supplied with steam heaters. Ventilation in the two new buildings and

STATISTICS OF INDIAN TRIBES, AGENCIES, AND SCHOOLS. 143

in the hospital is modern. In all the remaining buildings it is carried on by means of open windows, transoms, doors, and openings in the ceilings.

Water is had from the La Plata River, which is fed from springs and melting snow, in two ways, by a gravity system through an open ditch leading to a receiving reservoir, thence to a discharging reservoir situated about 75 feet above the level of the plaza or school campus and through a pumping station located on the west bank of the La Plata River, distant from the receiving reservoir about 1,000 yards. The water is excellent. The quantity, however, is not sufficient in summers following winters in which the snowfall has been less than normal.

The distribution of water in the school is through a system of iron pipes laid below frost line. There are hydrants and fire plugs as a part of this system. The main sewer pipe is 12 inches in diameter with 6-inch laterals, all emptying into the river. Bathing is by a swimming pool, the water of which is heated by iron pipes carrying steam, laid in the floor. In the girls' new dormitory there are ring baths.

Fire protection consists of a water system with two pumps so arranged as to have the force of both, when necessary, thrown together into the system, a hose cart, several thousand feet of hose, a fire company, stand pipes and hose in several of the buildings, and buckets kept constantly filled with water in all inhabited buildings.

The farm consists of 6,360 acres, good sandy loam, and known as mesa land, part of former military reservation and cost Government nothing. Value, about $5,000. All under fence. About 200 acres under cultivation. By clearing of small scrub oak 2,000 acres additional can be cultivated. Over 6,000 acres are used for pasturage. About 200 acres are irrigated.

This school was formerly a military post, which upon being abandoned by the troops was given over to the Interior Department for the purpose of an Indian school. Its existence in this character began in 1892.

Fort Mojave Indian Industrial School.

Located, 20 miles north of Needles, Cal., on the east bank of the Colorado River. Climate for about seven months of the year mild and pleasant; for about five months, very hot.

Boys' building.—Character, two-story frame. Use, dormitories, sitting room, clothes room, and wash room. Capacity, 150 pupils. Erected in 1899. Cost, $10,000. Present value, $10,000. Present condition, good.

Dormitory building.—Character, two-story frame. Use, girls' quarters. Capacity, 80 pupils. Erected in 1902. Cost, $14,994. Present value, $14,994. Present condition, excellent.

Superintendent's quarters.—Character, one-story adobe. Use, dwelling and mess kitchen and dining room. Capacity, 5 rooms. Present condition, good. Present value, $4,500.

Hospital and physician's office.—Character, one-story adobe. Use, care of sick. Capacity, 4 rooms. Present value, $4,000. Present condition, good.

Employees' quarters.—Character, 3 one-story adobe cottages. Use, employees' quarters. Capacity, 24 employees. Present value, $8,500. Present condition, good.

Commissary.—Character, one-story adobe. Use, storing goods and supplies. Dimensions, 3,090 square feet. Present value, $2,000. Present condition, good.

Engine house and blacksmith shop.—Character, one-story adobe. Dimensions, 900 square feet. Use, engineering, blacksmithing, etc. Present value, $800. Present condition, good.

Bakery.—Character, one-story adobe. Use, baking for school. Present value, $1,000. Present condition, poor.

Bath house.—Character, one-story frame. Used for bathing purposes. Erected in 1897. Cost, $2,000. Present value, $2,000. Present condition, good.

Barn.—Character, two-story frame. Use, housing live stock and storing feed, etc. Erected in 1901. Cost, $1,900. Present value, $1,900. Present condition, good.

Store.—Character, one-story adobe. Use, traders' store, etc. Present value, $250. Present condition, poor.

Office.—Character, one-story adobe. Use, keeping property accounts, papers, etc. Present value, $1,000. Present condition, good.

Miscellaneous outbuildings.—Character, all adobe. Use, wagon shed, bell house, storehouse, chicken house, etc. Present value, $650. Present condition, good.

The plant is lighted by acetyline gas. Automatic generator of 200 lights capacity installed in 1901. Cost, $1,700. Light good and sufficient. Heated by wood stoves and fireplaces sufficient. Ventilated by adjustment of windows and ventilators in ceiling, good but not modern.

Water supply excellent. Derived from Colorado River, through a well located about 30 feet from river. The water filters through sand and gravel into well, is pumped from well into water tanks of 30,000 gallons capacity, thence furnished to buildings and grounds by gravity pressure through pipes. Sewerage empties into Colorado River below source of water supply. Pipes of main sewer 6 inches, laterals 4 inches. Sewer flushed by automatic flush tanks. Is sufficient and in excellent condition. Water system, sewer system, and 1 large tank, 19,000 gallons capacity, installed in 1889 at a cost of $11,000. Bathing facilities, 14 shower baths; installed 1897. Cost, $2,000. Slightly out of repair and being repaired at present date; when completed will be in excellent condition and sufficient for needs of school, and its value will be $2,000.

This school has 14,966 acres of as good land as can be found in this desert. It consists of two reservations, one styled the military, in the center of which the school buildings are situated; the other, the hay and wood reservation, is located about 2 miles south of military reserve and extends along the east bank of the Colorado River toward the south. There are 80 acres under fence, nearly 50 acres under cultivation, the greater part in alfalfa, fruit, and garden vegetables. It is not possible to farm more with present irrigating plant. Fifty acres are irrigated by centrifugal steam pump. The rest of the land is needed for wood and is occupied by Indians.

This school opened October 8, 1890, with an enrollment of 31 pupils, which has been increased to 210.

Fort Shaw Indian School.

Located in the northwestern part of Montana, 40 miles east of the Rocky Mountains. Is situated on Sun River, 27 miles west of Great Falls, Mont., a city of about 30,000. Nearest railroad point, Vaughn, on the narrow-gauge railroad, 14 miles from the school. The climatic conditions are very favorable, as the heat of the long summer days and the cold of the short winter days is very much modified by the winds from the Pacific Ocean, making the climate on the whole a very moderate one.

Building No. 1, schoolroom and chapel.—Character, stone addition to adobe building—adobe weatherboarded. Use, chapel and schoolrooms. Capacity, chapel crowded with 250; schoolrooms, 30 each. Erected, adobe, 1872; stone addition, 1897. Cost, no data giving cost of adobe; stone addition cost $5,000. Present value, $5,000. Present condition, good.

Building No. 2, employees' rooms and dormitory.—Character, adobe, weatherboarded. Use, dwelling rooms for employees and dormitories for girls. Capacity, 45 pupils and 4 employees are quartered in this cottage. Erected in 1872. Present value, none. Present condition, poor.

Building No. 3.—This building is a facsimile of building No. 2, and same remarks will apply here.

Building No. 4.—Same as Nos. 2 and 3.

Building No. 5.—Same as Nos. 2, 3, and 4, only this building is used for employees' quarters, employees' kitchen and dining room, guests' room and employees' sitting room.

Building No. 6.—Same as Nos. 2, 3, and 4, only this cottage is used for boys instead of girls.

Building No. 7.—Same as No. 6.

Building No. 8.—Same as Nos. 6 and 7.

Building No. 9, boys' cottage.—Character, frame, a mere box. Use, dormitory for boys. Capacity, 40 boys are quartered in this building. Erected in 1872. Condition, poor.

Building No. 10, gymnasium, guardhouse, and employees' quarters.—Character, adobe, stone, and frame. Use, gymnasium, guardhouse, and employees' quarters. Capacity, would answer for a gymnasium for a school of 100. Erected in 1872. Condition, poor.

Building No. 11, cottage No. 11.—Character, adobe. Use, employees' quarters, shoe, and tailor shop, band room, and clothing room for boys. Capacity, 4 employees with families and purposes indicated above. Erected in 1872. Condition, poor.

Building No. 12, storehouse and office.—Character, adobe. Use, storehouse and office. Capacity, 2 office rooms and storeroom for supplies. Erected in 1872. If rooms now being used for offices were used for storing purposes it would answer for a school of this size. Condition, fair.

Building No. 13, hospital, sewing room, and employees' rooms.—Character, adobe. Use, hospital, sewing room, and employees' quarters. Capacity, hospital, sewing room, and 4 employees. Erected in 1872. Present value, nothing. Present condition, poor.

Building No. 14, steam laundry.—Character, frame. Use, laundry. Capacity, laundry for 300. Erected in 1901. Cost $1,690. Present value, $1,690. Present condition, good.

STATISTICS OF INDIAN TRIBES, AGENCIES, AND SCHOOLS. 145

Building No. 15, dining room and kitchen.—Character, adobe, with frame addition. Use, dining room and kitchen. Capacity, 300 children. Erected in 1872. Present condition, poor.

Building No. 16, carpenter and blacksmith shop.—Character, stone. Use, shop for manual training teacher and blacksmith. Capacity, 6,000 square feet. Erected in 1872; reconstructed in 1897. Cost, school labor. Present value, $2,500. Present condition, good.

Building No. 17, coal house.—Character, frame. Use, coal house and shed room. Capacity, 3,200 square feet. Erected in 1897. Cost, $750. Present value, $750. Present condition, good.

Building No. 18, lumber house.—Character, stone. Use, storing lumber, oils, and paints. Capacity, 1,080 square feet. Erected in 1872. Reconstructed in 1897. Cost, no data giving original cost. Reconstructed by school. Present value, $1,000. Present condition, good.

Building No. 19, tool house.—Character, frame. Use, storing machinery. Capacity, 952 square feet floor space. Erected in 1872. Present value, $20. Present condition, poor.

Building No. 20, cow shed.—Character, frame. Use, store hay for dairy herd and shed for 25 head of cattle. Capacity, 4,680 square feet floor space. Erected in 1872. Present value, $500. Present condition, fair.

Building No. 21, stock barn.—Character, frame. Use, horse and dairy barn. Capacity, 7,200 square feet floor space. No room for hay or grain. Erected in 1872. Present value, $500. Present condition, fair.

Building No. 22, wagon house.—Character, frame. Use, shedding wagons. Capacity, 1,440 square feet floor space. Erected in 1872. Present value, $25. Present condition, fair.

Building No. 23, ice house. Character, frame. Use, storing ice. Capacity, 816 square feet floor space. Erected in 1872. Present value, $50. Present condition, bad.

Building No. 24, boiler house.—Character, frame, Use, boiler house. Capacity, 320 square feet floor space. Erected in 1897. Cost, $100. School labor. Present value, $100. Present condition, fair.

Building No. 25, tank house. Character, frame. Use, tank house. Capacity, 256 square feet. Erected in 1897. Cost, $1,500. Present value, $1,500. Present condition, good.

Building No. 26, well house.—Character, stone. Use, well house. Capacity, 100 square feet. Erected in 1897. Cost, $600. Present value, $600. Present condition, good.

Buildings Nos. 27 and 28, cattle sheds.—Character, frame. Use, sheds for cattle. Capacity, 7,150 square feet each. Erected in 1897. Cost, $500 each. Present value, $500 each. Present condition, good.

Lighting by kerosene lamps and heating by coal stoves. No system of ventilation. Do the best we can according to uses of various buildings.

The water system consists of a steam pump and supply tank of 400 barrels capacity, from which the water is piped to the several buildings in 2-inch mains. The water is of good quality. The water is taken from Sun River. Six-inch sewer pipe from various buildings to Sun River. Bathing facilities, none. We are now putting in temporary facilities. Water is piped to various buildings.

There is now under contract a new water system, sewer system, and two outhouses, with necessary plumbing. Cost of this new work, $13,162.

Farm consists of 5,000 acres. Quality and character, bottom and first and second bench land. Soil varies and consists of gumbo, alkali, sandy loam, and gravel. On the whole, a most excellent soil. No original cost, and the present value of the 5,000 acres, under fence, is about $50,000. Number of acres under fence, 5,000; under cultivation, 125. Additional acres that can be cultivated, 2,000. Acres in pasture, 4,875. The land that is supposed to be irrigated, and so reported, and under a ditch, is in fact not irrigated, as the ditch that carries water to the upper bench has no capacity and can not supply sufficient water to irrigate the school campus. The irrigation ditches on the low bottom land were never laid out with any system and they do not run on any grade; besides this land is rather difficult to irrigate as farm land. It can be more successfully irrigated as hay meadows when ditches are properly constructed.

The school was organized during the year 1892. The plant was originally constructed and occupied by the military, most of the buildings being built about 1872. The walls of original buildings are of adobe, weatherboarded and plastered, with shingle roofs. The buildings have been altered and added too so as to make them as convenient as possible for school use. The school is now accommodating 300 pupils.

Genoa Indian School.

This school is located at Genoa, Nebr. (a thriving little town of about 1,200 population), five blocks east of post-office, and has a capacity of 325 pupils. The Union Pacific Railroad runs within 300 feet of, and in front of the main buildings. This is considered a very good site for an Indian school. The only objection is the nearness to the town. Climate is dry and very healthy. Soil is of sandy loam and quite productive in favorable seasons.

Boys' building.—Character, 2½-story brick, with basement. Use, boys' dormitories, office, employees' rooms, and mess dining room and kitchen. Capacity, 200. Main part erected in early days; two wings added in 1884. Present value, $10,000. Present condition, fair.

Girls' building.—Character, 3½-story, brick. Use, girls' dormitories, superintendent's rooms, and employees' rooms. Capacity, 125. Erected in 1891. Cost, $17,000. Present value, $15,000. Present condition, good.

Dawes Hall (chapel).—Character, two-story brick, veneered. Use, dining room, kitchen, chapel, music room, and domestic science department. Capacity, 300. Erected in 1892. Present value, $5,500. Present condition, good.

School building (new).—Character, two-story brick. Use, assembly hall and class rooms. Capacity, 325 pupils. Erected in 1902. Cost, $23,595. Present value, $23,595. Present condition, excellent.

School building (old).—Use, employees' quarters, mess dining room, kitchen, and sewing room. Character, two-story brick. Capacity, 8. Erected in 1890, remodeled in 1902. Cost, $6,560; remodeling, $3,000. Present value, $8,000. Present condition, good.

Power house.—Character, two-story brick, with basement. Use, steam and electric-lighting plant, laundry, bakery, and meat shop. Capacity, entirely inadequate; have three large buildings heated by stoves. Erected in 1897. Cost, $3,854. Present value, $3,500. Present condition, good.

Shop building.—Character, two-story frame. Use, carpenter, blacksmith, shoe, harness, and tailor shops. Capacity, 65. Erected in 1888. Cost, unknown. Present value, $2,500. Present condition, good.

Hospital (new).—Character, two-story frame. Use, isolation and care of sick. Capacity, 16 to 20 beds. Erected in 1902. Cost, $5,000. Present value, $5,000. Present condition, excellent.

Hospital.—Character, two-story frame. Use, for sick pupils, dispensary, and rooms for nurse. Capacity, 18. Erected in 1888. Present value, $500. Present condition, poor.

Warehouse.—Character, one-story brick, with basement. Use, storing supplies. Capacity, 250. Erected in 1899. Cost, $3,349. Present value, $3,000. Present condition, good.

Stable.—Character, 1½-story frame. Use, for horses and storing hay. Capacity, 12 horses, 15 tons hay. Erected in 1886. Present value, $300. Present condition, poor.

Dairy barn.—Character, one story frame. Use, for cows and storing hay. Capacity, 30 cows, 50 tons hay. Erected in 1902. Cost, $1,500. Present value, $2,500. (Erected by school.) Present condition, excellent.

Granary.—Character, one-story brick, with basement. Use, storing of grain and vegetables. Capacity, 2,000 bushels. Erected in 1887. Present value, $300. Present condition, fair.

Corn crib.—Character, one-story frame. Use, storing corn. Capacity, 2,000 bushels. Erected in 1897. Present value, $400. Present condition, excellent.

Cottages (3).—Character, 2 one-story frame, 1 two-story frame. Use, employees and families. Capacity, 3 employees. Erected in 1885-1888. Present value, average $200 each. Present condition, good to fair.

Miscellaneous buildings.—Character, all frame. Use, fire department, band room, lumber shed, coal sheds, piggery, tool house, etc. Erected in 1884-1897. Present value, $2,500. Present condition, poor to fair.

Main buildings, including shops and hospital, lighted by electricity, furnished by dynamo from power house. Capacity, 500 16-candle power incandescent lamps. Cottage buildings lighted by kerosene lamps. Sufficient light. Boys' building, girls' building, Dawes hall, and warehouse heated by steam from central station. School building, shops, hospital, and all other buildings heated by stoves. Heating facilities by steam inadequate. Boys' building, girls' building, Dawes hall, and all other buildings, no system of ventilation. New school building, modern system of ventilation.

Water for cooking, bathing, and all other purposes is furnished the school by the Genoa Town Company from wells in center of town. Water is pumped into reservoir at top of high hill and piped to school. Pressure is sufficient to throw water to top of any of the buildings. Quantity of water is generally sufficient. Purity of water is questionable, as the source is from wells in center of town with no protection from surface water draining into them. There are three old privies within 100 feet of well. Have failed to get city to properly clean up about wells.

Boys' building, girls' building, Dawes hall, and power house has sewerage connections. Main sewer pipe is 12 inches and conducts sewage to cesspool three-fourths mile from school. Sewer facilities sufficient for present need. Bathing facilities consist of 10 shower baths in boys' and 4 in girls' buildings, insufficient for present needs. Fire protection consists of standpipes with hose and hose racks on each floor and basement of boys' and girls' buildings and Dawes hall; also, fire hydrants located at convenient distances from buildings to which fire hose can be readily attached by fire department of school. Protection of main buildings is adequate.

The school farm consists of 300 acres prairie land of average quality for this section. Of sandy loam soil, and slopes from west to east. All is used for school buildings, barns and lots, campus grounds, orchard, farm, garden, and pasture. One hundred and sixty acres of this land was set aside by the Government for a school after the Pawnee Indians were moved to the Indian Territory. The present value of the school land is estimated to be $18,000. All of the land is fenced. One hundred and sixty acres under cultivation; 40 acres on which buildings, barns, lots, campus are located; 20 acres apple orchard. Additional acres that can be cultivated, none; all in use. Eighty acres in pasture and wild meadow. None irrigated.

This school is situated on land that was originally owned by the Pawnee Indians, and is the outgrowth of the Pawnee Industrial School of the early days, which consisted of the central portion of the present boys' building. After the Pawnees were moved to the Indian Territory in 1873-74, and provision made in 1876 for the sale of their Nebraska land, Congress, in 1882, appropriated $25,000 for the establishment of an Indian school for 150 children, to be located in the buildings of the Pawnee Reservation. These buildings, together with 160 acres of land, were withheld from the general land sale authorized in 1876. In the same year—1882, August 7—Congress appropriated $2,200 for the purchase of an additional 160 acres. About 12 acres of the school farm is taken up by the Union Pacific Railroad, which runs east and west near the center of the place.

On February 20, 1884, the Genoa Indian School opened with an enrollment of 74 pupils, which was increased to 136 before the end of the year. During this year there was added to the main building two wings, each 20 by 80 feet, three stories high. The school has an actual attendance of 328 pupils.

Grand Junction School.

Located 1½ miles east of Grand Junction, Colo., on the Colorado Midland and Denver and Rio Grande Railway. Located on an elevation of 4,500 feet, second rise from river; site only fairly good. Soil, hard adobe, on a substratum of sand and gravel saturated with sand and water.

Girls' building.—Character, two-story brick, with basement. Use, dormitory. Capacity, 65 pupils. Erected in 1901. Cost, $18,250. Present value, $18,250. Present condition, excellent.

Boys' dormitory.—Character, 1½-story brick. Use, dormitory, mess dining room and kitchen, and employees' quarters. Capacity, 86. Erected in 1886. Cost, $12,500. Present value, $8,110. Present condition, fair.

Little boys' dormitory.—Character, two-story brick. Use, little boys' dormitory, children's dining hall, children's kitchen, and employees' quarters. Capacity, 52. Erected in 1891. Cost, $11,975. Present value, $10,000. Present condition, fair.

Hospital.—Character, two-story frame. Use, isolation and care of sick. Capacity, 27 pupils. Erected in 1896. Cost, $1,500. Present value, $1,300. Present condition, fair.

Warehouse.—Character, two-story and basement, frame. Use, storing supplies. Dimensions, 20 by 40 feet. Erected in 1895. Cost, $175. Present value, $285. Present condition, good.

Warehouse.—Character, one-story brick. Use, storing supplies. Dimensions, 20 by 50 feet. Erected in 1901. Cost, $2,394.51. Present value, $2,394.51. Present condition, good.

Barn.—Character, two-story frame. Use, housing live stock and storing hay. Capacity, 8 horses, 16 cows, 35 tons hay. Erected in 1891. Cost, $1,500. Present value, $1,225. Present condition, fair.

Office.—Character, two-story brick. Use, office, shoe shop, and employees' quarters. Erected in 1891. Cost, $1,800. Present value, $1,700. Present condition, good.

Office.—Character, one-story brick. Use, transacting official business. Dimensions, 33 by 26 feet. Under construction. Cost, $2,300.

Lavatory.—Character, two-story frame. Use, boys' lavatory and clothes room. Erected in 1897. Cost, $1,500. Present value, $1,375. Present condition, fair.

School building.—Character, two-story frame. Use, class rooms. Capacity, 148. Erected in 1893. Cost, $5,894. Present value, $5,825. Present condition, good.

Assembly hall.—Character, one-story frame. Use, religious worship and entertainments. Capacity, 350 pupils. Erected in 1899. Cost, $2,396. Present value, $2,396. Present condition, good.

Laundry.—Character, two-story frame. Use, laundry. Capacity, inadequate to the necessities of the school in bad weather. Erected in 1886. Cost, $1,600. Present value, $1,500. Present condition, fair.

Miscellaneous outbuildings.—Character, all frame. Use, cattle sheds, wagon sheds, etc. Erected in 1886-1901. Present condition, fair.

Lighted by acetylene gas installed in 1902 at cost of $1,443 for piping, $305 for generator house, and $729 for one 400-light Drake acetylene machine and fixtures. Heated by coal stoves, with the exception of new dormitory, which is heated by steam. Ventilation in girls' dormitory and schoolhouse by foul-air flues leading above roof with registers at floor and ceiling. In new dormitory air is admitted under radiator by register leading through the wall under the windows. In schoolrooms and assembly hall air is admitted through windows and doors only. In all other inhabited buildings ventilation is by means of partially open windows protected in accordance with a plan of the Indian Office for window ventilation.

The water supply is fairly good. Its source is the Gunnison River, supplied by the city of Grand Junction through a large reservoir which is located 1 mile south of the city. The water is furnished to the school through a 2-inch pipe, which supply would be inadequate to the school in case of fire. Three dormitories, hospital and wash room are connected with sewer which empties onto a 10-acre surface disposal bed, located 2,000 feet south of the school. There are 6 ring baths and 1 bath tub in the girls' dormitory, located in the basement; little boys' dormitory, only 1 bath tubs. There are standpipes in each of the dormitories, also chemical fire extinguishers and fire buckets in each of the dormitories and hospital. Plans and specifications have been prepared for new water and sewer systems for which Congress has appropriated $18,000.

This school has 167 acres of very hard adobe soil with a great deal of alkali in it, which makes it very difficult to grow fruits and vegetables. All under fence. About 50 acres in alfalfa, 7½ acres in orchard, 109½ acres subject to the needs of the school. There are 1,280 acres of pasture lands 15 miles from the school. This school was opened July 1, 1886, with an enrollment of 64 pupils.

Greenville Indian Industrial School.

Located 54 miles northwest of Beckwith, Cal., the nearest railroad point on the Sierra Valley Railroad. Site is poorly adapted to school purposes. Climate is mild. Temperature rarely reaches 0 in winter or 90 in summer. The soil is very stony, but produces well if well dressed with manure.

School and dormitory building.—Character, two-story frame, T-shaped. Use, school, dormitories, employees' quarters, kitchen, dining room, sitting rooms, clothes rooms, sewing room, office, etc. Capacity, 100 pupils. Erected in 1897-98. Cost, $22,000. Present value, $20,000. Present condition, excellent.

Storehouse No. 1.—Character, one-story frame. Use, used as a general storehouse. Dimensions, 21 by 45 feet. Erected, about 1890 (first used as a day school). Cost, $200 (for materials alone. Built by teacher and Indians). Present value, $200. Present condition, fair.

Carpenter shop.—Character, one-story, rough-board shed. Use, used as a carpenter and repair shop. Dimensions, 12 by 40 feet. Erected in 1897. Cost, $50. Present value, $50. Present condition, fair.

Storehouse No. 2.—Character, one-story frame shed, rough board. Use, storehouse. Dimensions, 12 by 24 feet. Erected in 1897. Estimated cost, $50. Present value, $40. Present condition, good.

Storehouse No. 3.—Character, 1½-story rough-board frame. Use, storehouse for worn-out property. Dimensions, 16 by 24 feet. Erected in 1895. Estimated cost, $100. Present value, $60. Present condition, fair.

Poultry house.—Character, one-story shed, rough board, frame. Use, used as a poultry house. Dimensions, 14 by 15 feet. Erected in 1897. Estimated cost, $25. Present value, $20. Present condition, fair.

STATISTICS OF INDIAN TRIBES, AGENCIES, AND SCHOOLS. 149

Ice house.—Character, one-story frame, rough board shed. Use, to store ice. Dimensions, 14 by 20 feet. Erected in 1896. Estimated cost, $25. Present value, $20. Present condition, fair.

Water-closets (2).—Character, one-story frame. Use, water-closets. Dimensions, 10 by 22 feet. Erected in 1899. Cost (including water and sewer system), $7,048. Present value, $1,200. Present condition, excellent.

Laundry.—Character, 1½-story frame. Use, used as a laundry. Dimensions, 22 by 38 feet. Erected in 1900. Cost, $1,575. Present value, $1,500. Present condition, excellent.

Barn.—Character, 1½-story frame. Use, barn, stable, and wagon shed. Dimensions, 30 by 32 feet. Erected in 1900. Cost, $1,125. Present value, $1,100. Present condition, excellent.

The school and dormitory are lighted by means of lamps. Heated by means of wood stoves. Most of the rooms are ventilated by means of air shafts from without.

Water supply comes from a mountain spring and is stored in a reservoir about 200 feet higher than the main building. It is usually sufficient. The sewer system is ideal and all that could be desired. The main sewer pipe is of terra cotta, vitrified, and empties into an irrigation ditch about one-fourth mile from the building. All sinks, water-closets, etc., open into this sewer. Ring baths are in use in the boys' lavatory, but those in the girls' lavatory have never given satisfaction. Girls are therefore bathed in tubs at the laundry. There are hydrants at the four corners of the main building and 200 feet of rubber-lined hose on a reel kept in a place easily accessible. There are two standpipes in the building, with four openings, to each of which is attached 50 feet of of cotton hose.

One-half acre under fence; one-half acre under cultivation. Additional acres that can be cultivated, none (without more water). Number of acres in pasture, none. One-half acre irrigated. Cost of school farm, $600. Present value of school farm, $200. Number of acres, 40. Character, very stony.

The school was organized about the year 1891 as a day school in a log cabin near the site of the present plant. Later the Women's National Indian Association erected a dormitory building, changing its character to a boarding school. In 1897 the United States bought the plant, since which time it has been conducted as a nonreservation boarding school. The school and dormitory building burned March 20, 1897, and the Government at once began the erection of the present plant.

Haskell Institute.

Located 2 miles south of Lawrence, Kans., on the Atchison, Topeka and Santa Fe Railway. Site admirably suited for school purposes. Climate without extreme changes. Soil of immediate site, prairie loam on a substratum of rock. Farm land mostly a heavy black clay, known locally as a black gumbo soil.

Auditorium.—Character, stone, two-story. Use, assembly hall and gymnasium. Capacity, 700 pupils. Erected in 1898. Cost, $18,500. Present value, $18,500. Present condition, good.

Bake shop.—Character, one-story stone. Use, school baking. Capacity, sufficient for school baking. Erected in 1888. Cost, $1,500. Present value, $200. Present condition, very poor.

Superintendent's barn.—Character, 1½-story frame. Use, housing driving teams and feed for same. Capacity, 6 horses, 6 tons of hay. Erected in 1893. Cost, $600. Present value, $500. Present condition, good.

Farm barn.—Character, 1½-story frame. Use, housing stock and tools and storing hay. Capacity, 2 horses, 2 cows, and 2 wagons. Erected in 1885. Cost, $600. Present value, $250. Present condition, fair.

Farm barn.—Character, 2½-story stone and frame. Use, housing school stock, farm implements, and storing hay and feed. Capacity, 24 horses, school implements, 1,000 bushels small grain, 500 bushels of corn, and 75 tons of hay. Erected in 1901. Cost, $3,000. Present value, $3,000. Present condition, excellent.

Barn.—Character, one-story frame. Use, housing horses. Capacity, 20 horses. Under construction. Cost, $2,000.

Barn.—Character, one-story frame. Use, storing implements and grain. Under construction. Cost, $2,000.

Hay and cow stable.—Character, one-story frame. Use, housing school cattle and storing hay. Capacity, 96 cows, and 250 tons hay. Erected in 1893. Cost, $2,250. Present value, $2,500. Present condition, good.

Dining hall and dormitory.—Character, basement and 3½ stories stone. Use, girls' dormitory. Capacity, 250 girls. Erected in 1889. Cost, $40,000. Present value, $30,000. Present condition, good.

150 STATISTICS OF INDIAN TRIBES, AGENCIES, AND SCHOOLS.

Domestic science building.—Character, two-story stone, with one-story wing. Use, teaching domestic science. Dimensions, 82 by 56 feet. Erected in 1902. Cost, $23,474. Present value, $23,474. Present condition, excellent.

Dormitory for large boys.—Character, 3½-story stone. Use, large boys' dormitory. Capacity, 200 boys. Erected in 1884. Cost, $20,000. Present value, $12,000. Present condition, fair.

Dormitory for small boys.—Character, 3½-story stone. Use, small boys' domitory. Capacity, 200 boys. Erected in 1884. Cost, $20,000. Present value, $12,000. Present condition, fair.

Engine and pump house.—Character, one-story frame. Use, boiler for pumping station and for heating hospital. Capacity, 1 boiler. Erected in 1897. Cost, $500. Present value, $500. Present condition, good.

Guardhouse.—Character, one-story stone. Use, storage for masons' supplies. Capacity, 20 by 20 by 10 feet. Erected in 1886. Cost, $1,200. Present value, $300. Present condition, poor.

Hospital.—Character, two-story frame. Use, isolation and care of sick. Capacity, 30 patients. Erected in 1886. Cost, $2,500. Present value, $2,000. Present condition, fair.

House, farm.—Character, two-story frame. Use, physician's residence. Capacity, 1 family. Erected in 1885–1898. Cost, $2,000. Present value, $2,000. Present condition, good.

House, farm.—Character, 1½-story frame. Use, farmer's residence. Capacity, 1 family. Erected in 1885. Cost, $1,000. Present value, $1,000. Present condition, fair.

House, farm.—Character, 2½-story frame. Use, residence for superintendent of industries and teacher with family. Capacity, 2 families. Erected in 1894. Cost, $1,500. Present value, $1,500. Present condition, fair.

Laundry.—Character, one-story stone. Use, school laundry work. Capacity, sufficient for school of 700. Erected in 1900. Cost, $3,985. Present value, $3,985. Present condition, good.

Lavatory for large boys.—Character, two-story stone. Use, lavatories and baths. Capacity, 200 pupils. Erected in 1899. Cost, $3,750. Present value, $3,750. Present condition, good.

Lavatory for small boys.—Character, two-story stone. Use, lavatories and baths. Capacity, 200 pupils. Erected in 1899. Cost, $3,750. Present value, $3,750. Present condition, good.

Office building.—Character, one-story stone. Use, clerical work. Capacity, 5 office rooms. Erected in 1891. Cost, $2,156. Present value, $2,100. Present condition, good.

Superintendent's residence.—Character, two-story frame. Use, residence superintendent. Capacity, 1 family. Erected in 1899. Cost, $3,450. Present value, $3,450. Present condition, good.

Schoolhouse.—Character, old portion basement and two-story stone; new portion, three-story stone. Use, class rooms, reading and library rooms, domestic art department, and manual-training room. Capacity, 1,000 students. Erected in 1884 and 1901. Cost, $45,000. Present value, $37,000. Present condition, old portion, fair; new portion, excellent.

Shopbuilding.—Character, three-story stone. Use, steam-fitters' workshop, shoemaker and tailor shops. Capacity, steam fitters, 10 boys each day; shoemaker shop, 30 boys each day; tailor shop, 30 boys each day. Erected in 1887. Cost, $4,500. Present value, $3,500. Present condition, good.

Shopbuilding.—Character, one-story stone. Use, wagon, blacksmith, and paint shops. Capacity, wagon shop, 20 boys each day; blacksmith shop, 20 boys each day; painters' shop, 20 boys each day. Erected in 1891. Cost, $5,845. Present value, $3,500. Present condition, good.

Carpenter's shop.—Character, 1½-story frame. Use, carpenter's shop. Capacity, 10 boys each day. Erected in 1888. Cost, $1,200. Present value, $800. Present condition, fair.

Storehouse.—Character, basement, one-story and attic stone. Use, storing supplies. Capacity, 45 by 100 feet. Erected in 1891. Cost, $4,112. Present value, $4,150. Present condition, fair.

Mason's workshop.—Character, one-story stone. Use, mason's department; teaching brick and stone masonry and plastering. Capacity, 20 boys each day. Erected in 1900. Cost, $1,745. Present value, $1,745. Present condition, good.

Miscellaneous outbuildings.—Character, all frame. Use, arch entrance, band stand, band house, chicken house, 2 corncribs, farm tools and wagon shed, hog house, girl's playhouse, lumber shed, slaughterhouse, tool house, etc. Erected, from 1884 to 1893. Cost, $150, $150, $800, $100, $500, $300, $400, $500, $1,500, $120,

$110, $75, $100, $100, $350, respectively. Present value, 50 per cent. Present condition, fair.

Lighting by electricity—energy furnished by Lawrence Electric Light Company. There are 900 incandescent lights. The cost per year is approximately $2 per 16 candlepower lamp. Heated by steam from a central power station. Hospital heated by independent plant. The plant was originally installed in 1885, but was thoroughly repaired in 1901 at an expenditure of $10,000 and is now in good condition. The original plant is without system of ventilation. The auditorium, new school building, and lavatory buildings are ventilated by the gravity system, similar to the Smead system without the forced draft. The system is very satisfactory.

The water supplied is pure, but hard and slightly brackish. The school has an independent system consisting of five wells, forming a reservoir of 150,000 gallons; however, the supply from the wells is very limited, being sufficient for only about one day's use out of each week. This supply is pumped by a steam engine and pump into a wooden tank of 20,000 gallons capacity, on a steel trestle standing 80 feet high. The pressure is ample to force the water wherever required. As the supply is so limited, most of the water used by the school is secured from the Lawrence Water Company. This is forced from wells, driven in the sand near the Kansas River, into a reservoir from which the city water is supplied. This reservoir is about 2 miles from the school on a hill considerably higher than the site of the school, therefore the pressure is very great and provides the best of fire protection. A $2\frac{1}{2}$-inch stream of water can be thrown far above the highest building. The water from the city system is quite satisfactory in quality, except for drinking purposes. The water expense is, however, very heavy, being about $1,500 per year in addition to what the wells at the school supply. The independent plant was installed at the school in 1896 at a cost of $5,500.

All the buildings are connected with an 8-inch sewer pipe which empties into an open ditch at a distance of about one-half mile from the buildings. The grade of sewer is sufficient to insure good results. Connected with each of the boys' dormitory buildings is a two-story lavatory building, the upper stories being bathrooms. Each bathroom is supplied with 6 ring baths and 6 tubs, making in all for the boys 24 baths. Bathing facilities for the girls consist of 10 ring baths and 6 tubs located in the basement of the girls' building. There are standpipes in the main buildings with hose on each floor. Where there are no standpipes, water buckets are provided. Fire hydrants are provided on grounds near all large buildings.

There are 650 acres in the school farm. The upland, about 250 acres, is thin and unproductive, because of having been cultivated for such a length of time without proper variation of crops. The remainder of the land is lowland, and if properly drained is very fertile. This portion of the farm has not been of much value to the school on account of poor drainage, but steps are being taken for draining, which will make it very valuable. Records do not show cost of school farm. Present value, $75,000. There are 650 acres under fence; 370 acres under cultivation; 280 acres more can be cultivated. There are 90 acres in pasturage. None irrigated.

This school was opened in September, 1884, with a capacity of 300. The number present on the opening day was 17 pupils. Present enrollment, 765.

Morris Indian Industrial School.

Located three-fourths of a mile east of Morris, Minn., on the Great Northern and Northern Pacific Railways, 147 miles west of Minneapolis. Climate subject to extremes of temperature. Prairie country and windy. Soil, rich black loom with clay or gravel subsoil. School site healthful and beautiful, with good drainage.

Boys' dormitory.—Character, two-story brick with basement, 63 by 43 feet. Use, dormitory and boys' sitting room. Capacity, 80 pupils. Erected in 1900. Cost, $11,530. Present value, $11,000. Present condition, good.

Girls' dormitory.—Character, two-story brick with basement, 63 by 43 feet. Use, dormitory and sitting room. Capacity, 80 pupils. Erected in 1899. Cost, $9,400. Present value, $9,000. Present condition, good.

Girls' building, L-shaped.—Character, three-story, 100 by 30 feet, with new two-story addition, 125 by 24 feet. Use, pupils and employees dining halls and kitchens, employees' rooms, office, sewing room, bakery, and domestic science rooms. Capacity, 160 pupils. Erected in 1890, addition in 1902. Cost, $5,000; addition, $2,328. Present value, $3,500; addition, $2,328. Present condition, three-story portion, fair; addition, excellent.

Boys' building.—Character, one-story frame, 113 by 29 feet. Use, none; will repair for shops and gymnasium. Capacity, shops, 20, gymnasium, 40 pupils. Erected in 1892. Cost, $600 (as purchased from mission, 1897). Present value, $600. Present condition, bad.

Hospital.—Character, two-story brick. Use, isolation and care of sick. Capacity, 12 beds. Erected in 1902. Cost, $4,985. Present value, $4,985. Present condition, excellent.

Laundry.—Character, one-story frame, 24 by 40 feet. Use, laundry. Capacity, 12 pupils. Erected in 1893. Cost, $250. Present value, $150. Present condition, bad.

Henhouse.—Character, one-story frame with shed. Use, storehouse for worn-out goods. Dimensions, 40 by 25 feet with small attic. Erected in 1893. Cost, $75 (as purchased from mission, 1897). Present value, $50. Present condition, poor.

Cow shed.—Character, one-story shed, 108 by 26 feet. Use, housing milch cows and calves. Capacity, 36 head cattle. Erected in 1892. Cost (as purchased from mission, 1897), $200. Present value, $150. Present condition, poor.

Barn.—Character, one low story and small haymow, 14 by 56 feet. Use, horse stable and feed. Capacity, 12 horses, 1½ tons hay. Erected in 1893. Cost, $150. Present value, $50. Present condition, bad.

Barn.—Character, 1½-story frame. Use, housing stock. Capacity, 6 horses and 12 cows. Erected in 1903. Cost, $3,000. Present value, $3,000. Present condition, excellent.

Granary.—Character, 1½-story frame. Use, granary. Dimensions, 36 by 16 feet, 1½ story. Erected in 1894. Cost, $150. Present value, $100. Present condition, fair.

Ice house.—Character, frame, one-story, 14 by 18 feet. Use, storing ice. Capacity, 45 tons. Erected in 1895. Cost, $100. Present value, $75. Present condition, fair.

Carpenter shop.—Character, one-story box, frame. Use, carpenter's shop. Dimensions, 24 by 16 feet. Erected in 1899. Cost, $50. Present value, $40. Present condition, fair.

Wagon shed.—Character, shed. Use, housing wagons and farm tools. Dimensions, 76 by 16 feet. Erected in 1890. Cost, $100. Present value, $25. Present condition, poor.

Commissary.—Character, two-story frame. Use, warehouse for school supplies. Dimensions, 75 by 30 feet. Erected in 1900. Cost, $600 (much old material used). Present value, $4,000. Present condition, good.

School building.—Character, one-story brick. Use, class rooms and assembly hall. Capacity, school, 150; assembly, 180. Erected in 1900. Cost, $8,800. Present value, $8,800. Present condition, excellent.

Lighted by electricity from private plant in village. One hundred and eighty 8-candlepower lights now in use, with 3 outside lamps 32 candlepower. System in good condition and satisfactory, except on dark days current is on too short a time. Dormitories heated by hot water and school building by steam, separate plant for each building. Heating of dormitories inadequate and unsatisfactory at present. Other buildings heated by wood stoves. Ventilation of schoolrooms and dormitories is by the system devised by the Indian Office. Other buildings have no modern system.

The water supplied is pure, but very hard. Its source is the large well which supplies the village of Morris. The well is about one-fourth mile east of the school and the main to the village tank passes the school buildings. The pressure is ample for fire protection. No water is used for irrigation. Water is purchased from the village of Morris at a cost of 14 cents per 1,000 gallons. The pipes and fixtures were put in by the Government at an original cost of about $600. Subsequent extensions have been included in the cost of dormitories and school building.

The two modern dormitories and the school building have 6-inch sewers leading to a ravine about 300 yards west of the buildings, where they empty. There are 6 ring baths and 1 tub for each of the two dormitories. They are located on the first floor of these buildings. There are stand pipes in the new dormitories with hose on each floor, water buckets and barrels in other buildings. Fire hydrants in grounds.

This school has 240 acres of good land. Eighty acres were purchased from the Catholic Mission in 1897 and 160 acres from private parties in 1901. The present value, exclusive of buildings, is estimated at $7,200. The land is all under fence. About 115 acres under cultivation. About 4 acres devoted to small fruits and ornamental grounds. Nearly all the remaining land could be cultivated. There are 125 acres used for pasturage. No irrigation.

This school was established as a Catholic mission in 1890 and was purchased by the Government in 1897 at a cost of $14,519. The capacity at the time of its purchase was rated at 100. The construction of new dormitories and school buildings has increased the capacity to 160.

Mount Pleasant Indian Industrial School.

Located 1 mile northwest of Mount Pleasant, Mich., on the Ann Arbor and the Pere Marquette railways. Site is well adapted to school purposes as to buildings.

STATISTICS OF INDIAN TRIBES, AGENCIES, AND SCHOOLS. 153

Climate very healthful, and is not subject to great or rapid changes. Soil of building site, clay. Nearly all of the school farm is a sandy loam.

Boys' dormitory.—Character, two-story brick. Use, dormitory, office, tailor shop, hospital, and employee's rooms. Capacity, 150 pupils. Erected in 1898. Cost, $13,999. Present value, $12,000. Condition, good.

Girls' dormitory.—Character, three-story brick, with 2 two-story wings. Use, girls' quarters. Capacity, 150 pupils. Erected in 1902. Cost, $17,516. Present value, $17,516. Present condition, excellent.

School building.—Character, two-story brick. Use, 4 school rooms and an assembly room. Capacity, 150 pupils. Erected in 1898. Cost, $8,956. Present value, $8,500. Condition, good. An addition to this building is now under contract for $7,870.

Shop.—Character, two-story frame. Use, carpenter, blacksmith, and shoe shops, and storehouse. Dimensions, 32 by 40 feet. Erected in 1893. Cost, $900. Present value, $800. Condition, good.

Barn.—Character, frame, with stone basement. Use, housing stock, storing fodder, etc. Capacity, 10 horses, 30 head cattle, and 100 tons hay. Erected in 1894. Cost, $2,300. Present value, $2,000. Condition, good.

Storehouse.—Character, 2½-story frame, with basement. Use, storing supplies, sewing room, mess dining room and kitchen. Dimensions, 36 by 50 feet Erected in 1894. Cost, $1,500. Present value, $1,100. Condition, good.

Hay barn.—Character, frame. Use, storing fodder and implements. Dimensions, 40 by 80 feet. Purchased with school farm. Cost, estimated, $800. Present value, $600. Condition, good.

Hay barn.—Character, frame, with basement. Use, storing fodder and housing sheep. Dimensions, 40 by 60 feet. Purchased with the school farm. Cost, estimated, $800. Present value, $600. Condition, fair.

Laundry.—Character, two-story frame. Use, laundering and dormitory. Dimensions, 40 by 48 feet. Erected in 1896. Cost, $1,200. Present value, $1,000. Condition, good.

Mess hall.—Character, 1½-story brick, with basement. Use, dining room, kitchen, pantries, and employees' rooms. Capacity, 150 pupils. Dimensions, 32 by 63 feet. Erected in 1898. Cost, $3,666. Present value, $3,300. Condition, good. An addition to this building is now under contract for $4,895.

Boiler house.—Character, one-story brick, with basement. Use, holding boiler, machinery, and fuel. Dimensions, 31 by 61 feet. Erected in 1898. Cost, $2,893. Present value, $2,500. Condition, good.

Lumber shed.—Character, one-story frame. Use, storing lumber, etc. Dimensions, 24 by 40 feet. Erected in 1896. Cost, estimated, $150. Present value, $150. Condition, good.

Wagon shed.—Character, frame. Use, storing wagons, etc. Dimensions, 26 by 90 feet. Erected in 1897 and 1901. Cost, estimated, $300. Present value, $300. Condition, good.

Farm house.—Character, 1½-story frame. Use, employees' quarters. Dimensions, 24 by 32 feet. Purchased with the school farm. Cost, estimated, $600. Present value, $400. Condition, good.

Silo.—Character, frame. Use, storing ensilage. Dimensions, 12 by 16 feet. Erected in 1901. Cost, $300. Present value, $300. Condition, good.

Miscellaneous buildings.—Sugar house, 16 by 32 feet. Ice house, 27 by 30 feet. Old residence, 16 by 24 feet. Tool house, 24 by 32 feet. Hennery, 12 by 40 feet. Pump house, 12 by 16 feet. Pig pens, etc., not expensive; data omitted.

A hospital building is now under contract for $57,376.

Lighted by electricity furnished by a dynamo in the power house, which runs about 200-incandescent 16-c. p. lamps. The plant was installed in 1899, and cost $2,500. It is in good condition and very satisfactory. Heated by steam from the power house, and it was installed in 1899, and cost $6,375. The farmhouse, bake shop, and storehouse are heated by stoves, wood and coal. Ventilation of dormitory, school building, and mess hall is by the system devised by the Indian Office. Other buildings have no modern system of ventilation.

The water supplied is sufficient and is obtained from drive wells and a large open well, all located about 1,000 feet west of the buildings. The water is forced from wells by an electric pump, driven by the dynamo by steam power into a ten thousand-gallon wooden tank placed on a steel trestle 80 feet high, located near the buildings. The system was established in 1899, and cost, together with the sewer system installed at the same time, $4,773. The water is supplied at the barn, bake shop, storehouse, laundry, boiler house, dormitory, school building, and mess hall, and it is hard water. A new 6-inch well is being drilled near the boiler house, for an increase in the water supply.

Nearly all the buildings are connected with an 8-inch main sewer, which empties into the river 2,000 feet east of the buildings. The outlet is 50 feet below the school buildings. There are 7 ring baths in the lavatory on the first floor and the same number on the second floor. There are standpipes in several of the buildings, with hose attached at each floor. Fire hydrants are well located, and two fire companies are organized and drill often enough to keep in practice. A greater supply is needed of water, and the pressure, which is from a tank 80 feet high, only throws water from the ground to the eaves of the buildings.

The school farm contains 320 acres and cost $17,900. It is nearly surrounded by a good wire fence. About 190 acres are cultivated. This includes 10 acres set to fruit. Ten acres more, not yet entirely cleared, could be cultivated. Fifty acres are in pastures. Timber, 40 acres besides the 10 partly cleared. No irrigation is carried on.

The school opened January 3, 1893, in the city of Mount Pleasant, with an enrollment of 15 pupils. In April the school was transferred to the farm, where a new dormitory (capacity, 100 pupils) was in process of construction. A small farm house with sheds attached furnished quarters for the 50 pupils and the employees until July, when the new building was occupied.

Perris School.

(Under Superintendent of the Riverside Training School, California.)

Located 4 miles north of Perris, Cal., on the Southern California branch of the Atchison, Topeka and Santa Fe Railway. Site most unsuitable. Climate good, but subject to sudden changes. Soil poor and thoroughly impregnated with alkali.

Girls' building.—Character, two-story frame. Use, dormitory, dining room and kitchen, sewing room, employees' quarters. Capacity, 75 pupils. Erected in 1892. Cost, $12,250. Present value, $2,000. Present condition, poor.

Boys' building.—Character, two-story frame. Use, dormitory, schoolrooms, employees' quarters. Capacity, 75 pupils. Erected in 1892. Cost, $12,250. Present value, $2,000. Present condition, poor.

Cottage.—Character, frame, one-story. Use, employees' quarters. Capacity, 3 employees. Erected in 1899. Cost, $900. Present value, $500. Present condition, poor.

Hospital.—Character, one-story frame, 48 by 50 feet. Use, isolation and care of sick, employees' quarters. Capacity, 14 pupils, 3 employees. Erected in 1895. Cost, $1,825. Present value, $500. Present condition, poor.

Laundry.—Character, one-story frame, 28 by 30 feet. Use, laundry. Capacity, 200 pupils. Erected in 1895. Cost, $420. Present value, $100. Present condition, poor.

Boys' wash house.—Character, one-story frame, 25 by 45 feet. Use, bathrooms, lockers for clothing. Capacity, 100 pupils. Erected in 1892. Cost, $500. Present value, $75. Present condition, poor.

Storehouse.—Character, one-story frame, 24 by 47 feet. Use, storehouse for goods and supplies. Capacity, 200 pupils. Erected in 1894. Cost, $1,250. Present value, $250. Present condition, poor.

Engine house.—Character, one-story frame, 10 by 12 feet. Use, contains gasoline engine for pumping plant. Erected in 1897. Cost, $110. Present value, $15. Present condition, poor.

Shops building.—Character, two-story frame, 24 by 44 feet. Use, shoe shop, carpenter and paint shop, one dwelling room. Capacity, 20 pupils. Erected in 1893. Cost, $1,000. Present value, $100. Present condition, poor.

Barn.—1½-story frame, 56 by 78 feet.—Use, housing stock and wagons, storing hay. Capacity, 8 horses, 8 cows, 5 wagons, 20 tons hay. Erected in 1893–94. Cost, $600. Present value, $200. Present condition, poor.

Old shoe shop.—Character, one-story frame, 16 by 24 feet. Use, storage for condemned property. Erected in 1892. Cost, $125. Present condition, worthless.

School plant is lighted by coal-oil lamps and heated by coal and oil stoves. Ventilation of whole plant is good; system same as laid down by Indian Office.

The water supply is meager, the water being hard and full of alkali. Pumped from 10-inch well 420 feet deep, well being about 50 feet from boys' building on highest point on school grounds. Pumped into 20,000-gallon wooden tank, elevated 40 feet, by gasoline engine. Pressure is good, water easily reaching second story. No water is used for irrigation. The system in use at present was installed in 1897.

All main buildings are connected with 4-inch sewer pipe, which empties into a pond one-fourth mile from buildings on ground not the property of the United States. Outfall is about 8 feet below buildings. The system is very poor and defective. There are 8 shower baths for boys in boys' wash house, and 5 bath tubs for girls in second story of girls' building. There are standpipes in the two large buildings, with hose on each floor. Water buckets in halls.

This school has 80 acres of very poor land, the present value of which is estimated at not over $5 per acre. There are 10 acres under fence, 80 acres under cultivation, 20 acres used for pasturage. None irrigated.

The school was opened about January 1, 1893, with 3 buildings and a capacity for 100 pupils. Other buildings have been added from time to time, making the total 11, all of which are in a bad condition. The school was consolidated with the Riverside California School by Indian appropriation act for fiscal year 1904.

Phoenix School.

Located 3½ miles north of Phoenix, Ariz., on the Santa Fe, Prescott and Phoenix Railway and Maricopa and Phoenix Railway. Site suited for school purposes; climate temperate. Soil, 3 feet of adobe or heavy clay on hard lime and cement formation.

Girls' home.—Character, two-story frame, with porches. Use, dormitory, clothes rooms, and sitting rooms for girls only, except 7 rooms for employees. Capacity, 300 pupils. Erected in 1892. Cost, $30,000. Present value, $20,000. Present condition, good.

Boys' dormitory.—Character, two-story brick, with porches. Use, dormitory for large boys, except 5 rooms for employees. Capacity, 150 pupils. Erected in 1899. Cost, $9,000. Present value, $9,000. Present condition, excellent.

Addition to boys' dormitory.—Character, two-story brick. Capacity, 60 pupils and 2 employees. Cost, $9,713. Now under contract.

Small boys' dormitory.—Character, two-story frame, with porches. Use, dormitory for small and medium-sized boys and 7 rooms for employees. Capacity, 200 pupils. Erected, main, 1895; addition, 1899. Total cost, $14,800. Present value, $12,000. Present condition, fair.

Schoolhouse.—Character, two-story brick. Use, class rooms and school assembly hall. Capacity, 600 pupils. Erected in 1898. Cost, $15,000. Present value, $15,000. Present condition, excellent.

Superintendent's quarters.—Character, one-story frame, with porches. Use, superintendent's dwelling. Capacity, 6 dwelling rooms. Erected in 1895; addition in 1900. Total cost, $4,060. Present value, $3,500. Present condition, excellent.

Hospital (old).—Character, one-story frame, with porches. Use, isolation and care of sick. Capacity, 10 pupils. Erected in 1895. Cost, $2,400. Present value, $1,500. Present condition, poor.

Hospital.—Character, one-story brick. Use, isolation and care of sick. Capacity, 2 wards and 8 additional rooms. Cost, $5,700. Under construction (1903.)

Addition to hospital.—Character, one-story brick. Capacity, two wards and 3 additional rooms. Cost, $2,935. Under construction.

Employees' cottages (5).—Character, 5 one-story frames. Use, employees' quarters. Capacity, 10 employees. Erected in 1891, 1893, 1895, 1896, and 1897. Cost, $500, $575, $500, $960, $200. Present value, $500, $575, $500, $960, $200. Present condition, 4 cottages good, 1 cottage poor.

Warehouse.—Character, one-story brick, stone basement. Use, storing supplies. Dimensions, 47 by 100 feet. Erected in 1893; addition, 1899. Total cost, $4,600. Present value, $3,600. Present condition, fair.

Shops building.—Character, two-story brick. Use, carpenter, wagon, blacksmith, paint, printing, harness, and shoe shops. Capacity, 100 pupils. Erected in 1898. Cost, $3,800. Present value, $3,800. Present condition, good.

Barn.—Character, one-story brick. Use, housing horses and storing vehicles and farm implements. Capacity, 10 horses, 5 vehicles, and implements. Erected in 1897. Cost, $1,015. Present value, $1,000. Present condition, good.

Dairy barn.—Character, one-story frame. Use, housing and care of cattle. Capacity, 100 cattle. Cost, $5,700. Under construction (1903).

Manual training building.—Character, two-story brick. Use, sloyd, domestic science, tailor, and seamstress departments. Capacity, 75 pupils. Erected in 1899. Cost, $8,978. Present value, $8,978. Present condition, excellent.

Engine house.—Character, one-story brick. Use, boiler and pump house and for storing of coal. Capacity, two 100-horsepower and one 20-horsepower boilers, 3 steam pumps, heaters, and feed-water pumps (room for ice machine of 2,000 pounds capacity) and for 100 tons coal. Erected in 1899. Cost, $3,585. Present value, $3,585. Present condition, good.

Laundry.—Character, one-story brick. Use, steam laundry. Capacity, for laundering of clothing for 600 pupils. Erected in 1898. Cost, $1,000. Present value, $1,000. Present condition, good.

Bath house.—Character, one-story brick; front, two-story brick. Use, bathing purposes, plunge and ring baths, disciplinarian's office, clothes rooms, and storerooms. Capacity, 300 pupils (boys). Erected in 1898. Cost, $1,500. Present value, $1,500. Present condition, fair to good.

Employees' quarters.—Character, two-story brick and basement. Use, basement for club dining hall and kitchen, cold-storage rooms; first and second floors, employees' quarters. Capacity, 50 in club dining room. Erected in 1898. Cost, $13,500. Present value, $13,000. Present condition, good.

Reading room.—Character, one-story frame. Use, sitting room for boys. Capacity, 100 pupils. Erected in 1896. Cost, $1,460. Present value, $1,200. Present condition, fair to good.

Carpenter shop.—Character, two-story frame. Use, band room and storage of fire apparatus. Dimensions, 24 by 40 feet. Erected in 1895. Cost, $775. Present value, $500. Present condition, poor.

Office.—Character, one-story frame, with porches. Use, school office, superintendent and 3 clerks (3 rooms). Erected in 1895 and 1899. Cost, $3,500. Present value, $3,000. Present condition, good.

School mess hall.—Character, one-story brick. Use, dining hall; also for social gatherings of pupils. Capacity, 700, with addition. Erected in 1901. Cost, $7,313. Present value, $7,313. Present condition, excellent.

Addition to above building.—Character, one-story brick. Dimensions, 104 by 70 feet. Cost, $10,887. Now under contract.

Band stand.—One-story frame (open). Use, band stand. Capacity, 24 pupils. Erected in 1895. Cost, $157. Present value, $157. Present condition, good.

Machine shed.—Character, one-story frame. Use, storing farm implements and tools. Dimensions, 20 by 48 feet. Erected in 1893. Cost, $100. Present value, $100. Present condition, fair.

Outhouses (4).—One-story frame sheds. Use, barber shop (1) and poultry houses (3). Dimensions, 12 by 14, 16 by 16, 10 by 20, and 16 by 16 feet. Erected in 1893, 1894, 1896. Cost (all), $325. Present value, $300. Present condition, fair.

Lighted by electricity, furnished by Phoenix Light and Fuel Company, of Phoenix, Ariz., at a cost of about $2,000 per year; there are about 1,000 incandescent lights, no arcs. School building is heated by steam. All other buildings are heated by coal stoves. Ventilation of schoolrooms and all buildings is ample, owing to the great number of windows and doors in each, and the weather which at all times permits same to be open.

The water supply contains a great amount of alkali, but otherwise is good, and derived from a well located in the engine house. The water from this well is pumped into a wooden tank 60 feet above the ground, and from there distributed by gravity to all buildings. The pressure is ample to force water to all buildings for domestic use, but not for fire-protection purposes, for which the large steam pump forces water into the mains. None of this water is used for irrigation. Water system was installed in 1894 for $2,225, and afterwards improved and enlarged at a total cost of $15,000. Sufficient water is furnished from the well at present, but during time of drought the well may be pumped dry in one hour.

All the buildings are connected with a 6-inch general sewer pipe, which empties into a cesspool 1,000 feet north of the school. The fall to this cesspool is ample. The sewerage is pumped from cesspool by means of compressed air utilized by the "Shone system," and is used to irrigate a tract of land on which garden truck is raised. There are 10 ring baths (and a plunge, 30 by 60 feet, used in summer months, May to October) for the boys, located in the bath house, which has been used by both boys and girls. Ten ring baths and two tubs are located in the addition to the girls' home. With this addition the bathing facilities are ample. There are standpipes in all the buildings, cottages and hospital excepted, with 1½-inch hose on each floor. Water buckets also in each large building. Fire hydrants for 2½-inch hose in grounds. Hose wagon and hook and ladder truck, and thoroughly drilled fire company is maintained.

This school has 160 acres of good alfalfa land. The land was purchased in 1890 at a cost of $6,000. The present value of the bare land is at least $16,000. There are 160 acres under fence, 160 acres under cultivation—100 acres in alfalfa and hay land, 20 acres in building site, 20 acres in garden, 20 acres in grain and vineyard. The entire farm, 160 acres, is irrigated. Under a specific appropriation in 1902, 80 acres of land with a 33½-inch right in the Arizona Irrigation Canal was purchased from Frank E. Whitten for $4,300.

The school was opened May 5, 1892, with a capacity of 150 pupils. It had an enrollment in 1902-3 of 728.

Pierre Indian School.

Located 2 miles east of Pierre, S. Dak., at terminus of a branch of Chicago and Northwestern Railway. The site of the school is in the bottom lands of the Missouri River Valley, and consists of 20 acres of land. Soil of immediate site of a character unfit for farming purposes without irrigation. Climate, dry and healthy.

School building.—Character, two-story brick with one-story addition for kitchen. Use, dormitory, schoolrooms, chapel, dining rooms, kitchen, office, and employees' quarters. Capacity, 150 pupils. Erected in 1889 and 1891. Cost, $35,540. Present value, $30,000. Present condition, fair.

Hospital.—Character, two-story brick with one-story addition for kitchen. Use, employees' quarters and sewing room. Capacity, 8 employees; 10 rooms and 2 bathrooms. Erected in 1891. Cost, $6,980. Present value, $6,000. Present condition, fair.

Storehouse.—Character, 1½-story frame. Use, storing supplies. Dimensions, 42 by 110 feet. Erected in 1891 and 1897. Cost, $3,552. Present value, $3,000. Present condition, fair.

Horse stable.—Character, 1½-story frame. Use, housing horses and storing hay. Capacity, 6 horses and 10 tons hay. Erected in 1890 and 1891. Cost, $896. Present value, $800. Present condition, fair.

Cow stable.—Character, 1½-story frame. Use, housing cattle and storing hay. Capacity, 31 head of cattle and 10 tons of hay. Erected in 1891. Cost, $1,425. Present value, $1,300. Present condition, fair.

Laundry.—Character, two-story frame with one-story addition for engine. Use, steam laundry and drying room. Erected in 1890. Cost, $1,800. Present value, $1,500. Present condition, fair.

Superintendent's cottage.—Character, two-story frame. Use, superintendent's dwelling. Capacity, 8 rooms. Erected in 1893. Cost, $1,700. Present value, $1,600. Present condition, fair.

Miscellaneous outbuildings.—Character, all frame, one story. Use, poultry house, pig pens, oil house, ice house, outhouses, coal sheds, boiler house, hose house, root cellar, guardhouse, and shoe shop. Erected in 1891–1899. Total cost, $7,332. Present value, $5,500. Present condition, fair, except ice house, which is worthless. Brick workshops are now under construction at a cost of $3,498.

The school is lighted by kerosene lamps and heated by steam. The heating plant was installed in 1891 and connected with the school building, hospital, and storehouse; sufficient for the needs of the school. Ventilation very poor. No ventilation of schoolrooms and dormitories except by windows and doors.

Water is supplied to the school from the city of Pierre, S. Dak. The source of the water supply is the Missouri River. It is pumped from cisterns into a reservoir placed on a hill above the city, and from thence to the school by force of gravity. The amount is ample for domestic purposes, but the pressure is insufficient for complete fire protection. A new water system is now being installed at a cost of $4,374. The school building, hospital, superintendent's cottage, and laundry are connected with an 8-inch sewer which empties into the Missouri River at a point about three-fourths of a mile from the school and about 2 miles below the source of the water supply. There are 4 tubs for use in the boys' department and 6 tubs for use in the girls' department—insufficient for the wants of the school. There is an artesian well on the school grounds, the water from which is suitable for bathing purposes, but is not utilized for any purpose. There are standpipes in the school building, with hose on each floor. Water buckets are placed in the school building and hospital. One fire hydrant in the grounds.

This school has but 20 acres in its reserve, upon which the buildings are located. Cost unknown. There is no farming at the school. The present value of the reserve is estimated to be $1,000, exclusive of buildings.

This school was opened in February, 1891, with a capacity of 80 pupils. Since then additions have been made increasing the capacity to 150 pupils.

Pipestone Indian Training School.

Located 2 miles north of the town of Pipestone, Minn., on the Burlington, Cedar Rapids and Northern Railway, Chicago, St. Paul, Minneapolis and Omaha Railway, Chicago, Milwaukee and St. Paul Railway, and the Great Northern Railway. Site well suited for school purposes; climate healthful, with plenty of high winds and extreme cold temperatures in winter. Soil of immediate site a sandy loam with a gravelly subsoil resting on a substratum of rock.

Girls' building.—Character, 2½-story stone. Use, dormitory and sitting rooms. Capacity, 90 pupils. Erected in 1892. Cost, $21,840. Present value, $22,000. Present condition, good.

Schoolhouse.—Character, two-story stone. Use, class rooms and assembly hall. Capacity, 150 pupils. Erected in 1899. Cost, $11,480. Present value, $12,000. Present condition, good.

Boys' building.—Character, two-story stone. Use, dormitory and sitting room. Capacity, 45 pupils. Erected in 1901. Cost, $11,866.31. Present value, $12,000. Present condition, good.

Addition to dormitory.—Character, 2 two-story stone wings. Use, dormitories. Capacity, 65 pupils. Cost, $13,484. Under construction (1903).

Mess hall.—Character, one-story stone. Use, dining room, kitchen, and bakery. Capacity, 200 pupils. Erected in 1901. Cost, $12,013.57. Present value, $13,000. Present condition, good.

Barn and silo.—Character, two-story frame, circular. Use, housing stock and storing feed. Capacity, 60 cattle, 8 horses. Erected in 1902. Cost, $2,950. Present value, $2,950. Present condition, excellent.

Warehouse.—Character, one-story frame. Use, storing supplies. Dimensions, 50 by 20 feet. Erected in 1902. Cost, $1,980. Present value, $1,980. Present condition, excellent.

Miscellaneous outbuildings.—Character, all frame. Use, chicken house, cattle sheds, horse sheds, etc. Capacity, not sufficient for the needs of the school. Erected in 1892–1897. Cost, $2,441.60. Present value, about $1,500. Present condition, good to poor.

Laundry and boiler house.—Character, stone basement, one-story frame, 25 by 50 feet. Use, basement for boilers and steam pump and fuel, frame building for laundry. Capacity, sufficient for the school. Erected in 1892–93. Cost, $1,543.75. Present value, $1,000. Present condition, good.

Lighted by gasoline gas furnished by three Detroit heating and lighting gasoline plants. Installed in 1897 and 1901; cost unknown; installed with buildings. In good condition and satisfactory. Heated by steam by five automatic, low-pressure, cast-iron boilers, which are placed in the basements of the buildings. Ventilation of the schoolhouse and the boys' building is by the system devised by the Indian Office; the other buildings have no modern system of ventilation.

The water supply is pure and good. Its source is a well located 1,700 feet south of the buildings. The water is pumped by steam into a 500-barrel tank on a steel tower 60 feet high. The power is ample to force the water where required. Water system has been installed and added to as necessity occasioned, making the plant cost about $4,000. All of the buildings are connected with an 8-inch sewer pipe which empties through the rocks about a quarter of a mile southwest of the buildings and below the source of water supply. The outfall is 20 feet below the buildings. There are 4 ring baths and 1 tub for the use of the boys' building, situated in the basement. There are 4 bath tubs on the second floor of the girls' building. There are standpipes in the girls' and boys' buildings with hose on each floor. Water buckets in the buildings. Fire hydrants in the grounds.

This school has 684 acres of land, being the Pipestone Indian Quarry Reservation, and is set apart by treaty with the Yankton Sioux for quarrying purposes. It is estimated to be worth about $20,000. There are 400 acres under fence, 200 acres under cultivation and school grounds. Two hundred acres additional can be cultivated. Two hundred acres are used for pasturage, while balance is left for the use of the Yankton Sioux Indians for quarrying their pipestone.

This school was opened in February, 1893, with a capacity of 75 pupils. Its present enrollment is 135. It is situated for a good agricultural school of the Northwest. A small orchard of hardy fruits is established, but most of the attention is given to agriculture.

Rapid City School.

Located 2½ miles northwest of Rapid City, S. Dak., on the Freemont, Elkhorn and Missouri Valley Railroad. Site well suited for school. Climate is dry without extreme changes, except occasional cold waves during the winter season. Soil of immediate site is the table-land so common to this western country.

Dormitory.—Character, two-story brick, with stone basement under entire building. Use, dormitories, dining room and kitchen, boys' and girls' play rooms, heating plant. Capacity, 80 pupils. Erected in 1898. Cost, $22,700. Present value, $22,700. Present condition, good.

Addition to dormitory.—Character, one-story brick. Use, dormitory purposes. Dimensions, 33 by 32 feet. Cost, $7,300. Under construction (1903).

STATISTICS OF INDIAN TRIBES, AGENCIES, AND SCHOOLS. 159

Dormitory.—Character, two-story brick. Use, dormitory purposes and play rooms. Capacity, 110. Erected in 1902. Cost, $19,820. Present value, $19.820. Present condition, excellent.

Schoolhouse.—Character two-story brick. Use, schoolrooms and assembly hall. Capacity, schoolrooms, 160; hall, 350. Erected in 1902. Cost, $18,400. Present value, $18,400. Present condition, excellent.

Employees' quarters.—Character, two-story brick. Use, living rooms for employees. Capacity, 8 employees. Cost, $6,500. Under construction (1903).

Superintendent's cottage.—Character, two-story frame. Use, home for superintendent and family. Capacity, 7 rooms and bath. Cost, $3,820. Under construction (1903).

Hospital.—Character, one-story frame. Use, care of sick and dining room for employees. Capacity, 10 pupils. Erected in 1898. Cost, $1,444.65. Present value, $1,200. Present condition, good.

Shop.—Character, one-story frame. Use, blacksmith shop and commissary. Capacity, 4 pupils. Erected in 1898. Cost, $1,378.75. Present value, $1,378.75. Present condition, good.

Horse barn.—Character, 1½ stories, frame. Use, housing horses and storing hay and grain. Capacity, 4 horses, 7 tons hay, 5,000 pounds grain. Erected in 1898. Cost, $887. Present value, $887. Present condition, good.

Addition to laundry.—Character, one-story frame. Use, general laundry purposes. Dimensions, 40 by 25 feet. Cost, $2,110. Under construction.

Acetylene gas house.—Character, one-story frame. Use, to house gas plant. Dimensions, 23 by 14 feet. Cost, $1,416. Under construction (1903).

Cow barn.—Character, one-story frame. Use, housing milch cows and storing hay. Capacity, 7 cows, 15 tons hay. Erected in 1900. Cost, $600. Present value, $600. Present condition, good.

Miscellaneous outbuildings.—Character, all frame. Use, poultry house, laundry, ice house, cattle and pig sheds. Erected in 1898–1901. Cost, $925. Present value, $925. Present condition, good.

Lighted by gasoline gas; capacity, 125 lights. Expended in additional lights in 1903, $204. Heated by steam from boiler located under dining room; hospital heated by stoves. Cost of heating and lighting system included in cost of dormitory and school building. Ventilation is by the system devised by the Indian Office.

The water supplied is hard, but pure and good. The school is connected with the city system. All the buildings are connected with a 6-inch general sewer pipe, which empties into a small branch below the surface of water supply. The outfall is 35 feet below the buildings. Addition to sewer system made in 1902, costing $1,395. There are 4 ring baths for each of the two dormitories. They are located on the first floor. There are standpipes in the school and dormitory building, with hose on each floor; fire hydrants in grounds.

This school has 160 acres of land, purchased in 1898 for $3,000. All of said land is under fence. There are 5 acres under cultivation for garden purposes, and 30 acres used for hay land. Fifty acres could be cultivated if irrigation could be secured. There are 100 acres used for pasture—50 acres good, 50 acres poor. Balance of land in school campus. Negotiations now pending (1903) to add 160.61 acres, with water rights, to this school, at a cost of $11,644.22.

This school was opened September 12, 1898, with a capacity for 80 pupils.

Riverside School.

Located at Riverside, Cal., on the outskirts of the city, one-half mile from the Santa Fe Railroad, Arlington station; also located on the Riverside and Arlington Electric Railway. An ideal site for an Indian school; civilizing surroundings unequaled; climate the best in the United States. Soil, a rich sandy loam.

Mess hall.—Character, one-story brick, roughcast and pebble dashed. Use, dining rooms and kitchens for both employees and pupils. Capacity, 400 pupils and 36 employees. Erected in 1902. Cost, $15,975. Present value, $15,975. Present condition, excellent.

Laundry.—Character, one-story brick, roughcast and pebble dashed. Use, steam laundry uses. Capacity, 300 pupils. Erected in 1902. Cost, $2,950. Present value, $2,950. Present condition, excellent.

Schoolhouse.—Character, two-story brick, roughcast and pebble dashed. Use, 8 class rooms and auditorium. Capacity, 600 pupils. Erected in 1902. Cost, $26,245. Present value, $26,245. Present condition, excellent.

Warehouse.—Character, one-story brick, roughcast, etc. Use, storing supplies. Dimensions, 24 by 60 feet. Erected in 1902. Cost, $1,780. Present value, $1,780. Present condition, excellent.

Office.—Character, one-story brick, roughcast, etc. Use, 3 office rooms for clerks and superintendent. Erected in 1902. Cost, $1,710. Present value, $1,710. Present condition, excellent.

Employees' quarters (2).—Character, two-story brick, roughcast, etc., each. Use, reception rooms and sleeping quarters for employees. Capacity, 18 employees (9 to each building). Erected in 1902. Cost, $7,280 ($3,640 each). Present value, $7,280. Present condition, excellent.

Two dormitories, including two ambulatories, for small boys and girls, respectively.—Character, two-story brick, roughcast and pebble dashed. Use, dormitories and sitting rooms, etc. Capacity, 150 pupils (75 each building). Erected in 1902. Cost, $26,518 ($13,259 each). Present value, $26,518. Present condition, excellent.

Two dormitories for large boys and girls, respectively.—Character, two-story brick, roughcast and pebble dashed. Use, sleeping quarters, sitting rooms, bath, etc. Capacity, 150 pupils (each dormitory, 75 pupils). Erected in 1902. Cost, $27,174 ($13,587 each). Present value, $27,174. Present condition, excellent.

Barn.—Character, one-story frame. Use, housing stock and storing feed. Dimensions, 73 by 69 feet. Capacity, 14 horses and 16 cows. Cost, $5,400. Under construction (1903).

Lighted by electricity, purchased from the city of Riverside. About 1,000 electric bulbs and 4 arc outside lights. System installed during fiscal year 1902, at a cost of $7,147. Excellent condition and satisfactory. Heated by steam from 5 boilers, located respectively in two dormitories (large boys and girls), school building, and mess hall, from which other buildings are heated, except office, which is heated by stoves. Cost, $11,513. Excellent condition. Ventilation of schoolrooms and dormitories is by the system devised by the Indian Office and is most satisfactory. All buildings are thoroughly ventilated.

The water is pure and reasonably soft. The water is supplied by the city of Riverside Water Company. The water is furnished from artesian wells; the source is some miles above the city. The system is satisfactory in every particular; pressure is 80 pounds to the square inch. Water system was installed during 1902. The cost of water and sewer systems was $6,297. All the buildings are connected with a 6 and 8 inch sewer piping, conducted five-eighths of a mile below upon a sewer deposit tract. The outfall is probably 24 feet below. Cost of sewer and water systems was $6,297. There are 4 needle baths and 2 bath tubs in each of the 4 dormitories. They are ample and very satisfactory in every sense of the word. There are standpipes in each of the 4 dormitories, with hose on each floor. Fire hydrants on the grounds, with fire hose convenient to each.

This school has 140 acres connected therewith—40 for the school site, 10 acres for sewer deposit, and 100 acres of elegant land for agricultural purposes, located three miles south of the site, upon Magnolia avenue. Cost of the 140 acres, $18,900. Entire 140 acres has been under cultivation. The farm of 100 acres is being prepared for irrigation.

This school was opened September 1, 1902, with a capacity of 300 pupils. Its enrollment December 31, 1902, was 384.

Riggs Institute.

Located one-half mile north of Flandreau, S. Dak., on the Chicago, Milwaukee and St. Paul Railway. Site admirably suited for school purposes. Climate, dry, healthful, and invigorating. Soil, prairie loam, well adapted to diversified farming.

School and assembly building.—Character, two-story brick. Use, 10 schoolrooms, 3 offices, and assembly hall. Capacity, schoolrooms, 320 pupils; assembly hall, 400. Erected in 1899. Cost, $19,000. Present value, $20,000. Condition, excellent.

Girls' building.—Character, two-story brick with basement. Use, home for girls. Capacity, 175 girls' and 6 employees' rooms. Erected, main building, 1892; annex, 1898. Cost, $30,000. Present value, $27,000. Condition, good.

Large boys' building.—Character, two-story brick with basement. Use, home for large boys. Capacity, 100 boys' and 3 employees' rooms. Erected in 1898. Cost, $14,680. Present value, $14,000. Present condition, good.

Small boys' building.—Character, two-story brick with basement. Use, home for small boys. Capacity, 80 boys and 3 rooms for employees. Erected in 1892. Cost, $5,000. Present value, $4,000. Present condition, fair.

Industrial building.—Character, two-story brick. Use, employees' mess, tailor, harness, and carpenter shops, sewing room, and 3 employees' rooms. Capacity, mess for 40 employees, shops for 60 pupils, 3 employees. Erected in 1892. Cost, $5,200. Present value, $4,500. Present condition, good.

Work shops.—Character, one-story brick. Use, for teaching different trades. Dimensions, 92 by 42 feet. Under construction (1903). Cost, $6,113.

Dining hall.—Character, main, two-story; annex, one-story; brick. Use, kitchen, bakery, dining room for pupils. Capacity, 400 pupils and 12 employees' rooms. Erected in 1898. Cost, $14,630. Present value, 14,000. Present condition, good.

Laundry.—Character, one-story brick. Use, school laundry. Capacity, school of 300 pupils. Erected in 1892. Cost, $2,500. Present value, $2,000. Present condition, poor; no ventilation.

Laundry.—Character, one-story frame. Use, school laundry. Dimensions, 65 by 42 feet. Under construction (1903). Cost, $2,824.

Hospital.—Character, main, two-story; wings, one-story; frame. Use, isolation and care of sick. Capacity, 40 pupils. Erected in 1897. Cost, $5,400. Present value, $4,800. Present condition, fair; poorly constructed.

Superintendent's residence.—Character, two-story frame. Use, quarters for superintendent. Capacity, ordinary sized family. Erected in 1898. Cost, $2,300. Present value, $1,800. Present condition, fair; poorly constructed.

Office and warehouse.—Character, 1½-story brick. Use, official business and storing supplies. Dimensions, 70 by 41 feet. Under construction (1903). Cost, $5,793.

Employees' quarters.—Character, one-story frame. Use, living rooms for employees. Capacity, 4 rooms and bath. Erected in 1902. Cost, $1,500. Present value, $1,500. Present condition, good.

Barn.—Character, one-story and basement. Use, housing live stock and hay. Capacity, 20 cows, 6 horses, and 30 tons of hay. Erected in 1892. Cost, $2,500. Present value, $1,600. Present condition, poor.

Barn.—Character, two-story frame. Use, housing stock and storing feed. Dimensions, 52 by 108 feet. Erected in 1902. Cost, $4,995. Present value, $4,995. Present condition, excellent.

Barn.—Character, 1½-story frame. Use, housing stock; under construction (1903). Cost, $1,875.

Dairy building.—Character, one-story brick. Use, care and manipulation of milk. Dimensions, 36 by 20 feet. Erected in 1903. Cost, $1,875.79. Present value, $1,875.79. Present condition, excellent.

Storehouse.—Character, one-story frame. Use, storing supplies. Capacity, 24 by 60 feet; 12-foot posts. Erected in 1892. Cost, $1,000. Present value, $600. Present condition, poor.

Ice house.—Character, one-story frame. Use, storing ice. Capacity, 100 tons. Erected in 1902. Cost, $300. Present value, $300. Condition, new.

Power house.—Character, one-story and basement; brick and stone. Use, central steam and lighting plants. Capacity, 3 boilers, 2 engines, 2 pumps, and 1 dynamo. Erected in 1892. Cost, $2,800. Present value, $2,400. Present condition, good.

Miscellaneous buildings.—Character, all frame. Use, henhouse, hog house, and sheds. Capacity, 150 hens, 10 hogs, and 20 sheep. Erected in 1892 and 1899. Cost, unknown. Present value, $250. Present condition, fair.

Lighted by electricity furnished by dynamo in power house; there are about 400 incandescent lamps 16 and 32 candlepower and eight 64-candlepower incandescent lamps on campus. Dynamo is directly connected to engine and gives good service. Central plant was installed in July, 1900, at a cost of $2,500. Interior wiring was done when buildings were erected. Heated by steam from central station at powerhouse, which has been installed by installments from 1895 to 1899. Total cost of heating plant (approximately), $20,000. Hospital has local system, and superintendent's residence hot-water system. Improvements to heating plant, costing $1,635, made in 1903. Ventilation in schoolrooms and dormitories by system approved by Indian Office. Other buildings have no modern system.

Water is furnished by the village of Flandreau at an annual cost of $1,500. Water is pumped from the Big Sioux River and delivered without filtering, and is poor a good part of the year. New system owned and operated by the school is now complete and cost $9,312. All buildings on west side of campus are connected with a 12-inch sewer, which empties into the river about a half mile from the school and below the water supply. Buildings on the east side of the campus are connected with a 6-inch sewer which empties into a dry run about 600 feet from the buildings.

In the girls' building are 10 ring baths and 2 tubs on the first and second floors. Large boys' building has 4 tubs on first and second floors, and small boys' building has 4 tubs in basement. All tubs are iron, porcelain enameled. Hospital has 2 tubs, 1 on male ward side and 1 on female ward side. There are also 3 tubs in different buildings for employees' use. There are 4 standard size fire hydrants on the grounds. There are also 14 standpipes, with hose attached in the different buildings, at all times ready for use. Tubs and buckets of water are found where standpipes are not erected.

The school has 480 acres of land which was purchased by the Government. Its present value, exclusive of buildings, etc., is about $25,000. There are but 240 acres under fence. Nearly 120 acres are under cultivation. The entire farm can be cultivated. There are 140 acres used as pasture. None is irrigated.

This school was opened in 1893, with a capacity of 150 pupils. In 1898 and 1899 new buildings were added, increasing the capacity to 350 pupils.

Salem Indian School.

Located 5 miles north of Salem, the capital of Oregon, on the Southern Pacific Railway. The site is admirably suited for school purposes, the climate moderate both in winter and summer, and without sudden changes in temperature. The soil in the immediate vicinity of buildings is loam, with a clay subsoil and a substratum of gravel. Portions of school farm is peat, or lake bottom land.

Schoolhouse.—Character, two-story brick. Use, class rooms and assembly hall. Capacity, 400 pupils. Erected in 1899. Cost, $15,000. Present value, $15,000. Present condition, good.

Girls' home.—Character, 2½-story frame. Use, dormitory for girls and sewing room. Capacity, 150. Erected in 1885. Cost, $6,000. Present value, $4,500. Present condition, fair.

Dormitory building.—Character, two-story brick. Use, girls' quarters. Capacity, 150. Erected in 1902. Cost, $19,386. Present value, $19,386. Present condition, excellent.

Large boys' home.—Character, 2½-story frame. Use, dormitory for large boys. Capacity, 150. Erected in 1885. Cost, $5,225. Present value, $4,500. Present condition, fair.

Dormitory building.—Character, two-story brick. Use, boys' quarters. Capacity, 150. Under construction (1903). Cost, $24,700.

Small boys' home.—Character, 2½-story frame. Use, dormitory for small boys. Capacity, 60. Erected in 1891. Cost, $4,000. Present value, $3,000. Present condition, fair.

Superintendent's cottage.—Character, two-story frame. Use, superintendent and assistant superintendent. Capacity, 8 dwelling rooms. Erected in 1891. Cost, $3,500. Present value, $3,500. Present condition, good.

Employees' building.—Character, two-story frame. Use, rooms for employees and employees' mess. Capacity, 11 employees. Erected in 1891. Cost, $3,000. Present value, $2,500. Present condition, good.

Hospital.—Character, two-story frame. Use, isolation and care of sick. Capacity, 32. Erected in 1891. Cost, $4,500. Present value, $4,000. Present condition, good.

Trades' building.—Character, two-story brick. Use, teaching trades. Dimensions, 124 by 40 feet, divided into 7 rooms. Erected in 1902. Cost, $5,940. Present value, $5,940. Present condition, excellent.

Barn.—Character, two-story frame. Use, housing live stock and storing hay. Capacity, 14 horses, 32 cows, 80 tons hay. Erected in 1894. Cost, $1,600. Present value, $1,200. Present condition, poor.

Storehouse.—Character, two-story frame. Use, storing supplies. Dimension, 40 by 75 feet. Erected in 1896. Cost, $1,500. Present value, $1,500. Present condition, good.

Office.—Character, two-story frame. Use, office, printing department, post-office, and employees. Capacity, first floor, 3 office rooms, post-office, and 3 dwelling rooms (dining room, kitchen, and sleeping room); second floor, 2 employees' rooms and printing office. Erected in 1895. Cost, $2,000. Present value, $2,000. Present condition, good.

Blacksmith.—Character, two-story frame. Use, blacksmith, wagon maker, and painter. Capacity, 14 pupils. Erected in 1887. Cost, $1,000. Present value, $700. Present condition, fair.

Cottage (old bakery).—Character, two-story frame. Use, employees' families. Capacity, 2 families—6 small rooms. Dimensions, 25 by 30 feet. Erected in 1887. Cost, $1,500. Present value, $600. Present condition, poor.

Carpenter.—Character, two-story frame. Use, carpenter shop and storeroom for lumber. Capacity, 12 pupils. Dimensions, 30 by 60 feet. Erected in 1885. Cost, $750. Present value, $300. Present condition, poor.

Dining room and kitchen.—Character, two-story frame. Use, dining room and kitchen. Quarters for cook and matron. Capacity, 600. Erected in 1887. Remodeled in 1899. Cost, $9,214. ' Present value, $5,000. Present condition, good.

STATISTICS OF INDIAN TRIBES, AGENCIES, AND SCHOOLS. 163

Gymnasium, girls'.—Character, one-story frame. Use, for gymnastics and weekly socials. Dimensions, 30 by 100 feet. Erected in 1885 and 1896. Cost, $1,500. Present value, $1,500. Present condition, good.

Laundry building.—Character, one-story brick. Use, general laundry work. Dimensions, 90 by 43 feet. Erected in 1902. Cost, $5,144. Present value, $5,144. Present condition, excellent.

Laundry (old).—Character, one-story frame. Use, drying fruit. Dimensions, 60 by 35 feet. Erected in 1895. Cost, $500. Present value, $400. Present condition, fair.

Shoe and harness shop.—Character, two-story frame. Use, harness shop and band room. Dimensions, 30 by 36 feet. Erected in 1887. Cost, $1,000. Present value, $600. Present condition, fair.

Tailor shop.—Character, two-story frame. Use, tailor shop and shoe shop. Dimensions, 30 by 36 feet. Erected in 1887. Cost, $1,000. Present value, $600. Present condition, fair.

Power house.—Character, one-story brick. Use, for heating and lighting plant. Dimensions, 61 by 30 feet. Wing 20 by 11 feet. Erected in 1900. Cost, $2,850. Present value, $2,850. Present condition, good.

Miscellaneous outbuildings.—Character, all frame. Use, henhouse, beehouse, wood sheds, storing implements, coal, etc. Erected in 1887–1901. Cost, unknown. Present value, unknown. Present condition, bad to good.

Lighted by electricity furnished by a dynamo in the power house. There are 470 incandescent lights. The plant was installed, in connection with steam heating, in 1900. Heated by steam from a central power plant (excepting school building, which has separate boiler). Plant was installed in October, 1900, in connection with electric lighting, at a cost of $16,136. Several buildings are heated by wood stoves. Ventilation of school building devised by Indian Office. Other buildings have no modern system.

The water supplied is pure and soft. It is pumped from drilled wells located in the center of the plant, and is pumped by steam pump into a tank having a capacity of 25,000 gallons, and having a height of 85 feet. The pressure is ample to force the water wherever required, but it is arranged so that the direct pressure of pumps can be turned on the system. None of the water is used for irrigation. Water system was extended in 1897 at a cost of about $1,800. All the principal buildings are connected with an 8-inch sewer pipe, which empties into two tanks, and from thence filters into Lake Labish ditch, about one-half mile to the southeast of buildings. The outlet is 32 feet below the level of the buildings, and it flows from thence via Lake Labish drainage ditch to Willamette River, a distance of about 3 miles. Improvements to the drainage and sewerage made in 1902 at a cost of $5,570. There are in use 1 tub and 8 ring baths located in girls' lavatory, and 4 tubs and 8 ring baths in boys' lavatory. The equipment poor and unsatisfactory. There are standpipes with hose in school building and in large boys' and girls' homes. Water buckets and underwriters' fire extinguishers in these and other buildings. Fire hydrants on grounds, and 2 hose companies.

This school has 345.09 acres of land, as follows: 177.32 acres were donated by the citizens of Salem; 84.92 acres by the pupils from their earnings in the hop fields; 10.58 acres prune orchard, purchased in 1899 at $125 per acre; 60 acres of lake bottom purchased in 1900 at $80 per acre; and 12.27 acres of lake bottom purchased in 1901 at $100 per acre. Present estimate value of land, $24,000. There are 345 acres under fence; 250 acres under cultivation—30 acres orchard and small fruits, 70 acres farm and garden, 150 acres pasturage. Ninety-five acres timber and brush can be pastured. There are 150 acres of pasturage, aside from 95 acres timber and brush land. None irrigated.

This school was established on February 25, 1880, at Forest Grove, Oreg., and moved to its present location in 1884.

Santa Fe School.

Located 2 miles southwest of Santa Fe, N. Mex., on the Atchison, Topeka and Santa Fe Railway. Site admirably suited for school purposes. Climate, dry and equable. Soil is adobe clay; is fertile when irrigated.

Main building.—Character, two-story brick, 2 two-story wings, 2 two-story extensions, 1 two-story addition with basement. Use, dormitory, dining room, kitchen, assembly rooms, bathrooms, employees' rooms. Capacity, 300 pupils. Erected in 1890. Cost, $30,985. Present value, $30,000. Present condition, good.

School building.—Character, two-story brick. Use, class rooms and assembly hall. Capacity, 450 pupils. Erected in 1899 and 1901. Cost, $16,243. Present value, $16,000. Present condition, excellent.

164 STATISTICS OF INDIAN TRIBES, AGENCIES, AND SCHOOLS.

Employees' building.—Character, two-story brick. Use, employees' quarters. Capacity, 13 employees. Erected in 1892. Cost, $5,700. Present value, $5,000. Present condition, fair.

Hospital.—Character, two-story brick. Use, isolation and care of sick. Capacity, 40 pupils. Erected in 1896. Cost, $3,000. Present value, $3,000. Present condition, good.

Laundry.—Character, two-story brick, one addition one-story brick. Use, laundry purposes, engine and boiler room, sewing room. Capacity, 50 pupils. Erected in 1892; addition, 1898. Cost, $5,224. Present value, $3,000. Present condition, fair.

Shop building.—Character, two-story brick. Use, tailor, shoe and harness maker, carpenter, blacksmith. Capacity, 80 pupils. Erected in 1902. Cost, $6,000. Present value, $6,000. Present condition, excellent.

Employees' building (superintendent's quarters).—Character, two-story brick. Use, superintendent's dwelling. Capacity, 1 parlor, 1 sitting room, kitchen, dining room, bathroom, 5 bedrooms. Erected in 1902. Cost, $4,500. Present value, $4,500. Present condition, excellent.

Warehouse.—Character, one-story brick and basement. Use, storing supplies. Dimensions, 31 by 60 feet. Erected in 1901. Cost, $1,989.90. Present value, $1,989.90. Present condition, excellent.

Warehouse.—Character, one-story brick with basement. Use, storing supplies. Dimensions, 20 by 40 feet. Erected in 1892. Cost, $750. Present value, $750. Present condition, good.

Barn.—Character, 1½-story, frame. Use, housing live stock and storing feed and hay. Capacity, 10 horses. Erected in 1895. Cost, $1,200. Present value, $1,000. Present condition, good.

Miscellaneous outbuildings.—Character, frame, brick, and adobe. Use, oil house, hose house, henhouse, etc. Erected in 1892–1900. Cost, about $2,500. Present value, about $1,000. Present condition, bad, fair, and good.

Lighted by electricity furnished by Santa Fe Water and Light Company, of Santa Fe, N. Mex., consisting of 361 incandescent lights and 4 32-candlepower outside lights. Cost, $4 per year for each light. Heated by wood and coal stoves. Ventilation of school rooms is by the system devised by the Indian Office. Other buildings have no modern system.

The water is furnished by the Santa Fe Water and Light Company, of Santa Fe, N. Mex., from reservoir located about 2 miles above Santa Fe, N. Mex., in the Santa Fe Canyon. The water is pure and the pressure is strong. Sufficient quantity is furnished for all domestic purposes and for the irrigation of 15 acres. Cost, per annum, for water, $1,500. All the buildings, excepting new shop building and new employees' quarters, are connected with 10-inch general sewer pipe, which empties into a dry arroyo a sufficient distance from the buildings. The new employees' quarters and shop building have an independent sewer, 4-inch, which empties into same arroyo as 10-inch sewer. There are 14 bath tubs for use of pupils. Six porcelain-lined tubs have been installed in basement of new addition to girls' wing of main building. Eight old zinc tubs are in boys' wing of main building. The school has a well-equipped fire department. Buckets filled with water are kept in all of the buildings.

This school has 106 acres of land. This land was donated to the United States Government by the citizens of Santa Fe, N. Mex. Its present value is about $2,000. There are 106 acres under fence; about 20 acres under cultivation. One hundred acres can be cultivated if sufficient water could be obtained for irrigation. There are about 75 acres in pasturage; 20 acres are irrigated.

This school was opened in 1890, with a capacity of about 140 pupils. The school was closed in 1893 and the pupils were sent to the following schools: Albuquerque, Carlisle, Fort Lewis, and Ramona Indian School, at Santa Fe, N. Mex. The school was reopened in 1894, with a capacity of about 150 pupils. It has an actual attendance at the present time of 334.

Tomah School.

Located 1 mile north of Chicago, Milwaukee and St. Paul Railroad, Tomah, Wis., in a splendid farming and dairy country; winters cold, but not severe, and summers very pleasant; soil, sandy loam.

Boys' building.—Character, 2½-story brick with 2½-story wing. Use, boys' dormitory, sewing room, and employees' quarters. Capacity, 150 pupils. Erected in 1892. Cost, $22,000. Present value, $18,000. Present condition, good.

Laundry and boiler house.—Character, one-story brick. Use, laundry, boiler room, band room, and boys' closet. Erected in 1892. Cost, $5,800. Present value, $5,000. Present condition, good.

Schoolhouse and assembly hall.—Character, two-story brick. Use, school rooms and assembly hall. Capacity, 250 pupils. Erected in 1898. Cost, $9,139.68. Present value, $8,500. Present condition, good.

Girls' building.—Character, two-story brick. Use, girls' home and matron's quarters. Capacity, 75 pupils. Erected in 1900. Cost, $11,410. Present value, $11,000. Present condition, excellent.

Mess hall and kitchen.—Character, dining hall, one-story brick; wing, 1½-story brick. Use, dining room, kitchen, bakery and baker's, cook's, and assistant cook's quarters. Capacity, 250 pupils. Erected in 1900. Cost, $9,732. Present value, $9,500. Present condition, excellent.

Superintendent's residence and office.—Character, two-story frame. Use, superintendent's dwelling and office. Capacity, 2 office rooms and 5 dwelling rooms. Erected in 1900. Cost, $3,350. Present value, $3,000. Present condition, excellent.

Hospital.—Character, one-story frame. Use, care of sick and nurses' quarters. Capacity, 8 pupils. Erected in 1900. Cost, $2,870. Present value, $2,500. Present condition, good.

Shop and warehouse.—Character, two-story frame. Use, storing supplies and carpenter shop. Dimensions, 26 by 40 feet. Erected in 1898. Cost, $888. Present value, $888. Present condition, fair.

Tool house.—Character, 1½-story frame. Use, housing tools, spring wagons, harness, etc. Erected in 1895. Cost, $800. Present value, $650. Present condition, poor.

Barn.—Character, 1½-story frame with wing. Use, housing live stock and storing hay. Capacity, 5 horses, 20 cows, and 40 tons of hay. Erected in 1885. Cost, $1,000. Present value, unknown. Present condition, very poor.

Barn, straw.—Character, 1½-story frame. Use, storing straw, etc. Erected in 1885. Cost, $300. Present value, unknown. Present condition, very poor.

Barn, sheep.—Character, 1½-story frame. Use, housing horses and storing hay. Capacity, 4 horses and 3 tons of hay. Erected in 1895. Cost, $300. Present value, unknown. Present condition, very poor.

Warehouse.—Character, one-story frame. Use, storing school supplies. Dimensions, 80 by 30 feet. Cost, $1,746. Under construction (1903).

Barn and silo.—Character, two-story frame. Use, housing live stock and storing feed. Dimensions, 108 by 52 feet. Cost, $4,883. Under construction.

Ice house and wood shed.—Character, 1½ story frame. Use, storing ice and wood for kitchen and bakery. Erected in 1901. Cost, $425. Present value, $425. Present condition, good.

Hog house.—Character, one-story frame. Use, housing hogs. Capacity, 20 hogs. Erected in 1900. Cost, $200. Present value, $175. Present condition, good.

Lighted by electricity; current furnished from C. A. Goodyear, in city of Tomah. There are 250 incandescent and 3 arc lights. Heated by steam. A separate heating plant for each building. The ventilation of schoolrooms and dormitories was installed by Indian Office.

Water supply is pure and soft. It is supplied from a 6-inch drilled well 150 feet deep. The water is forced to a large tank on tower, the pressure from which carries the water to the top of all buildings excepting the barns, and in case of fire direct pressure may be had from the pump. All buildings are connected with an 8-inch sewer, which empties into a stream running through one corner of school farm. There are 6 ring and 1 tub baths in the boys' building, situated on the second floor, and 6 ring and 1 tub in girls' building, situated in basement; also 2 tub baths in hospital. There are standpipes in both the boys' and girls' buildings, with hose on each floor and fire hydrants in the grounds. The supply of water in the school well raises to within 10 feet of the surface, and so far have been unable to lower it with a 4-inch steam pump.

This school has 200 acres of land, present value, $10,000. The whole is under fence. There are 120 acres under cultivation, the balance is wet and used for pasture.

This school was opened January 19, 1893, with 90 pupils.

Wittenberg Indian School.

Located one-half mile northwest of Wittenberg, Wis., on the main line of the Chicago and Northwestern Railroad, between Chicago and Ashland, Wis. Good location; climate good; rains copious; no failures of crops; soil a clay loam, very productive, but stony.

Main building.—Character, two-story, with stone basement. Use, girls' dormitory, dining room, kitchen, bakery, schoolrooms, and office. Capacity, 50 girls. Erected in 1886. Cost, $8,000. Present value, $5,000. Present condition, good.

Boys' building.—Character, two-story frame in three parts. Use, boys' dormitory, play room, laundry, and shop. Capacity, 50 boys. Erected in 1890. Cost, $3,000. Present value, $1,000. Present condition, fair.

Superintendent's quarters.—Character, two-story frame. Use, superintendent's dwelling. Capacity, office and 5 dwelling rooms. Erected in 1897. Cost, $1,800. Present value, $1,800. Present condition, excellent.

Water tower.—Character, three-story frame. Use, water tank, store house. Dimensions, 24 by 24 feet. Erected in 1893. Cost, $1,100. Present value, $600. Present condition, good.

Barn.—Character, one-story and stone basement, frame. Use, housing live stock and storing hay and feed. Capacity, 4 horses, 14 head cattle, 20 tons of hay. Erected in 1891. Cost, $1,200. Present value, $600. Present condition, fair.

Implement and fuel house.—Character, one-story frame. Use, one room for implements and the balance for fuel. Capacity, 24 by 80 feet. Erected in 1895. Cost, $700. Present value, $400. Present condition, good.

Chicken and hog house.—Character, two-story frame. Use, chicken and hog house. Dimensions, 20 by 28 feet. Erected in 1894. Cost, $350. Present value, $200. Present condition, good.

Miscellaneous outbuildings.—Character, all frame. Use, 3 outhouses and small barn. Erected in 1890 and 1897. Cost, $300. Present value, $300. Present condition, good.

All buildings lighted by lamps. Heated by stoves, except superintendent's dwelling, which is heated by furnace. No modern ventilation system.

Water good and plentiful; furnished from two 50-foot wells. Windmill for power, not satisfactory. Eight-inch sewer pipe extending 500 feet from buildings to cesspool. Sewers not used for lack of power for flushing same. Outfall about 40 feet below buildings. Two bath tubs. Water heated through coils in common box stoves. In cold weather water pipes are not in use. Water buckets and fire extinguishers only.

This school has 80 acres of land, which cost $1,000. Present value, $1,800. There are 80 acres under fence; 40 acres under plow; balance in pasturage and hay.

This school was leased by Government in 1895 and purchased in 1900 for $11,000. It was formerly a mission school and owned by the Luthern Church.

DAY SCHOOLS OFF RESERVATION.

Birch Cooley Day School, Paxton Township, Minn.

The Birch Cooley Day School is under the jurisdiction of the Superintendent of the Pipestone Training School.

Located 1¼ miles south of Morton, Minn., on Minneapolis and St. Louis Railway. Site well suited for school purposes, climate good, soil of site prairie loam.

Schoolhouse.—Character, one-story frame, 3 rooms. Use, schoolroom 20 by 30 feet; 2 living rooms 20 by 20 feet. Capacity, 36 pupils. Erected in 1891. Cost, $1,400. Present value, $1,100. Present condition, good.

Lighted by lamps and heated by wood stove. No modern system of ventilation. Water supply, none. All water used for the school drawn from well, the property of Episcopal Mission, distant about 300 yards from school building. There is an excellent spring of pure water in abundant quantity upon school land, distant about 300 yards from school building, but not easily accessible for securing water by hand. The school has no sewerage, bathing facilities, or fire protection.

This school has, including site, 9 acres of land. There are 7 acres under cultivation farmed by Indians, 1 acre of timber, 1 acre of school site. Soil good.

This school was opened February 8, 1892, with capacity of 36 pupils.

Bay Mills Day School, Mich.

The Bay Mills Day School is under the jurisdiction of the Superintendent of the Mount Pleasant Boarding School.

Located 2 miles west of Bay Mills, Mich., on the Duluth, South Shore and Atlantic Railway. Site admirably situated for school purposes. Climate subject to extreme changes. Soil alluvial.

Schoolhouse.—Character, one-story frame. Use, schoolroom and kitchen. Capacity, 40 pupils. Erected in 1902. Cost, $930. Present value, $930. Present condition, excellent.

Employees' quarters.—Character, one-story frame. Use, living quarters for employees. Capacity, 3 rooms. Erected in 1902. Cost, $745. Present value, $745. Present condition, excellent.

The following day schools are each under the jurisdiction of its individual teacher, who reports directly to the Indian Office. These teachers are not bonded officers.

Manchester Day School, Cal.

Located 5 miles southeast of Manchester, Cal., 5 miles from stage route. Site suited for school purposes. Climate without extreme changes. Soil of immediate site, dark loam.

Schoolhouse.—Character, one-story frame building. Use, pupils recite and study. Capacity, 24 pupils. Erected in 1894. Cost, $150. Present value, $150. Present condition, good.

This school has 40 acres of land, consisting of 3 or 4 acres where the school building and the Indian houses are, 4 or 5 acres of sandy river bottom through which the Garcia River runs, and the remaining acres across the river, which are heavily timbered. This land was purchased June, 1901, through the kindness of friends interested in their welfare, as the Indians were told to "move on" from the place where they had lived for years. The present 40 acres on which they have just moved is held in trust for them by the Ladies' National Indian Association, of San Jose. Two hundred and fifty dollars was the price paid for the land, and that is its present value.

This school was opened February, 1894, and for six months was held in an Indian's house, with a capacity of 16 pupils.

Ukiah Day School, Cal.

Located 3 miles northeast of Ukiah, Cal., near the California and Northwestern Railway; site, good for school purposes. Climate mild. Soil, bench land, sometimes called second bottom land.

Schoolhouse.—Character, one-story frame. Use, common schoolroom. Capacity, 24 pupils. Erected in 1891. Cost, $400. Present value, $500. Present condition, good.

Miscellaneous outbuildings.—Character, all frame. Use, wood shed, horse shed, etc. Erected in 1891–1900. Present condition, fair.

Not lighted. Heated by wood stove. Ventilated by doors and windows. Water is brought for day school from shallow wells near by. No sewerage. No bathing facilities, and no fire protection.

No school farm.

This school was opened October, 1891, with an average of 30 pupils. The building is held by the trustees of the Methodist Episcopal Church of Ukiah, Cal. It is rented by the Indian Department.

Upper Lake Day School, Cal.

Situated at Upper Lake, Lake County, Cal., 30 miles from the California Northwestern Railway at Ukiah, Cal.

Site is at base of Mount Diablo; location, poor; soil, serpentine rock.

Schoolhouse.—Character, one-story, redwood. Use, class room and assembly hall, latter used for church purposes. Capacity, 30 pupils. Erected in 1893. Cost, $300. Present value, $300. Present condition, good, but unpainted. No accommodations for the teacher.

Miscellaneous outbuildings.—Character, all one-story frame. Use, shed for horse, etc. Erected in 1901. Cost, $17.50. Present condition, good.

The land for this schoolhouse was deeded by the Indians to the Methodist Episcopal Church in 1892 as the Ukiah Indian Mission, and was opened February, 1893, with a capacity of 30 pupils.

INDEX.

Agencies:	Page.	Schools—Continued.	Page.
Blackfeet	3	Albuquerque	133
Cheyenne River	9	Arapaho	5
Colorado River	11	Bay Mills Day	166
Colville	12	Blackfeet Agency Boarding	4
Crow	14	Black Pipe Creek Day	97
Crow Creek	15	Blackwater Day	69
Devils Lake	16	Bena Boarding	48
Eastern Cherokee	20	Big Pine Day	124
Flathead	21	Big White River Day	99
Fort Apache	21	Birch Cooley Day	166
Fort Belknap	23	Bishop Day	124
Fort Berthold	24	Bull Creek Day	100
Fort Hall	26	Bullhead Day	117
Fort Peck	27	Butte Creek Day	96
Grande Ronde	28	Cantonment Training	7
Green Bay	29	Cannon Ball Day	117
Hoopa Valley	32	Capitan Grande Day	53
Hualapai	34	Carlisle Industrial	134
Jicarilla	35	Carson	136
Kiowa	36	Casa Blanca Day	69
Klamath	40	Cass Lake Boarding	47
La Pointe	41	Chamberlain	137
Leech Lake	46	Chehalis Day	88
Lemhi	49	Cheyenne Boarding	6
Lower Brulé	50	Cheyenne River Boarding	9
Mackinac	51	Cheyenne River Day—	
Mescalero	51	No. 5	10
Mission-Tule River	52	No. 7	10
Moqui	54	No. 8	11
Navaho	56	Chilocco Industrial	139
Neah Bay	58	Coahuila Day	52
Nevada	59	Cochiti Day	84
New York	60	Colorado River Training	11
Nez Percé	60	Colville Agency Boarding	12
Oakland, Oto, and Ponca	78	Corn Creek Day	95
Omaha and Winnebago	61	Cross Lake Boarding	48
Osage	64	Crow Boarding	14
Oto, Oakland, and Ponca	78	Crow Creek Industrial Boarding	15
Ouray and Uinta	120	Cut Meat Day	101
Pima	66	Eastern Cherokee	20
Pine Ridge	70	Flathead Agency Boarding	21
Ponca, Oto, and Oakland	78	Fond du Lac Day	44
Puyallup	86	Fort Apache Boarding	21
Quapaw	90	Fort Belknap Agency	23
Rosebud	92	Fort Berthold Agency	24
Round Valley	101	Fort Berthold Day—	
Sauk and Fox (Iowa)	102	No. 1	25
Sauk and Fox (Okla.)	103	No. 2	25
San Carlos	104	No. 3	25
Santee	106	Fort Bidwell	140
Shoshoni	109	Fort Hall	26
Siletz	110	Fort Lapwai Training	61
Sisseton	111	Fort Lewis	142
Southern Ute	112	Fort Madison Day	119
Standing Rock	113	Fort Mojave	143
Tongue River	117	Fort Peck Agency	27
Tulalip	118	Fort Shaw	144
Uinta and Ouray	120	Fort Sill Boarding	36
Umatilla	122	Fort Totten Boarding	17
Union	123	Fort Yuma	131
Warm Springs	124	Genoa	146
Western Shoshone	125	Gila Crossing Day	68
White Earth	126	Grand Junction	147
Winnebago and Omaha	61	Grand Portage Day	44
Yakima	128	Grand River Boarding	115
Yankton	129	Grande Ronde	29
		Great Nemaha Day	81
Schools:		Green Bay Agency (Menominee)	30
Absentee Shawnee	3	Greenville Industrial	148
Acoma Day	82	Haskell Institute	149
Agricultural Boarding (Standing Rock)	114	Havasupai Day	35
		Hayward Boarding	43

169

Schools—Continued.	Page.
He Dog's Camp Day	100
Hoopa Valley Training	33
Independence Day	124
Ironwood Creek Day	98
Isleta Day	82
Jamestown Day	89
Jemes Day	84
Jicarilla Training	36
Kaw Training	65
Klamath Boarding	40
Kickapoo Training	81
Lac du Flambeau	42
Laguna Day	83
La Jolla Day	53
Leech Lake Agency	46
Lehi Day	69
Lemhi Boarding	49
Little Crow's Camp Day	96
Little Water	57
Little White River Day	93
Lower Brulé Agency	50
Lower Cut Meat Creek Day	98
Lummi Day	119
Manchester Day	167
Maricopa Day	69
Martinez Day	53
Menominee (Green Bay)	30
Mesa Grande Day	53
Mescalero	51
Milk's Camp Day	99
Moqui Training	54
Morris Industrial	151
Mount Pleasant Industrial	152
Nambe Day	85
Navaho Agency	56
Neah Bay Training	58
Nevada Agency Training	59
Normantown Day	44
Oak Creek Day	97
Odanah Day	44
Omaha Boarding	62
Oraibi Day	55
Osage Agency	64
Oneida Boarding	31
Oneida Day No. 2	32
Ouray Boarding	121
Oto Boarding	79
Pahuate Day	83
Paraje Day	83
Pawnee Training	66
Pechanga Day	53
Perris	154
Picuris Day	85
Pima Training	67
Pine Creek Day	96
Pine Point	127
Pine Ridge Boarding	70
Pine Ridge Agency Day—	
No. 2	71
No. 3	71
No. 4	71
No. 5	71
No. 6	72
No. 7	72
No. 8	72
No. 9	72
No. 10	73
No. 11	73
No. 12	73
No. 13	74
No. 14	74
No. 15	74
No. 16	74
No. 17	74
No. 18	75
No. 19	75
No. 20	75
No. 21	75
No. 22	76
No. 23	76
No. 24	76
No. 25	76
No. 26	77
No. 27	77
No. 28	77
No. 29	77
No. 31	78
No. 32	78
Pipestone Training	157

Schools—Continued.	Page.
Phoenix	155
Polacca Day	55
Ponca	78
Ponca Day	107
Porcupine Day	117
Port Gamble Day	89
Potawatomi Training	80
Potrero Day	53
Puyallup Boarding	87
Pryor Creek Boarding	14
Quileute Day	59
Quinaielt Day	89
Rainy Mountain Boarding	39
Rapid City	158
Redcliff Day	44
Red Lake Boarding	46
Red Leaf Day	94
Red Moon	9
Rice Station	105
Riggs Institute	160
Rincon Day	54
Ring Thunder Day	93
Riverside (Cal.)	159
Riverside (Okla.) Boarding	38
Rosebud Agency	92
Round Valley	101
Salem	162
Salt River Day	68
San Carlos Agency	104
San Felipe Day	83
San Ildefonso Day	85
San Juan Day	85
Santa Ana Day	84
Santa Clara Day	85
Santa Fe	163
Santee Training	106
Santo Domingo Day	86
Standing Rock	113
Standing Rock Day—	
No. 1	116
No. 2	116
Sauk and Fox Agency (Iowa)	102
Sauk and Fox Agency (Okla.)	103
Sauk and Fox Day	82
Seama Day	84
Second Mesa Day	55
Seger Colony	7
Seneca Training	90
Shebits	108
Sia Day	86
Siletz Training	110
Sisseton Training	111
Spring Creek Day	94
Springfield Training	107
Swinomish Day	119
Shoshoni	109
Skokomish Day	90
Soboba Day	54
Stockbridge Day	31
Southern Ute	112
Taos Day	86
Tesuque Day	86
Tomah	164
Tongue River Boarding	118
Tongue River Day	118
Tonkawa Day	79
Tulalip Boarding	118
Turtle Mountain Day—	
No. 2	16
No. 3	17
Truxton Canyon Training	34
Ukiah Day	167
Uinta Boarding	120
Umatilla Training	122
Upper Cut Meat Day	99
Upper Lake Day	167
Upper Pine Creek Day	98
Vermilion Lake	45
Walker River Day	123
Warm Springs Training	124
Western Navaho Training	57
Western Shoshone Training	125
Whirlwind Soldier Day	94
White Earth Boarding	126
White Thunder Day	95
Wild Rice River	128
Winnebago	62
Wittenberg	165
Yainax Boarding	41

INDEX. 171

Schools—Continued.	Page.
Yakima Training	129
Yankton Training	129
Zuni Boarding	132

Tribes and bands:	
Absentee Shawnee	3
Apache	36
Apache, Coyotero	104
Apache, Jicarilla	35
Apache, Mescalero	51
Apache, San Carlos	104
Apache, Tonto	104
Apache, White Mountain	21
Arapaho	4
Arapaho, Northern	109
Arickaree	24
Assinniboine	23, 27
Bannock	26, 49
Blackfeet	3
Blackfeet Sioux	9–113
Bloods	3
Brulé Sioux	92
Capote Ute	112
Cass Lake Chippewa	46–126
Carlos' band of Flatheads	21
Cayuga	60
Cayuse	122
Clackamas	28
Cedar band, Pah-Ute	108
Chehalis	86
Chemehuevi	11
Cherokee	123
Cherokee, Eastern	20
Cheyenne	4
Cheyenne, Northern	117
Creek	123
Chickasaw	123
Chippewa	80
Chippewa, Bad River	41
Chippewa, Boise Fort	41
Chippewa, Cass Lake	46, 126
Chippewa, Fond du Lac	41
Chippewa, Grand Portage	41
Chippewa, Lac Court d'Oreilles	41
Chippewa, Lac du Flambeau	41
Chippewa, Leech Lake	126
Chippewa, Mississippi	126
Chippewa and Ottawa	51
Chippewa, Otter Tail Pillager	126
Chippewa, Pillager	46
Chippewa, Red Cliff	41
Chippewa, Red Lake	46
Chippewa, Rice Lake	41
Chippewa, Turtle Mountain	16
Chippewa, Winnibigoshish	46, 126
Citizen Potawatomi	103
Choctaw	123
Cœur d'Alène	12
Columbia, Moses band	12
Colville	12
Comanche	36
Concow	101
Cow Creek	28
Coyotero Apache	104
Crow	14
D'Wamish	118
Digger	19
Eastern Cherokee	20
Eastern Shawnee	90
Flathead	21
Fond du Lac	126
Georgetown	86
Grass Valley band, Pah-Ute	108
Gros Ventre	23, 24
Havasupai	34
Hoopa	32
Hoh	58
Hopi (Moqui)	54, 56
Hualapai	34
Humptulip	86
Hunkpapa Sioux	113
Iowa	80, 130
Jicarilla Apache	35
Joseph's band, Nez Percé	12
Kaibabs band, Pah-Ute	108
Kalispel	12
Kalispel, Lower	21
Kanash band, Pah-Ute	108
Kaw (or Kansas)	64
Klamath	32, 40

Tribes and bands—Continued.	Page.
Kickapoo	80
Kiowa	36
Kootenai (from Idaho)	21
Lake	12
Lake Winnibigoshish Chippewa	46
Lakmiut	28
L'Anse and Vieux Désert	51
Leech Lake Chippewa	126
Little Lake	101
Loafer Sioux	92
Lower Brulé Sioux	50
Lower Kalispel	21
Lower Spokane	12
Lower Yanktonai Sioux	15
Lummi	118
Madison	118
Makah	58
Mandan	24
Maricopa	66
Mary's River	28
Menominee	29
Mescalero Apache	51
Mexican Kickapoo	103
Mdewakanton Sioux	46, 51
Miami	90
Minneconjou Sioux	9
Mission	52
Missouria	78
Mississippi Chippewa	126
Mississippi Chippewa, White Oak Point band	46
Moapa River (Paiute)	54
Modoc	40, 90
Mohave	11, 104
Moqui (Hopi)	54, 56
Moache Ute	112
Moses' band, Columbia	12
Muckleshoot	118
Munsee	29, 80
Navaho	54, 56
Nespilem	12
Nez Percé (Joseph's band)	12
Nez Percé	60
Nisqually	86
Nomelackie	101
Northern Arapaho	109
Northern Cheyenne	117
Northern Sioux	92
Oglala Sioux	70
Okanogan	12
Omaha	61
Oneida	29, 60
Onondaga	60
Osage	64
Ottawa	51, 90
Otter Tail Pillager Chippewa	126
Oto	78
Pahranagat band, Pah-Ute	108
Pah-Ute	123
Pah-Ute, Cedar band	108
Pah-Ute, Grass Valley band	108
Pah-Ute, Kaibabs band	108
Pah-Ute, Kanash band	108
Pah-Ute, Pahranagat band	108
Pah-Ute, Pyramid Lake	59
Pah-Ute, Rabbit Valley band	108
Pah-Ute, San Juan band	108
Pah-Ute, Shewits band	108
Paiutes	56, 125
Paiute, Moapa River	54
Paiute, Pitt River	40
Papago	56, 66
Pawnee	66
Pembina	126
Pembina Chippewa	46
Pend d'Oreille	21
Peoria	90
Piegan	3
Pillager Chippewa	46
Pima	66
Pitt River	40, 101
Piute	124
Ponca	78
Potawatomi (Prairie band)	79
Potawatomi of Huron	51
Ponca of Nebraska	106
Pueblo	82, 132
Puyallup	86
Quapaw	90
Quaitso	86

Tribes and bands—Continued.	Page.
Quileute	58
Quinaielt	86
Rabbit Valley band Pah-Ute	108
Red Lake Chippewa	46
Redwood	101
Rogue River	28
San Arcs Sioux	9
San Carlos Apache	104
Santiam	28
San Juan band, Pah-Ute	108
San Poil	12
Santee Sioux	106
Sauk and Fox of Mississippi	102, 103
Sauk and Fox of Missouri	80
Shawnee, Absentee	3
Shawnee, Eastern	90
S'Klallam	86
Snake (Shoshoni)	109
Seminole	108, 123
Seneca	60, 90
Sheepeater	49
Shewits band, Pah-Utes	108
St. Regis	60
Siletz	110
Sioux	16
Sioux, Brulé	92
Sioux, Blackfeet	9, 113
Sioux, Hunkpapa	113
Sioux, Loafer	92
Sioux, Lower Brulé	50
Sioux, Lower Yanktonai	15
Sioux, Mdewakanton	46, 51
Sioux, Minneconjou	9
Sioux, Northern	92
Sioux, Oglala	70
Sioux, San Arcs	9
Sioux, Santee	106
Sioux, Sisseton	111
Sioux, Two Kettle	9, 92
Sioux, Yankton	129
Sioux, Yanktonai	27, 113
Sioux, Wahpeton	111
Sioux, Waziaziah	92
Sisseton Sioux	111
Swinomish	118
Shoshoni	26, 49, 109, 125
S'Kokomish	86
Stockbridge	29
Spokane	49

Tribes and bands—Continued.	Page.
Spokane, Lower	12
Spokane, Upper and Middle	12
Supai (Havasupai)	34, 35
Squaxon	86
Tenino	124
Tonkawa	78
Tonto Apache	104
Two Kettle Sioux	9, 92
Tulalip	118
Tule River	52
Turtle Mountain Chippewa	16
Tuscarora	60
Umatilla	122
Umpqua	28
Ute, Capote	112
Ute, Moache	112
Ute, Uinta	120
Uncompahgre Ute	120
Ute, White River	120
Ute, Wiminuchie	112
Upper and Middle Spokane	12
Uinta Ute	120
Ukie and Wylackie	101
Wahpeton, Sioux	111
Walapai (Hualapai)	34
Walla Walla	122
Wapeto	28
Warm Springs	124
Wasco	124, 128
Waziaziah Sioux	92
White Mountain Apache	21
White Oak Point band of Mississippi Chippewa	46
White River Ute	120
Wichita, and affiliated tribes	36
Winnebago	61
Wiminuchie Ute	112
Winnibigoshish Chippewa	126
Wyandotte	90
Wylackie and Ukie	101
Yakima	128
Yakima, Wild	128
Yam Hill	28
Yankton Sioux	129
Yanktonai Sioux	27, 113
Yanktonai Sioux (Lower)	15
Yuma	104, 130
Zuni	132

O